ETHICS

A PLURALISTIC APPROACH TO MORAL THEORY

Lawrence M. Hinman
University of San Diego

HARCOURT BRACE COLLEGE PUBLISHERS

Fort Worth Philadelphia San Diego New York Orlando Austin San Antonio Toronto Montreal London Sydney Tokyo

Editor-in-Chief *Ted Buchholz*
Acquisitions Editor *David Tatom*
Developmental Editor *Kristin Trompeter*
Project Editor *Barbara Moreland*
Production Manager *Cynthia Young*
Art Director *Nick Welch*

Cover Art: Paul Gauguin. *Among the Mangoes in Martinique*, 89 × 116 cm.
Vincent Van Gogh Foundation/Van Gogh Museum, Amsterdam.

Address editorial correspondence to:
301 Commerce St., Suite 3700, Fort Worth, TX 76102

Address orders to:
6277 Sea Harbor Dr., Orlando, FL 32887
1-800-782-4479 (outside Florida), 1-800-433-0001 (inside Florida)

ISBN 0-15-500367-4

Library of Congress Card Number 93-79504

Printed in the United States of America

4 5 6 7 8 9 0 1 2 3 016 9 8 7 6 5 4 3 2 1

For my parents

Preface

This book is for those who seek to understand better how to live a morally good life. Several important assumptions guide the approach taken here.

First, *we can learn from tradition.* Each of the major ethical traditions has important truths to contribute to our understanding of the moral life, even if none of them is able to capture all the truths about that life. This book approaches each tradition in this spirit, asking what light it can shed on the moral life. This does not mean that criticism will be absent—far from it. However, even the criticism is designed to help us to see what is right, not just what is wrong, in each tradition.

Second, *we can learn from each other.* Diversity is a source of strength in the moral life, and this book provides a conceptual foundation for understanding and appreciating diversity. This attitude is explicitly present the treatment of relativism in Chapter Two, the account of pluralism in Chapter Three, and the discussion of both gender and ethnic diversity in Chapter Eleven. It is implicitly present in the choice of examples and the discussion of particular topics throughout the book.

Third and finally, *you can learn from yourself.* This book begins with an ethical inventory that is intended to provide each student with the opportunity to take stock of his of her own moral beliefs. The discussion questions at the end of each chapter follow up on those initial responses, stressing the examination and refinement of the arguments underlying each student's initial position. Ultimately, each of us must make a personal assessment of the theories and arguments presented in this book.

Several features of this book are intended to make the journey easier as the reader moves through these often complex matters. *Extended examples* from real life have been used throughout the book to illustrate theoretical matters. *Discussion questions* have been provided for every chapter that encourage students to apply theoretical points to their own experience. A *glossary* is given at the end of this book. *Bibliographical essays* provide a guide through the thicket of primary and secondary literature. An *appendix* on writing ethics papers offers stylistic, technical, and substantive help on such things as choosing a topic, finding resources, and refining arguments.

In addition to these features, a number of optional discussion questions referring to movies, especially *The Mission, Gandhi, The Color Purple,* and *Glory,* have been included. They are marked with a special symbol for movies. Use of these questions is optional, but they provide certain common points of reference for comparing different ethical theories. Since they are easily available in video rental stores, they may be assigned for viewing outside of classroom time as well as used in class. I use them for two reasons. First, the strengths and weaknesses of various theories can be more vividly assessed by bringing the theories to bear on a particular scene in a movie. The movie provides the richness of detail and context that promotes insightful and lively discussion. Second, as we shall see in Chapter Nine, morality is often a matter of *perception*. Discussion of movies can be a powerful tool for developing the moral perceptions that are characteristic of each theory.

I would like to thank a number of people whose comments and support have helped to make this a better book than it would otherwise have been. The reviewers contracted by Harcourt Brace, Donna Bestock, Skyline College; George Graham, University of Alabama at Birmingham; Robert Hollinger, Iowa State University; Bruce Miller, Michigan State University; Anne Morrissey, California State University-Chico; Walter O'Briant, The University of Georgia; and John Serembus, Widener University, helped refine the text. Kathleen Dugan, Greg Kavka, Vali Nasr, Lance Nelson, Rodney Peffer, Linda Perry, Mike Wagner, and Virginia Warren offered numerous helpful comments on various chapters. Dennis Rohatyn read the entire manuscript and offered a number of insightful suggestions. Monica Wagner typed the original bibliography. My wife, Virginia Lewis Muller, has been a source of continuing love and support, intellectual as well as emotional.

TABLE OF CONTENTS

C H A P T E R 1

THE MORAL POINT OF VIEW

WHY STUDY ETHICS?

There are many things in life that we can avoid studying without any dire consequences. Few of us study, for example, molecular biology or quantum mechanics, but most of us (except for scientists in certain fields) are able to live quite well without any of the knowledge that comprises such disciplines. Yet there are other areas that we neglect only at hazard to ourselves and others. Consider nutrition. Most of us, myself included, have never had a course in nutrition or even read much about it. Yet many of us do have some general knowledge of the field. We know, for example, that there are several basic food groups, that a well-balanced diet involves items from each of these different groups, that we need a certain amount of protein each day, and that certain foods (usually ones we like) are bad for us. But we also realize that we make mistakes about these things. We discover that certain foods that we originally thought to be nutritious are actually quite harmful to us, sometimes in subtle ways that are evident only over a period of many years. We may also realize that there are foods we do not like that are nevertheless quite healthful. Even though we are not naturally inclined to eat them, we may find that we include some of them in our diet because in the long run we are going to feel better for it and be healthier because of it.

The Inevitability of Moral Questions

Morality is a lot like nutrition. We cannot avoid confronting moral problems, because acting in ways that affect the well-being of ourselves and others is as unavoidable as acting in ways that affect the physical health of our own bodies. We inevitably face choices that hurt or help other people, choices that may infringe on their rights or violate their dignity or use them as mere tools to our own ends. We may choose not to pay attention to the concerns of morality such as compassion or justice or respect, just as we may choose to ignore the concerns of nutrition. However, that does not mean we can avoid making decisions about morality any more than we can evade deciding what foods to eat. We can ignore morality, but we cannot sidestep the choices to which morality is relevant, just as we cannot avoid the decisions to which nutrition is pertinent even when we ignore the information that nutritionists provide for us. Morality is about living, and as long as we continue living, we will inevitably be confronted with moral questions—and if we choose to stop living, that too is a moral issue.

The Role of Moral Experts

There is a second respect in which ethics is like nutrition. We all have some general nutritional information that is part of our everyday stock of knowledge. We know, for example, that an ice cream cone is less healthful than a fresh garden salad and we really do not need to consult a specialist to figure that out. Similarly, we know that torturing a little baby is morally wrong—and we do not need to ask a philosopher's advice to see that. Yet in both fields there are whole groups of specialists who spend their entire lives trying to refine and provide a solid foundation for the everyday beliefs that we do have. Sometimes nutritionists, for example, discover things that are surprising (such as the health benefits of fish oil), sometimes things that are disturbing (such as the harmful effects of certain food additives). At other times, they just confirm our everyday beliefs, but they do so in a way that gives those beliefs a more solid foundation than they had before. The relation between our everyday moral beliefs and the work done by professional ethicists (that is, philosophers and others who specialize in ethics) seems to follow this same pattern. At times, they provide a secure foundation for things that we already know, such as the fact that we should not torture other people for our own amusement. At other times they may discover unsettling things, such as the idea that we may have stronger obligations to people starving in other countries than we originally thought or that our society in general may not be treating the elderly with sufficient respect. Thus we consult these moral experts for at least two reasons: they provide a firmer foundation for many of our existing beliefs, and they provide new insight into some moral issues that confront us in our everyday lives.

Moral Disagreement

There are several other points to note here in relation to the analogy between research in nutrition and the specialized knowledge of ethicists. The first of these concerns the problem of moral disagreement. Just as there is disagreement among nutritionists about the health value of certain foods and just as their opinions change as they understand nutritional matters better, so it is also with ethicists. They may disagree about some important matters, and their views may change over time. The best we can do is listen to them, understand their arguments, weigh their relative merits, and come to the best decision we can. Just as we should not give up on nutrition because the final answers are not yet completely available, so too we should not abandon ethics just because there is not complete agreement on all the important issues. We shall return to this issue in more detail in several of the following chapters.

Ethics as an On-Going Conversation

The comparison with research in nutrition is enlightening in another respect. If we were to pick up a recent issue of a professional journal devoted solely to nutrition, we might well be lost. Not only would there probably be an extensive technical vocabulary that was largely foreign to us, but also the articles would be dealing with questions that seem so minute or detailed that they are hardly helpful to us in the daily business of eating well. We might also feel as though we suddenly were thrown into the middle of a set of discussions that had been going on for a long time—and no one has bothered to fill us in on what has been said before.

Reading the work of professional ethicists can have the same effect on us, and it is easy to understand why this is so. Philosophers have been discussing these issues, sometimes in great detail, for decades if not centuries. As happens in any discipline, the discussion becomes more finely tuned. Distinctions are drawn, concepts refined, arguments criticized and reconstructed, rebuttals developed, rejoinders to the rebuttals framed. All of this dialogue makes perfect sense to those engaged in the conversation over a long period of time, but to newcomers it will often seem overly technical, much too picky, and too removed from everyday experience. If you are new to ethics, you may feel that you have just walked into a room where a conversation has been going on for a very long time. The people already in the room understand one another's positions well and have been working on these issues for quite a while. They may be right in the middle of a heated debate about some small point in an argument advanced by one of the participants. One of the functions of this book is to be the good host: to introduce you to the people in the room, to fill you in on what has been said, and to ease you into participating in the conversation yourself. A portion of each chapter of this book will be devoted to supplying you with the necessary background knowledge to participate in the on-going conversation among philosophers about the particular moral issues found in that chapter.

Ethics as an On-Going Task

There is another way in which reading an ethics book is rather like reading a book on basic nutrition: we inevitably are confronted with more information than we could possibly absorb in a single sitting. This is simply to be expected, and again, should not be a source of discouragement. Just as we would not change our eating habits overnight after reading a book on nutrition but instead would gradually become more aware of nutritional concerns and perhaps change our diet in certain areas over a period of time, so too with reading an ethics book. It forces us to notice things we have not noticed before and to pay attention to issues that we previously had been unaware of or ignored. Generally, however, it will not result in a total and immediate change in our lives—and with good reason. Most of us live basically good lives, and it is unlikely that an exposure to formal work in ethics would necessitate a complete revamping of our moral outlook. Moreover, we need to test these ideas through our own experience, and that is a gradual process of living with a new idea and beginning to get a feel for how our daily experiences are changed when seen through the lens of that new insight. This back-and-forth process, in which both the idea and our experience gradually become refined, changed, and developed, is a process that we will examine more closely later in this book when we discuss moral change. For the moment, however, it is sufficient to remember that reading a good ethics book is like reading a good book on nutrition: if it is really good, we will not absorb it all at once but will continually come back to it, refining and developing our ideas and reshaping our lives.

Morality and Ethics

Playing the good host, let me mention at this point a distinction between morality and ethics that recurs throughout this book. Philosophers generally draw this distinction in the following way. Every society has its set of moral rules or guidelines that set the boundaries of acceptable behavior. Often these rules are about behavior that might harm other people (killing, stealing), behavior that is concerned with the well-being of others (helping those in need, responding to the suffering of others), or actions that touch on issues of respect for other persons (segregation, using other people for one's own ends without concern for their welfare). Often the rules about such behavior are expressed in statements about what you *ought* to do or *should* do. These rules fit together, more or less consistently, to form the moral code by which a society lives.

Moral codes are seldom completely consistent. Our everyday life raises moral questions that we cannot answer immediately. Sometimes that is because there are contradictions among our different values and we are uncertain about which value should be given priority. For example, Oliver North was caught in a conflict between what he saw as the value of loyalty to his country and the value of telling the truth, even to Congress. At other times, our traditional values do not cover new situations and we have to figure out how to extend them. We believe in the value of privacy, but in an age of increasing computerization, what rules should we establish to govern access to information in computer data banks about private individuals? When we step back and consciously reflect on our moral beliefs, we are engaging in ethical reflection. **Ethics,** then, **is the conscious reflection on our moral beliefs** with the aim of improving, extending, or refining those beliefs in some way. This book is an invitation for you to participate in the activity of ethical reflection.

Public and Private Moral Beliefs

Let us take our analogy with nutrition a step further. If they are at a party with many health food fanatics, it is unlikely that most people will volunteer that their favorite breakfast food is Hostess Twinkies and Pepsi-Cola or that they would like to have pizza and beer for dinner every night. For most people, the atmosphere is not conducive to such confessions, although there are certainly some people who would not hesitate to make such unwelcome statements.

We encounter a similar situation in regard to our moral beliefs. There are certain things that it is acceptable to say, others which it is not. In most circles, it is socially quite acceptable to say that one is in favor of honesty, fairness, respect for other people, and so on; it is frowned upon to claim that lying, cheating, or using other people as mere means may sometimes be quite acceptable to you. Indeed, for many of us there may be a difference between our public (overt, official) moral beliefs and our private (covert, personal) moral beliefs. We may publicly endorse paying one's debts, but if a major purchase on our credit card never shows up on our bill, we may be quite content not to call it to the company's attention. We may proclaim the importance of truthfulness, but lie to a friend about what we did last weekend.

This discrepancy between overt and covert moral beliefs causes a problem for ethics. Imagine that you went to a nutritionist to get some information on a better diet and, in response to questions about what you ate during a typical day, you lied and said, for example, that you had tofu and a spinach salad for dinner instead of pizza and beer. If your goal is to change your eating habits, lying in this way simply keeps you from dealing with reality and thus prevents you from changing. Similarly, if we are going to enter into the on-going conversation that constitutes ethical reflection, we have to become clear what our real (at times, covert or unacknowledged) moral beliefs are and then examine those actual beliefs, rather than simply talking about the overt, publicly acceptable moral values that most of us espouse as a matter of course. This refocus may be quite difficult. Not only is there social pressure against expressing some of our personal values, but also sometimes we do not know what our actual beliefs and values are. At times we must look at our behavior to see what we actually believe. We say that honesty is the best policy, but do we in fact act in that fashion? We talk about the importance of respect for other persons, but how do we actually treat those around us? Coming to know ourselves is a difficult but essential step in ethical reflection.

This book is an invitation to enter into a discussion about your own beliefs, private as well as public. It is an invitation to examine, develop, and perhaps even improve those beliefs as you see fit in light of the insights that others have had into the moral life. In order for that process to be most meaningful to you, you need to examine the private as well as the public values you hold. This reflection may be work you want to do in complete privacy, looking at those personal values alone. Or you may want to discuss them with classmates, friends, or professors. Those are choices each of us must make as individuals. I would urge you, however, to dig for those real values by which you actually live and—in whatever way you find appropriate—bring them into the on-going conversation that constitutes ethical reflection. It is in this way that the material contained in this book will be most meaningful to you.

Moral Health

There is one final point to make about our comparison between nutrition and ethics: both are concerned with good health. This point is obvious in the case of nutrition, which focuses on our physical health. Ethics has a corresponding focus on our *moral* health. It seeks to help us determine what will nourish our moral life and what will poison it. As such, it seeks to enhance our lives, to help us to live better lives. Just as nutrition sometimes is experienced primarily as telling us what we cannot eat, so ethics may seem to be concerned mainly with telling us what we cannot do. But this negative aspect is simply a by-product of a more positive focus. In the case of nutrition, the central question is how we should eat in order to experience more of the vibrancy associated with genuine physical healthiness. Similarly, in the case of ethics, our principal concern is how we should live in order to experience the joy and satisfaction of a morally good life. The negative prohibitions arise, not out of a desire to be negative, but rather as by-products of a much more positive concern about moral health.

An Ethical Inventory: Discovering Your Own Moral Beliefs

All of us already have some idea of what our moral beliefs are, but often it is necessary to make these explicit. Since the rest of this book provides you with an opportunity for developing and refining your views on moral theory, it is helpful to begin by taking stock of the views with which you begin this investigation. The following checklist is intended to provide the opportunity to make an initial survey of your views. Read each of the following statements carefully and indicate whether you strongly agree, agree, are undecided or do not know, disagree, or strongly disagree with each statement.

	Strongly Agree	Agree	Undecided	Disagree	Strongly Disagree	
						Relativism, Absolutism and Pluralism
1.	☐	☐	☐	☐	☐	What is right depends on the culture a person is in.
2.	☐	☐	☐	☐	☐	People should always do whatever the majority thinks is right.
3.	☐	☐	☐	☐	☐	What is right is up to each individual.
4.	☐	☐	☐	☐	☐	No one has the right to judge what is right or wrong for another person.
5.	☐	☐	☐	☐	☐	No one has the right to intervene when he or she thinks someone else has done something morally wrong.
						Theories about Theories
6.	☐	☐	☐	☐	☐	It is hopeless to try to arrive at a final answer to ethical questions.
7.	☐	☐	☐	☐	☐	I need to look at the particular situation before I can know the right thing to do.
8.	☐	☐	☐	☐	☐	Morality is primarily a matter of considering the *consequences* of actions.
9.	☐	☐	☐	☐	☐	Morality is primarily a matter of considering the *intentions* people have when they act.
10.	☐	☐	☐	☐	☐	Morality is primarily a matter of considering the *character* a person has.
11.	☐	☐	☐	☐	☐	Ultimately, there is one and only one right standard of moral evaluation.
12.	☐	☐	☐	☐	☐	Morality is just a set of rules people all agree upon in order to make living together better.
						Religion and Ethics
13.	☐	☐	☐	☐	☐	What is right depends on what God says is right.
14.	☐	☐	☐	☐	☐	There is only one true religion.
15.	☐	☐	☐	☐	☐	What my religion says (in the Bible, the Qu'an, or whatever its sacred text is) is literally true.

	Strongly Agree	Agree	Undecided	Disagree	Strongly Disagree	
16.	☐	☐	☐	☐	☐	All major religions have something important to tell us about what is right and what is wrong.
17.	☐	☐	☐	☐	☐	We do not need to depend on religion in order to have a solid foundation for our moral values.
18.	☐	☐	☐	☐	☐	Religion is just a narcotic that lulls people into feeling better about their misery.

Psychological and Ethical Egoism

	Strongly Agree	Agree	Undecided	Disagree	Strongly Disagree	
19.	☐	☐	☐	☐	☐	Everyone is just out for himself or herself.
20.	☐	☐	☐	☐	☐	Some people think they are genuinely concerned about the welfare of others, but they are just deceiving themselves.
21.	☐	☐	☐	☐	☐	People are not really free. They are just products of their environment, upbringing, and other factors.
22.	☐	☐	☐	☐	☐	Everyone should watch out just for himself or herself.

Utilitarianism

	Strongly Agree	Agree	Undecided	Disagree	Strongly Disagree	
23.	☐	☐	☐	☐	☐	I do not care what motivates other people; I judge them solely on the basis of what they do.
24.	☐	☐	☐	☐	☐	When I am trying to decide what is the right thing to do, I look at the consequences of the various alternatives open to me.
25.	☐	☐	☐	☐	☐	The right thing to do is whatever is best for everyone.
26.	☐	☐	☐	☐	☐	We should look at the overall consequences of our actions in each and every case.
27.	☐	☐	☐	☐	☐	If someone tries to do the right thing but it works out badly, that person still deserves moral credit for trying.
28.	☐	☐	☐	☐	☐	Pleasure is the most important thing in life.
29.	☐	☐	☐	☐	☐	Happiness is the most important thing in life.

Kant, Duty, and Respect

	Strongly Agree	Agree	Undecided	Disagree	Strongly Disagree	
30.	☐	☐	☐	☐	☐	It is important to do the right thing *for the right reason.*
31.	☐	☐	☐	☐	☐	Morality is primarily a matter of doing one's duty.
32.	☐	☐	☐	☐	☐	What is fair for one is fair for all.
33.	☐	☐	☐	☐	☐	People should always be treated with respect.
34.	☐	☐	☐	☐	☐	We should never use other people merely as a means to our own goals.

	Strongly Agree	Agree	Undecided	Disagree	Strongly Disagree	
						Rights Theories
35.	☐	☐	☐	☐	☐	Morality is basically a matter of respecting people's rights.
36.	☐	☐	☐	☐	☐	Some rights are absolute.
37.	☐	☐	☐	☐	☐	I have a right to do whatever I want as long as it does not impinge on other people's rights.
38.	☐	☐	☐	☐	☐	People have a right to health care, even if they cannot afford to pay for it.
39.	☐	☐	☐	☐	☐	Animals have rights.
40.	☐	☐	☐	☐	☐	In personal relationships, rights usually are very important.
						Theories Against Theories
41.	☐	☐	☐	☐	☐	We should always strive to do what is best, not just the moral minimum.
42.	☐	☐	☐	☐	☐	Morality applies to friends in just the same way that it applies to strangers.
						Virtue Ethics
43.	☐	☐	☐	☐	☐	Morality is mainly a matter of what kind of person you are.
44.	☐	☐	☐	☐	☐	Sometimes courage seems to go too far.
45.	☐	☐	☐	☐	☐	Compassion for the suffering of others is an important character trait.
46.	☐	☐	☐	☐	☐	It is important to care about yourself.
						Ethics and Diversity
47.	☐	☐	☐	☐	☐	Men and women often view morality differently.
48.	☐	☐	☐	☐	☐	Morality should reflect an individual's ethnic and cultural background.
49.	☐	☐	☐	☐	☐	Moral disagreements are a good thing in society.
50.	☐	☐	☐	☐	☐	Compromise is bad.

In the discussion questions at the end of each chapter, we shall return to your answers to these questions. At this juncture, however, it is helpful to have some initial idea of the issues raised by these questions and the place of those issues in this text. I will briefly comment on each group of questions in turn.

Relativism, Absolutism, and Pluralism. We live in a world of differing and at times conflicting values. How do we deal with differences in value? Is there a single moral standard that is correct for everyone? Are standards completely relative to each culture? to each individual? What right do we have to make moral judgments about other people, whether in our own culture or in another culture? If we can make moral judgments about the behavior of others, are we ever justified in intervening in their affairs? If so, when? These are crucial questions about how we understand the relationship between our own moral values and the moral values of others. We shall deal with them in detail in Chapter Two, where I shall sketch out a middle ground between the two extremes of relativism and absolutism.

If you find yourself agreeing or strongly agreeing with the first two statements, your initial position is most compatible with *ethical relativism.* If you agree or strongly agree with the third statement, you are initially aligned with *ethical subjectivism.* Chapter Two is primarily concerned with a clarification and assessment of these positions. A corollary of both these positions is the belief that we ought not to judge others. Statement 4 indicates your position on that issue. Finally, relativists and subjectivists also often maintain that one cannot intervene in the affairs of others, an issue dealt with in statement 5. If you agree or strongly agree with statements 4 and 5, you will find Chapter Two interesting because it presents some reasons for reconsidering and revising your agreement with these items.

Theories about Theories. Most of us have some initial beliefs about the nature and limits of moral theories in general, and statements 6–9 are intended to make some of those beliefs explicit. Both statements 6 and 7 deal with how much you think we can know about moral matters. They indicate, respectively, whether you are an *ethical nihilist* (that is, one who holds that no moral knowledge is possible at all) or an *ethical skeptic* (that is, one who believes that our moral knowledge is modest and limited to particular contexts). Statements 8, 9, and 10 deal with what you think is the primary focus of moral evaluation. Do we look primarily at consequences, intentions, or character? These options will be examined, respectively, in Chapters 6, 7, and 10 of this book. Statement 11 deals with the issue of whether there is some single standard of moral value (*moral monism*) or whether there are several different and legitimate standards (*moral pluralism*). If you checked "agree" or "strongly agree" for more than one of statements 8–10, you are already committed to a pluralistic account of moral evaluation. If you agreed with statement 11, you will find the approach articulated in this book very challenging, for it defends an explicitly pluralistic account of morality. The final statements deal with the nature of moral values. Those who (strongly) agree with statement 9 are usually called *contractarians.* For contractarians, moral values are neither objective nor subjective, but intersubjective; they are the result of a (perhaps implicit) social contract that establishes the basic moral rules for a society.

Religion and Ethics. Chapter Four discusses the relationship between moral values and religious beliefs. For many people, religion plays a crucial role in their moral values, whether as a formative factor in their development or as their principal foundation. Your position on statement 13 gives a partial indication of where you stand on this issue; those who agree with it are often called *divine command theorists*. Some people, often called *fundamentalists*, hold that their religious beliefs are literally true (statement 15) and are the only truth (statement 14); others maintain that the truths of their religion are better understood as metaphorical. Those who see religious truth as metaphorical are more likely to see all major religions as being sources of moral truth (statement 16).

In contrast to those who hold that there is a positive and supportive relationship between religion and ethics, many people maintain that moral questions should be resolved independently of any religious beliefs. Those who agree or strongly agree with statement 17 would hold this position, which is called the *autonomy of ethics* theory. Some advocates of this position (Marxists are one of the main groups here) also believe that religion is harmful to the moral welfare of human beings. Your response to statement 18 partially reveals where you stand on this issue.

The Ethics of the Self: Egoism. Some thinkers have maintained that the only thing that matters in the moral life is the self. This position, called *egoism*, encompasses two distinct beliefs. *Psychological egoists* maintain that we all act selfishly all of the time (statement 16) and those who think they do not are just deceiving themselves (statement 17). Often, in order to support their belief, psychological egoists invoke some version of *determinism*, that is, the claim that human behavior is causally determined rather than freely chosen (statement 18). Other egoists—called *ethical egoists*—admit that people can act altruistically, but argue that they *ought* to act selfishly. Statement 19 measures the degree to which you agree with this position. Perhaps the best known advocate of this position is Ayn Rand. Chapter Five is concerned with evaluating this theory and showing that, while it does contain an important insight into the moral life, it falls far short of giving a comprehensive account of how we ought to act.

The Ethics of Consequences: Utilitarianism. When we address ourselves to moral issues, many of us are particularly concerned with evaluating the *consequences* of specific actions or rules. Both ethical egoists and utilitarians are consequentialists, but there is a crucial difference between the two. The ethical egoist is concerned only with the consequences for the individual agent; the utilitarian is concerned with the consequences for everyone. The extent to which you agree with statements 23 and 24 indicates the extent to which you are a *consequentialist*. If you agree or strongly agree with statement 25, this indicates that utilitarian considerations are a significant part of your moral theory. Your agreement with statement 26 is an indication that you will be more favorably disposed toward *act* utilitarianism than rule utilitarianism. If you agree or strongly agree with statement 27, you will find that Kantian criticisms of utilitarianism are appealing to you.

Statements 28 and 29 deal with the standard that utilitarians use to judge consequences. *Hedonistic utilitarians* (statement 28) say that consequences must be judged in terms of their ability to produce pleasure, while *eudaimonistic utilitarians* (statement 29) maintain that happiness is the proper standard in terms of which consequences should be judged.

The Ethics of Intentions: Duty and Respect. Whereas utilitarians concentrated on consequences, many ethical theorists—Immanuel Kant is the most famous representative of this tradition—claim that *intentions* are what really count in the moral life. If you found yourself strongly agreeing or even agreeing with statements 30 and 31, you will probably find the Kantian viewpoint initially attractive. As we shall see in Chapter Seven, Kant held that everyday life was simply too unpredictable to allow the moral worth of an action to depend on consequences. Once we have performed an action, it is out of our control; anything might happen as a result. The only thing which we are truly responsible for, and the only thing for which we can claim moral credit, is the intention behind our action.

Kant used several criteria in evaluating intentions, and your responses to statements 32–34 indicate how you view those criteria. For Kant, rules must be applied impartially to everyone. Your reaction to statement 32 indicates the extent to which you agree with Kant on this issue. In addition to fairness, Kant emphasized the importance of *respect*. Statements 33 and 34 measure the degree to which you agree with Kant that we should always treat people with respect and never use them merely as a means to our own goals.

The Ethics of Rights. During the last fifty years, philosophers and political leaders have come to see *rights* as occupying an increasingly important place in the moral life. We shall discuss this movement in Chapter Eight. Your reaction to statement 35 indicates the degree to which you agree with this trend; if you strongly agree with this statement, you will be among those thinkers who hold that morality is *only* a matter of rights. Statement 36 highlights a central issue for rights theorists: Are there any rights which are absolute, which can never legitimately be violated? Some thinkers—in the political realm these are often libertarians—hold that the only restriction on our actions should be the rights of others to non-interference; statement 37 shows the extent to which you initially agree with this claim.

One of the troublesome issues faced by rights theorists is how far the notion of rights should be extended. Does it include positive rights to welfare, such as a right to health care? Do animals have rights as well as human beings? Do rights have an important place in personal relationships? Your responses to statements 38, 39, and 40, respectively, indicate where you stand initially on these issues.

Theories Against Theories. In recent years, ethicists have indicated a number of reservations about moral theories. Some have complained that the notion of moral perfection implicit in most theories is actually very undesirable. Others have argued that most of traditional morality does not apply very well to personal relationships. Your position on statements 41 and 42 indicate the extent to which you are initially sympathetic to these criticisms. These issues will be explored in Chapter Nine.

The Ethics of Character: Virtues and Vices. Although much of ethical theory centers around the evaluation of actions (in terms of intentions or consequences or both), ever since Aristotle there has been another tradition in ethics which concentrates on the development of *character.* If you agree or strongly agree with statement 43, you will probably find this tradition compatible with your own ideas. Your responses to statements 44, 45, and 46 indicate where you stand on several specific virtues (courage, compassion, and self-love, respectively) that are discussed in detail in Chapter Ten.

The Ethics of Diversity: Gender and Ethnicity. During the past two decades, there has been a rapidly growing interest in the relationship between morality and gender. Some thinkers, such as Carol Gilligan, have argued that males and females view morality differently. Statement 47 measures your initial position on this issue, while 48 indicates a comparable issue in regard to ethnicity and culture. Both of these issues will be discussed in Chapter Eleven, which focuses on the ethics of diversity. Diversity often brings disagreement, and the final two statements are intended to gauge your initial attitude toward disagreements and your initial position on how they are to be resolved.

Save your answers to these questions. We will return to them throughout the course of this book.

The Moral Point of View

When I was on vacation a few years ago, I visited a farm in Pennsylvania where chickens were raised. Although I had heard about the conditions under which chickens were kept for laying eggs, I had never seen them first-hand. I was appalled. The chickens were squeezed so tightly into the cages that they could not move at all. They would spend their entire lives in the particular cage in which they were confined, which struck me as a terribly *cruel* thing to do to the chickens, and I found myself going outside just to avoid looking at them. For the first time, I could appreciate on an emotional level one of the reasons why some people in our society are strict vegetarians. They refuse to be a part of a process that they consider cruel and inhumane. I found myself wondering whether it was immoral for me to eat chicken or even to eat eggs. Was I participating in something morally bad by doing so? Let us look more closely at some of the elements in this example. Was it even a moral issue?

Consider, first, the process through which we usually recognize that something is a nutritional issue. When we call something a nutritional issue, we are singling it out both in terms of its *content* (that is, it has to do with food or other sources of bodily nourishment) and in terms of the *perspective* we take on that content (that is, we consider food in terms of its effect on health rather than primarily in terms of its color, price, and so on). Similarly, when we claim that something is a moral issue, we usually are indicating that:

- its content is of a particular type (duties, rights, human welfare and suffering, and so on.)
- we are approaching it from a particular point of view (impartial, caring, and so on.)

Moral issues are thus a matter both of *what* we see and *how* we see it.

Let us look at an example of a typical moral issue and then outline some of the major theories about what makes it a moral issue.

An Example

Imagine that you are a student in a very large undergraduate course at a university that has a clear honor code about cheating and the duty to report cheating to appropriate authorities. During a very difficult mid-term exam, you notice that many students—including one of your best friends—are cheating on the test. The proctor, a teaching assistant for one of the sections, is reading a novel and seems oblivious to the cheating. At one point, a friend of yours even leans over to ask you the answer to one of the questions. You pretend not to hear the request for help. A week later, the professor returns the exams. A number of students, including some of your close friends, receive "As" and "Bs," higher grades than they otherwise would have gotten if they had not cheated. You would have received a "B," which you feel is a reasonably accurate assessment of your grasp of the material, but because of the high curve, you actually receive a "C" on the exam.

The Moral Content

Consider those things in the *content* of this situation that make it a moral issue. Several things stand out. First, some people are *hurt* in the situation. They receive lower grades than they otherwise would because of the cheating and the fact that grading is done on a curve. Second, there is *deception* in the situation, which is usually a moral "red flag," an indication that moral scrutiny is in order. Third, it seems *unfair* that people who cheat get ahead because of their cheating, while those who are honest seemingly are penalized because of their honesty. Fourth, there are questions of *conflicting values*, and these are usually principal sources of moral questions. In this case, loyalty to friends conflicts with possible duties to inform a professor about cheating. Finally, there may be a concern about *character* and the effects that cheating or informing on cheaters has on a person's character. All of these are elements that typically are recognized as part of the moral content of this situation.

The Moral Standpoint

For something to be a moral issue, it is not enough for it simply to have a certain content. We must also approach it in a particular way. If we approached this cheating example solely as sociologists interested in describing the various social forces at work in the situation, we would not be raising a moral issue. For something to be a moral issue, we have to raise it from a particular standpoint or point of view. If, for example, we are asking what is *right* to do in the situation, we are approaching it from a moral point of view. So, too, our concern is a moral one if we ask what our duty is in a particular situation. Similarly, if we are concerned with what makes a person a *good* person rather than popular or witty, we are approaching the issue of character from a moral point of view. We will examine several attempts to describe the moral standpoint below.

Non-Moral Concerns

There are a number of questions you could ask about this situation that would *not* be specifically or directly moral in character. For example, you might ask questions about what the correct answers were, about what pages from the textbook were covered in the exam, about how many people missed a particular question, and the like. None of these questions is specifically moral in character.

The Language of Moral Concerns

Many philosophers have attempted to specify the nature of the moral point of view by looking at the language we typically employ when we are talking about moral issues. Recall the cheating example given above. We may ask whether it is our *duty* to inform on students who cheat. Is the proctor *obligated* to pay close attention to signs of cheating? Is cheating *bad* or *wrong* or *immoral?* Is it always *right* or *good* to be honest? *Ought* we to always be honest? Do students have a *right* to demand that cheating not be permitted? Will a policy of strict honesty have the greatest *overall amount of good consequences for everybody?* Who will be *hurt* by such a policy?

These are questions that are characteristically moral questions that you could ask about this situation, and the italicized words are characteristically moral vocabulary. Indeed, one of the ways philosophers describe the moral point of view is that it typically employs the kind of moral vocabulary emphasized in the previous paragraph. We will look at this concept in more detail later in this book, so for the moment you need to get only a rough idea of what type of language usually is associated with the moral point of view.

Impartiality

There is another characteristic of each of these approaches to morality, one that many philosophers take to be at the heart of the moral point of view. Typically, the moral point of view is an *impartial* one. When we make a moral judgment, we do not just ask what would be good for ourselves. We set aside our own personal, selfish interests and attempt to do what is right, even if it involves sacrifice on our part. (One ethical system, ethical egoism, disagrees with this notion and defends the moral value of selfishness. We shall examine this issue in Chapter Five). We have all certainly experienced this phenomenon: doing the right thing even when it hurts, when it would be easier to do the selfish thing. For example, consider what happens when a salesperson gives us back too much change in the store. Especially if you know that the clerk will have to pay for any shortages at the end of the day, you may give back the extra money, even though you could use the additional cash. You may do so because it is the right thing to do or because it would hurt the other person not to do it, but in any case you set aside your self-interest to do what morally is demanded of you. Many philosophers maintain that setting aside narrow personal interests in this way is at the heart of the moral point of view.

Compassion

Some philosophers have described the moral point of view in quite a different way, one that initially seems far from the impartiality discussed above. Morality, they maintain, is essentially about *compassion*, about the ability to understand and to help alleviate the suffering of other people. (Indeed, the etymology of compassion is from the Latin meaning "suffering with.") The moral point of view, according to this approach, is characterized by our ability to understand, appreciate, and help relieve the suffering of others.

Although compassion may initially seem quite distant from impartiality, there is actually an important underlying link between the two. Josiah Royce, an American philosopher, once characterized the essential moral insight as the realization that "Such as that is for me, so is it for him, nothing less." Compassion is the ability to appreciate that all suffering is equal, that my own suffering counts for no more than the suffering of any other person. Compassion is a unique combination of the impartial and the personal: it is an intensely personal concern for the suffering of others, but it is applied impartially to the suffering of everyone.

Universally Binding

There is yet another way in which some philosophers characterize the moral point of view. They see morality as being primarily a matter of commands or, as they usually put it, imperatives that are binding on everyone in an impartial manner. We encounter many imperatives in life. Some of them are *hypothetical* in character, that is, that we should do some particular thing only *if* we want to achieve a specific goal. "If you want to see an enjoyable movie, see the new James Bond film." "If you want to get an 'A' in this course, you must write an excellent term paper." These are everyday examples of hypothetical imperatives. Yet some imperatives are not hypothetical in character. They claim to be binding without qualification. According to Immanuel Kant, an eighteenth-century philosopher whose work has had a profound impact on ethics, these unconditional or **categorical imperatives** are at the heart of ethics. Kant maintains that the moral point of view is distinguished by the fact that its imperatives are categorical rather than merely hypothetical in character. "Never treat people merely as a means to your own ends." "Always respect people as ends in themselves." "Always act in such a way that you could will that everyone follow the same rule that you are following." These are examples of typical moral categorical imperatives. Notice that none of them was hypothetical; none began with an "If . . ." clause. Morality is not a matter of choice. It binds us absolutely. Part of the moral point of view, according to many philosophers, is that we feel bound by moral imperatives, not just hypothetically, but categorically.

Our everyday experience of morality often confirms this claim that morality is universally binding, especially in serious moral matters. Think, for example, of our moral prohibitions against sexually abusing children. Virtually none of us think that this prohibition is just a matter of personal opinion. We feel it is wrong to sexually abuse children, and we believe that this prohibition is binding on *everyone*. Morality, at least at its core, is universally binding.

Concern for Character

Each of the previous ways of characterizing morality (moral language, impartiality, and categorical imperatives) presumes that morality is concerned primarily with the assessment of particular *acts*. But as we have already mentioned, there is another tradition in ethics, stretching back at least to Aristotle's time over 2,200 years ago. This tradition, called **virtue ethics,** suggest that morality is primarily a matter of individual character. Within this tradition, the moral point of view primarily is concerned with the question of what it means to be a good person. The focus is on excellence of character. Indeed, the Greek word for virtue (*areté*) originally meant excellence. Courage, compassion, self-love, and generosity are some of the moral virtues that we will be discussing in this book. Along with these, we will also be looking at the opposite of virtues: vices such as hatred, envy, jealousy, and cowardice.

THE POINT OF ETHICAL REFLECTION

In the preceding sections, we discussed the question of why we should study ethics, and we looked at various answers to the question of what puts an issue into the moral ballpark. There is one final topic to consider here: what is the *point* of ethical reflection? More specifically, is it primarily supposed to help us judge others or to better understand and guide our own lives?

Ethics as the Evaluation of Other People's Behavior

We certainly are aware of those who see ethical reflection primarily as a means of making judgments about the morality (usually, actually, the immorality) of other people. Think, for example, of some of the nastier debates about the morality of abortion, euthanasia, the death penalty, or nuclear armaments. Very often, advocates on all sides of these issues use ethical arguments to press a case against their opponents, to show their audience that the course of action recommended by their opponents is morally objectionable. Sometimes they will even attack the moral character of their opponents, claiming that they are bad people. Ethics, in this context, is often used to condemn other people, or at least to denounce the actions that they advocate.

Mistrust about Moral Judgments

This idea is certainly an important and legitimate use for ethics, and I have no desire to urge its elimination. However, some people feel a certain mistrust about this aspect of ethics. There seem to be several sources of this mistrust, and I would like to discuss five of them here.

Hypocrisy The first source of mistrust centers around the issue of consistency and motivation. Some people wonder whether ethics is being used, when it is convenient to do so, to attack others but ignored when it raises difficult questions about one's own conduct. They mistrust, in other words, the *motives* of those who advance such arguments and are concerned that ethical arguments may be being used selectively to support particular positions. Such critics do not necessarily deny the soundness of the arguments, but rather they have doubts about the motives behind their use.

Sometimes such mistrust about motivation may be justified, but it certainly does not need to be extended to all moral judgments. Not everybody who makes moral judgments is unwilling to look at themselves and apply the same moral standards to themselves that they apply to others. Moreover, we need to distinguish between the motivation for making a moral judgment and its validity. Moral judgments may be self-serving, but that does not mean that they necessarily lack any validity. Indeed, the converse is also true. The fact that a particular moral judgment is not self-serving does not mean that it is valid. There is no shortage of well-intentioned mistakes.

Knowing Other People The second source of mistrust that I have encountered is primarily epistemological; that is, it has to do with how much we can *know* about other people. (Epistemology is a branch of philosophy that deals with the nature and justification of our knowledge claims.) How, many people ask, can we ever know enough about what other people are thinking or feeling to pass judgment on their actions?

This argument has merit, but perhaps not as much as its proponents believe. We probably can never *completely* know and understand another person. (Indeed, we can probably never completely know and understand ourselves, either.) But this division is a matter of degree. We partially can know and understand some people, just as they can at least partially know and understand us. Moreover, we can increase our knowledge and understanding of another person—a natural part of the process of getting to know someone. Indeed, think of what an incredibly lonely world we would inhabit if we could never really know or understand another person at all.

There is another problem with these epistemological doubts. Sometimes we do not need to know another person's inner beliefs and feelings and motives in order to make a judgment about the moral worth of an act. Sometimes our concern is with the act and its consequences, not with motives or intentions. It is primarily when we are making moral judgments about persons rather than actions or consequences that we need to know about the person's intentions and feelings.

The Right to Judge The third source of mistrust is captured in the question, "Who am I to judge other people's actions?" By what right, in other words, do I claim to be in a position to pass judgment on someone else's life? This is a good question—and, like all good questions, it deserves an answer. Clearly, we are not entitled to make such judgments simply because it is what we want. It would seem, in order to exercise the right to make moral judgments (about oneself as well as others), at least two conditions must be met. First, we must have some standards that we do not think are arbitrary. The standards must, in other words, be justified. Much of the rest of this book is an exploration of how such standards may be justified. Second, we must have some knowledge of the situation we are judging. Moral judgments, in other words, must be well grounded in both justified moral standards and in appropriate knowledge of the situation. Of course, when some people ask the question "Who am I to judge?" they are not really looking for an answer. They are using a rhetorical question to assert that no one has a right to make moral judgments, which is a strong, important claim that must be examined directly. We will do so in the next chapters when we discuss moral skepticism and moral nihilism.

Intervention Another source of mistrust centers around the issue of intervention. What good, it is often asked, does it do to try to change the way someone else lives? We cannot live other people's lives for them. They have to do it themselves.

Several things need to be said about this mistrust. First, judgment is not the same thing as intervention. Therefore, even if it is true that intervention is not justified in a particular case, that does not mean that judgment is impossible. We may very well say that what someone is doing is wrong but decide that the best thing for us to do is not to intervene. Second, while it may often be true that intervention is not effective, it is not *always* true. Intervention can sometimes both be justified and effective. Certainly there are times when we intervene in order to protect innocent people from the potentially harmful effects of someone's actions. Think about drunk driving. We may refuse to let someone drive home drunk after a party because we do not want to see anyone hurt or killed by such driving, whether it be the driver or any unsuspecting victims. Such intervention may well be effective. It may not ultimately eliminate the behavior, but it will prevent it on that occasion and reduce the chance that anyone will be hurt or killed that evening by that drunk driver.

Finally, we should emphasize that intervention is an art that often requires quite a bit of skill. Most of us have been in situations where we knew that we ought to do something but we did not know what—and we were afraid that if we did the wrong thing, it would just make matters worse. Part of the moral life is learning how to intervene in ways that are both caring and effective. That is not an easy or a simple task.

Judging and Caring There is a final possible source of mistrust about making moral judgments that deserves special attention here. Making moral judgments sometimes feels harsh and uncaring. To judge someone seems equivalent to condemning them, which seems antithetical to caring about them.

Once again, we can safely say that sometimes this mistrust is justified. At times people do judge one another harshly and uncaringly. But two points need to be noted. First, we do not *always* judge in such an uncaring and harsh way. Second, if moral judgments are sometimes objectionably harsh and uncaring, that does not mean that we should get rid of the entire process of making moral judgments. Rather, we need only reject the objectionable part—the harsh, uncaring part. We need to learn how to make moral judgments in a caring, sometimes even loving, fashion and to express them when appropriate in a similar way.

Ethics as the Search for the Meaning of Our Own Lives

There is, however, another tradition in ethics which has a quite different focus. Within this tradition, ethics is concerned primarily with reflection about the quality of one's own life. Here ethics is less a matter of judging and more a matter of understanding and seeing things more clearly. It is less concerned with other people's lives than with our own. Finally, it is less concerned with the negative than with the positive. Let me illustrate this difference first by means of an example.

Most of us probably have had the following kind of experience, one which exemplifies this difference well. Imagine that you are facing a difficult moral choice—let us say, whether to have an abortion. We easily can imagine going to someone who has very firm views on the subject and who tells you there is only one thing to do. Often we go away from such conversations with a feeling of dissatisfaction, for the other person's advice does not seem to have anything to do with us personally. We realize anyone would have gotten the same answer. Contrast that to the experience of talking with someone who does not give us an immediate and absolute answer, but joins with us in the search for what will be the right answer for us. Such discussions involve probing the details of the situation, trying to see one's own motives more clearly, looking for additional courses of action that might have been neglected, and searching for an answer that reconciles the various moral challenges we experience in the situation. Often the participants are not concerned primarily with determining what the moral minimum is that anyone must do in the situation, but rather are concerned with figuring out what is the morally appropriate course of action for me as a unique individual to do. This activity may well involve more than what is minimally necessary.

Ethics and Moral Health

Let me conclude with an invitation. We have seen some of the ways in which ethics is concerned with moral health. In the following chapters, we shall consider some of the major theories that have been advanced to help us understand what the morally good life is like. I invite you to approach this topic in the same spirit in which you might approach the study of nutrition. Most of us want to live a healthier life, even if we do not always want to eat in the ways necessary to achieve this end. Similarly, most of us want to live a morally better life, but we may also be reluctant to do what is necessary to achieve it. Yet in both cases, we often encounter pleasant surprises, discovering that there is a greater overlap between what is good and what is ultimately enjoyable than we suspected. Just as we are sometimes surprised that something can taste great and still be good for us, so we may be pleasantly surprised to discover that there is joy in doing the right thing.

And in both cases, we discover that there is no unanimity on how we can achieve health. There are conflicting theories, and all of them contribute in varying degrees to our understanding how to live a healthy life. Similarly, the various theories discussed throughout the rest of this book help us to understand how to live a good life, but none of them provides the single and exhaustive answer to our questions. That is hardly surprising, since the moral life is no less complex than the life of the body. Yet despite the fact that none of these theories provides the complete answer, each does provide a part of the answer.

There is a final point about our comparison between nutrition and ethics. In the last analysis, no matter how much we know about nutrition, it makes no difference if we do not act on that knowledge. Similarly, our knowledge of moral theories will be of little benefit to us unless we are willing to incorporate it into our own lives. This text cannot make that decision for any of us. It can only provide knowledge and insights that will be useful if we decide to live a moral life. Each of us must decide individually the extent to which we want to do so. The invitation of this book is a simple one: take the insights offered by the theories presented in the following chapters and use them in making your own life a better one. Use them in your own quest for a better life.

Bibliographical Essay

There are a number of other good **introductions to ethics** that present some of this same material in other ways. Among the best are James Rachels, *The Elements of Moral Philosophy*, 2nd ed. (New York: Random House, 1993); Louis Pojman, *Ethics: Discovering Right and Wrong* (Belmont, Calif.: Wadsworth, 1990) and his anthology, *Ethical Theory: Classical and Contemporary Readings*, edited by Louis P. Pojman (Belmont, Calif.: Wadsworth, 1989); J. L. Mackie, *Ethics: Inventing Right and Wrong* (Harmondsworth England: Penguin Books, 1977); also see D. D. Raphael, *Moral Philosophy* (Oxford: Oxford University Press, 1981). For a short but exceptionally nuanced view of the place of ethics in contemporary thought (including the social sciences and the humanities), see Frederick A. Olafson, *Ethics and Twentieth Century Thought* (Englewood Cliffs, N.J.: Prentice-Hall, 1973). For an excellent introductory approach that emphasizes moral realism and the development of moral sensitivity, see David McNaughton, *Moral Vision: An Introduction to Ethics* (Oxford: Blackwell, 1988).

There are several excellent **reference works** in ethics that may be helpful to those who wish to pursue further the ideas presented in this book. Among the most helpful are the eight volumes of *The Encyclopedia of Philosophy*, edited by Paul Edwards (New York: Macmillan, 1967) and, more recently, *A Companion to Ethics*, edited by Peter Singer (Oxford: Basil Blackwell, 1991) and the excellent *Encyclopedia of Ethics*, edited by Lawrence and Charlotte Becker (New York: Garland Press, 1992). Singer's anthology contains articles covering a wide range of topics, including non-traditional areas such as Buddhism, Islam, and Confucianism. The Becker's *Encyclopedia* has articles covering virtually all the major topics in ethics.

Several **histories of ethics** are also available. Vernon Bourke's *A History of Ethics* (Garden City, N.J.: Doubleday, 1968) provides a solid, reliable historical guide. Alasdair MacIntyre's *A Short History of Ethics* (New York: Macmillan, 1966) is more tendentious and insightful. For a brief survey of contemporary Anglo-American ethical theories, see Mary Warnock, *Ethics Since 1900*, 3rd ed. (Oxford: Oxford University Press, 1978) and G. J. Warnock's *Contemporary Moral Philosophy* (New York: St. Martin's Press, 1967). Frederick A. Olafson's *Principles and Persons: An Ethical Interpretation of Existentialism* (Baltimore: Johns Hopkins Press, 1967) is an exceptionally insightful treatment of existential ethics. Among the anthologies in this area, see Michael Wagner, *An Historical Introduction to Moral Philosophy* (Englewood Cliffs, N.J.: Prentice-Hall, 1990) and J. B. Schneewind's *Moral Philosophy from Montaigne to Kant*, two volumes (Cambridge: Cambridge University Press, 1990).

On the **definition of the moral point of view**, see Paul Taylor's "On Taking the Moral Point of View," *Midwest Studies in Philosophy*, III (1978), 35–61, which contends that six characteristics are necessary for a standard or rule to be a moral one: (1) generality, (2) universality, (3) priority, (4) disinterestedness, (5) publicity, and (6) substantive impartiality. Wallace and Walker's excellent anthology, *The Definition of Morality* (London: Metheun, 1970) contains reprints of important papers on the definition and limits of morality by Alasdair MacIntyre, William Frankena, Neil Cooper, Peter Strawson, Philippa Foot, Kurt Baier, G. E. M. Anscombe, David Gauthier, and others. For a more detailed presentation of Baier's views, see Kurt Baier, *The Moral Point of View* (Ithaca, N.Y. Cornell University Press, 1958). For a vigorous defense of the claim that the moral point of view is impartial, see Thomas Nagel, *Equality and Partiality* (New York: Oxford, 1991). Josiah Royce's characterization of the moral insight is found in his *The Religious Aspects of Philosophy* (Boston: Houghton Mifflin, 1885); reprinted in part in Sommers and Sommers, *Vice and Virtue in Everyday Life*, 2nd ed. (San Diego: Harcourt Brace Jovanovich, 1989), pp. 55–59.

For a sustained argument that the **moral ballpark** is smaller than often believed, see Peter A. French, *The Scope of Morality* (Minneapolis: University of Minnesota Press, 1979). Shelly Kagan's *The Limits of Morality* (Oxford:

Clarendon Press, 1989) provides a forceful critique of those who see morality's demands as limited.

Discussion Questions

1. Imagine that you are a hospital administrator and that you have been asked to set up an Ethics Committee in the hospital. The Committee will deal with moral dilemmas that may confront hospital staff and advise in establishing ethical guidelines for the treatment of patients. (a) What kind of persons would you look for to fill this position? What values would you want them to hold? For what types of moral sensitivity would you be looking? (b) What basic moral principles would you advise the Committee to follow?
2. Imagine that you have been charged with the same task described in Question #1, but this time for an advertising agency instead of a hospital. What would the differences be? If there are any differences, what conclusions would you draw about the way we define the moral ballpark?
3. What are your own deepest moral values? What moral qualities do you look for in other people as well as in yourself? Are these values that you think everyone shares, or are some of your values ones that you feel are not always observed by our culture as a whole? How have your values changed, if at all? What influenced their development?
4. A friend asks you to pick out a tie for him to wear at a social occasion. Is this a moral issue? Why or why not? If you refuse, is that immoral, or just rude? If you pick out the wrong tie (one that causes him shame or great embarrassment in public), is that immoral or just a mistake? Does it make a difference if you pick out the wrong tie intentionally or accidentally? The same friend asks you to transport some merchandise across state lines so that he can avoid paying sales tax on it. Is this a moral issue? Why or why not?
5. When (under what circumstances) is it right to tell a lie? Give some examples from everyday life. What does your answer reveal about the scope (or relevance) of morality in general?
6. Recently, an undergraduate student from Rutgers published *Cheating 101*, a guidebook to help students learn how to cheat. What moral issues do you see associated with publishing such a book? Should the campus bookstore carry it? Why or why not? Should the campus newspaper carry advertisements for the book? Similarly, should the

campus newspaper carry advertisements for companies that will write students' research papers for them? Again, what are the relevant moral considerations here? Are these issues in the moral ballpark? Why or why not?

7. What is the moral issue about which you are most undecided? Describe the pros and cons in regard to this issue. How do you go about arriving at a decision when it is unavoidable?
8. We have suggested that ethics is about moral health. When you think of a morally healthful life, what sort of a life do you imagine? What would be some examples of lives that (at least in some respect) are not morally healthy? Give examples from your own experience.
9. When asked to explain his batting technique, Yankee catcher Yogi Berra said, "Just watch me do it." To what extent is this advice applicable to morality, as well? Can we convey it to others or learn it by following someone's example? Or must we teach it to ourselves?

CHAPTER 2

The Role of Relativism in the Moral Life

When in Rome, so the saying goes, do as the Romans do. Yet what do you do if you are an American executive of a multinational corporation in Rome and income tax time comes around? Many Italians consider an income tax report to be like an opening bid in what often prove to be complex and challenging negotiations. It would be silly to give away your entire hand on the first bid, so typically much is initially concealed. Nor would the Italian government expect complete honesty at this stage. To an Italian, this covert activity does not feel like cheating; it is simply the way business is done. Yet to an American businessperson, to file a false tax return is to cheat. When in Rome, what does the American executive do?

Nor, obviously, is this example just an issue about Rome. What should American business people with factories in South Africa have done during the decades of apartheid? When in South Africa, did one do as the Afrikaaners did and exploit the native population? Should one have actively participated in the oppression, or perhaps just benefited economically from it? Or, to shift locations, how should the American businessperson behave in countries in which a bribe, *la mordida* or the *baksheesh,* is considered a normal and acceptable part of almost any business deal? How are we to act in such situations, especially given the moral restrictions in our own culture against bribes?

Nor are these just questions faced outside our own country. Consider the problems faced by our State Department when a man from Saudi Arabia applies for a visa for himself and his wives. Polygamy is forbidden morally as well as legally in our country, but it is both legal and morally acceptable in Saudi

Arabia. Do we issue visas for all his wives, for just one (if so, who chooses which one), or for none? Indeed, do we even issue him a visa, since he is a polygamist? Even closer to home, how would we have dealt with polygamous Mormon families in the United States a hundred years ago when possessing multiple wives was still sanctioned by some of their leaders? More recently, consider the question of the religious use of peyote in Native American religious ceremonies. Should the moral standards of the dominant white society in the United States override the moral and religious standards of the indigenous population?

These are difficult questions, and we will not be able to answer them all in this chapter. However, we will answer that part of the questions which relates to the issue of ethical relativism. **Ethical relativism** is a doctrine that is expressed (inadequately and misleadingly) in adages such as "When in Rome, do as the Romans do." More precisely, it is the belief that moral values are relative to a particular culture and cannot be judged outside of that culture. In examining ethical relativism, we shall be concerned with understanding what makes it attractive to many of us, for it is a doctrine that many people accept, or at least *think* they accept. Yet we shall also ask whether ethical relativism actually succeeds in delivering on its promises, in providing the things that seem to make it attractive. Then we shall look at the standard alternative, moral absolutism, and examine some of its strengths and weaknesses. Finally, we shall suggest a middle ground between relativism and absolutism, one which combines the attractions of both without their liabilities.

The Attractions of Ethical Relativism

Ethical relativism is an attractive doctrine, and in this section we shall see some of the reasons *why* it is attractive. People are drawn to it for any of several possible reasons. First, ethical relativism seems to encourage moral tolerance and understanding, attitudes that most of us find highly desirable. Second, it seems to fit the facts about moral diversity much better than any alternative. Third, it seems that no one has produced a moral system that has commanded universal assent and it seems unlikely that anyone will in the foreseeable future. Fourth, some people hold that everything is relative, and for them ethical relativism is just a corollary of a more general relativism about all beliefs. Finally, we often feel that we have no right to make moral judgment about other people because we ourselves have led far from perfect moral lives. Ethical relativism is often a way of saying, "Don't judge me and I won't judge you." Let us examine each of these lines of argument.

The Need for Tolerance

A Plea for Tolerance and Understanding

Ethical relativism is initially attractive to many of us because it offers the promise of *tolerance* and *understanding*, attitudes most of us value highly. All too often in the past, we have rushed to judgment, letting condemnation eliminate the need for tolerance, allowing superiority to substitute for understanding. Ethical relativism holds the promise of a tolerant attitude of "live and let live."

Moral absolutism, on the other hand, can be a morally intolerant and insensitive position, one which is all too willing to condemn what it does not understand. This argument sometimes is placed within the context of the history of anthropology, which is one of the disciplines most directly involved with issues of cultural relativism. Early anthropology, so the argument goes, was absolutist, measuring the entire world in terms of its own standards and generally finding the rest of the world lacking. So, for example, anthropologists would often refer to the peoples they studied as "barbarians" or "primitive societies." Anthropology made progress, they contend, when it moved toward a more relativistic stance, when it recognized that societies that are different from our own are not necessarily primitive or inferior. Indeed, *we* often appear barbaric to these so-called primitive societies. (When Europeans first reached China, the Chinese were appalled at the Westerners' lack of cleanliness and manners; to the Chinese, it was the Europeans who were the barbarians.) Each society, relativism suggests, should be judged in terms of its own standards rather than be measured in terms of our ethnocentric expectations. We shall return to this comparison with anthropology in the final part of this chapter, and at that point I want again to argue in favor of a third possibility. We shall consider some of the problems with this argument about tolerance shortly.

Tolerance and Understanding

Oddly, given that relativism frequently is associated with a plea for greater understanding as well as tolerance, it often is associated with a belief that we can*not* understand other cultures. Indeed, it is often the conclusion of an argument that begins with a premise such as "We can never (fully) understand another culture." The conclusion then drawn is that we ought not to judge any other culture, and the implicit premise is "We ought not to judge anything which we do not (fully) understand." We will discuss the merits of this argument below.

The Fact of Moral Diversity

Morality and the Ik

For decades, anthropological research has produced countless examples of moral diversity. One of the most striking of recent examples is a mountain tribe in

Africa called the Ik. The Ik seem to explode any belief that we have in a universal morality. They do not even bother to cook their food—they just eat it as soon as they find it. They hide from one another so that no one can see them eating and steal their food. The adults do not bring food back to the village for the children, the aged, or the infirm. If they see a weak old man eating, they will sometimes even take the food out of his mouth and eat it themselves. Children are breast-fed until they are about three years old, and then unceremoniously kicked out and left to fend for themselves. The kids form gangs to hunt for food, but they never develop enduring friendships. Even the name of their tribe—the Ik—seems oddly appropriate to English-speakers. Colin Turnbull, whose *Mountain People* is the most detailed study of the Ik, refers to them as the "Loveless People." They pose a deep question to those who believe that there are certain fundamental values common to all societies, since they seem to lack almost all the moral qualities that we admire in people. They appear to provide an almost irrefutable example that proves that moral goodness is not universal and is not found in all societies.

It is worth noting, however, that the Ik were not always this way. Once they were a proud, nomadic tribe of warriors whose hunting grounds were turned into a national park. Their values were hardly unusual for nomadic tribes, and there is little evidence of their current lack of compassion. However, the government forced them to settle in a mountainous area of northern Uganda plagued by droughts and famine. It was during this period that their moral code declined rapidly.

Initially, one of the most attractive aspects of the relativist's position is that it gives adequate recognition to this kind of moral diversity. Different cultures have such widely divergent moral codes that the notion of a universal morality of any kind simply seems to defy the facts: there is radical moral diversity in our world. Indeed, even individuals within a single society seem to exhibit great diversity in the range of moral values they accept. The only adequate way of recognizing this fact, according to the relativist, is by accepting ethical relativism.

The Lack of a Plausible Alternative

Relativists have another argument at their disposal, one which seems to supplement and strengthen the first argument. They issue the following challenge: "If you claim that ethical relativism is mistaken, then show me a plausible alternative. Show me a set of moral values that everyone accepts, or even that everyone plausibly could accept." In other words, they are suggesting that we may come to agree with ethical relativism by default: no alternative moral system has managed to represent everyone. Not only, they continue, is this fact true of the world at large, it is also true of moral philosophers. These are the people one would expect to agree on basic moral principles, if anyone could, because they spend their lives thinking and talking and writing about such things. Yet when we look at the opinions of many moral philosophers today, we see that there is a tremendous amount of disagreement, even about fundamental moral values. Finally, relativists argue, this situation is in sharp contrast to science and medicine. Certainly there is disagreement in those areas, but there is also widespread agreement on many fundamentals. Since morality has never exhibited that kind of consensus, it is pointless to expect that it ever will.

The Relativity of All Understanding

There is yet a fourth route that leads to ethical relativism, and it begins with the conviction that *all* knowledge and understanding are relative. In its strongest version, this position even claims that truth in the natural sciences is relative to the culture and conceptual framework within which it is expressed. Other cultures may develop quite different ways of understanding and controlling the natural world. In some cultures, magic occupies the place that science holds in our society. Strong relativists would claim that we cannot say that science is right and magic wrong; rather, each is appropriate to, and only to be judged in terms of, the culture in which it is situated.

Other more moderate versions of relativism make a slightly more modest claim. They say that *the meaning of human behavior is always relative to the culture in which it occurs.* In one desert society, it is a sign of friendship and respect to spit at the foot of another person; such behavior means something quite different in our own society. In some cultures, eating dogs is as acceptable as eating cows is in Western societies. In our society, we consider killing dogs cruelty to animals; in India, killing cows is a sacrilege. The meaning of the act is different, depending on the society. In India, how we act toward cows is a *religious* issue, and this attitude is what gives it special meaning. In our country, how we treat dogs is a matter of how we relate to pets, which is almost an issue of *friendship*. More generally, the meaning of any action depends on the cultural context within which it is performed. Consequently, the relativist argues, the moral dimension of our actions is similarly dependent on cultural context for meaning.

Don't Cast the First Stone

There is a final consideration that often weighs in favor of relativism, and it centers around doubts whether we have the *right* to judge other people. Often people are hesitant to pass judgment on someone else's actions because they feel that if they had been in that same situation, they might have done the same thing. Since few people like to condemn themselves, it is just a short step to saying that they should not condemn other people either. In one sense, this attitude is a self-protective strategy: if I do not condemn others, then they cannot condemn me. Yet in another sense, it is a position that emphasizes consistency: if I am unwilling to judge myself harshly, then I forfeit my right to judge others in such a manner. In yet a third sense, it is a position of humility, recalling Jesus's injunction, "Let one who is without sin cast the first stone." Whatever way one takes it, it is a position that denies that one has a *right* to pass judgment on other people. It is, moreover, a position that becomes even more plausible in times when there seems to be fundamental disagreement about basic moral values. "Who," my students often ask, "am I to judge someone else?" We will discuss possible answers to this important question below.

The Definition of Ethical Relativism

We have begun to consider some of the reasons why ethical relativism is attractive, but we have not really looked closely at what ethical relativism maintains. As we shall see, there are several different positions that often are lumped together under this single name. It will be important to distinguish among these various doctrines, for some versions of ethical relativism may prove to be true, while others turn out to be false.

Ethical Relativism: Descriptive and Normative

There is a sense in which there is little disagreement among philosophers about the truth of one type of ethical relativism. It is clear, simply as a matter of fact, that different people have some different moral beliefs—sometimes radically so. Various societies in the past have engaged in such practices as cannibalism or sacrificing human beings to the gods, and those practices were viewed within those societies as morally acceptable, often even as morally commendable. Indeed, even in our own day, there exist some isolated societies that until recently have approved of such actions.

Descriptive Ethical Relativism

Simply to state that different people in fact have different moral beliefs, without taking any stand on the rightness or wrongness of those beliefs, is to accept **descriptive ethical relativism,** which is, as I have already implied, a rather uncontroversial claim, for it does not in any way commit us to saying that these other moral beliefs are also *correct.* Thus someone could be a moral absolutist (that is, someone who believes that there is one and only one true morality) and still accept descriptive ethical relativism, since the absolutist would simply say that those who do not accept this true moral code are wrong. Descriptive ethical relativism does not entail any beliefs about whether the moral codes of various societies are right or wrong.

Types of Ethical Relativism

Descriptive	Claims as a matter of fact that different cultures have different values.
Normative	Claims that each culture's values are right for that culture.

Normative Ethical Relativism

The more controversial and interesting position is what we can call **normative ethical relativism.** The normative ethical relativist puts forward a crucial additional claim not found in descriptive ethical relativism, namely, that each moral code is only *valid* relative to the culture in which it exists. Thus, for example, if cannibalism is acceptable according to the moral code of society X, then members of that society are right in permitting their people to practice cannibalism, even though it would not be permissible for people in our society to do so. A controversial doctrine, normative ethical relativism suggests that what is right in one culture is not right in another and that members of one culture either should not pass any moral judgments on any other culture or else must endorse the moral judgments of other cultures as right for those cultures. (Because normative ethical relativism is both the interesting and controversial claim and the one we will center our discussion on, when I refer to "relativism" or "ethical relativism" I will mean "normative ethical relativism" unless otherwise noted.)

If normative ethical relativism is correct, then the kind of truth that we find in morality is far different from the kind of truth characteristic of everyday factual knowledge, scientific knowledge, or mathematics. If I know that the Morning Star and the Evening Star are the same celestial body (Venus), then I know that it is true for everyone. If some society believes they are two different stars, that society is simply wrong. Similarly, many societies in the past have held that the earth is flat, but we would not hesitate today to state that their belief is false. So, too, we can say with assurance that $2 + 2 = 4$ absolutely, even if some societies do not believe that to be the case. Those who do not believe it are just mistaken. However, if the normative ethical relativist is correct, we cannot say that intentionally killing innocent human beings is always wrong in the same way, because if there is some society that believes that sacrificing innocent victims to the gods is a morally good thing to do, then it is not wrong *for them* according to the normative ethical relativist.

We have now seen one of the basic ambiguities in the claim that morality is relative: it may be either a descriptive or a normative claim. Now we need to get a clearer idea of precisely what we may mean by ethical relativism. We can do so by looking more closely at two important questions: what is morality relative *to*, and *what portion* of our morality is relative? We shall see that there are widely divergent answers to these questions.

Relative to What?

Individuating Cultures

So far, we have presumed that the ethical relativist believes that morality is relative to a particular *culture*. That, however, is no easy notion. What, precisely, do we mean by a culture? Typically, we tend to think of some isolated tribe in New Guinea or some other secluded place, and this idea does provide a clear-cut example of another culture that is radically different from our own and which generally is isolated from our own. However, such examples are quickly becoming the exceptions. There are few such isolated cultures remaining in the world today, and it is likely that their number and degree of isolation will rapidly diminish in the near future. The simple fact of the matter is that most cultures interact with and mutually influence other cultures. In fact, the issue is even more complicated because cultures often seem to contain quite a bit of internal diversity.

Consider American culture. We may refer to it as though there were some single culture, but when we look more closely, we uncover much diversity. A generation ago there were many neighborhoods in major cities where one did not need to know English. German, Lithuanian, Polish, Italian, Greek, or any number of other European languages might have sufficed. Were these part of American culture or should they be seen as part of the culture of their original country? Today Vietnamese, Korean, Tagalog, Cambodian, Laotian, and other Asian and Pacific languages predominate, some in these same neighborhoods. Again, should we see the culture as American or as belonging to another country? This problem concerns how we *individuate a culture*, that is, how we draw the lines to separate one culture from another. It is rare in these days of shifting political systems and mass migrations of people that cultural boundaries coincide strictly with geographical ones. Furthermore, in an age of increasing mass communication and ever-expanding international trade, individual cultures are less and less likely to remain isolated.

The problem of individuating a culture is by no means an abstract issue created solely by philosophers who enjoy drawing logical distinctions. It is very much a problem of everyday living. Consider the moral conflicts that individuals encounter who find themselves on the borderline of two such cultures. For instance, imagine that you were teaching grammar school in an area of the Southwest where a number of the students came from Hopi Indian families. When one student does not know the answer to a question in grammar school, the teacher often calls on other students until one comes up with the correct answer. Yet Hopi schoolchildren would regard it as an insult to provide the answer when the first student did not know it, for they have quite different views on the morality of competition. As a teacher, do you follow the morality of the dominant white group or the morality of the minority Native American group? (Indeed, do we determine which group is "dominant" by sheer numbers or by the power they have in the political and economic system?) Do we have one culture here or two?

In a similar way, think of the problems encountered by American businesspeople in other countries. In South Africa, for example, much of the white population still strongly supports apartheid; some of the white population and virtually all of the black and mixed race population oppose it strongly. If we have businesses with branch offices there, whose values do we follow? Our own? The values of the majority of whites? Those of the majority of blacks and a minority of whites? Again, do we have one culture here or two? These are the questions about the individuation of cultures that are faced everyday by people and which directly raise the question of ethical relativism.

From Relativism to Subjectivism

It is easy to see one direction in which this argument can lead. Some people have taken the question "what are our moral values relative to?" and given increasingly specific answers to it until they finally conclude that those values are relative to each individual person. If our values are partially shaped by the culture in which we live, are not our own individual values also shaped by more specific factors such as geographical location, period in history, family background, religion, schooling, early childhood experiences, and so on? Is it not plausible to believe that if our values are shaped by our culture, they are just as significantly influenced by our individual life histories? Soon we reach the point where instead of seeing values as relative to a culture, we see them as relative primarily to individual life histories. Those who maintain this position are claiming that *cultural ethical relativism collapses into ethical subjectivism.* They maintain, in other words, that cultural ethical relativism inevitably leads to a more radical position, **ethical subjectivism,** which claims that moral values are relative to each unique individual.

One of the reasons given in support of the claim that relativism leads to subjectivism already has been discussed: the difficulty in individuating cultures. The other reason usually given has also been hinted at: there are a number of individual factors (such as family background, religious training, economic status, and education) that seem to be at least as powerful as general cultural factors in shaping an individual's moral beliefs. Yet when our argument is stated in this way, something very interesting starts to emerge. We see that the relativist's claim is at least in part about the *causes* of our moral beliefs. Indeed, as we look more closely, we shall see that the relativist can be making several different claims—one about *understanding* and *judging* moral values, one about the *causes* of those values, one about their *justification,* and one about how to *act.* We will look more closely at this distinction when we discuss the nature of the relativist's claim, but first we must address the question of how much of our morality is relative according to the relativist.

When we claim that morality is relative, our claim is still vague. We have not answered the question of *how much* of morality is relative, which is a question of the *scope* of the relativist's claim. There are at least three ways of defining the scope of relativism. It is important to distinguish among these three, for it may well turn out that only one or two of these claims are true.

The Relativity of Behavior

The first thing that the relativist could be saying is that *moral behavior is relative to a particular culture* (or some other aspect of a person's background). This idea is certainly true in non-moral areas. In some cultures, for example, the polite way of expressing approval of the dinner is to belch; in our own society, such behavior would be considered ill-mannered. Approval would properly be expressed in some other way, such as complimenting the host on the meal. Similarly, spitting at another person's feet is a way of expressing respect in some desert cultures; the same behavior in our culture expresses contempt. Notice that there may be agreement here that it is a good thing to show appreciation of a meal, but the *way* in which that is expressed (that is, the behavior) differs from culture to culture. It seems uncontroversial to say that polite behavior is often relative to a particular culture.

The Relativity of Peripheral Values

The second thing that may be said to be relative is what I shall call peripheral values, the non-fundamental or somewhat secondary values of a culture. In our own culture, for example, respect for innocent human life is taken to be a fundamental moral value; individual privacy is a less fundamental one; freedom to smoke cigarettes is becoming comparatively peripheral and low-level. Here, then, is the second claim that the relativist could be making: *peripheral values vary from culture to culture.* So, for example, the value of private property may be quite important in one society and of relatively little significance in another. One culture may value monogamy quite strongly, another may endorse polygamy; but both might value the basic family, especially for child rearing, even though they differ in their respective definitions of the family unit.

Of course, there is no clear-cut line that separates low-level values from fundamental ones, and one point of disagreement between two cultures may be precisely whether a particular value should be taken as fundamental or peripheral. The distinction is unavoidably vague, but nonetheless useful, as we shall now see.

The Relativity of Fundamental Values

Imagine, in discussing ethical relativism, that someone supports the relativist's position by claiming that morally acceptable behavior varies from culture to

What Is Relative?

Behavior	How different values are expressed in action varies from one culture to another
Peripheral Values	Secondary or peripheral values vary from one culture to another
Fundamental Values	Basic values vary from one culture to another

culture and that, furthermore, moral values such as privacy or monogamy are different in various cultures. You easily could imagine someone replying to this assertion in the following way.

> Yes, I agree that there are these differences among cultures. However, while many things are relative, there are some things that are absolute. Virtually no culture believes in torturing and killing innocent children—and if it does, it is simply wrong in holding that value. There are some values, such as respect for innocent human life, which, though they may be few in number, are not relative. Cultures that do not accept these values are simply wrong.

The person who maintains this position is conceding the first two forms of relativism discussed in this section (the relativity of behavior and the relativity of low-level moral values), but disputes the relativity of fundamental values. There are, as I hope to show below, good reasons for rejecting the relativist's claim when it comes to fundamental values.

What Kind of Doctrine Is Ethical Relativism?

There is another kind of ambiguity in the relativist's position, one which can cause serious confusion if not brought to light. When relativists say, "Moral values are relative to culture," they may mean several rather different things. Once again, it is necessary to distinguish among these different meanings because one or two of them may be true while the other(s) may be false. For the sake of clarity, I will present this ambiguity in terms of different versions of the adage "When in Rome, do as the Romans do." In this saying, Rome stands for any culture different from our own.

Action

The first sense in which ethical relativism may be intended is as a doctrine about action, a doctrine that tells us how to act. Here we see the full and straightforward force of the saying "When in Rome, do as the Romans do." It tells us to **always act in a way that is consistent with local customs**

and values, which in fact turns out not only to be a guide to behaving in other cultures, but also in our own. It says that we should act in a way that is consistent with the moral standards of whatever culture we are in, including our own when we are at home.

As a doctrine of action, relativism is incomplete in three ways. First, it does not tell us how to act when two cultures overlap—an increasingly important issue, as we shall see below. Second, it does not tell us *why* we should act in this way. In order to do so, relativism as a doctrine of action usually depends on one of the other following versions of relativism for its justification. Third, it does not provide any leverage to convince the majority to change, since by definition whatever the majority believes to be right simply is right.

Understanding

The second claim that the relativist may be making is that *in order to understand a person's values and behavior, we must understand the cultural background out of which they arise.* We must, in other words, understand the Roman's behavior in terms of Roman society. This claim is relatively uncontroversial, at least in regard to behavior. The meaning of most behavior is embedded in a context of social meanings that at least to some extent vary from one culture to another. If we are to understand what a particular action or value means to a person in another culture, it is often necessary to understand that stock of background meanings which underlie its significance. To fail to do so is often to misunderstand and distort the meaning of the behavior we observe in another society.

There is an ambiguity in relativism as a doctrine of understanding, and it is one that is important in our assessment of the relativist's claim. When the relativist claims that behavior can be understood only relative to the specific cultural context within which it occurs, it is unclear whether an outsider to the culture can understand the behavior at all. In its **strong version,** this doctrine claims not only that all behavior must be understood relative to the cultural context, but also that the cultural context can be understood only by participants; consequently, outsiders cannot genuinely understand behavior in a society in which they are not participants and thus they are not entitled to make value judgments about that behavior. In its **weak version,** this doctrine maintains that meaning is relative to culture, but that outsiders can understand other cultures. This weaker version leaves the door open for dialogue between cultures and for mutual understanding. The stronger version seems to close the door to such dialogue and perhaps even precludes the possibility of anthropology.

Judgment

At this juncture, we encounter another ambiguity within relativism as a doctrine of understanding, and this ambiguity rests on the relation between understanding and judgment. Assuming that behavior must be understood relative to its cultural context, what does this assessment tell us about the moral judgments we make about the actions and values of other societies? There are three possibilities: 1) such behavior may not be judged at all by outsiders; 2) it may be judged by outsiders only in relation to the society's own values; and 3) it may be judged by outsiders even in relation to values which the society itself does not share. Relativism as a doctrine of judgment maintains that behavior within a society can be judged only by the standards of that society. We should judge Romans only by Roman standards. Again, this theory has a strong version and a weak version. The **strong version** maintains that only Romans can judge Romans by their own standards; the **weak version** allows anyone in principle to judge Romans as long as they employ Roman standards.

Explanation

In arguing in favor of relativism, some people claim to explain the origins of our moral values by showing that *moral values are caused or determined by cultural forces.* This claim, our fourth possible one, is equivalent to saying that if you were raised in Rome, you would have the values that the Romans have. The fact that people grew up in a particular culture explains *why* they have the specific values they do. Our own culture forces us to accept particular values, while living in another culture would cause us to believe in a different set of values, a concept closely related to what philosophers call **determinism**, that is, the belief that (in this case) our moral values are determined causally. In contrast, some philosophers claim that our values are, at least to some extent, *freely chosen.* They maintain that although our culture may initially shape our values, as we mature we come to make our own independent choices about what our values will be. This notion is a version of the dispute between freedom and determinism, which will be discussed in Chapter Five in our consideration of psychological egoism.

There is little chance that we will be able to unravel all the knotty issues surrounding freedom and determinism here, but we can at least note the following objection to the determinist's position. If we have no choice in our moral values, then there really is not much point in talking about them at all, because we will believe whatever we are determined to believe anyway. If there is not *some* room for freedom of choice, then we will just have whatever values we are determined to have. Yet the whole point of these discussions is that we have to make choices, and making choices presumes some degree of freedom. If determinism is true, there is no point in discussing what we ought to do. (This issue will be discussed in more detail in the chapter on Egoism.)

Justification

There is a fifth claim that the relativist may make: *moral values may be justified only relative to the standards of a particular culture.* In other words, when values

Relativism as a Doctrine about:

Action	People ought to act according to the values of the culture in which they live
Understanding	People's values must be understood within their cultural context
Judgment	People's values can be judged only within their cultural context
Explanation	People's values are causally determined by cultural forces
Justification	People's values can be justified only in terms of their own culture

are challenged or called into question in some way, the only appropriate way of justifying them is by an appeal to the standards of the culture. When in Rome, the only way of justifying one's actions and values is to appeal to fundamental values accepted by Roman society. This claim is distinct from any of the four preceding claims. One could, for example, maintain that values initially may be understood within the context of a particular culture and yet deny that they can be justified only in relation to that culture.

The question of justification of values is a tricky one, and it is important to realize what the alternatives are. Those who support the claim that moral values can be justified only in terms of the values of that culture encounter a possible problem: the fundamental values of the culture are not themselves open to justification. Those values simply have to be accepted as they are. Yet we can imagine cases, at least as outsiders to a particular culture, where we would want to question some of a society's values and claim that they should *not* be accepted as they are. The anti-Semitism of Nazi Germany, for example, became a fundamental value for a number of people in that society, but most of us today would want to deny that that value was justified, even for those in that situation. Yet the relativist's position on justification would seem to leave no basis for those in Nazi Germany to have questioned that value. We shall consider this problem in more detail below when we discuss relativism and moral change.

We have now seen some of the important distinctions that need to be drawn in talking about relativism. They are summarized in the chart at the top of this page.

As we shall see by the end of this chapter, relativism as a doctrine of action is largely useless, unable to answer the questions that confront us today. Relativism as a doctrine of judgment, of explanation, and of justification is seriously incomplete. But relativism as a doctrine of understanding has a lot of merit and should be accepted. Let us now turn to a consideration of some of the reasons why ethical relativism will not suffice as a doctrine of action or justification, even though it is partially valid as a doctrine of understanding.

THE LIMITS OF ETHICAL RELATIVISM

Despite its attractiveness, many philosophers have been hesitant to accept ethical relativism. A number of arguments have been advanced against it, some of which are put forward primarily by philosophers, others of which are shared by the general public. In this section, we shall consider five of these arguments: (1) the facts of moral diversity do not actually justify ethical relativism; (2) the refutation of relativism through the defense of one's own absolutist position; (3) the claim that relativism is self-defeating, leading to the acceptance of absolutism or intolerance; (4) the concern that ethical relativism is really a form of moral isolationism or indifference that ignores the fact that moral judgments are unavoidable; and (5) the claim that relativism is unable to provide an adequate basis for moral change. Let us consider each of these arguments in turn.

The Fact of Moral Diversity Reconsidered

We can already see in light of some of the distinctions drawn above that the argument for moral diversity is less strong than it originally appeared to be. First, the fact of moral diversity is certainly sufficient to establish *descriptive ethical relativism*, but taken by itself it does not necessarily commit us to *normative ethical relativism*. We could argue, for example, that there are many bizarre scientific views in the world (today as well as in the past), but the mere fact of different views does not entail the conclusion that each of them is right within its own culture or context. Similarly, there are many people with unusual medical beliefs, but we do not hesitate to label at least some of them quacks. The mere fact of diversity, in other words, does not suffice alone to support the conclusion that we cannot make judgments about the moral values held by other cultures.

Second, we have to be wary of the level of generality on which the relativist's argument is stated. Recall the earlier distinction among behavior, low-level values, and fundamental values. We may well want to concede that respect for the dignity of the person is shown in different ways in different cultures and that other cultures should not necessarily be compelled to manifest this value through the same kinds of behavior that we find appropriate. But most of us certainly would draw the line at *some* point. The Nazis' attempted extermination of Jews, Gypsies, homosexuals, and others is certainly one such point. It may have *seemed* right to some of them within their culture, but I clearly would want to say that they were wrong if they held that belief.

The Appeal to an Absolute Position

Perhaps the most common way of arguing against ethical relativism is to present an alternative, that is, a position that one claims is absolute. We find absolutes in everyday life quite often. Sometimes it is a religiously based viewpoint which is being advocated to the exclusion of all others, at other times it may be grounded in a particular political idealogy. Sometimes it is rooted in philosophical systems, and in the following chapters we shall critically assess five of the primary attempts to provide a philosophical basis for an absolutist morality: the libertarian program of the ethical egoist, Kant's ethics of duty, a utilitarian ethics of consequences, modern attempts to see ethics primarily as rights, and recent attempts to revive Aristotle's approach to the ethics of character. Certainly the strongest refutation of relativism would be the introduction of a moral system which not only claimed to be absolute, but also which everyone actually accepted as such.

There is no simple way of evaluating here all of these attempts at an absolutist morality, although we shall examine several of the strictly philosophical positions in subsequent chapters. Yet there are many other absolutist positions which have not received elaborate philosophical expression, and an examination of these is simply beyond the scope of this book. It is important to note, however, what relativists would say to all of these attempted refutations. None, they would claim, has *in fact* achieved anything approaching universality. While there are groups of people who believe strongly that each of these positions is absolute, relativists see it as simply supporting their claim. Different groups, they would argue, have different sets of moral beliefs, and relativism is the only plausible way of accounting for these differences.

Relativists are not only demanding that an absolutist system of morality *claim* to be absolute, they are also demanding that it be *accepted* by everyone (or at least a very large percentage of people) as absolute if it is to count as a refutation of relativism. Claiming to be absolute is simply not enough, for many moral systems already do that. Indeed, it is precisely the fact that many such systems *claim* to be absolute that creates the problem relativism tries to solve. Until we all agree about which system of morality is absolute, the absolutist refutation of relativism falls short of the mark.

Is Relativism Self-Defeating?

The Relativist in an Absolutist Society

There is a paradoxical implication in relativism as a doctrine of action. If you should do in Rome as the Romans do, what happens if the Romans assume a very absolutist attitude toward everyone else in the world? What if the Romans turn out to be highly ethnocentric, taking their own culture's values and customs as the absolute measure of everyone else's? Then, it would seem, if we are in

Rome, and if the Romans are absolutist and ethnocentric, then we should be absolutist and ethnocentric. Yet this absolutism is precisely the kind of culturally chauvinistic attitude that the relativist is trying to convince us to give up. If relativism tells us to do as the Romans do, and if the Romans are not relativists, then relativism tells us to act like non-relativists. Such an injunction appears to be self-defeating.

The Relativist in an Intolerant Society

There is another closely related difficulty with relativism as a doctrine of action. One of the principal attractions of relativism is that it seems to promise tolerance. Yet what if the other culture is intolerant? Do we then accept intolerance as one of our values when in that culture? If, to return to our standard example, the Romans are intolerant, should we also be intolerant when we are in Rome? It would seem that relativism as a doctrine of action commits us to this approach, and that threatens to undermine one of its attractions.

This fault is also true of relativism as a doctrine of understanding and judgment, but in a slightly different way. As a doctrine of understanding and judgment, relativism seems to be the clearest example of tolerance imaginable. It recommends a highly tolerant attitude toward others, and yet it becomes a problem when those others are themselves intolerant. If relativism says do not judge the Romans, be tolerant of them, and if the Romans themselves are very judgmental and intolerant, then relativism commits us to being tolerant toward intolerance.

The Value of Tolerance

As we have seen, one aspect of relativism that makes it initially so attractive is that it promises a more tolerant attitude toward other cultures. We also have seen that this promise may at times be illusory, since relativism as a doctrine of action might oblige us to adopt intolerant values if we were in a society which valued intolerance. Yet there is another difficulty with tolerance which we have not yet addressed here. Granting that tolerance should be an important value for us, should we place it above all others? Should tolerance be our *highest* value?

There are clearly some areas in which most of us are inclined to be tolerant. Other cultures may have different moral codes governing, say, business relations or family obligations, and most of us would probably tolerate and respect those differences, even if we would not personally want to live by them. Yet in other areas, we are more likely to draw the line. Racism in South Africa, for example, is something that calls forth protest from many of us. The Nazis' attempted genocide against the Jews, the Turkish massacre of the Armenians, and Pol Pot's genocide in Cambodia are but a few examples of the wanton killing that outrages almost all of us. When faced with atrocities such as these, tolerance has to take second place to other more important values, such as respect for innocent human life and justice. Tolerance, in other words, is an important value—it just is not appropriate as our *highest* value.

Relativism as Moral Isolationism

There is yet another difficulty with ethical relativism: all too often it seems to lead to a kind of moral isolationism in which we simply do not care about the rest of the world. There are several aspects to this isolationism.

Relativism as a Conversation Stopper

In order to understand relativism, we need to consider not only what relativism actually says, but also the *function* of the appeal to relativism in moral discourse. Consider, in this regard, the typical way that appeals to relativism function in a conversation. Imagine two persons discussing and disagreeing about some moral issue such as abortion or capital punishment. If one of them says, "Well, after all, it's all relative, isn't it?", this serves to bring the conversation to a halt. What, after all, can you say *after* you've said it is all relative? It is crucial to see how the appeal to relativism works in such situations. When someone says, "it's all relative," they are often also *implicitly* saying that something follows from this claim, namely, "therefore, we cannot criticize it." It is this implication which is, I think, most doubtful. If the appeal to relativism were used to begin a conversation rather than end it, we would have quite a different picture of its rhetorical function.

Relativism as a Protection from Criticism

There is another aspect of the way in which relativism is used in conversation which is the opposite side of the implicit claim that we cannot criticize others. If we cannot criticize others because "it's all relative," then neither can *they* criticize *us*. In a sense, this approach may be the payoff that relativism has for many people: it insulates them against criticism from the outside. It nullifies in advance any possible objection to their behavior or values that anyone outside their culture could present.

The full force of this hidden implication of relativism becomes apparent when we recall that relativism often collapses into subjectivism, namely, the belief that values are relative to each individual person. If that were true, then the hidden implication of relativism might be that no one has a right to criticize us. We are each, as it were, worlds unto ourselves, and no one is entitled to criticize a person's choices because no one is in the same situation. The appeal to relativism thereby becomes an insulation against possible criticism, a way of protecting oneself against any possible moral objections to one's behavior or values.

What is Wrong with Moral Isolationism?

What, one might plausibly ask, is wrong with this hidden implication of the appeal to relativism? There are at least three problems with this isolationist attitude: 1) it fails to provide an answer about how we should resolve moral disagreements between cultures; 2) it ignores the fact that we live in a constantly shrinking world which necessitates inter-cultural moral judgments; and 3) it overlooks the ways in which intra-cultural as well as inter-cultural moral judgments are necessary parts of everyday life.

The Absence of an Answer

First, the appeal of relativism claims to function as a way of dealing with moral conflict and with disagreements about moral values. But the difficulty is that often relativism is not an answer to the question of how to deal with such differences, but is rather *the absence of an answer*. Faced with moral disagreements, the relativist says, in effect, "let's not talk about it," which is not an answer, but instead is the refusal even to search for an answer. But why, we may well ask, are answers necessary?

Relativism in a Shrinking World

Relativism as an attitude toward other cultures made more sense when cultures were in fact much more isolated from one another. A century ago it was not uncommon to find isolated cultures, often tribes that lived in remote jungles or mountains, that had had virtually no contact with our own culture. In such instances, relativism might have expressed an attitude of respect toward those cultures, an unwillingness to interfere with the culture or to judge it too quickly. Such an attitude of non-interference would be particularly appropriate to a scientific, anthropological approach to such a society.

Such societies are increasingly rare today, and it seems highly improbable that they can escape interacting with other more powerful societies. When interaction occurs, the problem is to decide whose values should prevail. And here, precisely where it is needed most, ethical relativism fails to deliver an answer. As different cultures interact more and more, we need to develop rules that govern the *intersection* of two cultures, and this union is what relativism fails to offer. When in Rome, relativism as a doctrine of action suggests, do as the Romans do. Yet there is an area of overlap, an area that is neither purely Roman nor purely American, in which the two cultures meet—and it is here that we need guidance. This overlap emerges most clearly in our world in two ways. First, cultures overlap through trade and commerce. Nations must deal with each other and consequently must develop rules of interaction that are acceptable to *both* cultures. Second, the rapid growth of communications and of the news and entertainment media has increased the amount of influences cultures have on one another. In both of these areas, the larger, more powerful, and more productive cultures threaten to overwhelm the smaller, weaker, and less productive ones. German children grow up watching a number of American television programs; American children watch American programs. We are, in other words, living in a shrinking world, and we need guidance about how to interact with other cultures. To the extent that relativism simply says that each culture is a world unto itself, it fails to give us such guidance.

The Unavoidability of Moral Judgments

Relativism, we have seen, often collapses into subjectivism. Just as cross-cultural moral judgments are increasingly unavoidable in our world, so, too, is it impossible to avoid interpersonal moral judgments. Yet when ethical relativism collapses into moral subjectivism, it is precisely such judgments that it seeks to avoid. To the extent that interpersonal moral judgments are unavoidable, and to the extent that ethical relativism fails to offer us any guidance in making those judgments, relativism does not provide us with an answer to the moral questions that face us.

There can be no doubt that interpersonal moral judgments are unavoidable. We continually make decisions that affect other people, just as their decisions affect us—and in both cases, we need to make moral judgments about the acceptability of such decisions. Nor can we remain neutral about such issues, for we often are forced to make decisions which implicitly take a stance on moral issues. Consider abortion, for example. We may not have to make a personal decision about whether to have an abortion, but we often make decisions that either support or condemn such a practice. The allocation of our tax dollars, the political candidates we support, the kind of sex education we encourage in schools—these are but a few of the ways in which we indirectly take a stand on the morality of abortion.

Even in matters that do not require a decision, we make moral judgments. Recall that moral judgments do not need to be negative. When we say that someone is good, we are making a moral judgment just as much as if we were condemning the person. If we try to avoid moral judgments, then we have to give up positive judgments as well as negative ones. We even have to give up such things as blaming or gossiping, both of which have a significant component of moral judgment. Moral judgments, in other words, permeate our everyday life, and it is hard to imagine what life would be without them.

Relativism and Moral Change

There is an additional set of difficulties associated with ethical relativism, and these relate to the issue of moral progress. Let us examine each of these.

Pressure to Change

There was a cartoon years ago in the *New Yorker* that captured well one of the difficulties with relativism. It showed a group of people marching down a street, carrying signs such as "It's a point of view," "This is just my opinion," "My perspective," and "This is just another way of looking at things." Although the signs were not explicit appeals to relativism, they were close enough to illustrate one of its drawbacks. When we claim that everything is relative, we say that our own point of view is valid only for ourselves. Once we do this, we lose any moral leverage for claiming that other people ought to heed what we say.

Consider the civil rights movement in America. If Martin Luther King, Jr., had been a relativist, in effect he would have said, "I have a dream—but, of course, that's only my limited point of view, valid within my context but not binding on anyone outside of that context." For the full-fledged moral relativist, there is no vantage point from which to exert moral pressure, for each person is considered right relative to his or her culture.

There is, of course, one way in which relativists do have some moral leverage: they are justified in objecting to anything which is *not* consistent with the values of the culture. Yet this makes relativism a profoundly conservative doctrine in ways that may be unacceptable. In a racist society, relativists are justified only in objecting to those who are *opposed* to racism, those who are in favor of equal treatment. This is not to suggest, of course, that relativists are necessarily racists, or anything of the kind. Rather, it is to say that relativists in a racist society can offer no *reasons* why someone should not be a racist, no *justification* for rejecting racism.

Moral Progress

Another difficulty that relates to this issue is whether the relativist can offer a satisfactory account of moral progress. When relativists say that morality is relative to a culture, they usually also are saying that a culture changes over time. Consequently, what might be morally right at one time might be morally wrong at some other time. Just as we cannot legitimately impose one culture's values on another, so, too, we are not permitted to impose one *epoch's* values on those of another epoch. Each era must be understood and judged in terms of its own values.

The difficulty with this claim is that each epoch is, in effect, right unto itself; consequently, it is impossible to say that one is any better than any other. Yet if we cannot make this judgment then it makes no sense to talk about moral progress (or moral decline, either). Just as we cannot say that one society is better than another, neither can we say that one historical period is better than any other. Each has to be judged only in relation to itself. For the relativist, there is no overarching standard in terms of which the various epochs could be judged.

This argument contrasts sharply to our attitude toward, say, science or medicine. A century ago, people were bled with leeches when they had infections; now physicians administer antibiotics. This is progress. Antibiotics are more effective than leeches in eliminating infections. Yet the relativist cannot make similar judgments about moral progress. If we used to hang pickpockets and now we give them a jail sentence, the relativist can say only that we now have different standards, not that we have *better* standards. Similarly, if we used to condone slavery and we now value and strive toward genuine freedom and equality, the relativist can see the development only as change, not as progress. To claim that these changes were improvements would be to claim that there was some standard in terms of which they could both be judged—and it is precisely this understanding which relativism precludes. Each age can be judged only by its own standards.

Where Do We Go from Here?

Where, then, are we left in our attempt to decide whether ethical relativism is true or not? It seems that we have some strong arguments in favor of both sides, and we have some very powerful objections to both sides. Are we to give up, or do we perhaps just ignore the arguments on one side and continue to believe whichever position we prefer? As long as we see ourselves as confined to these two options, relativism and absolutism, there will appear to be no satisfactory answer. However, I think there is a third option, a middle ground between relativism and absolutism that combines the attractive features of both without the liabilities of either. It is to this option that we now turn.

Fallibilistic Ethical Pluralism

Some Preliminary Conclusions

The Inadequacy of Ethical Relativism

Several conclusions emerge from the preceding remarks. First, *ethical relativism is simply inadequate*. As a doctrine of action, it fails to provide us with guidance precisely where we need it most—at the intersection of two cultures. As a doctrine of judgment, it leads to an unacceptable and unrealistic moral isolationism. As a doctrine of causal explanation, it commits us to a determinism that creates more problems than it solves. Yet as a doctrine of understanding, it makes an important contribution, especially through its emphasis on tolerance and the contextuality of our understanding of moral practices. It is precisely this dual emphasis on tolerance and contextuality which we must retain.

The Failure of Ethical Absolutism

Second, *ethical absolutism also fails as a moral theory*. Certainly there are plenty of candidates for such absolutism, but that is precisely the problem. There is no single absolutist position which virtually everyone acknowledges as correct, nor is there any reason to expect that such a consensus will emerge in the near future. Moreover, absolutism seems to carry precisely those dangers that relativism avoids. The twin dangers of intolerance and lack of understanding, although not a necessary part of absolutism, are certainly dangers that often accompany it. It is precisely these which we want to avoid.

The Inevitability of Moral Disagreement

Third, it is reasonable to assume that we will continue to have moral disagreements for the foreseeable future and that, given the shrinking character of our world, such disagreements will become increasingly unavoidable. *Disagreement and difference are standard features of the moral landscape.* We need a moral theory that recognizes this fact and provides an appropriate interpretation of it. Two interpretations seem to me to be unsuitable: (1) those which see such disagreement as a sufficient basis for simply giving up on ethical reflection, for saying the undertaking is futile; and (2) those which see such disagreement simply as an indication of how wrong other people can be. In both cases, disagreement is not something that we can learn from; it is not a positive source of understanding.

Fallibilistic Ethical Pluralism

Thus what we need is an account of moral discourse that recognizes these three claims and shows us how we can meaningfully engage in ethical discussions under these conditions. We need, in other words, a way of doing ethics until we find the absolute truth.

Chapter Three, which deals with the diversity of ethical theories, provides such an account of moral discourse. It offers a position that marks out the middle ground between relativism and absolutism, a position I shall call *fallibilistic ethical pluralism.* It incorporates insights both from relativism and absolutism. From relativism, it retains the sensitivity to the contextuality of our moral beliefs and the recognition that moral disagreement and conflict are permanent features of the moral landscape. From absolutism, it retains the commitment to the relevance of reasoned discourse in the moral life and the belief that some moral positions are better than others. It offers a way of appreciating such diversity and disagreement as sources of richness in our moral lives and it suggests ways in which we can live together in the face of such disagreements. It also provides an account of the ways in which various ethical theories relate to one another.

Chapter Eleven will complete the themes introduced here by considering in more detail the positive role of diversity in ethics and presenting an account of how we can resolve conflict in the moral life.

Let us now turn to Chapter Three, which outlines an alternative to the dichotomy between relativism and absolutism.

Bibliographical Essay

Ruth Benedict's "A Defense of Moral Relativism," *The Journal of General Psychology*, Vol. 10 (1934), pp. 59–82, is one of the most influential and often-reprinted contemporary defenses of ethical relativism by a leading figure in twentieth-century anthropology. It is reprinted in numerous anthologies, including *Vice and Virtue in Everyday Life*, edited by Christina Sommers and Fred Sommers (San Diego: Harcourt Brace Jovanovich, 1989), pp. 148–56. Also see Edward Westermarck, *The Origin and Development of the Moral Ideas* (London: MacMillan, 1912) and, more recently, Richard A. Shweder, "Anthropology's Romantic Rebellion against the Enlightenment: Or There's More to Thinking than Reason and Evidence," *Culture Theory: Essays on Mind, Self and Emotion*, edited by R. A. Shweder and R. A. Levine (Cambridge: Cambridge University Press, 1984). Colin Turnbull first described the Ik in his book *The Mountain People* (New York: Simon and Schuster, 1972). For a thoughtful commentary on the implications of Turnbull's work for ethics, see Christine Battersby's "Morality and the Ik," *Philosophy*, Vol. 53 (1978), pp. 201–14, and Jonathan Lear's "Moral Objectivity," *Objectivity and Cultural Divergence*, edited by S. C. Brown (Cambridge: Cambridge University Press, 1984), pp. 135–70. For a fascinating study of the history and morality of **bribes,** see John T. Noonan, Jr.'s *Bribes* (Berkeley: University of California Press, 1984).

There are several good **introductory anthologies** containing a number of the basic articles on moral relativism, including *Relativism: Cognitive and Moral*, edited by Michael Krausz and Jack W. Meiland (Notre Dame: University of Notre Dame Press, 1982), which contains essays on moral relativism by Philippa Foot, Bernard Williams, Gilbert Harman, David Lyons, and Geoffrey Harrison; and *Relativism: Interpretation and Conflict*, edited with an Introduction by Michael Krausz (Notre Dame: University of Notre Dame Press, 1989), contains an excellent selection of articles primarily by philosophers but also contains articles by two eminent anthropologists, Clifford Geertz and Richard Shweder. Also see *Objectivity and Cultural Divergence*, edited by S. C. Brown (Cambridge: Cambridge University Press, 1984), which contains a number of insightful papers on the possibility of objectivity (including, but not limited to, moral objectivity) in light of cultural differences. For an excellent **survey of recent work on moral relativism,** see Robert M. Stewart and Lynn L. Thomas, "Recent Work on Ethical Relativism," *American Philosophical Quarterly*, Vol. 28 (April, 1991), pp. 85–100; also see the extensive bibliography on relativism in Harvey Seigel, *Relativism Refuted* (Dordrecht, Netherlands: Reidel, 1987).

On the relationship between **relativism and tolerance,** see Joshua Halberstam's "The Paradox of Tolerance," *Philosophical Forum*, Vol. 14 (1982/83), pp. 190–206; Geoffrey Harrison's "Relativism and Tolerance," *Ethics*, Vol. 86,

No. 2 (January, 1976), pp. 122–35; Max Hocutt's "Must Relativists Tolerate Evil?", *The Philosophical Forum*, Vol. 17 (Spring, 1986), pp. 188–200; Nicholas Unwin's "Relativism and Moral Complacency," *Philosophy*, Vol. 60 (1985), pp. 205–14; Jay Newman's "Ethical Relativism," *Laval Théologique et Philosophique*, Vol. 28 (1972), pp. 63–74, and his "The Idea of Religious Tolerance," *American Philosophical Quarterly*, Vol. 15 (1978), pp. 187–95. On the related notions of compromise and accommodation, see Martin Benjamin, *Splitting the Difference: Compromise and Integrity in Ethics and Politics* (Lawrence, Kans.: University of Kansas Press, 1990) and David Wong, "Coping with Moral Conflict and Ambiguity," *Ethics*, Vol. 102, No. 4 (July, 1992), pp. 763–84.

One of the more persuasive arguments in favor of relativism from the fact of **moral disagreement** is to be found in J. L. Mackie's *Ethics: Inventing Right and Wrong* (New York: Penguin Books, 1976). Also see Thomas L. McClintock's "The Argument for Ethical Relativism from the Diversity of Morals," *The Monist*, Vol. 47 (1963), pp. 528–44; Judith Wagner DeCew, "Moral Conflicts and Ethical Relativism," *Ethics*, Vol. 101, No. 1 (October, 1990), pp. 27–41; Amy Gutmann and Dennis Thompson, "Moral Conflict and Political Consensus," *Ethics*, Vol. 101, No. 1 (October, 1990), pp. 64–88; Kai Nielsen, "On the Diversity of Moral Beliefs," *Cultural Hermeneutics*, Vol. 2 (1974), pp. 281–303; Carl Wellman, "Ethical Disagreement and Objective Truth," *American Philosophical Quarterly*, Vol. 12 (1975), pp. 211–21; James D. Wallace, *Moral Relevance and Moral Conflict* (Ithaca, N.Y.: Cornell University Press, 1988); and Michael Stocker, *Plural and Conflicting Values* (Oxford: Clarendon Press, 1990). For a recent defense of a middle ground on moral realism, see Richard W. Miller, *Moral Differences: Truth, Justice, and Conscience in a World of Conflict* (Princeton, N.J.: Princeton University Press, 1992).

For critical assessments of Mackie's position, especially in regard to the question of **moral realism**, see David O. Brink's "Moral Realism and the Skeptical Arguments from Disagreement and Queerness," *Australasian Journal of Philosophy*, Vol. 62 (1984), pp. 111–25, and William Tolhurst, "The Argument from Moral Disagreement," *Ethics*, Vol. 87, No. 3 (April, 1987), pp. 610–21. The anthology *Morality and Objectivity: A Tribute to J. L. Mackie*, edited by Ted Honderich (London: Routledge & Kegan Paul, 1985) contains essays by Simon Blackburn, Philippa Foot, R. M. Hare, Susan Hurley, Steven Lukes, John McDowell, Amartya Sen, David Wiggins, and Bernard Williams on the issues raised by Mackie. Geoffrey Sayre-McCord's *Essays on Moral Realism* (Ithaca, N.Y.: Cornell, 1988) contains a number of excellent essays (including one by Mackie) for and against moral realism. Also see Robert L. Arrington, *Rationalism, Realism, and Relativism: Perspectives in Contemporary Moral Epistemology* (Ithaca, N.Y.: Cornell University Press, 1989) for an overview of recent work in this area.

Some of the most interesting work on the issue of ethical relativism stems from **Alasdair MacIntyre's** *After Virtue*, 2d ed. (Notre Dame Ind.: University of Notre Dame Press, 1984). He has carried this work forward in two later books: *Three Rival Versions of Moral Inquiry* (Notre Dame, Ind.: University of Notre Dame Press, 1990), which examines competing conceptions of moral discourse, and *Whose Justice? Whose Rationality?* (Notre Dame Ind.: University of Notre Dame Press, 1988), which is devoted to an examination of changing conceptions of justice and rationality. Also see his "Relativism, Power and Philosophy," *Proceedings and Addresses of The American Philosophical Association,* Vol. 59 (September, 1985), pp. 5–22. In this same tradition, also see Jeffrey Stout's *Ethics After Babel. The Languages of Morals and Their Discontents* (Boston: Beacon Press, 1988); and James Boyd White's *When Words Lose Their Meaning. Constitutions and Reconstitutions of Language, Character, and Community* (Chicago: University of Chicago Press, 1984).

Gilbert Harman has offered a vigorous **defense of ethical relativism** in "Moral Relativism Defended," *Philosophical Review,* Vol. 84 (1975), pp. 3–22; in his "Relativistic Ethics: Morality as Politics," *Midwest Studies in Philosophy,* Vol. 3 (1978), pp. 109–21; and in his "What Is Moral Relativism?" in *Values and Morals,* edited by Alvin I. Goldman and Jaegwon Kim (Dordrecht, Netherlands: D. Reidel, 1978). Steven Darwall's "Harman and Moral Relativism," *The Personalist,* Vol. 58 (1977), pp. 199–207; and Louis P. Pojman's "Gilbert Harman's Internalist Moral Relativism," *The Modern Schoolman,* Vol. 68 (November, 1990), pp. 19–39, present some insightful criticisms of Harman's position. For a recent defense of a version of **causal relativism**, see S. F. Sapontzis, "Moral Relativism: A Causal Interpretation and Defense," *American Philosophical Quarterly,* Vol. 24, No. 4 (October, 1987), pp. 329–37.

Discussion Questions

1. Recall statement 1 in your Ethical Inventory: "What is right depends on the culture a person is in."
   (a) How would you reformulate this statement to make it more precise?
   (b) Has your rating on this item changed after reading this chapter? If so, in what way? If your rating has not changed, are your reasons for your rating any different now than they were when you first responded to this statement?
2. Recall statement 2 in the Ethical Inventory: "People should always do whatever the majority thinks is right."
   (a) What is the proper name for this theory?
   (b) What arguments can be offered in support of this claim? against it?
   (c) Has your rating of this item changed after reading this chapter? If so, in what way? If your rating has not changed, are your

reasons for your rating any different now than they were when you first responded to this statement?

3. Recall statement 3 in the Ethical Inventory: "What is right is up to each individual."
   (a) What is the proper name for this theory?
   (b) What arguments can be offered in support of this claim? against it?
   (c) Has your rating of this item changed after reading this chapter? If so, in what way? If your rating has not changed, are your reasons for your rating any different now than they were when you first responded to this statement?
4. Statement 4 of the Ethical Inventory—"No one has the right to judge what is right or wrong for another person"—concentrates on our right to make moral judgments about other people.
   (a) Has your rating of this item changed after reading this chapter? If so, in what way? If your rating has not changed, are your reasons for your rating any different now than they were when you first responded to this statement?
   (b) Take a specific example of someone who has committed a morally extreme act, whether exceptionally good or bad. What arguments could be advanced to claim that we are not entitled to make a judgment about that act? What replies could be offered?
5. Recall statement 5 of the Ethical Inventory: "No one has the right to intervene when he or she thinks someone else has done something morally wrong."
   (a) When, if ever, do you think intervention is morally justified? morally required? Give examples of actual situations.
   (b) Has your rating of this item changed after reading this chapter? If so, in what way? If your rating has not changed, are your reasons for your rating any different now than they were when you first responded to this statement?
6. A friend of mine taught English as a second language to a group of Southeast Asian students in Southern California. Over the months she developed an excellent rapport with the students. When she became pregnant, they were all happy for her and her husband, even having a baby shower after class one night. My friend was delighted when she delivered a beautiful, healthy seven pound girl. She was shocked and puzzled when, several days after the students in her class had heard of the birth, she began to receive cards of *condolence* from them! It soon became clear. In their culture, having a son as a first child is a matter of great joy, and they all sympathized with what they presumed was her sense of deep disappointment that she had had a girl.

Discuss the issues that this example raises about moral relativism. If you were in my friend's position, how would you deal with the situation?

7. Near the Taos Pueblo of New Mexico, Native Americans for centuries have considered Blue Lake, on the slopes of Mount Wheeler, a sacred place, as holy to them as a church is to Christians. During the 1970s, residents of the Pueblo engaged in a long and ultimately successful judicial and legislative battle to regain control of Blue Lake. While Blue Lake meant one thing to Native Americans, it meant something quite different to most non-Native Americans. How do you think such differences should be resolved? What principles do you appeal to in deciding who should have control of the land?
8. In Peter Weir's movie *Witness,* we find an interesting clash of two cultures: the pacifist world of the Amish and the violence-ridden world of a Philadelphia police detective played by Harrison Ford. What would the normative ethical relativist have to say about their interaction, and especially about how Harrison Ford should behave while living with the Amish? Do you agree with the relativist's normative recommendations? Why or why not?
9. The move *The Mission* opens with a startling scene: a Catholic priest is being tied alive to a cross and then is pushed out into a river that eventually goes over a huge waterfall, killing the priest. What would the normative ethical relativist have to say about this event? Was it just another case of "when in Rome. . . ," or did it violate some basic principle of morality that we should all uphold? Why or why not?
10. In *The Mission,* Jeremy Irons plays a Jesuit missionary in South America and Robert De Niro depicts a slave trader who gives up his former life and becomes a Jesuit as well. Both bring foreign values to the native inhabitants. What would the normative ethical relativist say about Jeremy Irons' activities among the natives as a missionary? What would the same relativist say about Robert De Niro's slave trading among the natives? In the eyes of the relativist, are there any morally relevant differences between the two? If so, what are they? If not, why not? How would you assess the behavior of both men in light of the discussion of moral relativism?

C H A P T E R 3

PRELUDE: THE DIVERSITY OF THEORIES

Introduction

In the following chapters, we will be considering a number of different ethical theories, theories that often seem to conflict with one another. Before we begin discussing them in detail, it is important to reflect on this diversity, our possible attitudes toward it, and the ways in which we might be able to reconcile these diverse approaches to the moral life. The purpose of this chapter is primarily to offer a framework within which we can understand this diversity of theories. In the process, we also can develop an overview of the moral theories discussed in subsequent chapters. It will furthermore be important to reflect on this issue *after* we finish our detailed consideration of these theories, so we will return to this topic again at the end of the book to determine whether our initial considerations here still seem valid.

In a nutshell, the issue is this: Each of the moral theories we will be considering, at least in its strong version, makes a claim to being *exclusively correct*. In other words, each claims that its theory, and only its theory, is right. For example, the **divine command theorist** alleges that *morality is determined by God's commands*. The **Kantian** claims that *morality is a matter of having the correct intention, one which can be willed universally for all human beings*. The **egoist** thinks that *morality is solely a matter of self-interest*. The **utilitarian** says that *morality is solely a matter of consequences*. The **rights theorist** *sees the only moral issues as being issues as being issues of rights and correlative duties to respect the rights of others*. The **virtue theorist,** finally, maintains that *morality is primarily about character*, not actions. Therefore, the problems is: What are we to make of this diversity and conflict among moral theories?

In this chapter, we shall develop a framework which makes sense of this diversity and conflict. First, we shall examine possible attitudes toward moral theories. The focus of this section is not on *what* we believe, but rather *how* we believe it. Rejecting nihilistic and absolutist attitudes toward our moral beliefs, we argue in favor of one particular attitude, *moral fallibilism.* Moral fallibilists may hold their beliefs deeply and passionately, but they always hold them open-mindedly as well; they are willing to admit their own fallibility and to revise their beliefs if necessary. The second section contains a sketch of *moral pluralism*, a theory of moral value which recognizes the legitimacy and importance of diversity and even conflict in the moral domain. There are, as we shall see in this section, several kinds of moral values, each important, none exclusive. In the third part, we shall turn to the question of whether moral values are objective or not. This section has two purposes: (a) to present a theory about the ways in which moral values are subjective, intersubjective, and objective; and (b) to provide a comparative survey of major moral theories in regard to their views on the objectivity of moral value. Finally, we turn to a consideration of what it is reasonable to expect from a moral theory.

What attitude should we have toward this diversity of theories? At least four attitudes seem possible. Let us examine them.

OUR ATTITUDES TOWARD THEORIES

The Moral Nihilist

Certainly one possible attitude is clear: we can look at the multiplicity of theories and give up, concluding that philosophers cannot agree on anything and one theory is as good (or as bad) as any other, which is the attitude of the **nihilist,** that is, the person who believes in nothing. (The word "nihilist" comes from the Latin *nihil*, which means "nothing.") Moral nihilists have given up hope of ever really knowing anything in the area of morality. Thus they either believe in nothing or, even if they do believe in something, look upon their own beliefs (and everyone else's as well) as arbitrary.

The German existentialist philosopher Friedrich Nietzsche (1844–1900) provided one of the most trenchant and influential analyses of modern nihilism. He predicted that the twentieth and twenty-first centuries would be characterized by the spread of nihilism; increasingly, people would find that the traditional values that had held their world together were disintegrating. Human life would seem to lack a goal, and there would be no ultimate answer to the question of the meaning of life. People would give up on even trying to find answers to the most fundamental questions of life. Morality would become meaningless.

Moral nihilism seems like an extreme position, but it is sometimes easy for students to become nihilists if moral theories are presented in the wrong

The German philosopher Friedrich Nietzsche (1844–1900) claimed that nihilism would be the major philosophy of the twentieth century.

way. When the theories are presented, one right after the other, with all the main arguments for and against each theory, it is easy to conclude that the situation is hopeless. It looks as if there is something wrong with every theory, and so after a while some students give up and just say that there are no good reasons at all for preferring one theory to another. Indeed, they often feel that philosophers can come up with arguments for or against virtually any theory. Why bother, they ask, when you can prove or disprove anything?

Why bother? It is a good question. The answer is twofold: (1) because resolving some of these issues is *not* a hopeless quest; and (2) because reflecting on these issues will yield a better life for both yourself and other people. The rest of this book is a detailed attempt to show that this quest is not hopeless at all. When we finish, you can judge for yourself to what extent it has been successful. Each of us must test, through our own lives, whether these theories can lead to a better life or not. One thing is clear: whether we keep moral theories or not, we are still faced with unavoidable moral choices in everyday life. There is no question that we have to make moral choices. The question is simply whether moral theories can help us to make those choices in a better way. I think they can.

The Moral Skeptic

There is a second, less extreme response to the fact of moral disagreement: moral skepticism. While moral nihilists simply give up on the very possibility of any value or truth in the moral domain, moral skeptics are suspicious of theories that would talk us out of the evident truths of our own moral experience. This classical tradition, which stems from the ancient Greek philosopher Sextus Empiricus (around 200 A.D.), is quite different from modern skepticism, which is typified by a modern philosopher such as René Descartes. Modern skepticism is founded on a radical doubt of the reliability of sense experience, and that doubt often is motivated by a commitment to a theory. Classical skepticism is just the opposite: it doubts *theories* and seeks to preserve the integrity of particular moral experiences. We will take this classical sense of skepticism as the principal sense here.

Moral skeptics find truth in the realm of the particular rather than the general, in details rather than in grand theories. Whereas many ethical theorists might seek to develop a theory of the nature of the good as pleasure or happiness or duty, skeptics would be more likely to look at particular instances of goodness or evil and to investigate those. (The Greek word for skeptics, *skeptikoi*, literally means "inquirer" or "investigator.") A good contemporary example of this idea is found in the work of Philip Hallie, who labels himself a skeptic in the tradition of Sextus Empiricus. When Hallie became interested in the issue of moral evil, he did not try to develop a general theory of good and evil. Instead, he undertook a number of case studies of particular examples of evil (including work on the Marquis de Sade and on American slavery). Eventually, he turned his attention to the Holocaust. Once again, his studies were specific rather than general, concerned with actual individuals rather than abstract concepts. His book, *Lest Innocent Blood Be Shed*, told the story of a pacifist French Huguenot village in Nazi-occupied France during the Second World War. (We will consider this example in more detail in Chapter Ten.) Moral skepticism does not deny the possibility of moral truth, but it does tell us to look for the truth in concrete experience rather than in the domain of theory.

Moral Fallibilism

The third possible attitude toward moral theories is what we will call *moral fallibilism*. Simply put, fallibilism is the conviction that, no matter how strong our beliefs are, we might be mistaken. Consequently, we are always open to the possibility that we have to reconsider and revise those beliefs. Open-mindedness is the corollary of fallibilism.

Fallibilism does not exclude commitments to theories, even deep and passionate commitments. Fallibilists may have strong, deep beliefs, but they are always aware of the possiblity that they might be mistaken or incomplete. While moral fallibilists may be passionate about their beliefs, they are not dogmatic. Their passion is for finding the truth, for uncovering the morally most enlightening way of understanding a given situation or problem. They may be devoted to their moral beliefs, but their devotion does not stem from the fact that they are *their* beliefs but from their conviction that they are the *best* beliefs available. They are open to the possibility that if someone can present good reasons for revising those beliefs, they should then be revised. The moral fallibilist thus treads a narrow line between open-mindedness and commitment, managing to combine the best elements of both.

The True Believer

The final attitude to be considered here is that of the true believer. The true believer believes in one and only one of these theories and treats all the other theories as simply wrong. Many have this approach and it certainly has a strong appeal. We find ardent believers and advocates for each of these theories. Indeed, their conviction and devotion often play a crucial role in developing and promoting the theory. Precisely because they are so certain that this approach is the one and only adequate moral theory, they are often devoted passionately to articulating and defending the theory, showing how it applies to difficult cases, replying to critics, and so on.

Despite its appeal, there are good reasons for not adopting this attitude. Common sense suggests that each of these major theories has been developed by insightful and intelligent people; it would be surprising if each of them did not contain at least part of the truth about moral life. While none of them may have the whole story about morality, each of them probably has *part* of the story. The difficulty with the true believer's attitude is that it closes us off from the possibility of finding truth outside of our theory.

Choosing an Attitude

These four attitudes are not primarily about *what* we believe, but *how* we believe. There are good reasons for rejecting both the nihilist's attitude and the true believer's. Whether we are skeptics or fallibilists, or some combination of both, depends in part on our more substantive views on moral theories. Most of the rest of this book is devoted to such assessment, and by the end of this book you should be in a position to decide which attitude is most reasonable for you to assume. Our choice of attitude will be dependent in part on the outcome of that detailed evaluation of moral theories. Yet it is also dependent on the expectations with which we approach those theories. There are two areas in which those expectations are of particular importance:

- whether moral value is a unitary phenomenon (monism) or a multiplicity of different values (pluralism);
- whether moral values are subjective, intersubjective, or objective.

Let us now turn to a consideration of these questions.

Moral Pluralism

One of the most important expectations that we have in approaching moral theories is whether we expect to find only one kind of moral value or not. Theories that maintain that there is only one kind of moral value are *monistic* theories, while those that are open to the possiblity of more than one kind of value are *pluralistic* theories. The approach underlying this book is pluralistic. Before looking at the strengths of moral pluralism, let us first consider why moral monism is so attractive and powerful.

Moral Monism and the Deductive Model

Central to all monistic moral theories is the belief that there is one and only one kind of moral value or one and only one method of resolving moral disputes. Consider an example that will be examined in more detail in Chapter Six: *hedonistic utilitarianism*. The hedonistic utilitarian holds that we should always act in a way that produces the greatest overall amount of pleasure. Maximizing pleasure is the sole standard of moral value for judging anything. Because it has one and only one standard of moral value, hedonistic utilitarianism is a monistic moral doctrine.

Part of the appeal that comes from such doctrines is that they promise a high degree of certitude in our moral judgments. Although not every case will be clear-cut, many will be. We add up the pleasure and pain associated with each alternative course of action open to us, and we have to choose the one that maximizes pleasure and minimizes pain. In some cases, two or more alternatives might be roughly equivalent in terms of the amount of pleasure/pain produced, and then we are free to choose either. Most of the time, however, the choice will be clear-cut and follow directly from our single moral principle and the analysis of the empirical situation.

The Deductive Model

This expectation of a deductive relationship between a moral theory and particular cases is a tremendously attractive one. Given the theory and the facts about a specific case, one should be able to deduce (that is, conclude *necessarily*) what ought to be done in that case. For example, if we have a monistic theory with the basic principle that we ought to treat other people the way that they treat us, and if we have an empirical premise that says that Bill has always treated you with courtesy, then one can conclude that you ought to treat Bill with courtesy. The structure of this argument is as follows.

Theoretical premise:	I ought to treat other people in the same way that they have treated me;
Empirical premise:	Bill has always treated me with courtesy in the past;
Normative conclusion:	I ought to treat Bill with courtesy.

Of course, the theoretical premise actually may be much more complex than the one that I have just given, and there may be a number of empirical premises spelling out the details of a particular case, but the structure of the deductive model is essentially this: a normative conclusion about how one ought to act is drawn from the conjunction of a theoretical premise that contains some norm or principle for acting and an empirical premise that describes a particular case or type of case.

If there is one and only one possible normative premise (that is, if monism is true), then such an argument is not open to doubt. But what if there are several possible moral standards? What if, in addition to maximizing pleasure and minimizing pain, we have another basic moral principle stating that we ought also to respect other people. We might get an argument that looks like the following.

Theoretical premise:	I ought to act in a way that respects other people;

Empirical premise:	Treating Bill with courtesy is a necessary part of respecting him;
Normative conclusion:	I ought to treat Bill with courtesy.

The difficulty is clear: the conclusion of this argument appears to contradict the conclusion of the previous argument. If ethical monism is true, then there would be only one ultimate moral principle—such as maximizing pleasure or respecting persons—which would be applicable. Monism guarantees that necessity by eliminating the possibility that any other moral principle is relevant and potentially overriding. It offers the promise that we can provide conclusive reasons for acting in a particular way.

The Use of Counter-Examples

The power and attractiveness of this deductive model is responsible for a particular style of philosophical argumentation that is quite common in ethics: the use of counter-examples. This technique depends on a particular characteristic of deductive arguments: it is impossible for the conclusion of a deductive argument to be false if the argument is valid and all the premises are true. So if the conclusion is false and the argument is valid, then one of the premises must be false. This basis for the most common strategy in moral arguments involves counter-examples. If you can construct a moral argument that is *valid*, that has *true empirical premises*, and that has a *false conclusion, then the theoretical premise has to be false.*

Consider a typical anti-abortion argument.

Theoretical premise:	It is morally wrong to kill innocent human beings;
Empirical premise:	Abortion is the killing of an innocent human being;
Normative conclusion:	Abortion is morally wrong.

In order to refute this argument by means of a counter-example, we would try to develop another argument that has the same theoretical premise, true empirical premises, and a false conclusion. Here is a possible example.

Theoretical premise:	It is wrong to kill innocent human beings;
Empirical premise:	The American bombing of Germany in World War II killed many innocent human beings (for example, German children);
Normative conclusion:	The American bombing of Germany in World War II was wrong.

While some would agree with this conclusion, many would maintain that this normative conclusion is wrong. The American bombing of Germany in World War II was justified. Thus there must be something wrong with one of the premises. Since the empirical premise seems uncontroversially true, the problem must be with the theoretical premise.

Definitions and Revisions

It is easy to see what the next step is in this debate: we need to amend our theoretical premise, often by defining some terms more precisely than before. What about the word "kill"? Murder involves an intentional killing of another human being; killing involves taking the life of another person, whether intentionally or not. But where do we draw the line between taking a life (killing) and doing something that results (whether intentionally or not, whether foreseeably or not) in the death of another person? A surgeon might perform surgery on a critically ill patient and the patient might die subsequently, but do we want to say the doctor *killed* the patient? But what about the bombing attacks against a military target that has the unintentional but foreseeable effect of killing innocent civilians? Is it just like the doctor's unsuccessful surgery? If not, what are the relevant differences? We may also need to look more closely at the meaning of the words "innocent" and "person." (The latter issue becomes particularly relevant to the abortion issue in discussions of whether the fetus is a person or not.) These are the questions that naturally are generated in this type of discussion.

Moral Dilemmas

A final characteristic of monistic theories should be noted. They reduce the possibility of moral dilemmas. A moral dilemma is a case in which we are obligated both to do something and to not do that same thing. (A dilemma is different from a case in which two alternatives are equally acceptable.) Moral dilemmas arise when different moral principles are applied to the same situation and yield conflicting obligations. Yet if there is only one moral principle, as monism holds, then the possibility of such a conflict seems to disappear.

The Problem with Monism

While there is much that is appealing in ethical monism, it has at least one major drawback: philosophers have been unable to agree on what the single moral principle is. There has been no shortage of candidates for that position, as the subsequent chapters of this book will show, but none of them is irrefutable, which alone is a good reason for revising any expectations we might have that a moral theory be monistic, considering the possibility that an adequate moral theory may be pluralistic.

There is a second, even more serious reason for rejecting any specific monistic theory. As we shall see in the remainder of this book, each of these major theories has been subjected to penetrating criticisms that help reveal each theory's shortcomings. Each of these candidates for a monistic account of moral value falls short of the mark. None of them is able to provide a complete account of moral value. Yet this reason is not sufficient for rejecting them completely. Instead, we must preserve what is sound in each theory, discard that which misses the mark, and look to other theories to help us understand those aspects of the moral life which are still obscure.

Moral Pluralism

Moral pluralism is the alternative to monism. Pluralism is simply the conviction that the truth, at least in the moral life, is not singular or unitary. There are many truths, sometimes partial and sometimes conflicting, which does not mean that there is no truth, as the subjectivist claims. Nor does it mean that all truth is relative, as the relativist maintains. But it does mean that, at least in some situations, there is not just a single truth.

A Baseball Analogy

The best example of this type of pluralism comes from Bernard Gert, a philosopher who teaches at Dartmouth. He asks his students, "Who is the best hitter in major league baseball today?" Invariably, he gets several different answers. As the discussion proceeds, it becomes evident that there are different standards for judging who the "best hitter" is. Some point to the number of hits per year, others to the number of runs batted in (RBIs), and some even point to the number of home runs a year. This excellent example of pluralism shows that there are several different standards, each of which is reasonable, none of which is exhaustive. Notice, though, that pluralism does not mean that "anything goes." There is room for mistakes in two ways. First, despite the plurality of standards, clearly most baseball players do not qualify as the best hitter. Second, not every standard is legitimate. If someone tried to define "best hitter" as "batter most often hit by a pitched ball" or "batter most often in a television commercial," we would immediately reject their proposed definitions. Pluralism does not mean "anything goes."

The Plurality of Moral Values

Moral pluralism is similar, but somewhat more complicated. Imagine that someone asked, "Who's the best baseball player today?" Several answers would be possible, depending on whether one focuses on hitting, fielding, team spirit, or some other criterion. Similarly in ethics, if we asked an abstract question such as "What is goodness?", we might get several different answers. Most philosophers would focus on actions, although some would look primarily at moral agents. Some consider a combination of both. Among philosophers who concentrate primarily on the **morality of actions,** some are concerned primarily with *formal characteristics* of the acts while others look at the acts' *consequences*. Among those who focus principally on the formal characteristics of acts are Kant, some divine command theorists, and many rights theorists.

Kant is concerned with whether the maxim behind an action can be consistently willed as a universal law. Some divine command theorists ask whether acts conform to God's law. Rights theorists concentrate on whether actions avoid infringing on the rights of other persons. Other act-oriented approaches consider the way in which actions produce consequences of a particular type, such as increasing the overall amount of happiness in a society (utilitarianism) or maximizing one's own self-interest (ethical egoism). All of these approaches take acts as the principal focus of moral evaluation, but there is another way of approaching the moral life. Some philosophers take the **morality of the agent** as the principal focus. Among those who focus on the agent are Kantians who ask if an act is being done for the sake of duty and those divine command theorists who are concerned that actions are done for God's sake. Both of these approaches look primarily to the agent's *intention* as the key moral factor. Other philosophers such as Aristotle see the agent's *character* as the primary focus. Such theorists see virtues as those strengths of character that promote human flourishing and vices as those weaknesses of character that restrict our flourishing. Thus the different traditions illuminate a plurality of values. Some of these standards of value, as we shall see in later chapters, are better than others, but all have some merit. The good is not some single factor, but a plurality of factors. And there are different standards of moral value. Each is reasonable; none is the *only* reasonable standard.

Just as in the case of "best baseball player," this concept does not mean that "anything goes." There are many baseball players who will never qualify

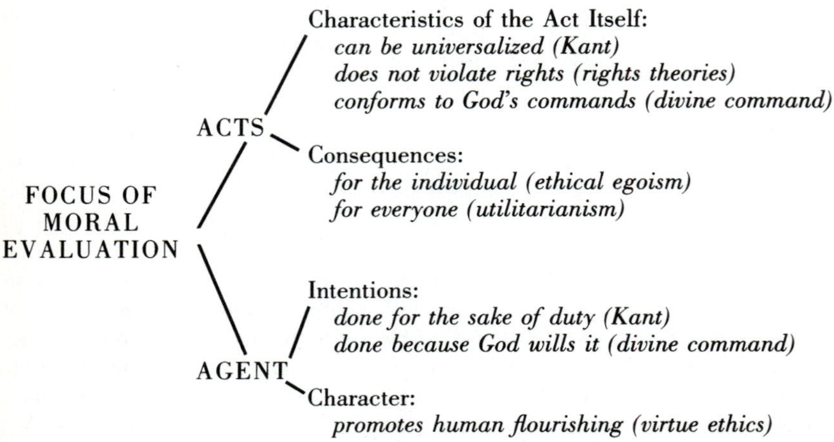

for the title of best player, no matter what standard we use. There are also plenty of standards (for example, most foul balls hit in a single season) that no reasonable person would accept as legitimate. Pluralism simply means that not all moral situations admit of a single evaluation. Several moral standards may be relevant. Sometimes these various standards may yield the same results, sometimes they may produce conflicting evaluations.

We learn from both the agreements and the disagreements. In the "best baseball player" case, we sometimes find that there is one player who excels in all areas. Then there is no doubt who deserves the title, and we are delighted to acknowledge that the choice was so clear-cut. At other times, various players will have strengths in a particular area, but none of them will be best in all areas. Then we have genuine ambiguity about who the best player is, and we may be willing to acknowledge that others are almost as deserving of the title as the one we choose. When someone edges out the competition by a small margin, it is appropriate to acknowledge that the margin was a small one. Reporting the final score of a tennis match, a sports commentator once captured this idea well by prefacing the score with the phrase, "In a match that neither opponent deserved to lose . . ."

It is similar in the moral life. When all the standards agree—for example, in prohibiting the torture of innocent children for fun—we usually discover that we have a clear-cut moral issue and acknowledge it as such. When the standards disagree—for example, in judging the morality of voluntary euthanasia—we discover that we have a genuinely complex moral problem. This ambiguity is precisely the complexity of the moral life, and it is appropriate to acknowledge it as such. The fact that some moral issues are difficult does not mean that moral theory is useless. It simply tells us that there are times in the moral life when we have to make close calls.

Pluralism and Consistency

Once we accept the possibility that there are many standards in the moral life, we need to address the question of whether they can conflict or not. There are at least three possible positions here, although only two of them are genuinely pluralistic.

The Identity Thesis

Perhaps the most extreme position one could take on this issue is to claim that the pluralism of moral theories is only apparent. Underneath the surface, all these major moral theories are saying the same thing, just in different words. Yet this approach clearly will not work. It is either too general to be useful or too specific to be true. On the one hand, one might argue that there is some common message to all the theories, such as "Do unto others as you would have them do unto you." The difficulty is that this doctrine is so vague as to be unhelpful. On the other hand, if we look in any detail at these different theories, we see that there are important differences between them. Any account that denies that there are genuine differences and disagreements among these various theories is, I think, doomed to failure.

Weak Pluralism

There is a second way of looking at the plurality of moral theories which is more illuminating. Imagine a large sculpture in a completely dark room—you cannot see it at all. Now imagine switching on a strong spotlight in one of the top corners of the room. It would illuminate the sculpture strongly, at least on those portions which faced the light. However, those parts of the sculpture which were in shadow would be less well illuminated and harder to see. In order to correct this problem, we could switch on another spotlight, perhaps in the opposing lower corner. The additional light would subject more of the sculpture to direct illumination, although there might still be parts that receive little direct light. Other spotlights might be introduced to illuminate them.

Moral theories can be likened to these spotlights. They throw light, from a particular angle, on the moral life and illuminate it. They elucidate aspects of our moral life that might otherwise be left in shadow. In this sense, they are like spotlights on the moral life. The different standards of value embedded in those theories may be genuinely different, but in this account they do not conflict with one another, which is considered pluralism without moral dilemmas. We shall call it *weak pluralism.*

One argument that supports this way of seeing the plurality of moral values centers around the claim that to some extent, these theories are different because *they attempt to answer different questions.* It is not that they are all providing competing answers to the same question; rather, they are giving different answers to different questions. (There will, of course, be instances where they offer genuinely different answers to the same question, and we will note these disagreements as well as we proceed.)

In the following chapters, we will explore the context of questions for each of the moral theories we discuss. Here I offer only a small preview. Kant claimed that what made an action morally good was that it was done for the right motive, namely, done for the sake of duty as well as in conformity to duty. Utilitarians such as John Stuart Mill claimed that what made an action good was the consequences that resulted from it. These two viewpoints seem to be in irreconciliable disagreement; but when we look more closely, we see that significantly different questions are being asked here. On the one hand, Kant is interested in evaluating the moral agent, the *person* who performs the act—and for answering this question, intention is of the utmost importance. On the other hand, Mill is interested more in evaluating the *action* itself, and to do so a consideration of consequences is quite relevant. Although there are certainly real disagreements between Kant and Mill, some of the apparent disagreements stem from the fact that they are asking significantly different questions.

Of course, even if we grant that to some extent these different theories are responses to different questions, we still need to know *when* to ask which question. Part of the answer to that will be an account of the different spheres of existence and what kinds of questions are most relevant to each. Questions about rights, for example, are most appropriate in relationships among strangers, but it is unusual—unless something is going drastically wrong—that *friendships* are approached in terms of rights. Thus part of our answer is that certain types of questions are most appropriate in certain types of contexts. We will make this notion more specific in the following chapters.

Despite its apparent merits, this account of the pluralism of moral standards has at least one principal drawback: we have no guarantee that it is true. There is virtually no way of being sure in advance that these various theories will not contradict each other. While we may hope that the different moral standards do not yield consistent demands when applied to particular cases, we can never be sure of that beforehand.

Robust Pluralism

The final interpretation of pluralism is the strongest. It entertains the possibility that we may have not only many standards of value, but also that they may not necessarily be consistent with one another. This position, which we will call *robust pluralism*, does not give up the hope of compatibility, but neither does it make compatibility a necessary requirement.

Robust pluralism is best captured by a metaphor suggested by Amélie Rorty in another context. We might imagine these various theories in a relationship similar to that of the three branches of government. The legislative, executive, and judicial branches exist in a network of *checks and balances* with one another. Not only are they not necessarily in harmony, but also their disagreement is often a good thing. So, too, with moral theories. Each, as it were, keeps the others honest. Just as we should not hope for the eventual victory of one branch of government over the other two, so we should not hope that one moral theory will finally vanquish all competitors from the field.

One of the intriguing aspects of this metaphor is that it suggests that disagreement can be positive. The fact that different moral theories point to different courses of action is not necessarily bad; indeed, the disagreement can help us ultimately arrive at the best course of action. Yet we should not be misled by this metaphor, for the American political system has certainly known periods of relative paralysis that was in part due to the checks-and-balances system. Sometimes, if the disagreements are too great and the possibility of genuine dialogue and compromise too small, the system of checks-and-balances can immobilize us, preventing us from choosing any course of action at all.

This text approaches moral theory within the context of robust pluralism. It assumes that there are many standards of value, and that these are not necessarily consistent with one another. It does offer a way of addressing the danger of paralysis inherent in the checks-and-balances metaphor. In order to begin seeing what that answer is, let us now turn to a consideration of the question of whether moral values are subjective, intersubjective, or objective.

Are Moral Values Objective?

Our attitude toward moral theories is not only shaped by our expectation that moral value be either unitary or pluralistic. It also depends on whether we expect moral values to be objective or not. Philosophers have developed widely divergent positions on this issue. In this section, we will be doing two things. First, we will be "surveying the territory" in regard to the question of whether moral values are objective, much of which is conceptual cartography, making a map that helps us locate many major moral theories in relation to each other on this issue. Second, we shall be developing and defending a particular position on this topic, a position that incorporates elements from several different traditions.

The central question that we are facing here is whether moral values are objective or not. It often is assumed that there are only two possibilities here—objective or subjective. Either moral values are purely subjective or else they are purely objective in some way. However, there is a middle ground between these two alternatives: the claim that moral values are intersubjective. The chart on the next page provides a rough "road map" of the possibilities and some of the major philosophers associated with those possibilities. (Please note that labels such as naturalist or conventionalist hardly ever capture the subtlety and range of the thought of the philosophers associated with them. These labels are intended as a first step toward understanding, not a final stopping point.)

Let us consider each of these three main approaches.

The Subjectivity of Value

The Meaning of "Subjective"

We often hear people make claims such as "That's purely subjective." Yet what exactly does "subjective" mean? It often seems in context to be equivalent to saying, "It's arbitrary" or "There are no good reasons for that." Yet this sense of "subjective" is derivative. The original meaning of "subjective" is simply "of, or pertaining to, a subject." We arrive at the meaning of "subjective" as "arbitrary" only when we add an additional premise: the belief that subjects are (completely) different. Given this premise, one subject's values might be

THE PLURALITY OF MORAL VALUE

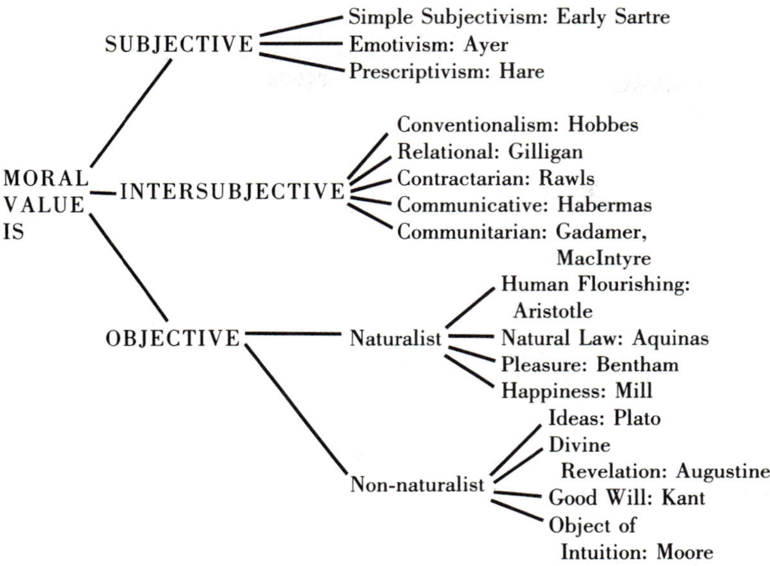

completely different from another subject's and the choice between the two is purely arbitrary. Alternatively, we can arrive at the same meaning of "subjective" as "arbitrary" if we think of subjects as emotional and think of emotions as arbitrary.

We really need to answer two questions: (1) are values subjective, and (2) what do we mean by "subjective"? *Values*, as we shall see, *are (partially) subjective, but that does not mean that they are arbitrary.* In order to understand let us consider some of the standard accounts of the subjectivity of moral values.

Existentialism

Existentialist philosophies typically have emphasized the primacy of human freedom and creativity. As a result, most existentialist approaches to ethics have seen moral values as exclusively human creations, as the results of our free choices. One of the strongest statements of this type of position is found in the work of Jean-Paul Sartre, especially his "Existentialism Is a Humanism" (1946). Sartre sees human beings as radically free. Consequently, not only are human beings able to choose *whether* to be good or not, but they are also free to decide *what* is good.

Few thinkers hold to such radical subjectivism today, and even Sartre revised his views on the extent of human freedom in his later years. Such radical subjectivism seems to defy our everyday moral experience. While many of us would be willing to allow a fair degree of latitude in the creation of human value, few would jettison all limits on what we could decide to value. If someone were to claim that genocide is good, most of us would maintain that the person was wrong. Opposition to genocide is neither arbitrary nor merely a matter of personal taste.

Relativism

We have already seen the way that moral relativism provides a path to subjectivism. Moral relativism usually begins with the claim that morality is relative to a particular culture, but as proponents of relativism recognize smaller and smaller subdivisions within a culture, they may eventually be driven to the claim that morality is relative to each individual. Relativism thus provides the second path to subjectivism.

Generally in this context "subjective" is taken to be roughly equivalent to "arbitrary." Yet this equivocation is misleading. We can say that taste in food is to some extent relative to cultures, but that hardly means that it is arbitrary or that "anything goes" in culinary matters. Some meals are better than others, and there is even some cross-cultural agreement possible in such matters. To be sure, it does not mean that there are absolute standards in regard to the taste of food; but the absence of absolute standards does not mean that there are *no* standards.

Emotivism

In the first half of the twentieth century, philosophers became increasingly enchanted with natural science and the way in which scientific disputes seemed open to resolution through empirical tests. The natural sciences became the model for genuine truth. At the same time, the claims of ethics came under increasing suspicion because they were not subject to empirical verification in the same way that scientific statements were. A. J. Ayer's *Language, Truth and Logic* (1936) was one of the earliest and most influential works to claim that ethical language was merely an expression of negative or positive emotions. The sentence "Abortion is wrong" is simply equivalent to saying, "Boo for abortion!" Our moral language, in other words, is nothing but an expression of our feelings of approval or disapproval. Feelings are neither true nor false, nor are they not subject to rational evaluation. Emotivism thus claims that moral judgements are simply expressions of feeling; they contain no cognitive content at all. Later refinements in this theory, particularly by Charles Stevenson in *Ethics and Language* (1944), focused on the way in which moral judgments express attitudes rather than simply emotions, but the common element remained.

Emotivism thus provides a second path to subjectivism because emotions and attitudes were seen as purely subjective and arbitrary. Each person's feelings are right for that person, and there is no rational standard for assessing any individual's feelings. Ethics becomes subjective because emotions and attitudes are subjective.

The emotivists were partially right, but their account falls short of the mark in four respects. First, while moral values are partially subjective, they are not *solely* subjective. We care intensely about our moral values, and for this reason there is a subjective connection to them which is not present in other areas, such as scientific knowledge. Yet this subjectivism does not mean that they are arbitrary; it simply means we are subjectively committed to them.

Second, while emotivists were right in emphasizing the role of emotions in the moral life, their account of emotions was primitive and distorted. They viewed emotions as either positive or negative. Thus traditional moral prohibitions against murder were reinterpreted simply as, "Murder—boo!" Yet emotions are much more subtle, complex, and cognitive than that. Consider a moral emotion such as shame, which can often be immediate and intense. We experience it in the moment without being aware of its complex structure, but when we step back and examine it, we see that shame has a complex structure. In order to experience shame, we exercise fairly sophisticated normative, cognitive, and emotive capacities. We must make a normative judgment about what standards of morality are appropriate to us; we must make a cognitive judgement that we have not met those standards; and we must have the appropriate negative feelings accompanying those judgments. Emotions are rarely simply positive or negative. Emotivists were right in recognizing that emotions play an important role in the moral life, but they failed to develop their understanding of the emotions sufficiently.

Third, emotivists failed to recognize that there may be some common emotional ground among human beings. Values might be grounded in emotions, but this fact alone does not mean that they necessarily differ from one individual to another. Virtually all human beings would shrink back in horror at the sight of an infant being tortured, and we would have serious moral questions about any person who was indifferent to such a sight. Emotivists failed to realize that there might be a common emotive ground which could in part give a foundation to moral judgements. Not only do we begin with a common emotional ground, but our connectedness with other people is often primarily through emotions. An ethics of compassion, to take just one example, is one in which the emotion of compassion and its concomitant actions form the basis for a moral community. Having compassion is necessary for the moral life, and compassion itself is a moral value.

Finally, emotions are valuable in the moral life because they may help us to see more clearly. Again, think of compassion. All other things being equal, compassionate people are more likely than non-compassionate people to notice the suffering of others as suffering. Their compassion makes them more "attuned" to suffering in the world.

The Subjectivity of Moral Values

There is some truth in these efforts to explore the subjectivity of moral values, but no one in this tradition has come close to capturing the whole story. Moral values are partially subjective, but as we shall see they are also objective and intersubjective. Moreover, in saying that they are subjective, we are not claiming that they are completely arbitrary. Rather, one of the characteristics of moral values is that they are held—often deeply and passionately—by subjects, and emotions play a crucial role in the way in which subjects are committed to those values. This emotive dimension of moral value is far more complex than a simple "yes" or "no" feeling. Emotions often shape our perception of the moral landscape and provide our principal connection to other people.

Objective

Many philosophers have argued that moral values are objective. Broadly speaking, we can divide such philosophers into two camps: naturalist and non-naturalists. Both maintain that moral value is objective and consequently that moral disagreements can be settled at least in part by an appeal to facts, but they differ about what kind of facts these are. On the one hand, *naturalists* maintain that moral value is grounded in, or equivalent to, something objectively knowable in the external world: pleasure (Bentham), happiness (Mill), natural law (Aquinas), or human nature (Aristotle). (Bentham and Mill will be considered in Chapter Six; there is a brief discussion of Thomas Aquinas's views on natural law in Chapter Eight; Aristotle's account of human nature is to be found in Chapter Ten.) On the other hand, *non-naturalists* also claim that moral value is something objectively knowable, but that it is grounded in some fact outside of the natural order. Plato sees the Good as an Idea which we seek to know. Augustine and others see divine revelation as providing the objective criterion for judging the goodness of particular actions. Kant (who is discussed in Chapter Seven) sees it as the Good Will. G. E. Moore sees the good as the object of an intuition. What all of these approaches have in common is the conviction that there is an objectivity to moral value, even if they disagree on the objects in which value resides.

A large portion of this book will be devoted to a critical evaluation of theories that claim that moral values are in some sense objective. Consequently, it is not necessary to survey this territory closely at this point. We can, however, anticipate the conclusion of those chapters. We shall see that there is an objectivity to moral values, especially accounts in the naturalistic tradition. Yet this objectivity is not the whole story. Moral values are *partially* objective (in ways to be shown in later chapters below), but not completely so. We have already seen that they have (to a limited extent and in a specific sense of that term) a subjective dimension. Let us now turn to consider the third dimension of moral values, their shared or intersubjective character.

Intersubjective

There is a middle ground between these two extremes, one which sees moral values as *inter*subjective, which is a position that often is overlooked. However, there are actually a number of moral theories which have a strongly intersubjective dimension to their account of value. Let us briefly examine some typical intersubjective accounts of morality.

Conventionalism

One of the most common intersubjective accounts of morality is conventionalism, the claim that moral values are simply those values which we as a society have agreed to accept. Most moral relativists fall into this camp, since they hold that moral values are relative to the conventions of one's society. Thomas Hobbes is one of several philosophers who have defended some version of conventionalism. It is also a position that occurs with some degree of frequency in every day morality among people who believe that moral values are whatever a society agrees to accept.

Relationships

One of the most interesting works on moral psychology to appear in recent years has been Carol Gilligan's *In a Different Voice*. Gilligan presents a view of ethics, one she finds is predominately among women, in which the moral life is essentially about caring and relationships. We discuss her work in detail in Chapter Eleven.

Contractarian

One of the most influential ways of understanding the moral life has been in terms of a social contract. Rousseau was certainly one of the most influential modern representatives of this tradition, but it continues today in thinkers who have no explicit intellectual ties to Rousseau. Both John Rawls and David Gauthier have strongly contractarian elements in their moral philosophies. Their work is discussed in both Chapter Six and Chapter Eight.

The essence of contractarian ethics is the claim that moral values are legitimized through some kind of (largely implicit) social contract, an agreement to which all members give their voluntary consent to be governed by certain laws. In theories such as Rousseau's, the contract is a metaphor that refers to a mythical state of nature in which people freely choose to come together under certain self-imposed constraints that they recognize would ultimately be beneficial to all. In an account such as Rawls presents in *The Theory of Justice*, it is the contract that we would all agree to if we were behind "the veil of ignorance," that is, if we were trying to decide the basic moral rules of society without knowing in advance what our own personal position in society would be. In Gauthier's *Morals by Agreement*, the contract is a cooperative one which any rational agent would accept if that agent were seeking to maximize benefits. What is common to all these approaches is that morality is essentially a matter of a social contract.

Communicative

A number of contemporary German philosophers have been moving in this same direction. They, too, believe that moral values gain their legitimacy through some kind of social contract, but one which involves *dialogue.* Not just any contract will do. German philosophers such as Jürgen Habermas and Karl-Otto Apel have their own equivalent of Rawls's veil of ignorance. They maintain that the only legitimate moral values are those which could be freely agreed upon by all individuals participating in what Apel calls an ideal speech community. Such situations are characterized by mutual respect, symmetry, and reciprocity. The contrast with Rawls helps us to understand what is unique in this approach. Rawls asks whether people would agree to a basic moral rule if they were behind "the veil of ignorance," but those behind this Rawlsian veil of ignorance do not talk with one another. Each accepts or rejects proposed basic moral rules in isolation from one another. In the communicative approach, on the other hand, members of the ideal speech community discuss such proposals with one another and arrive through dialogue at an agreement.

This approach to morality is thus essentially *procedural* and *dialogical.* It holds that the best guarantee of arriving at a good and just social order is to follow certain procedures in constructing a dialogue about fundamental moral values. One of the central procedural requirements of such dialogues is their public character, what philosophers in this tradition call their "publicity." This tradition is partially Kantian in inspiration, going back to what Kant in "Perpetual Peace" called the transcendental formula of public right: "All actions affecting the rights of other human beings are wrong if their maxim is not compatible with their being made public." The public character of the dialogue provides a procedural guarantee against accepting unjust moral rules.

Communitarian

There is an on-going debate in contemporary ethics between communicative theorists such as Habermas who are trying to develop a universal decision procedure for ethics and those who maintain that all moral thinking is necessarily embedded in the context of a particular community. Representatives of this tradition usually deny that we can ever attain any kind of strongly objective, culture-independent moral truth. They also deny that there is any kind of universal decision procedure that could be relied upon in all situations. Instead of an infallible decision procedure, we must rely on good judgment, discernment, and ultimately wisdom in reaching decisions in the moral life. The moral life is closer to art than it is to science. This tradition has been developed in European philosophy by figures such as Hans-Georg Gadamer and in the

Anglo-American tradition by such diverse thinkers as Alasdair MacIntyre and Michael Walzer.

On the Limits of the Intersubjective

Intersubjective accounts of moral value rarely hold that there are no constraints on what people can agree to as a basic moral value. Some philosophers have maintained that *self-interest* provides that underlying limit. They believe that no agent would rationally agree to a fundamental moral value that contradicts that agent's self-interest. Someone like Buber sees the mutual recognition of the other person's subjectivity as the essential limit on what we can legitimately value. Others in this tradition maintain the *rationality* limits what people will consent to. It would, for example, be irrational (in the sense of inconsistent) for people to consent to becoming slaves, for they would be freely choosing to be unfree. Yet others such as Rawls and Habermas see some sort of *procedure* as setting the limits on shared values. For Rawls, this limitation is determined by what we would agree to behind the veil of ignorance. For Habermas, it is what we would agree upon in an ideal speech community.

What is common to both objective and most intersubjective approaches to morality is that there is some kind of discursive procedure through which moral values can be legitimized and moral conflicts resolved. While that discursive procedure involves an appeal to some kind of moral fact (whether natural or non-natural) for objectivists, intersubjectivists turn to a procedure to guarantee moral values. Both of these approaches stand in sharp contrast to most subjectivist accounts of moral value in which moral values just are; there is little, if anything, that can be said in their support or justification. Consequently, subjectivism offers little or no opportunity for the *reasoned* justification of moral values or resolution of moral conflicts.

Reconciling the Objective and the Subjective

One of the principal moral challenges we face is (a) reconciling conflicting objective accounts of moral value and (b) reconciling those objective accounts with our subjective experiences of value. It is precisely this reconciliation which the intersubjective dimension of value primarily concerns. As we shall see in subsequent chapters, each of the major moral theories has an element of truth.

If we accept the pluralistic model discussed above, we can see that conflicts among theories have a different point than they did when the focus was either to articulate or else to refute a theory. Rather than concluding from such conflicts that something is wrong with a particular theory, we may rather see each theory as shedding differing light on the moral complexity of the decision that we are facing. Of course, we need to know how to weigh these conflicting theories—but that is a question we cannot answer here. I will, however, address it later in this book, both in the chapter on virtue ethics and in the concluding discussion of moral conflict.

What to Expect from a Moral Theory

The Power of Theory

Theories attract and fascinate us. The extent to which they ultimately satisfy us as well depends at least in part on our expectations for a moral theory. What do we think moral theories are able to do? Our expectations center around five areas.

Description and Explanation

Theories help us understand how things actually work, how apparently diverse elements fit together into a single whole. Moral theories are no exception to this general rule. They help us understand the ways in which people structure their lives, the ways in which their diverse actions fit together into a coherent whole. These theories are primarily *descriptive* in character, that is, they focus on describing how people actually act and thus understanding the underlying coherence of their actions.

We have already seen one example of such a theory, descriptive ethical relativism. In Chapter Five, we will examine another example of this type of theory, descriptive psychological egoism, which maintains that people always act in their own self-interest. In Chapter Eleven, we will consider two contemporary descriptive theories which aim to increase our understanding of moral development: Lawrence Kohlberg's cognitive-developmental model and Carol Gilligan's account of females' moral development. Other descriptive accounts are structured in terms of narratives about individual lives. For example, Robert Bellah et al.'s *Habits of the Heart: Individualism and Commitment in American Life* describes and helps explain the moral interplay between the strong current of individualism in American life and the difficulty of developing an adequate language of commitment in our society. Robert Coles, a child psychiatrist at Harvard Medical School, has written with particular insight into the moral lives of children in many of his works, including his *Children of Crisis* and most explicitly in his *The Moral Life of Children.*

Strength

When Captain James Stockdale was shot down over North Vietnam and taken prisoner, he began three years of hell. He was tortured frequently and ruthlessly in an attempt to get him to confess to war crimes against the Vietnamese people and to collaborate with the enemy. (Since he was the senior officer in captivity, he was the commanding officer of all the American prisoners of war in North Vietnam; a confession from him would have been a tremendous public relations coup for his captors.) He spent months in solitary confinement, and throughout his ordeal some of his principal sources of strength were the Roman Stoic philosophers, especially Epictetus. Their philosophy provided him with wisdom and solace in a time of desperate need. As such, Stockdale was simply continuing a long tradition, beginning with Plato's *Apology* and immortalized in Boethius's *The Consolations of Philosophy*, of turning to philosophy in times of adversity to find comfort and moral security.

Critique

Moral theories also help us to see moral blind spots, both our own and those of other people. For example, I was once working out an example of what Marx meant by the alienation of capitalist society by talking about education as a commodity. In the course of the article, I found myself seeing grades in a new light. They are, I realized, like money. Part of the alienation we find in societies like our own arises when people simply work for the sake of money, not caring about the value of the job they do or the quality of the product they produce. They work only in order to get paid. Similarly, part of the alienation of education occurs when people start working only for the grades themselves rather than for anything inherently meaningful or interesting in the work itself.

As I began to play with the example, I also started to reflect on the curve in grading and began to see a moral dimension to the curve that I had not appreciated before. When grades in a class are curved in such a way that a certain percentage of the class must receive As, Bs, Cs, Ds, and Fs, we set up a competitive model of learning in which one person's progress necessarily is bought at the price of someone else's (relative) failure. In other words, if you are a student in a course with such a curve, it is not in your best interest to have your fellow students learn well. Indeed, there are two ways in which you can improve your own grade: either score higher on your own exams or see to it that your classmates score lower on their exams! It is far preferable, from a moral point of view, to establish in the classroom a model which permits everyone to do well (if they are able to do so) and which encourages cooperation in learning rather than competition.

New Possibilities

One of the most striking characteristics of the twentieth century, one which will undoubtedly be carried over into the next century, is the sheer amount of *newness* in our lives. We continually are confronted with new problems and new possibilities. Good theories work to unveil new possibilities for us and to offer solutions to new problems.

Consider the perplexities posed by advances in reproductive medicine. It is now possible for a woman to have one of her eggs fertilized outside of her body and then implanted in another woman for the period of the pregnancy and birth. Who then would be the mother? Genetically, the baby has nothing in common with the woman who gives birth to it. On the other hand, the fetus has not spent any time at all in the womb of the woman from whose egg it sprang. Developments such as these force us to develop our theories in two ways. First, when disagreements arise and turn into court cases, we must reflect on the rights of the various parties. Second, even when no disputes occur, we need to reflect on our notion of a family. What is the source of its coherence? What does it mean, for example, to be a mother? Is it a genetic concept, a social one, or some combination of both?

Wonder

Aristotle claimed that philosophy begins in wonder, and there has always been a dimension to philosophy that values it as an activity done for its own sake. Philosophy done in this way is pursued for its own sake, for the sheer joy of discovery and exploration.

Each of us must determine what we as individuals expect moral theories to do, and then use these expectations as a focus for our investigations of the theories presented in the following chapters.

Conclusion

Moral theories, we have seen, are diverse and potentially conflicting. In this chapter, we have sketched out a model for understanding and appreciating that diversity. It is a model that takes diversity as a strength rather than a weakness. Just as our government is stronger because it has three branches rather than one, so too the moral life is richer because of the competing theories which are applied to it. Far from being a reason for nihilism, moral diversity is a source of strength. It keeps us from falling into moral complacency and reinforces the fallibilistic attitude crucial to moral openness. Just as there is no need to eliminate two of our three branches of government in order to have a good political life, so there is no need to eliminate competing moral theories in order to achieve a good moral life. Our diversity is our strength, not our weakness.

We turn now to a detailed consideration of some of the major moral theories that have helped to shape our moral consciousness. When we finish that analysis, we shall return in Chapter Eleven to a consideration of one of the most vexing issues posed by the plurality of moral theories: how we resolve moral disagreements and conflicts.

Bibliographical Essay

Nietzsche offers some of the most insightful comments on the issue of **moral nihilism** in his work. See Friedrich Nietzsche, *Beyond Good and Evil: Prelude to a Philosophy of the Future*, translated, with commentary, by Walter Kaufmann

(New York: Vintage Books, 1966), and *The Will to Power*, translated by Walter Kaufmann and R.J. Hollingdale (New York: Random House, 1967). For a discussion of Nietzsche's ethics as a whole, see especially Tracy B. Strong, *Friedrich Nietzsche and the Politics of Transfiguration*, revised edition (Berkeley: University of California Press, 1988); Alexander Nehamas, *Nietzsche, Life as Literature* (Cambridge, Mass.: Harvard Press, 1985); and Lester H. Hunt, *Nietzsche and the Origin of Virtue* (London and New York: Routledge, 1991).

For more recent discussions of nihilism see Michael Novak, *The Experience of Nothingness* (New York: Harper and Row, 1990) and Stanley Rosen, *Nihilism. A Philosophical Essay* (New Haven, Conn.: Yale University Press, 1969). Chapter three of Richard W. Miller's *Moral Differences: Truth, Justice and Conscience in a World of Conflict* (Princeton, N.J.: Princeton University Press, 1992) contains an insightful and sympathetic discussion of nihilism.

The sense of **moral skepticism** discussed here begins among the Greek *skeptekoi*. One of the most interesting and forceful contemporary representatives is Philip Hallie. See his work on compassion, *Lest Innocent Blood Be Shed. The Story of the Village of Le Chambon and How Goodness Happened There* (New York: Harper Colophon, 1979) and his *Cruelty* (Middleton, Conn.: Wesleyan University Press, 1982). Also see his articles "From Cruelty to Goodness," reprinted in *Vice and Virtue in Everyday Life*, edited by Christina Hoff Sommers and Fred Sommers (San Diego: Harcourt Brace Jovanovich, 1989), pp. 9–24, and "Skepticism, Narrative, and Holocaust Ethics," *Philosophical Forum*, Vol. XVI, Nos. 1–2 (Fall-Winter, 1984–85), pp. 33–49.

The classic tests for **emotivism** are A.J. Ayer, *Language, Truth and Logic* (New York: Dover, 1947) and Charles L. Stevenson, *Ethics and Language* (New Haven, Conn.: Yale University Press, 1944). For a perceptive analysis of values that criticizes the unidimensionality of the emotivist understanding of value, see Frithjof Bergmann, "The Experience of Values," *Inquiry*, Vol. 16 (1973), pp 247–79.

For a subtle account of the ways in which philosophical theories are connected to certain **contexts of questions,** see Virginia Held, *Rights and Goods: Justifying Social Action* (New York: Free Press, 1984). For a variant of the **spotlight metaphor,** see Dorothy Emmet, *The Moral Prism* (New York: St. Martin's Press, 1979). On the **checks-and-balances metaphor,** see Amélie Rorty's essay, "Two Faces of Courage," in her *Mind in Action* (Boston: Beacon Press, 1988) where this metaphor is used to a different purpose. Her essay, "The Advantages of Moral Diversity," *Social Philosophy & Policy*, Vol. 9, No. 2 (Summer, 1992), pp. 38–62, appeared after the draft of this chapter was finished and pursues, with more subtlety than I have achieved, some of the same ends.

For a number of perceptive essays on **moral pluralism,** see the Symposium on Pluralism and Ethical Theory in *Ethics*, Vol. 102, No. 4 (July, 1992), especially Susan Wolf's "Two Levels of Pluralism," pp. 785–98, and David

Wong's "Coping with Moral Conflict and Ambiguity," pp. 763–84. I am indebted to Wolf's essay for the reference to Gert and his "best hitter" analogy. Also see John Kekes, "Pluralism and Conflict in Morality," *Journal of Value Inquiry*, Vol. 26 (1992), pp. 37–50, for an insightful discussion of this issue. Onora O'Neill's "Ethical Reasoning and Ideological Pluralism," *Ethics*, Vol. 98, No. 4 (July, 1988), pp. 705–722 deals with the relationship between pluralism and liberalism; William A. Galston's "Pluralism and Social Unity," *Ethics*, Vol. 99, No. 4 (July, 1989), pp. 711–726 examines the issue of pluralism within the context of Rawls's thought.

Michael Walzer's *Spheres of Justice: A Defense of Pluralism and Equality* (New York: Basic Books, 1983) develops a pluralistic approach to distributive justice. Neil Cooper's *The Diversity of Moral Thinking* (Oxford: Clarendon Press, 1981) presents a justification of the rationality of altruism within the context of a theory of diversity in moral judgments. Michael Stocker's *Plural and Conflicting Values* (Oxford: Clarendon Press, 1990) presents a subtle account of the relationship between pluralism and conflict in morality and a perceptive analysis of the reasons why contemporary moral philosophers find such conflict so disturbing.

Citations. The quotation from Kant's essay, "On the Disagreement Between Morals and Politics in Relation to Perpetual Peace," is from *Kant's Political Writings*, edited by Hans Reiss (Cambridge: Cambridge University Press, 1977), p. 126.

Discussion Questions

1. Recall statement 7 in your Ethical Inventory: "I need to look at the particular situation before I can know the right thing to do."
   (a) What position discussed in this chapter is most closely correlated with this statement?
   (b) Has your rating of this item changed after reading this chapter? If so, in what way? If your rating has not changed, are your reasons for your rating any different now than they were when you first responded to this statement?
2. Recall statement 11 in your Ethical Inventory: "Ultimately, there is one and only one right standard of moral evaluation."
   (a) Has your rating of this item changed after reading this chapter? If so, in what way? If your rating has not changed, are your reasons for your rating any different now than they were when you first responded to this statement?
   (b) Contrast statement 11 with the account of moral pluralism given in this chapter. Which position do you think is stronger? Why?

3. Recall statement 12 in your Ethical Inventory: "Morality is just a set of rules people all agree upon in order to make living together better."
   (a) What philosophical theory of position does this statement express?
   (b) If you think that morality is more than what statement 12 indicates, please specify what that additional element is.
4. What is the origin of the term "theory"? Does the meaning of the word provide a clue as to what moral theories do or what they are about?
5. What is the difference between a moral theory and a scientific theory? Can either one be tested, proved, or established by rational means? On what basis would you reject, or at least be suspicious of, a scientific theory? of a moral theory?
6. Suppose we always knew just what to do without knowing why we ought to do it. Would that make every moral theory redundant? Is intuition a substitute for explanation?
7. If two (moral) theories conflict, do they just cancel out or can we use the "checks-and-balances" approach to decide between them? Consider an example from your own experience in which you have conflicting conclusions about what the right course of action is.
8. We have suggested several possible attitudes toward moral theories: nihilistic, skeptical, fallibilistic, and absolutist. Which of these best describes your own attitude at this point? Return to this question when you have finished the book and see if your answer has changed at all. If it has, describe the reasons for that change.

C H A P T E R 4

The Ethics of Divine Commands: Religious Moralities

In the twenty-second chapter of Genesis, God talks to Abraham and tells him that he must sacrifice his son Isaac, who was born very late in Abraham's life after he had given up all hope of having children. Abraham had longed for children for years, and Isaac meant almost everything to him. Thus imagine Abraham's dismay when God said to him:

> Take now thy son, thine only son Isaac, whom thou lovest, and get thee into the land of Moriah; and offer him there for a burnt offering upon one of the mountains which I will tell thee of.

Abraham took his son Isaac to the mountain, prepared to offer the sacrifice. Isaac, who did not know what God had said to his father, was puzzled, for he noticed that his father seemed to have everything for the sacrifice but the offering itself. When his father actually tied him up and put him on the sacrificial altar to be sacrificed, Isaac presumably realized what was happening. Eventually, just before Abraham was ready to sacrifice Isaac, God told him to stop. "Lay not a hand upon the lad," God told Abraham, "neither do thou any thing unto him: for now I know that thou fearest God, seeing thou hast not withheld thy son, thine only son, from me."

Many of us feel that such a case could never happen in our own society. Today, Abraham probably would be taken into custody and sent for (involuntary) psychiatric evaluation. The fact that he heard voices might be sufficient in some states to hold him for several days; the fact that the voices told him to sacrifice his only son would often be sufficient to justify a much longer period of restraint and involuntary treatment.

Yet is this example really so far removed from what many of us accept today? Many in our society still feel the essential tension that Abraham experienced: the tension between the officially sanctioned morality of our society and the commands that come to us from some higher power that transcends human society. Consider two types of cases that have received much media attention in our society. Christian Scientists are required by their religious beliefs to withhold medical treatment in many circumstances, even for their own children. The essential tension that they experience is the same as Abraham's: the (apparent) commands of God require them to act in ways that (apparently) conflict with their love for their children. Yet to turn to modern medicine is to betray their faith in God. Similarly, when religiously motivated opponents of abortion disobey civil laws in order to stop abortions, they are responding to a higher law which requires them to disobey the laws of the state.

What all three of these examples have in common is the conviction that religion tells us how to act. As such, religion either replaces or overrides the demands of society's morality. This issue is at the heart of a heated longstanding debate on the relationship between religion and ethics, a debate which in the Christian tradition has its roots in centuries of discussion and disagreement about the nature and limits of religious morality. Yet this Christian tradition is not by any means the only one within which this issue exists. Although it is impossible in the short space available here to survey even the major religious traditions, we can look briefly at some of the diverse ways in which the relationship between religion and ethics has been understood in various religious traditions. Then we can turn to an examination of the general conceptual issues raised by these examples.

The Diversity of Religious Traditions

It is misleading to talk about the relationship between "religion" and "ethics" as if both of these words referred to a single, uniform phenomenon. In fact, neither of them does. Most of this book will be devoted to a discussion of the diversity of traditions contained within the single word "ethics" in traditional Western thought from Aristotle to the present. In this section, we will examine the ways in which religion and ethics are related to each other in three quite different traditions: the Navajo view of the harmony between human beings and the natural world; the Muslim vision of a religious state that unifies religion, ethics, law, and politics; and the Buddhist view of the place of a morality of compassion in the eightfold path. In the process of doing so, we will see that the term "religion" can refer to as widely diverse a set of practices and beliefs as the word "ethics" does.

Each of these traditions presents us with a distinctive ethical perspective, and each provides a different view of the relationship between religion and ethics. The Navajo provide us with an *ethic of harmony*, in which a balance in the relationship between human beings and the natural world is central. Islam offers us an *ethic of law*, based on the Qu'an and other sacred texts, in which obedience to the will of Allah is the highest good. Buddhism presents an *ethic of compassion* in which the alleviation of suffering and the purification of the soul become principal concerns. In the Navajo worldview, there is little need to draw a line between religion and ethics, for the natural and the supernatural permeate one another much more than in scientifically oriented cultures. Islam, in contrast, makes ethics clearly depend on religion—indeed, the good is ultimately whatever Allah wills it to be. For the Buddhist, the path to enlightenment or *nirvana* is one which blurs traditional Western distinctions between faith and reason and between religion and ethics. Buddhism provides a model in which enlightenment lies beyond rationality.

Each of these religious traditions is also distinctive in another sense. The Navajo worldview contains a plurality of gods and spirits, and these are not necessarily in agreement with one another or with human beings. The Islamic worldview, in contrast, is starkly monotheistic. There is only one God and Allah is His name. Buddhism presents yet a third model, for it is virtually a non-theistic religion. It has no notion of a personal or individual god at all. Each of these religions thus exemplifies a different relationship between God and the world. In the polytheistic model, different gods may issue different, and at times conflicting, moral commands to human beings. In a monotheistic model, the possibility of such conflict is eliminated. Presumably one cannot be caught between conflicting divine commands within a monotheistic world view. Finally, the non-theistic model offered by Buddhism necessitates the grounding of moral commands in some kind of order outside of God—in this case, in the order of *karma*. Thus we see quite different ways in which religion and ethics can be related.

Let us begin by examining the Navajo worldview. Be aware in our study of each of these traditions that it is difficult to avoid oversimplifying in such brief presentations. Consider the following discussions of Navajo, Muslim, and Buddhist ethics as a first step toward understanding these traditions rather than as the final word, or as an invitation to learn more rather than as a guarantee of understanding.

The Navajo Holy Wind

One of the benefits of studying other cultures is that we come to see and understand our own assumptions more clearly. Rarely is this consideration more clearly shown than in the contrast between the Navajo understanding of the moral life and our own. There are a number of key points of divergence, points that help us to see our own world more clearly just as we come to understand theirs better. Before we consider some of those points of contrast, let us begin with a brief examination of the distinctive character of an ethic that for centuries existed in a comparatively small society with an oral tradition.

Traditions and Societies

Initially, one of the most obvious differences between the Navajo and many white cultures is simply one of size. For centuries, Navajo ethics was oriented largely toward guiding the actions of Navajo toward Navajo, that is, toward guiding the actions of people who usually knew one another or at least knew one another's families. This attitude is in sharp contrast with much of Western European ethical thought, which—as we shall see in Chapter Nine—is directed primarily toward regulating the behavior of people who are strangers to one another.

There is a second, related difference. Navajo ethics is almost exclusively practical; there is virtually no interest in theory. Part of the reason is that the concept of ethics is passed from one person to another. There is nothing impersonal about the process of transmission of moral values for the Navajo, which was even more strongly the case before the development of a written language. Abstract theories rarely exist without the support of the written word. A corollary of this idea is that it is more difficult for outsiders to come to understand the Navajo worldview insofar as the tradition is still an oral one.

Dualisms and Antagonisms

Whereas classical modern European ethical thought has been dominated for the past several centuries by fundamental dualisms, the Navajo understanding of morality is generally free of such dualities. As we shall see in later chapters, dualism is pervasive in these European traditions: body versus spirit, emotion versus reason, and sensuous inclination versus duty are but a few of the dualities that recur continually in these traditions. Typically, these traditions try to resolve such dualities by choosing one side—usually spirit, reason, and duty—over the other.

Not only are these classical European dualities foreign to the Navajo way of understanding the world, but also the idea of choosing one side of a duality would be completely incongruous with their way of dealing with tensions and antagonisms in their world. Like the Chinese *yin* and *yang*, both sides of any antagonism need the other. When one exists without the other, it is incomplete. The principal tension is that of male and female, and virtually everything in the Navajos' world is either male or female. Together, both sides create a dynamic union in tension. Good and evil do not exclude one another. Each needs the other. The Navajo idea of harmony thus involves embracing both sides of an antithesis rather than choosing one and banishing the other.

The difference between Western medicine and Navajo medicine illustrates the way in which the Navajo worldview simply has no trace of the mind-body dualism so prevalent in Western medicine. Navajo medicine is directed toward the whole person, what we (as non-Navajo) would call body and spirit. Western medicine, in contrast, strictly separates body and spirit. Indeed, the body itself is compartmentalized through medical specialization. Healing in the Navajo tradition is a process that involves the entire person.

A corollary of this antagonistic worldview is to be found in the Navajos' attitude toward evil, which is often puzzling to the outsider. In large measure, evil—like good—just "is" for the Navajo, an idea found both in their view of a person's character and in their view of the everyday world. People are a mixture of good and evil, and there is very little that one can do to adjust the balance in any given individual. Similarly, evil exists in the world, and its presence is as necessary as the presence of goodness. A Navajo might well look for ways to avoid evil, but would not think of trying to create a world free from it.

Hozho

In the Navajo worldview, the principal goal toward which they strive is *hozho*, which is variously translated as harmony, beauty, peace of mind, goodness, health, well-being, or success. Although some scholars have interpreted this in a dualistic way in which *hozho* is contrasted with its opposite (*hochxq*), this interpretation does not seem to be the way in which the Navajo themselves traditionally have understood it. Rather, they seek a dynamic harmony with their environment that is characterized by a proper balance of all things. The function of morality is to guide individuals toward achieving such a balance by marking out alternatives that prevent the achievement or maintenance of such harmony.

Three levels must be harmonized in the Navajo world: the natural, the human, and the supernatural. Rather than trying to control nature, the Navajo tries to achieve harmony with it. Again, we find a sharp contrast here to the Western approach which emphasizes the technological subjugation of the natural world. Where representatives of Western technology would deal with flooding on a river by building a dam, the Navajo would simply move to higher ground.

The Holy Wind

How, then, do the Navajo determine how they should act? Clearly they learn patterns of behavior from the myths and stories that comprise their oral tradition, but that tradition also tells us that there is another source of guidance: the holy wind. The wind is a major force in the Navajo worldview, and it provides a superb example of a concept that escapes traditional dualities. The wind is physical (we can feel it on our faces when it blows), yet strangely ephemeral (we cannot hold it or capture it as we can physical objects). It is pervasive but shifting in its direction and intensity. It is both one (there is one wind just as there is one ocean) and many (we distinguish among several different oceans even though they are all connected). The winds come from the four principal directions, are associated with the four mountains where the gods dwell, and in some Navajo creation stories are even responsible for the creation of the world.

The wind, moreover, acts in a way similar to the Christian conscience. It becomes a Messenger Wind, often called a Little Wind or Wind's Child, that swirls around and enters the individual through a hidden point in the ear. The wind then warns individuals of impeding dangers, discouraging them from pursuing courses of action that would upset their *hozho*. Like Socrates' *daimon* and some versions of the Christian conscience, this little wind is primarily a negative voice. Rarely does it provide positive guidance about what we must do, but rather just negative warnings about possibilities that could lead to disaster. The individual is then free to pay attention to those warnings or to disregard them. In a striking contrast to most Western worldviews, the wind does not punish. Individuals suffer the natural consequences of their own actions, but there is no divine final reckoning that punishes the evil and rewards the good.

One Who Lacks Faults

The person who heeds these Messenger Winds becomes what the Navajo call "one who lacks faults." Their concept of a person without faults gives us a clear idea of what they consider a good person to be. Here are two representative Navajo descriptions of what such a person is like.

> This person who lacks faults thinks in a good way, he thinks well of one, one thinks well of him. He usually smiles, comes up to one slowly and, showing his relationship, shakes one's hand. (HB)
>
> "One lacks faults" means . . . he does not argue with a person. He does not steal. He is not mean. . . . Nothing bad is said about him. He is obliging towards everything. (CM) (Quoted p. 41)

The person who is without faults thinks in a good way, and because of this attitude, he talks and acts in a good way.

Practical Ethics

As we have mentioned already, the Navajo do not have a theory of ethics. Their ethics is purely practical. It may help to get the flavor of their ethics to consider some of their typical guidelines, many of which follow closely from one of the basic premises of Navajo life, namely, that "*life is very, very dangerous*." Kluckholm and Leighton describe some of the practical directives which follow from this view of life for the Navajo.

- "Maintain orderliness [that is, harmony] in those sectors of life which are little subject to human control."
- "Be wary of non-relatives."

- "Avoid excesses."
- "When in a new situation, do nothing."
- "Escape."

The practical value of some of these injunctions is obvious to outsiders. In other cases, it is initially harder to see. The wariness of non-relatives, for example, is partially a function of the strength of kinship ties, but it is intensified by a fear of witches, who are more likely to go unrecognized among strangers. Similarly, the idea of doing nothing in a new situation derives from a deep mistrust of the unknown. Safety is found in remaining still and quiet—or escaping. Instead of taking control of a situation, one tries to remain untouched by it. Again, we see the connection to the idea of harmony. If you find yourself in a new situation, then *you* are the foreign, potentially disharmonious element. As such, you need to do as little as possible until you understand how to act in a way that will restore harmony.

The Role of Ritual

The preceding injunctions help the Navajo to avoid disrupting harmony whenever possible. Sometimes, however, such disruptions are impossible. Illness, death (especially sudden and violent death), and other catastrophic events may disrupt that harmony. When that occurs, harmony must be re-established. One of the principal ways in which that is accomplished is through rituals. Indeed, the repetitive character of the chants contributes greatly to restoring a sense of orderliness to the Navajo's world. Whereas to an outsider this repetition might appear monotonous, to a Navajo their repetitiveness is a source of order and safety. The role of the rituals such as the Blessingway (*hozhooji*) is crucial in the re-establishment of a harmony (*hozho*) that has been disrupted in one way or another. When the Blessingway is performed, the Holy People who first brought the Navajo out onto the surface of the earth are present through the Holy Wind. Through their presence, moral harmony is re-established in the world.

An Ethic of Harmony

Thus we see that the central focus of Navajo ethics is the establishment of balance and harmony among the natural, the human, and the supernatural world. Rather than seek to control by brute force or to flee into an other-worldly existence, the Navajo seek to establish a harmony and balance in their lives. Their ethics is intended to promote precisely this balance.

The Islamic Shari'ah

Sometimes little details tell us much. When I began looking for books on Islam at local bookstores, I noticed a strange division which may well be reflective of our larger attitudes as Americans toward Islam. In many stores, there simply were no books on Islam. Many of these had a section entitled "Religion," in which all the books were about Christianity. Some had an additional section called "Judaica." Many had one on astrology. A few had a "Religion—General" section that included a few books on Islam. This general neglect of Islam is perhaps reflective of our ignorance and of our lack of interest, both of which have been changed only slightly as the result of recent conflicts in the Middle East. Yet the world of Islam is vast, with over 900 million believers, and long-standing, stretching back fourteen centuries to Mohammed himself in the seventh century. Within 100 years after Mohammed's death, the Islamic empire already had become larger than the Holy Roman Empire ever was.

The world of Islam is also vastly different from our own Western tradition, especially in regard to the place of religion in the moral and political lives of its believers. Since the Enlightenment in modern Europe, the West usually has maintained a tradition of separation of church and state, a tradition that has found one of its strongest expressions in the political system of the United States. The image of the late Ayatollah Khoumeni, dressed in stark black clerical garb, is in sharp contrast to the secular images of Western leaders such as George Bush, Margaret Thatcher, or Helmut Kohl. In Iran, there is no separation of church and state, and in fact that state has an explicitly religious mandate to support the growth of Islam.

Not only does Islam wipe out the traditional Western separation of church and state, but it also eliminates the distinction between ethics and religion. Two factors account for this fusion. First, Islam is concerned primarily with behavior rather than dogma. Whereas Christians are intensely concerned with theology, which deals with the proper interpretation of dogma, Muslims are concerned primarily with *law*, which deals with proper action. Indeed, the very word "*islam*" means "surrender to the will of God." Second, not only are Muslims concerned with behavior, they are concerned with virtually all behavior. Their code of behavior is a remarkably extensive one, covering virtually every area of daily life. Islam thus provides a striking model of a worldview in which religion completely determines ethics. However, it is important to note that neither the Christian separation of church and state nor Islam's fusion of the two were always reflected in history. Some Christians during the Holy Roman Empire fused religion and politics in "Caesaropapism," while Muslims separated the affairs of *sultans* from those of the *ulama*.

The Three Canonical Elements of Islam

In suggesting that Islam emphasizes the importance of right action, we do not mean to claim that behavior is all that comprises Islam. Traditionally, there are three canonical elements to Islam: belief or faith (*imam*), practice or action (*islam*), and virtue (*ihsan*). Islam is staunchly monotheistic in its faith, with its central belief is in a single God (Allah) and in Mohammed as God's prophet.

Yet Islamic belief also encompasses faith in God's angels, revelations, and other prophets. We shall consider the Muslim concept of virtue below.

As shall be seen later in this chapter, Islam exemplifies what we will call the *divine command theory of moral goodness.* Actions are right in Islam because God commands them. The question "What should I do?" is seen as equivalent to the question "What is Allah's will?" The will of Allah is embodied in Shari'ah, the religious and civil law that governs Muslim life. An action is good simply because Allah wills it, and there is comparatively little room in mainstream traditional Islam for reason to determine Allah's will. It is the authority of revelation contained in the Qu'an and the other sacred texts comprising the Shari'ah that determines what is good.

There are two other traditions in Islam. One, the mystical tradition of the Sufis, is beyond our scope here. There is, however, another tradition in Islam, dating from the ninth century and deeply affected by the Greek rationalism of Aristotle, that is necessary to our study because it maintained that reason is crucial to the interpretation of the Qu'an. Those in this tradition, the Mutazila, emphasized the importance of philosophy and rational reflection upon belief. The Mutazila further argued that God is not absolutely omnipotent and unconstrained by any limitations; rather, since God's nature is good and just, God is able to act only in ways that are good and just. Although the Mutazila did not survive as a distinct group in Islam any more than the Gnostics did in Christianity, the philosophical tradition as a whole did. The Mutazila approach soon proved, however, to be a minority position in Islam, and proponents of Greek rationalism and philosophy came to be seen as infidels, unbelievers, and thus as not true Muslims. (This same dispute, as shall be seen later in this chapter, also occurred in Christianity with quite a different outcome.) The removal of reason has profound implications for ethics, for it discards any possible rational restrictions on what can be taken to be God's will. There is no foundation in principle for denying that God could command us to torture or kill other human beings. (None of this reasoning, of course, denies that Allah can be compassionate; indeed, Allah commands believers to be compassionate, to care for widows and orphans, and so on.)

Shari'ah: *The Islamic Law*

Muslim religious law covers virtually all areas of human behavior, telling believers in great detail what behavior is (a) required, (b) recommended, (c) permitted, (d) discouraged, and (e) forbidden. As members of a religion that places very strong emphasis on the importance of right action, Islamic scholars have devoted tremendous energy to articulating the laws that govern actions. These fall, roughly, into two categories. On the one hand, there is that body of law that governs the behavior of Muslims toward God. These include laws about prayers, fasting, alms-giving (which is principally a duty to God, although the alms themselves are given to human beings), pilgrimages, and the like. These laws are not directly comparable to Western ethical codes since they are not primarily about the interactions of human beings among one another but rather of the actions of human beings toward a transcendent God. The most important of these laws are described in the Five Pillars. The second type of Islamic law directly regulates the ways in which human beings treat one another, covering approximately the same territory as Western ethical systems and can be seen as a direct counterpart to them. This law includes the penal code, regulations governing commercial interactions, and laws structuring family life. Let us first consider the Five Pillars that govern how believers should act toward God.

The Five Pillars

Central to Islam's understanding of itself are the Five Pillars of Islam, the five elements which comprise the core of the Muslim religion. No true Muslim is allowed openly to disavow any of these five pillars, although in practice it is only the first of these that every Muslim has to observe actively. The pillars are:

- *Shahadah:* the profession of faith that "there is no god but God (Allah) and that Mohammed is the Messenger of God";
- *Salah:* ritual prayer and ablutions, undertaken five times a day while facing the holy city of Mecca;
- *Zakah:* the obligatory giving of alms (at an annual rate of approximately 2.5 percent of one's net worth) to the poor to alleviate suffering and promote the spread of Islam;
- *Saum:* ritual fasting and abstinence from sexual intercourse and smoking, especially the obligatory monthly fast from sun-up to sun-down during the month of Ramadan to commemorate the first revelations to Mohammed; and
- *Hajj:* a ritual pilgrimage, especially the journey to Mecca which traditionally occurs in the month after Ramadan and which Muslims should undertake at least once in a lifetime.

Detailed and elaborate rules govern every aspect of the believer's behavior in each of these areas. In a *hajj,* for example, the pilgrims are supposed to wear very plain, unsewn clothes that resemble burial shrouds and they must wear nothing that distinguishes social or economic class. Similarly, there are detailed rules governing the ritual ablutions and prayer that Muslims participate in five times a day. All of these are part of the Shari'ah that governs the way in which believers relate to God.

Muslim Civil and Family Law

One of the most striking developments in Islamic countries during recent years has been a gradual return to Shari'ah as the basis of criminal, civil, and family law. In contrast to Western nations in which the separation of church and state usually is taken for granted, this movement establishes a religious state under which all citizens are subject to a religiously based civil law. The contrast between Islamic and Western states is not, of course, complete in this regard. Christian religious groups in Western countries often push for bans on abortion and homosexuality on primarily religious grounds.

The family is central to traditional Islamic society, and much of Muslim law is devoted to strengthening the Islamic conception of the family. Although to contemporary Westerners Islam often seems to diminish the status of women, we get a somewhat different picture when Islamic practices are seen against the tribal background to which they were in part a reaction. Generally, Islamic family law raised and insured the status of women in Islamic society as compared with the tribal cultures of the Middle East. Prior to Islam, there were no limitations on the number of wives a man might take, and a woman had no right to refuse an offer of marriage and did not receive the dower that the man gave. All of these restrictions changed with the advent of Islam. Centuries before their rights to inheritance were recognized in the West in the nineteenth century, Islamic family law guaranteed inheritance rights for women in families. Similarly, when we place contemporary Islamic next to classical Judaic and Christian practices in treating women, the similarities may be more striking than the differences.

Virtue

Ihsan, or virtue, constitutes the third essential element of Islam, in addition to faith and action. Traditionally, there have been two quite different ways of characterizing virtue. On the one hand, virtue has been defined in terms of worshipping God. In this sense, virtue is roughly equivalent to piety or holiness. On the other hand, virtue is sometimes also defined in a way strikingly reminiscent of Aristotle as excellence in the pursuit of some end or goal. Thus Mohammed said, "Allah has prescribed *ihsan* for everything; hence if you kill, do it well; and if you slaughter, do it well; and let each one of you sharpen his knife and let his victim die at once" (quoted in Glassé, p. 182). As we shall see toward the end of this book, this attitude is remarkably similar to Aristotle's conception of virtue.

The Role of the Ulama

Any worldview which sees right actions as depending on God's will needs some way of determining what God's will is, and traditional Islam deals with this issue by stressing the role of the clergy, the *ulama*, in providing the way for giving definitive interpretations of God's will. Although the clergy often occupy a similar interpretative role in Christianity, what sets Islam apart from Christianity in this respect is that the *ulama* provide interpretations that have political as well as theological implications.

One of the most striking examples of the changing role of the *ulama* in contemporary Islam was Ayatollah Ruhollah Khoumeni's rise to political power in Iran, which signaled a growing Islamic conviction that Muslim clergy should assume positions of political power in order to promote the development of Islam. Thus the *ulama* not only have an interpretive role, but also an executive function in implementing the law as well.

Jihad

The word "*jihad*" often conjures up frightening images in the minds of Westerners, and the popular press has not hesitated to exploit the sensationalism associated with this fear in the past. Although there may be occasional justification for such fears, in large measure the Islamic concept of *jihad* is much different than the popularly feared concept of a "holy war." The word "*jihad*" literally means "striving," and its focus is on resisting evil. Muslims commonly distinguish the internal striving against evil desires within oneself and the external striving against forces that threaten the way of Islam. The former, internal striving, is called the Greater Jihad and the latter, externally directed striving usually is referred to as the Lesser Jihad. What is common to both types of *jihad* is the conviction that the path to holiness requires a constant vigilance and striving against the forces of evil.

Although most Muslim traditionalists have focused on the Greater Jihad, in recent years some Islamic radicals have emphasized the connection between the Lesser Jihad and revolutionary movements toward social justice. Although traditionally *jihad* has been seen as almost exclusively defensive in character, a few have begun to interpret it in a more aggressive manner. Some commentators maintain that such interpretations are not representative of traditional Islam, while others argue that the early spread of Islam depended directly on conquest.

Morality, Compassion, and the Eightfold Path

The moral code of the Buddha is best understood against two background beliefs that profoundly shape the Buddhist's perception of the moral life: the character of existence and reincarnation. Only within this context can we understand the eightfold path and the central role of compassion in Buddhism. Buddhists traditionally emphasize the importance of the ethic of renunciation for the clergy (monks and nuns) and stress the ethic of *karma* and reincarnation for laypersons. We will begin by considering this ethic of renunciation and then turn to the ethic of *karma*.

The Four Noble Truths and the Character of Existence

Life, according to the Buddha in his sermon in "The Deer Park," inevitably involves *suffering*. Indeed, suffering is the principal fact of existence that we must recognize—the inevitability of suffering is the first of the Four Noble

The Buddha (563–483 BCE) gave his followers a message of deep compassion for all living beings.

Truths preached by the Buddha, and the remaining three truths deal with the sources of suffering, the elimination of suffering, and the path that leads to its elimination. In an analysis that bears striking resemblance to the Stoics, the Buddha saw suffering as arising from a discrepancy between the way things are and our desires for how we want them to be.

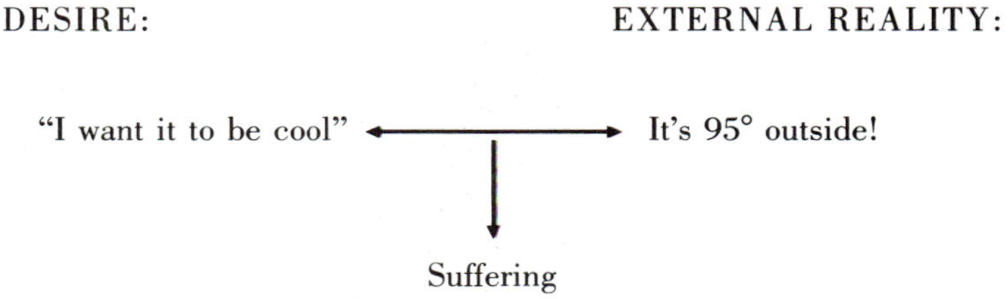

DESIRE: EXTERNAL REALITY:

"I want it to be cool" ⟷ It's 95° outside!

↓

Suffering

When we understand suffering in this way, we see that it can only be alleviated or eliminated if we are able to reduce or eliminate this discrepancy.

There are two ways of reducing this discrepancy between reality and desire. On the one hand, we can attempt to transform reality so that it matches our desires, thereby reducing suffering. Typically, this path is the one that the West has taken, especially insofar as it has become a technological society. Each approach to suffering has its characteristic strengths and weaknesses. We in the West seek to eliminate suffering by transforming the material world through technology. If we are suffering because the weather is hot and we want it to be cool, we invent air conditioning. This approach stands in stark contrast to the Buddha's way of ameliorating suffering. He saw the same discrepancy, but tried to change the other pole of the relationship by reducing human desire. If we can eliminate our desire to have the climate be cool, then we can eliminate our suffering as well. The path to the overcoming of suffering, for the Buddha, lies in overcoming our desires—and the purpose of morality is to help us in this task. Of course, Buddhists recognize the importance of changing external conditions as well. Indeed, there are well-developed traditions of Buddhist medicine, often practiced by Buddhist monks. But the crucial point is that externals can never be controlled totally to our advantage, and even if they could be, this control would not deal with our deeper frustrations, dissatisfactions, and sufferings.

Each of these approaches to suffering has its merits, and each leads to a different moral outlook. The Western understanding of suffering seems particularly well-suited to certain kinds of suffering that arise from physical conditions, such as excessive heat, that are subject to change. It leads to an ethic of action that emphasizes intervention and control. There are several limitations to this approach. First, some physical conditions, such as death, are not subject to such change. Second, some kinds of suffering, such as the pain that comes from losing the love of someone close, are not primarily about physical conditions, but rather center around psychological or spiritual issues. Third, the Western approach has a tendency to treat all issues as physical, even when they are not. Western medicine exemplifies this attitude, for it often equates healing the body with healing the person. Such an approach increases dependence on technology, leading to what some critics see as the technological "quick fix." On the other hand, the Buddhist approach also has its limitations. It is well-suited to the psychological and spiritual aspects of suffering but is more likely to neglect the ways in which changes in physical conditions can ameliorate suffering. Where the Western attitude focuses on the morality of action and leads to an ethic of activism, the Buddhist approach to suffering is more likely to emphasize the morality of desire and lead to an ethic of acceptance.

Reincarnation

There is a second key background belief that shapes the Buddhist understanding of morality, and that is the belief in reincarnation. The dominant metaphor that Buddhists use is that of the passing of a flame from one candle to another. The personal self moves through the wheel of existence in the same way in which the flame moves from one candle to another: it is both the same flame and yet a different flame. So, the same personal ego is not reborn in a different body; instead, some spark of life passes on to a new individual. Hence, Buddhists do not believe in an eternal personal soul, setting them apart from Christians. Christians typically believe in the immorality of each individual soul, and often within Christianity the function of morality is to insure the salvation of the soul. Each individual soul, after a single life on earth, thus gains eternal existence, either in heaven or in hell. Yet Buddhists typically are striving to *extinguish* the personal self through the overcoming of desire. It is hardly surprising, then, that they do not believe in an eternal self. The self is but a fleeting bundle of sensations, and wisdom lies in the recognition of the ephemeral character of the self. Instead of seeking to strengthen a purified self as Christians do, Buddhists take the extinguishing of the individual self as their goal.

Yet the doctrine of *karma* still plays an important role for Buddhists and has important ethical implications. Each individual action either helps to free us from the personal self or to increase our attachment to it. Since *nirvana* is achieved through a detachment from that personal self, actions that increase that attachment—greed, jealousy, and envy are some of the possible motives for such actions—force us to remain in the cycle of existence longer, until we can break the attachment. The cycle of reincarnation is a gradual process through which we struggle to free ourselves from our past unwholesome acts and achieve a state of ever-increasing detachment that culminates in the extinguishing of the personal self, or *nirvana*. Thus the goal is not the salvation of the individual soul, but rather its extinction.

The Eightfold Path

The moral teachings of the Buddha offer a way of extinguishing that self, a way of reducing suffering by overcoming the desires which conflict with the facts of existence. This path to *nirvana* is the Fourth Noble Truth, and the path is an eightfold one. It consists of the following.

- right views
- right intention
- right speech
- right action
- right livelihood
- right effort
- right mindfulness
- right concentration

The first two of these require the development of Wisdom (*prajna*); the next three are the proper domain of Morality (*Sila*), while the final three are developed through Concentration (*Samadhi*). The emphasis in the eightfold path is on right understanding and right thought, for right speaking and acting follow from them. Right meditation provides the mental discipline necessary to overcome desire. Anything that clouds the mind's true perception of itself is to be avoided. Thus drugs and alcohol, for example, are to be shunned. So, too, powerful emotions such as anger should be avoided, for they also cloud our perceptions and fetter us to the everyday world of illusion. Thus Buddhism preaches an *ethic of detachment*, one which claims that the ultimate state is one in which the personal self has been overcome and left behind.

Compassion

After the Buddha's death, Buddhism developed along two distinctive paths. In Mahayana Buddhism, which is the Buddhist path followed in many northern Asian countries, the realization of the fact of suffering leads in a different direction than is found in the Theravada Buddhism of southern countries such as Cambodia, Laos, and Sri Lanka. Whereas Theravada Buddhism stresses the importance of self-purification and a striving for detachment from this world, Mahayana Buddhism emphasizes the way in which compassion for the suffering of others leads one back into the world in order to help others to overcome their own suffering. In Mahayana Buddhism, compassion for the suffering of others leads the Buddhist back into the world, relinquishing the possibility of immanent *nirvana* in order to help others free themselves from their earthly bounds, from the wheel of life and death. Indeed, we find here one of the strongest statements of *altruism* imaginable. In the Diamond Banner Sutra, for example, followers of the Buddha are urged to take the entire suffering of the world onto themselves. The rationale is simple if daunting: how much better the world would be if all its suffering fell on me alone and everyone else was without woe.

Nowhere is this emphasis on compassion more prominent than in Tibetan Buddhism, where training in compassion and loving kindness is one of the mainstays of Buddhist disciplines. Indeed, the fourteenth Dalai Lama, who is the spiritual leader of many Buddhists, is one of the most powerful voices today for compassion, kindness, and world peace. This message of compassion, kindness, and peace extends to all living creatures, including animals, which are not to be killed. All suffering, not just the suffering of human beings, deserves our compassion.

Religious Ethics Without God

One of the distinctive characteristics of Buddhism is that there is no reference to a personal god of any sort. Indeed, some even have characterized Buddhism as a "non-theistic religion." The absence of God has profound implications for our understanding of the relationship between religion and ethics. In monotheistic religions, God's commands often are seen as the basis of right and wrong. Islam provides an excellent example, for in Islamic thought "morally right" is equivalent to "willed by Allah." Yet Buddhism allows no such foundation for morality, since it contains no idea of an individual god who could be a source of ethical commands.

Instead of grounding moral commands in God's will, Buddhism ultimately grounds them in the notion of *karma,* a doctrine of ethical causation whose operation is almost akin to the laws of Western physics. In a sense, this consequentialist moral doctrine maintains that the rightness or wrongness of actions depends on their consequences. But two points need to be noted here. First, consequences are not judged by the same standards that many versions of Western utilitarianism (which we shall examine in Chapter Six) employ. Second, the motives behind our actions are not irrelevant to the consequences as they are in Western utilitarianism. Indeed, a common Buddhist saying is "I call the motive to be the deed." The rightness or wrongness of actions (including their accompanying intentions) depends on their karmic consequences.

How, then, are karmic consequences determined? Here we find a fundamental tension in Buddhism already alluded to above. On the one hand, karmic consequences are determined by the extent to which they contribute to individual self-purification, to the attainment of *nirvana.* Actions which purify us, which loosen our ties to bodily pleasures and distorting emotions, are thus good precisely because they move us along the path to self-extinction, which is the tradition of Theravada Buddhism. On the other hand, Mahayana Buddhism understands karmic consequences more in terms of an action's contribution to reducing the overall amount of suffering in the world for all creatures. Thus for the Mahayana Buddhist, the right action may well be to forgo immediate salvation and go back into the world in order to help free others from the wheel of life and death.

The sayings of the Buddha and the numerous commentaries upon them have, of course, a central place in the moral life of Buddhists. However, in most versions of Buddhism, the moral truths enunciated in these texts are not true *because* the Buddha said them, rather they are true because they express the fundamental and inexorable character of existence. Similar considerations apply to the precepts (which are different for monastics and laypersons) and the *vinaya* (the monastic rule).

Respecting Religious Diversity

The preceding examples bring to light an important aspect of the relationship between religion and morality. In many cultures, moral codes are either directly or indirectly dependent on religious beliefs. Religion either dictates certain behavior as good or bad, or else at least provides the background beliefs about the character of existence within which normal codes are then developed. Moreover, religion often provides or supplements the motivation to be moral, especially in difficult times. Finally, religion may provide the consolation necessary to deal with the unavoidable injustices of our world.

One of the central moral issues that we all face, whether we espouse religious beliefs or not, is how we ought to deal with the diversity of religious beliefs. Let me make several suggestions here. First, we ought to respect the religious beliefs of others and their right to hold those beliefs. (Respect, it should be noted, is not synonymous with approval.) Second, since religious beliefs are often essential components of fundamental worldviews, we should try to understand and appreciate those worldviews and thereby understand more about our own conception of the world. Third, it is important to seek out common ground between different religious traditions. Even when the differences are great, the similarities may be greater. An awareness of common elements, such as the importance of respect and compassion, can provide the basis for developing agreements about how we can live together with our differences. Fourth, it seems appropriate in certain circumstances to make judgments about how deeply we are willing to let other people's religious beliefs impinge on our own behavior, which is perhaps the most difficult issue raised by religious pluralism, since it is the area in which the possibility of conflict is highest and in which there are often no shared rules for negotiating disagreements.

Religious Belief and Moral Rules

Those who have been involved in the discussion of the relation between religion and ethics have focused on questions about the morality of specific types of

Possible Relationships between Religion and Ethics

	Supremacy of Religion	*Compatibilist Theories*	*Autonomy of Ethics*
Strong version	All morality based on divine commands	Reason and religion are identical	Ethics based only on reason; atheistic or agnostic
Weak version	Teleological suspension of the Ethical	Reason and religion may be different but do not conflict	Even God must follow dictates of reason

actions (war, abortion, euthanasia, and so on). They generally have fallen into one of three different camps. First, some have maintained that whenever there is a conflict between religion and ethics, **religion** provides the correct guide for our behavior and **should take precedence over ethics.** God's commands determine what we ought to do. We shall consider two representatives of this tradition, **divine command theorists** and those who admit the autonomy of ethics but claim that in case of conflict **the ethical is suspended in favor of the divine.** At the other end of the spectrum are those who maintain that in cases of such conflict, ethics ought to take precedence over religion. Reason provides the criterion for judging which actions are right and wrong. Some in this tradition, whom we shall call the **autonomy of ethics theorists,** are theists who claim that even God must do what is right simply because it is right, while others (**atheistic ethicists**) reject any religiously based morality whatsoever. There is a middle ground between these two traditions which we shall refer to as **compatibilist theories,** which claim that religion and ethics are compatible with each other and that they do not conflict. The *strong version* of this position maintains that ethics and religion are saying the same thing, although perhaps in different language; the *weak version* claims that religion and ethics may be saying different, but not incompatible, things. Let us examine each of these positions.

Theories that Give Precedence to Religion Over Ethics

Those who claim that God's commands take precedence over societal morality fall into two distinct groups. On the one hand, there are the **divine command theorists** who maintain that there is no real conflict between

God's commands and genuine morality because *whatever God commands is what is right simply because God commands it.* In other words, the only reason something is right is that God commands it. Conversely, the only reason something is wrong is that God forbids it. Consequently, those in this tradition claim that there can never be a genuine conflict between religion and ethics because ethics just *is* what God commands. A corollary of this view is that if God does not exist, then neither does ethics, which is the sense of Dostoyevski's dictum, "If God does not exist, then everything is permitted." On the other hand, there are those (advocates of what Søren Kierkegaard called the **teleological suspension of the ethical**) who maintain that ethics has an independent foundation (usually in reason) but that God's commands override the rules of morality in those cases where a conflict occurs. Representatives of this position are willing to accord an independent validity to ethics, so they would not say that if God does not exist, everything is permitted. However, they do maintain that there is a higher law than the ethical, that God's word takes precedence over the commands of morality. Let us consider both of these traditions more closely.

Divine Command Theorists

In his dialogue *Euthyphro,* Plato poses the question of whether the gods love what is holy because it is holy or whether it is holy because the gods love it. The corresponding question in the realm of ethics is whether God loves the good because it is good or whether it is good because God loves it. Divine command theorists give a clear and unequivocal answer to this question in the area of ethics: they maintain whatever is good is good only because God wills it to be good.

This belief has serious implications for how divine command theorists live their everyday lives. Moral decisions are made ultimately on the basis of what God commands, not what reason tells us. We have to turn to God for the answer to all our questions about how to act. No matter what God commands, it is right just because God commands it. There simply is nothing more to say about it.

Divine command theories fit best within a monotheistic religion in which God is all-good. Christianity and Islam both meet this requirement. Yet divine command theories make little or no sense within either a Navajo or a Buddhist worldview. For the Navajo, two things count against the divine command view of ethics. First, for the Navajo there are many gods (what they call the Holy People), not just one, and they are not necessarily in agreement with one another. Second, the gods are not all-good. They, too, are a mixture of good and evil. Despite the fact that they are called "the Holy People," the gods of the Navajo neither always act good nor always give good advice to The People. Indeed, Kluckhohn and Lieghton, whose *The Navaho* is one of the finest studies of The People by outsiders, report no trace of the belief that an action is right simply because God commands it. The situation is quite different in Buddhism, for there simply is no personal God in the Buddhist religion. Consequently, the idea that something is good because God wills it simply has no basis.

The Teleological Suspension of the Ethical

Abraham believed that God's commands took precedence over morality. Many today share this belief in the priority of religious convictions over moral rules, even if they disagree about which religious convictions are to be given precedence. Fundamentalist Muslims believe very strongly that their religious beliefs take precedence over any demands of secular morality. Similarly, Christian religious fundamentalists take a comparable position, although it is the commands of Jesus rather than Allah that override secular morality for them. Orthodox Jews hold comparable beliefs about the commands of the God of the Old Testament. What all of these positions have in common is the conviction that God's commands, not human reason or local *mores*, are the ultimate guide to human behavior.

Søren Kierkegaard, a nineteenth-century Danish philosopher who is often seen as one of the founders of the religious strain of existentialism, devoted much of his work to a discussion of the relation between religion and ethics. In *Fear and Trembling*, his analysis of the case of Abraham, Kierkegaard argues that there are times when God's commands override the demands of morality. In contrast to divine command theorists who maintain that morality is simply a matter of God's commands, Kierkegaard acknowledges that morality has its own independent basis in reason. Thus, for Kierkegaard, if God did not exist, morality would not be eliminated. It would still have its own independent foundation. However, if we genuinely believe in God, we must believe that God has ultimate supremacy, even over reason. If God commands something, then it overrides the commands of morality.

Criticisms of Divine Command Theories

Divine command theories of ethics have been subjected to strong criticisms from both theistic and atheistic philosophers who maintain that God's commands cannot override an ethics based on reason. Let us consider three of these criticisms.

How Can We Know God's Will?

One of the most difficult issues for divine command theorists to answer is the question of how we can come to know God's will. The difficulty is not that no one claims to know God's will. Rather, the problem is just the opposite: *too many* people claim to know God's will, and they have quite different ideas of what it is. Why, critics ask, should we believe that any one of them has any greater claim to being right than any other? Perhaps God's will is revealed in sacred texts—but which ones? Do we look to the Bible, the Qu'an, or the writing of Mary Baker Eddy? While the answer is clear to the believer, to the outside there appears to be no reason to think that one group has any greater access to God's genuine commands than any other group. Even if one accepts a particular religious tradition, there is still a significant problem in determining exactly what God's will is. Typically, sacred texts tell us too much and too little: too much, because they often contain contradictory statements; too little, because they are often not specific enough.

Sacred texts are not the only way in which people claim to know God's will. Many religious thinkers claim that God speaks to individuals through some kind of voice. In the Christian tradition, this voice is the conscience; among the Navajo, the Holy Wind speaks to individuals by means of a Messenger Wind that enters through the person's ear. In most religions, there is an institutionalized code of conduct that is refined, transmitted, and often enforced by an institutionalized clergy. The *ulama*, the Muslim clergy, are in charge of the interpretation of the *sharia*. Similar structures are found in most organized religions.

Some religions still see signs in the natural world as indications of God's will, although these are usually religious traditions that have remained largely untouched by Western natural science. Animistic religions, for example, often see many natural events, ranging from cataclysmic occurrences such as volcanic eruptions to much less noticeable things such as the appearance of a brown owl, as giving clues to God's will and the course of future events. These perspectives depend on a concept of nature that is far different from that found in Western thought since Descartes. Remnants of this view remain, for example, in the Christian belief in miracles, astrology, and sometimes in superstitions.

The difficulty with all of these sources is not that they tell us too little, but that they claim to tell us too much. If they are all correct, they give us a wealth of varied and often contradictory information—and no way of resolving the contradictions satisfactorily.

God and Criteria for the Divine

The example of God asking Abraham to sacrifice his only son offers an interesting and difficult challenge to divine command theorists. Some philosophers, such as Robert Adams at UCLA, have argued that God cannot require cruelty for its own sake, for this contradicts the notion that God is love. If we did not have some concept of God, and with this criteria (such as love) for what legitimately counts as the divine and what does not (such as cruelty), the door would be open for saying that God could command us to do *anything*, even rape or pillage or kill. But the difficulty is that if we do establish some criteria for the divine, such as love or compassion, then it seems that these stand above God's commands, thereby limiting Him. Consequently, these no longer seem to be divine command theories; that is, they no longer maintain that actions are good solely because God commands them. There is a higher standard to which even God must conform. The divine command theorists seem to be caught on the horns of Euthyphro's dilemma. Either they maintain that a good action simply is whatever God commands, in which case they permit the possibility that God might command us to kill or pillage, or they maintain that there are some limits on what God can legitimately command, in which case they are not genuine divine command theorists any longer, since they say that there are independent limits on God's commands.

This issue is sometimes seen as a comparatively abstract one with little real import for our behavior. William of Ockham, for example, held a strong version of the divine command theory in which he believed that whatever God might command was good simply by virtue of the fact that God commanded it, but he never seriously entertained the possibility that God might command murder or mayhem. Yet this issue becomes absolutely crucial when religious authorities command in God's name a course of action that involves behavior that would usually be considered immoral. Holy wars, whether crusades or *jihads*, would be but one example. The Holy Inquisition is certainly another, as is persecution of any kind that appeals to religion for its foundation. If one is a believer and a strong divine command theorist, there is little basis for opposing such actions unless it is to challenge the legitimacy of the religious authority's claim to be speaking in God's voice. The one thing opponents cannot say, if they believe in the divine command theory, is that God would never condone a particular type of activity. Strong divine command theories eliminate such appeals because they hold that whatever God wills is good simply because God wills it. Thus, if God wills war or torture or even genocide, then it must be good. The divine command theory removes any kind of moral leverage that others, whether believers or non-believers, could use to convince authorities that such actions were not good.

Divine Commands and Human Autonomy

The third major difficulty that divine command theories pose centers around the issue of human autonomy. By claiming that the good is simply whatever God wills it to be, this position makes human moral life depend solely on God's will. What place, then, does human reason have? Are human beings simply reduced to the role of obedient puppets, to pets that respond to whatever the master's will is at the moment? In their strongest forms, divine command theories of ethics seem to leave human beings little room for independent thought or reasoned choice.

Defenders of divine command theories also are concerned about autonomy, but not primarily the autonomy of human beings. One of the principal motivating concerns in their position is to preserve God's autonomy, the divine sovereignty. The guiding insight for divine command theorists is that God is all-powerful; consequently, there is no reason to think that there are any necessary limits on God's power that are imposed from the outside. They seek to preserve the omnipotence of God at all costs.

Autonomy of Ethics Theories

Many philosophers have been unwilling to accept the claims of divine command theorists and have argued that the justification of ethics does not depend on God's will and that, in cases of conflict between the dictates of reason and God's commands, reason ought to override apparently divine commands.

Defenders of the autonomy of ethics may be either theists or atheists. Among theists, *autonomy of ethics philosophers* argue that even God must do what is right. God's choices are constrained by what is morally right. Theists are attracted to this position for at least two reasons. First, it provides a way—the appeal to reasoned arguments—for settling moral disputes without an appeal to religious authority. Furthermore, it provides a bridge to the non-believer, a common ground for moral deliberation that would not be available to the divine command theorist. *Agnostic and atheistic philosophers* also are attracted to the autonomy of ethics position, for it gives ethics an independent existence and justification in a world without a god.

Before looking at both the theistic and atheistic version of the supremacy of ethics position, it is helpful to consider the historical and conceptual background against which they arose.

The Heritage of the Enlightenment

The principal characteristic of the Enlightenment in seventeenth- and eighteenth-century Europe was the *belief in the power of reason.* Developing against the background of the rise of modern science, Enlightenment thought was captured by the dream that it could provide an absolute and presuppositionless starting point for itself. The model was geometry, which seemed to offer absolute certitude in its proofs. The Enlightenment captured a rising faith in the power of the human intellect, especially through modern science, to understand the world and to provide a meaning to life. Enlightenment philosophers hoped that philosophy could emulate mathematics and achieve an absolute foundation for its belief. Reason could then at last be free from dependence on religion.

The principal heritage of the Enlightenment is its belief in the power and the autonomy of reason. These two beliefs about reason—its autonomy and its efficacy—lie at the foundation of much of modern ethical thought. To understand our Enlightenment heritage in this regard is to better understand ourselves. Let us consider each of these two beliefs.

The Autonomy of Reason

The belief in the *autonomy* of reason is the belief that reason does not need to take anything outside of itself for granted. This belief, which pervades the history of modern thought, is most evident in the various attempts of modern philosophers to start anew and provide a solid foundation for all our ideas. René Descartes, a precursor of the Enlightenment, provides a perfect example of this faith in reason in his *Meditations.* At the beginning of the *Meditations,* he casts everything in doubt in order to avoid inadvertently assuming something that is not true. Then, purely through the power of reason, he tries to establish a solid foundation for all our well-founded beliefs (especially those of mathematics and physics). From the indisputable truth of the statement that "I think, therefore I am" (*cogito, ergo sum*), Descartes hopes to build a foundation for knowledge that is absolutely certain and secure without taking anything for granted at all, which includes, but is not limited to, religious beliefs. Three hundred years later, at the beginning of the twentieth century, we find essentially the same dream still alive, this time in logical positivism. Once again, philosophers sought a presuppositionless starting point for grounding all our knowledge claims. Reason, now reduced to the laws of logic, was thought to provide that foundation.

It is precisely this belief in the role that reason should play that provides the background for much contemporary thinking about the relationship between reason and religion. Even those who have lost their faith in the autonomy of reason are still children of the Enlightenment in the sense that they believe reason *should* have been autonomous. This expectation that reason should be autonomous is a principal heritage of the Enlightenment, even among those who feel that reason has failed to fulfill this expectation.

The Efficacy of Reason

The other principal heritage of the Enlightenment is the belief in its *efficacy* of reason. This belief is an understandable correlate of the tremendous advances of modern science. The Enlightenment belief was that reason could change the world and could change us. Reason could motivate, could move us to action. Immanuel Kant, for example, firmly believed that reason could not only tell us what was good, but could motivate us to act in accord with its demands. G. W. F. Hegel saw the whole of human history as the gradual unfolding and development of reason throughout history.

Theistic Versions of the Autonomy of Ethics

When Immanuel Kant developed his ethics, his guiding belief was that reason alone could tell us what to do and could motivate us to do it. As a theistic adherent of the belief in the autonomy of ethics, Kant believed that reason was the same for everyone, both God and human beings alike, and that both were obligated to follow its dictates.

In the eyes of many theists, the advantage of this approach to ethics is that it eliminates any necessary barrier between believers and non-believers in regard to their moral convictions. Since everyone has the same access to reasoned arguments, both theists and non-theists stand on equal footing in their search for the moral life.

Agnostic and Atheistic Versions of the Supremacy of Ethics

Many philosophers who maintain agnostic or atheistic positions as the basis for their views on the autonomy of ethics simply do not address the issue of the relationship between reason and religion in ethics because in their opinion there is no relationship. They are *de facto* agnostics or atheists. Some philosophers have, however, spoken out directly against the influence of religion on ethics. In the final section of this chapter, we will consider two nineteenth-century philosophers in this tradition, Friedrich Nietzsche and Karl Marx. In the twentieth century, two of the most eloquent voices in this tradition were the French existentialist Jean-Paul Sartre and the British logician and analytical philosopher Bertrand Russell. Sartre saw God as the ultimate threat to human freedom and in his "Letter on Humanism" argued that God had to die in order to make room for human freedom. Similarly, Russell saw belief in God as a pernicious fiction which, if believed, could rob human beings of their freedom.

Both Russell and Sartre see human beings as existing in a natural world that is essentially indifferent to them and see morality as a purely human phenomenon which has no deeper roots in either a natural or a transcendent order. This attitude stands in sharp contrast to theistic positions that often claim that there is a continuity between the moral order and the natural world and that see morality as woven more deeply into the fabric of existence. Recall, for example, the Navajo vision of moral harmony, which includes harmony with nature as an essential dimension of *hozho*. Nature and morality reflect one another. In a quite different way, the Christian traditions often see the natural order as fundamentally good, condemning that which runs counter to nature. When contrasted with their theistic counterparts, agnostic and atheistic accounts of ethics typically seem to be much less deeply rooted in any order outside that of purely human creation.

Compatibilist Theories

Among those who maintain that there is no conflict between religion and ethics are some, such as the eighteenth-century philosopher Georg Wilhelm Hegel, who argued that faith and reason could not conflict. According to Hegel, religion and philosophy were simply saying the same thing in different languages. While religion spoke in the language of symbolism and myth, philosophy spoke in the language of reason. The basis of such positions, which we will refer to as *strong compatibilism*, is a deeply rooted metaphysical conviction that the divine and the natural are in fundamental harmony and profoundly reflect one another. According to the strong compatibilist, God would not create a universe in which reason was at odds with God's thinking, nor would God create a world in which the natural order was opposed to the divine. Rather, according to the strong compatibilist, the natural order is a reflection of the divine. Reason and revelation are but two paths to the same truth.

Weak compatibilism is more modest in its claims. It begins with the conviction that God would not create a natural or a moral order that was opposed to the divine or a human reason that was contradicted by revelation. Yet, even though they are not in conflict, revelation (according to the weak compatibilist) may tell us more than reason is ever able to disclose. A weak compatibilist, such as the medieval theologian Thomas Aquinas, maintains that there may well be religious beliefs that are not reducible to reason and that cannot be achieved through any means except revelation. Although this content does not contradict reason, it does go beyond it. Weak compatibilism thus combines some of the strengths of both divine command theories and autonomy of ethics positions. It recognizes that religion has some distinctive contribution to the moral life that is not completely reducible to reason, yet at the same time it recognizes that reason has its own proper domain.

Saints and Moral Exemplars

In the previous section, the focus of our discussion was the morality of specific actions and whether the rightness or wrongness of such actions ultimately depended on an appeal to God. Yet, as we shall see in more detail in Chapter Ten, there is another approach to morality that focuses on the morality of *character* rather than on specific actions. Its principal question is about what kind of person we ought to be, rather than about how we should act. Good actions are seen as flowing from good character.

Saints

Consider the religious traditions and their leaders that we discussed at the beginning of this chapter. We see very different models of moral goodness and of the relationship between religion and morality. In Christianity and Buddhism, there are strong monastic traditions which see the pursuit of holiness as involving a renunciation of the world, which stands in sharp contrast to Islam, where there is more emphasis on the establishment of Muslim states and the pursuit of religious goals through political power. In Native American religions, there is a long tradition that maintains that spiritual leaders do not seek positions of power.

Despite these differences, we see a greater level of fundamental compatibility among religious leaders than we find among religious dogmas. Imagine, for example, the Dalai Lama, Mother Teresa, Bishop Tutu, and Black Elk coming together. They are all deeply religious persons of good will, and it is difficult to believe that they could not find common moral ground. We will discuss the issue of saints in more detail in Chapter Nine.

Stories

So, too, is the method of teaching different when the focus is on persons rather than dogmas. We learn about people through stories, and there is less of a chance of attributing an absolute and exclusive quality to stories than there is to dogma.

This tradition promises greater compatibility between religion and ethics, primarily because the focus is on individual persons rather than principles. Principles stand in logical relations to one another: they can be identical, compatible, or inconsistent. The relations among people have an elasticity not found in dogmas or arguments.

The Role of Religion in the Moral Life

Philosophers over the centuries have been strongly divided over whether religion is a positive or a negative influence in the moral life, whether it enhances or diminishes morality. Let us begin with those who argue that religion is a threat to the moral life.

Is Religion Harmful to Morality?

The last 150 years in the West have witnessed a number of scathing critiques of religion and, in particular, of the effects of religion on the moral life of humanity. The claim that has been made is that religion undermines human dignity and robs people of the autonomy necessary for making moral decisions. Let us briefly examine the ideas of two major representatives of this line of argument: Karl Marx and Friedrich Nietzsche.

Marx and the "Opiate of the People"

Over a century ago, Karl Marx claimed that religion was the "opiate of the people." Like opium, religion—in Marx's opinion—dulled the senses, lulled people into a false sense of security, and undermined their motivation to bring about effective social change to remedy conditions of injustice. When virtues such as humility and meekness are extolled, when people are told that injustices will be righted in the afterlife, and when suffering in this world is praised as preparation for salvation, few people will be motivated to challenge the existing social, political, and economic order.

Indeed, there is some historical justification for Marx's charges. In many countries in Latin America, for example, peasant populations were kept in a state of virtual slavery for generations, and religion played an important role in maintaining an oppressive socioeconomic system. While a large percentage of the population lived in staggering poverty and often worked under brutal conditions, a privileged few reaped great profits. To the extent that Christianity was used—or abused—to sanction this situation, it certainly functioned as an opiate for the people and as an enemy of social justice.

Nietzsche, Morality, and the Death of God

Friedrich Nietzsche, the other major nineteenth-century voice against religion, also criticized Christianity for its effects on people, including the way in which it has prevented the development of a genuine morality of strength. According to Nietzsche, Christianity is founded on *ressentiment,* the desire of the weak to gain control over the strong without themselves developing strengths. It is an example of what Nietzsche called the "herd morality" or "slave morality." The Christian virtue of humility provides a perfect example in Nietzsche's eyes. Humility, according to Nietzsche, is a sign of weakness, a lack of power, a failure to believe in oneself. Christianity takes this weakness and pretends that it is a strength, and then criticizes those with genuine strength—in this case, those with pride—as bad. Thus Christianity inverts the moral world, making the weak strong and the strong weak. The result, Nietzsche argues, is a world of mediocrity and sameness, a weak world from which genuine individuality has vanished.

When Nietzsche proclaimed that "God is dead," he was also making a statement about morality. In the traditional Christian worldview, moral values had an ultimate guarantee in God. This outlook had at least two important implications for ethics. First, since God is good, goodness is not just a human creation. It has an objectivity independent of human choice. Second, God's goodness guarantees that justice ultimately will prevail, that the wicked will be punished and the good will be rewarded, providing an important answer to the question "Why should I be moral?" God's goodness insures that a lifetime of being good will be rewarded in the long run. When Nietzsche said that God is dead, he meant (among other things) that morality had lost any transcendent foundation for its values and any guarantee that the scales of justice will be righted in a later life. In Nietzsche's view, morality must cease to be other-worldly. Instead, it must become purely a morality of this world, a morality of strength and self-affirmation that does not depend on a God or an afterworld.

Historical Accidents Versus Necessary Connections

The common message in this criticism is that religion is harmful to morality. It encourages a false morality and undermines human autonomy.

The central question that these critiques pose is whether religion *necessarily* has the effects that Marx and Nietzche attribute to it. It may well be that religion has at least to some extent had the negative influence that Marx and Nietzsche identified, but religious thinkers could well join Marx and Nietzsche in condemning such effects. Insofar as religion does undermine an individual's sense of autonomy, then religion is contradicting its own goals, falling short of its potential for human liberation. Far from shackling human beings, religion can liberate them to achieve a more fulfilling life in this existence as well as in the next. In order to examine the merits of this reply, let us now turn to a consideration of the arguments that claim that, without religion, morality would be impoverished.

Does Morality Need Religion?

Although arguments have been advanced in support of divine command theories, there is a sense in which such arguments are beside the point. Divine command theories claim that God's word takes precedence over reason, so there would be something logically odd if they were to appeal to reason to support their position. Divine command theorists can, however, point to several advantages or strengths of their position. They do not claim that they accept the position for this reason—rather, they accept it because it is the word of God. Nonetheless, they can point to strengths in their position which defenders of the autonomy of ethics cannot claim. Let us examine two of these strengths.

Ultimate Justice

One of most vexing difficulties for ethicians is that morality demands on some occasions that we set personal advantage aside and act for the sake of some larger good. Morality may require, for example, that we behave honestly, even when those around us are accepting bribes and never getting punished for it. Why should we behave morally when we lose by doing so? Divine command theorists have an answer to this question which is not available to others: they claim that ultimately God will balance the scales. The just will be rewarded and the unjust punished. If so, it certainly provides followers of divine command theories with a motivation to be moral that is not present for others. All of this presumes, of course, that God is just.

Religion as a Motivation to Be Good

In considering the relation between religion and ethics, we have seen that there are really two distinct issues, one relating to the *content* of morality, the other pertaining to its *motivation*. Our discussion has focused primarily on whether the content of morality derives from divine commandments or from reason. Yet even philosophers such as Kant who concluded that reason was the source of morality were troubled by whether reason alone could provide a sufficient motivation to be moral. Kant himself vacillated on this issue. On the one hand, he argued that reason did provide a sufficient motivation in the feeling of respect for the law which it created. On the other hand, he felt that from a practical point of view it was necessary to postulate the existence of God and the immortality of the soul in order to make sense of morality.

There are several senses in which religion is able to provide that motivation. First, as we have seen above, the thought that the just will be rewarded may often be a sustaining motivation for people in morally difficult times, guaranteeing that their virtue will be rewarded. Second, the other side of this same motivational coin is the threat of punishment and damnation, which also can be a powerful motivating force. Both of these factors presuppose a religion containing beliefs about personal immortality and some divinely administered system of rewards and sanctions. Third, in addition to these factors, we should note that religion provides practices and structures that support its values. There is usually a church of some kind and a community of the faithful who provide mutual support to one another. Ethics lacks a comparable support structure. Even religions that lack a belief in personal immortality can provide such communal support.

Religion as Liberating

Critics of religion such as Marx and Nietzsche saw religion as a profound source of social conformity, as a means of maintaining the status quo and keeping people confined to their existing social and economic positions. Yet there is another face of religion, one which was perhaps less visible in the nineteenth century, that suggests religion may be a profoundly liberating force in individuals' lives and an important force for social change.

Consider the role of religion in some of the most important moral transformations of our day. In the civil rights movement in America, religious faith was a central source of both vision and motivation for those involved in the fight for equality. Many of the black leaders of the civil rights movement, both major figures such as Rev. Martin Luther King, Jr., and countless minor figures were ordained ministers. Similarly, throughout the world religious leaders have been tremendously important forces for peaceful change. The story of Archbishop Romero in El Salvador is a powerful example of the transformation from a conservatively minded view of religion to a more radical, liberation-oriented perspective. Much of liberation theology in Latin America is an eloquent testimony to the way in which religion can allow people to escape the status quo and develop a vision of genuine human equality. So, too, in other parts of the world; Bishop Desmond Tutu remains one of the most eloquent and powerful voices for peaceful change in South Africa and Gandhi certainly sought to bring an equality and respect to India that changed the face of that nation—again, without resorting to violence. While religion may sometimes serve the functions that Marx and Nietzsche attributed to it, the evidence of the twentieth century is that it can also be a powerful force for moral progress and human dignity.

Religious Belief: Diversity and Dialogue

Benjamin Barber, a professor of political science at Rutgers, has suggested that our world is torn between two tendencies, which he calls Jihad and McWorld, respectively. On one hand, there is "a Jihad in the name of a hundred narrowly conceived faiths against every kind of interdependence, every kind of artificial social cooperation and civic mutuality." On the other hand, we find ourselves increasingly in "one McWorld tied together by technology, ecology, communications, and commerce." We are caught up in both these opposing trends. "The planet," Barber continues, "is falling precipitately apart *and* coming reluctantly together at the very same moment." One of the central challenges that faces us within this context is to create ways of living together that respect diversity but provide a sufficiently broad common ground to insure comparatively peaceful and harmonious interaction. The movement toward McWorld threatens to obliterate most differences and is hardly respectful of diversity. The movement toward Jihad, on the other hand, threatens to pull us back toward regional warring tribes, each pitted ferociously against all the others.

Where does religion fit in this picture? Clearly there is a strain—present in most religions, but stronger in some than in others—toward what Barber calls Jihad. (Indeed, the very word "Jihad" is an Arabic word that Westerners take as referring only to a Moslem war against infidels. As we have seen, in traditional Islam this word actually refers primarily to an internal struggle rather than an external war.) Jihad is the strain in religion which is convinced that it has found the absolute truth and that those who deny this truth are not to be tolerated. It is the spirit of the Inquisition, which tried and executed people for heresy. It is the spirit of all those who have died—and killed—for religion. We can call this spirit the fundamentalist tradition in religion.

Fundamentalism is not limited to any single religion, and it is not itself a religious belief; rather, it is better described as a way of holding particular beliefs. As such, it has three characteristics. First, it tends to see its beliefs in *literal* rather than metaphorical or allegorical terms. Fundamentalists of all religious persuasions usually have a very specific, explicitly spelled out set of beliefs. Second, fundamentalism tends to take its beliefs as *absolute*. It sees its beliefs as true for everyone and for all times. Fundamentalism usually sees itself as incompatible with relativism. Third, fundamentalism tends to be *intolerant* of those who do not agree with its beliefs, of course, to a matter of degree. In some cases, it is simply an intolerance that emerges when its dogmas are challenged directly. In other more extreme cases, it is an intolerance that demands that everyone accept its beliefs, even if others present no direct or indirect challenge. In such cases, fundamentalism goes out into the world to convert it. Fundamentalism is, to a greater or lesser degree, intolerant of differences and disagreements.

There is, however, another strain in most religious traditions which is quite different from the fundamentalist approach. I shall refer to it as the **ecumenical tradition,** although it may go by different names in different religious contexts. It differs from fundamentalism in regard to each of the three characteristics mentioned above. First, it usually tends to treat its statements of belief as more metaphorical or allegorical in character, which alone opens the door to tolerating greater diversity, since metaphors and allegories cannot contradict one another in the same direct way that literal statements can. Consequently, ecumenism usually does not hold its own beliefs to be absolute in the same way that fundamentalism does. It is more likely, for example, to be aware that any language it uses inevitably distorts and fails to completely capture the reality to which it refers. Finally, at least in part because of the first two differences, ecumenism tends to be more tolerant toward disagreements, often holding that there are many paths to the same God.

The ecumenical spirit in religion corresponds to the pluralistic and fallibilistic approach to ethics that is developed in this book. Both see diverse traditions as containing important truths, and both emphasize the ways in which we can learn from one another. Indeed, both see diversity as an opportunity for learning and insight, rather than as an impediment to them. Both ecumenism and pluralism recognize that none of us has the whole truth, and that all of us can learn from one another in our continuing search for greater insight.

Bibliographical Essay

For an introduction to **Navajo ethics,** see especially James Kale McNeley, *Holy Wind in Navajo Philosophy* (Tucson: University of Arizona Press, 1981), John R. Farella, *The Main Stalk. A Synthesis of Navajo Philosophy* (Tucson: University of Arizona Press, 1984), and Leland C. Wyman, *Blessingway* (Tucson: University of Arizona Press, 1970). For a classic and insightful introduction to Navajo culture, see Clyde Kluckhohn and Dorothea Leighton, *The Navaho* (Cambridge, Mass.: Harvard University Press, 1946). There are several excellent essays on Navajo culture, language, worldviews, religion, and culture in the *Handbook of North American Indians,* edited by William C. Sturtevant (Washington, D.C.: Smithsonian Institution, 1983), Vol 10: *Southwest,* edited by Alfonso Ortiz; unfortunately, none of the essays deals directly with morality or ethics. Gladys A. Reichard's *Navajo Religion. A Study of Symbolism* (Princeton, N.J.: Princeton University Press, 1977) contains a helpful chapter on

Navajo ethics. John Ladd's *The Structure of a Moral Code* (Cambridge, Mass.: Harvard University Press, 1957), which is a study of Navajo ethics, is one of the few studies of Native American ethics by an American philosopher. (Richard Brandt's *Hopi Ethics: A Theoretical Analysis* [Chicago: University of Chicago Press, 1954] is the only other such book-length work that I have been able to find.) One of the principal sources for information about the Navajo are the manuscripts of Fr. Berard Haile, many of which are available at the superb Museum of Northern Arizona in Flagstaff. Also, mention should be made of the mystery novels of Tony Hillerman, which have done much to bring an appreciation of Navajo culture to a wider audience; see especially *The Blessing Way*. For an eloquent statement of the plight of contemporary Native Americans, see especially Peter Matthiessen, *Indian Country* (New York: Penguin Books, 1979) and his *In the Spirit of Crazy Horse* (New York: Penguin Books, 1992). Mourning Dove's *Coyote Stories* (Lincoln: University of Nebraska Press, 1990) is an excellent collection of stories about this distinctive figure.

On **Islamic ethics,** see John L. Esposito, *Islam: The Straight Path* (New York: Oxford University Press, 1988) and also Seyyed Hossein Nasr's works, especially his *Ideals and Realities of Islam* (London: Unwin Hyman, Ltd., 1985). Cyril Glassé's *The Concise Encyclopedia of Islam* (New York: HarperCollins, 1991) is an excellent reference work. Azim Nanji's "Islamic Ethics," *A Companion to Ethics*, edited by Peter Singer (Oxford: Basil Blackwell, 1991), pp. 106–120, discusses Islamic ethics specifically within the context of Western thought. Also see G. Hourani, *Reason and Tradition in Islamic Ethics* (Cambridge: Cambridge University Press, 1985); Majid Khadduri, *The Islamic Conception of Justice* (Baltimore: Johns Hopkins University Press, 1984); I. Lapidus, "Knowledge, Virtue and Action: The Classical Muslim Conception of *Adab* and the Nature of Religious Fulfillment in Islam," *Moral Conduct and Authority*, edited by B. Metcalf (Berkeley: University of California Press, 1984); and the essays in *Ethics in Islam*, edited by R. Houvannisian (Malibu, California: Undena Publications, 1985). For a short survey of recent developments in Islam, see John L. Esposito, *Islam and Politics*, 3d edition (Syracuse, N.Y.: Syracuse University Press, 1991); Nazih Ayubi, *Political Islam* (New York: Routledge, 1991); and Emmanuel Sivan, *Radical Islam*, 2d edition (New Haven, Conn.: Yale University Press, 1991).

There are numerous collections of texts from, and articles about, **Buddhism.** For a good collection of basic texts, see *The Buddhist Tradition in India, China, and Japan*, edited by William Theodore de Bary (New York: Modern Library, 1969) and *Buddhist Texts Through the Ages*, edited by Edward Conze, I. B. Horner, B. Snellgrive, and Arthur Waley (New York: Harper Colophon, 1964); also see Conze's own presentation of Buddhism in his *Buddhism: Its Essence and Development* (New York: Harper Colophon, 1975) and Peter Harvey's *An Introduction to Buddhism* (New York: Cambridge University Press, 1990). For a discussion of Buddhist ethics that relates it to the categories of Western philosophy, see Padmasiri de Silva, "Buddhist Ethics," *A Comparison to Ethics*, edited by Peter Singer (Oxford: Basil Blackwell, 1991), pp. 58–68, and Ninian Smart, *Worldviews: Crosscultural Explorations of Human Beliefs* (New York: Charles Scribner's Sons, 1983), especially chapter six, "The Ethical Dimension," which contains an excellent discussion of comparative religious ethics. Arthur Danto's *Mysticism and Morality* (New York: Basic Books, 1972) is a philosophically sensitive discussion of the ethical implications of Buddhism. Additional works on Buddhist ethics include G. Dharmasiri, *Fundamentals of Buddhist Ethics* (Singapore: Buddhist Research Society, 1986); K. N. Jayatilleke, *Ethics in Buddhist Perspective* (Kandy, Sri Lanka: Buddhist Publication Society, 1972); H. Saddhatissa, *Buddhist Ethics* (London: Allen and Unwin, 1970); and Charles S. Prebish, *Buddhist Ethics: A Cross-Cultural Approach* (Dubuque, Iowa: Kendall Hunt Publishing Company, 1992). Also see Padmasiri de Silva, *An Introduction to Buddhist Psychology* (London: Macmillan Press, 1979) for a perceptive discussion of the psychology implicit in Buddhism, and Lenore Friedman, *Meetings with Remarkable Women: Buddhist Teachers in America* (Boston and London: Shambhala Publications, 1987) for the distinctive and often neglected voice of women in Buddhism. Mary Pat Fisher and Robert Luyster's *Living Religions* (Englewood Cliffs, New Jersey: Prentice-Hall, 1991) contains clear presentations of the basic doctrine of both Buddhism and Islam.

Much of the contemporary discussion of the **divine command theory of ethics** stems from the contemporary defense of this theory by Robert Merrihew Adams, "A Modified Divine Command Theory of Ethical Wrongness," *Religion and Morality: A Collection of Essays*, edited by G. Outka and J. P. Reeder, Jr. (New York: Doubleday and Company, Inc., 1973), pp. 318–34, and his "Divine Command Metaethics Modified Again," *Journal of Religious Ethics*, Vol. 7, No. 1 (Spring, 1979), pp. 71–79. On this same topic, see John Chandler, "Is the Divine Command Theory Defensible?" *Religious Studies*, Vol. 20(1984), pp. 443–52, and his "Divine Command Theories and the Appeal to Love," *American Philosophical Quarterly*, Vol. 22, No. 3 (July, 1985), pp. 231–39. Also see Philip Quinn, *Divine Commands and Moral Requirements* (Oxford: Clarendon Press, 1978). Many of the most influential articles on this topic are gathered together in *Divine Commands and Morality*, edited by Paul Helm (Oxford: Oxford University Press, 1981), and in R. G. Swinburne, "Duty and the Will of God," *Canadian Journal of Philosophy*, Vol IV, No. 2 (December 1974). For an insightful discussion of whether God's omnipotence entails the claim that God is able to sin, see Nelson Pike, "Omnipotence and God's Ability to Sin," *American Philosophical Quarterly*, Vol. 6, No. 3 (July, 1969), pp. 208–216. On the relationship of divine command theories to utilitarianism, see Edward Wierenga, "Utilitarianism and the Divine Command Theory," *American Philosophical Quarterly*, Vol. 21, No. 4 (October 1984), pp. 311–18.

On the question of whether it is possible to have **morality without religion**, see William K. Frankena, "Is Morality Logically Dependent on Religion?," *Religion and Morality: A Collection of Essays*, edited by Gene Outka and J. P. Reeder, Jr. (New York: Doubleday, 1973); E. D. Klemke, "On the Alleged Inseparability of Religion and Morality," *Religious Studies*, Vol. 11 (1975); Kai Nielsen, *Ethics Without God*, Rev. ed. (Buffalo, N.Y.: Prometheus Books, 1990); Alasdair MacIntyre and Paul Ricoeur, *The Religious Significance of Atheism* (New York: Columbia University Press, 1969); George Mavrodes, "Religion and the Queerness of Morality," *Rationality, Religious Belief and Moral Commitment: New Essays in the Philosophy of Religion*, edited by Robert Audi and W. Wainwright (Ithaca, N.Y.: Cornell University Press, 1986); Patrick Nowell-Smith, "Religion and Morality," *Encyclopedia of Philosophy*, edited by Paul Edwards (New York: Macmillan, 1967), pp. 150–58; Robert Young, "Theism and Morality," *Canadian Journal of Philosophy*, Vol. VII, No. 2 (December, 1977), pp. 341–351. For the argument that worshipping God is incompatible with human dignity and autonomy, see James Rachels, "God and Human Attitudes," *Religious Studies*, Vol. 7 (1971), pp. 325–327, and the reply by Philip Quinn, "Religious Obedience and Moral Autonomy," *Religious Studies*, Vol. 11 (1975), pp. 265–281.

On the **Marxist critique of religion**, see the excellent anthology of Marx's own writings in Karl Marx, *On Religion*, edited by Saul Kussiel Padover (New York: McGraw-Hill, 1974). Robert B. Tucker's *Religion and Myth in the Philosophy of Karl Marx* (Cambridge: Cambridge University Press, 1961) offers an insightful discussion of Marx's views on religion; the best discussion of religious alienation is still the untranslated work by Jean-Yves Calvez, *La pensée de Karl Marx* (Paris: Editions du Seuil, 1956). Also see Bertell Ollman, *Alienation: Marx's View of Man in Capitalist Society* (Cambridge: Cambridge University Press, 1976). **Nietzsche's critique of religion** is found throughout his writings, but especially his *Beyond Good and Evil: Prelude to a Philosophy of the Future*, translated, with commentary, by Walter Kaufmann (New York: Vintage Books, 1966); *On the Genealogy of Morals*, translated by Walter Kaufmann and R. J. Hollingdale (New York: Vintage Books, 1989); and *The Will to Power*, translated by Walter Kaufmann and R. J. Hollingdale (New York: Random House, 1967).

On the relationship between **religion, narrative, and character**, see especially Stanley Hauerwas, *Vision and Virtue. Essays in Christian Ethical Reflection* (Notre Dame, Ind.: Notre Dame University Press, 1981) and Richard J. Regan, S. J., "Virtue, Religion, and Civic Culture," *Midwest Studies in Philosophy. Ethical Theory: Character and Virtue*, Vol. XIII (1988), pp. 342–51. On the **emotive dimension of religious experience**, see especially Gareth Matthews, "Ritual and the Religious Feelings," *Explaining Emotions*, edited by Amélie O. Rorty (Berkeley: University of California Press, 1980), pp. 339–54.

Citations. The Navajo descriptions of the person who lacks faults come from McNeley, *Holy Wind in Navajo Philosophy*, p. 42. The practical ethical guidelines are found in Kluckhohn and Leighton, *The Navaho*, pp. 304–07. The quote by Benjamin Barber is found in "Jihad vs. McWorld," *The Atlantic Monthly*, Vol. 269, No. 3 (March, 1991), p. 53.

DISCUSSION QUESTIONS

1. Recall item 13 in the Ethical Inventory: "What is right depends on what God says is right."
   (a) What is the proper name for the theory that this statement exemplifies?
   (b) Has your rating of this item changed after reading this chapter? If so, in what way? If your rating has not changed, are your reasons for your rating any different now than they were when you first responded to this statement?
2. Recall statement 17 in our Ethical Inventory: "We do not need to depend on religion in order to have a solid foundation for our moral values."
   (a) What is the proper name for the theory this statement exemplifies?
   (b) Has your rating of this item changed after reading this chapter? If so, in what way? If your rating has not changed, are your reasons for your rating any different now than they were when you first responded to this statement?
3. Review your response to statement 16 in the Ethical Inventory: "All major religions have something important to tell us about what is right and what is wrong."
   (a) If you agree with this statement, discuss a moral insight that you have gained from a religious tradition other than your own.
   (b) Has your rating of this item changed after reading this chapter? If so, in what way? If your rating has not changed, are your reasons for your rating any different now then they were when you first responded to this statement?
4. Recall your evaluation of statement 18 in the Ethical Inventory: "Religion is just a narcotic that lulls people into feeling better about their misery."
   (a) What philosophers have supported a position like the one found in this statement?
   (b) Has your rating of this item changed after reading this chapter? If so, in what way? If your rating has not changed, are your reasons for your rating any different now than they were when you first responded to this statement?

5. The Russian novelist Fyodor Dostoyevski (1821–1881) often said, "If God is dead, everything is permitted." What does this quotation mean? How does it affect divine command morality? Would you live your own life any differently if you concluded that God is dead?
6. Many cultures, such as ancient Greek culture, are polytheistic, that is, they believe in many different gods. How would a polytheist interpret a divine command? What problems would the polytheistic divine command theorists encounter that their monotheistic counterparts do not have to confront? Is the (alleged) existence of more than one god an argument for moral relativity? (See Chapter Two.)
7. In Genesis Chapter 22, God orders Abraham to sacrifice his only son Isaac. Should Abraham (or any father) obey such a command? Why or why not? In your own experience, have you ever encountered a conflict between your religious beliefs and your moral convictions? If so, how did you resolve the conflict? What does your way of resolving the conflict say about your position on the autonomy of ethics?
8. Does religion provide believers with consolations not available to the non-theist? For example, is there a difference between the ways in which theists and non-theists deal with injustices and the suffering of the innocent? Is there a difference between the ways in which they experience guilt and forgiveness? What are the strengths and weaknesses of each perspective?
9. In the Amish and Mennonite sections of Pennsylvania, one can often see black horse-drawn buggies on the highways. Not only do their religious beliefs dictate using horse-drawn buggies instead of cars powered by mechanical engines, but their religious convictions also prohibit the Amish and Mennonites from displaying images—including the image of the red reflective triangle that the state requires that they put on the rear of their carriages to lessen the danger of collision with cars. How do you think we should resolve conflicts such as these? What does your answer reveal about your more general beliefs about the relationship between religious beliefs and moral standards?
10. The movie *The Mission* presents a subtle and complex portrait of the relationship between religion and ethics. Which characters in the movie advocate the divine command theory of ethics? Which oppose it? What reasons do they have in both cases? One of the principal issues in divine command theories of ethics is the question of how one determines what God's will is. Different characters in the movie deal with this issue in different ways. Which characters claim to know what God's

will is? Which do not? What is the position of the character played by Jeremy Irons?

11. In the movie *Gandhi*, Gandhi at one point says, "I am a Moslem; I am a Hindu; I am a Christian; I am a Jew." What did he mean by that? In what sense, if any, was it true? In what sense, if any do you feel that it is true about you?

12. We have seen the way in which some philosophers have argued that religion is harmful to the moral life while others have claimed that it is necessary to it. What view of the relationship between religion and ethics do you find in the movie *Gandhi?* Do you agree with this view? Why or why not?

CHAPTER 5

THE ETHICS OF SELFISHNESS: EGOISM

"As a basic step of self-esteem, learn to treat as the mark of a cannibal any man's *demand* for your help. To demand it is to claim that your life is his property—and loathsome as such claim might be, there's something still more loathsome: your agreement. Do you ask if it's ever proper to help another man? No—if he claims it as his right or as a moral duty that you owe him. Yes—if such is your own desire based on your own selfish pleasure in the value of his person and his struggle. Suffering as such is not a value; only man's fight against suffering, is. If you choose to help a man who suffers, do it only on the ground of his virtues, of his fight to recover, of his rational record, or of the fact that he suffers unjustly; then your action is still a trade, and his virtue is the payment for your help. But to help a man who has no virtues, to help him on the ground of his suffering as such, to accept his faults, his need, as a claim—is to accept the mortgage of a zero on your values. A man who has no virtues is a hater of existence who acts on the premise of death; to help him is to sanction his evil and to support his career of destruction. . . .

"I swear—by my life and my love of it—that I will never live for the sake of another man, nor ask another man to live for mine."

—A speech by John Galt in Ayn Rand, *Atlas Shrugged*

In her novel *Atlas Shrugged,* Ayn Rand presents a portrait of a man who lives his entire life for himself alone, asking nothing of other people, feeling no obligation to help anyone else. Her hero, John Galt, is a model of the person who practices what she calls the virtue of selfishness. Every man is an island, responsible for himself and for no one else, where genuine morality consists

Types of Egoism

Type of Egoism	*Type of Claim*	*Main Thesis*
Psychological	Descriptive	Claims that everyone acts in his or her own self-interest
Ethical	Normative	Claims that everyone ought to act in his or her own self-interest

precisely in striving not to give in to temptations such as compassion. In the fictional figure of John Galt, egoism has become a moral ideal. This chapter is devoted to a consideration of the value of that ideal.

Egoism has two forms that we will consider in this chapter, both of which center around the concept of acting in one's own self-interest. **Psychological egoism,** which advances a purely descriptive claim, **maintains that people always act in their own self-interest.** In contrast to this purely descriptive thesis, **ethical egoism maintains that people *should* always act in their own self-interest,** which is a normative claim because it tells us how we *ought* to act. (Recall the distinction between descriptive and normative claims that we drew in our discussion of moral relativism.)

Let us look at both of these versions.

Psychological Egoism

At first glance, psychological egoism is a plausible and appealing doctrine to many. Indeed, it is so plausible that many economic analyses of human behavior take psychological egoism as their basic premise. It also seems to be a fairly straightforward theory. What, after all, could be clearer than saying that people act out of their own self-interest?

Some Initial Distinctions

This initial clarity is deceptive. Psychological egoists claim that *people act out of their own self-interest.* Yet exactly what are they asserting when they make this claim? Several questions need to be posed:

- Do people *always* act out of their own self-interest or do they just *predominantly* act out of their own self-interest?
- Do people act out of their *genuine* self-interest or what they (perhaps mistakenly) *think* is their self-interest?

- Do people act *exclusively* out of self-interest or are other motives present as well?
- What part of the "self" is affirmed when people act out of self-interest? Is it the self that experiences pleasure and pain (*the hedonistic self*) or the self that has projects and interests (*the project-creating self)?*
- Do people *freely choose* to act out of their own self-interest or are they *determined* to do so?
- When egoists claim that people act out of their own self-interest, what *evidence* do they offer for their claim?

The plausibility of the psychologist's thesis will depend on how each of these questions is answered. Let us examine them.

Exclusive Egoism versus Predominant Egoism

In its stronger versions, psychological egoism claims that people act *exclusively* out of self-interest. It follows from this theory that altruistic behavior, behavior done solely for the sake of the other person, does not exist. Even when someone such as Mother Teresa appears to be acting purely for the sake of other people, in actuality she is doing what she does because—according to the exclusive psychological egoist—it makes her feel better. Everyone, the exclusive psychological egoist claims, always acts solely out of self-interest.

Predominant psychological egoism, on the other hand, advances a more restricted claim. According to the predominant egoist, "self-interest tends to be overriding in people's motivational structures . . . at least until they have reached a stable and satisfactory level of well-being and security." For most people in most situations, except where the ratio of altruistic gain to personal loss is very large or where they are dealing with people or projects that they care deeply about, self-interest will override any altruistic motives.

Which of these two versions of psychological egoism is stronger? Exclusive egoism is by far the more controversial and interesting position, for if it is true then some of our most deeply held beliefs about human goodness, compassion, and love must be revised. Predominant psychological egoism is much more likely to be true, but precisely because it is not an extreme position, its truth will be of much less interest to most people. If predominant egoism is true, most people's basic beliefs about human motivation largely will be unaffected.

Maximizing versus Non-Maximizing Self-Interest

If we assume the exclusive psychological egoist's position for a moment, we may ask a second related question about the strength of the egoist's claim. There is a significant difference between saying:

People always act in such a way as to promote *some* of their self-interest;

and saying:

People always act in such a way as to *maximize* their self-interest.

The strongest possible position here would be maximizing exclusive egoism, which would maintain that people always and only act to maximize their own self-interest.

It makes a significant difference whether one defends maximizing or non-maximizing egoism. The principal advantage of the non-maximizing versions of egoism is that they leave open the possibility of a significantly greater degree of social harmony, since people are not all trying to get the *most* for themselves. Again, the stronger thesis is less likely to be true. Maximizing psychological egoism can be falsified simply by showing that some people do not try to get the maximum benefit possible for themselves. Non-maximizing egoism, by contrast, is much harder to disprove, for one must show that some people act in ways that do not involve trying to get *anything* for themselves. Non-maximizing egoism, in other words, can be shown to be false only by proving that some people are genuine altruists some of the time.

Genuine versus Apparent Self-Interest

Psychological egoists claim that people act out of self-interest, but what do they say about people who smoke three packs of cigarettes a day? Are they acting out of self-interest? Clearly, most of us would say that heavy smoking is not in fact in anyone's self-interest. Does that prove that psychological egoism is false, since a number of people are heavy smokers?

The psychological egoist replies to this question by drawing a distinction between genuine self-interest and apparent self-interest. Everyone, the psychological egoist may claim, does what he or she *believes* is in his or her self-interest, even though that belief may be mistaken. Yet does this distinction really solve the problem? Many smokers willingly admit that their continued smoking is not in their self-interest, and yet they do it anyway. (Of course, for some people, the pleasure associated with smoking may be so great that it does not conflict with non-maximizing egoism.) So, too, some people *believe* that they are acting purely out of love or concern for the other person. The psychological egoist wants to say that they are really acting out of self-interest, but clearly they cannot be said to be consciously doing so or to believe that they are doing so.

Defining the "Self" in "Self-Interest"

When psychological egoists claim that human beings act out of self-interest, they usually presuppose a particular notion of the self which is the basis of that self-interest. Although there are a number of possibilities, we will consider only two of them here; a third will be added when we consider ethical egoism.

The Hedonistic Self In its most primitive form, the "self" of "self-interest" is a hedonistic self, that is, a self that seeks pleasure and tries to

Seeing human beings as "brutish and Nasty," the British philosopher Thomas Hobbes (1588–1679) developed a moral and political theory based on egoism.

avoid pain. This self is also a largely unconscious self; that is, we can imagine people seeking pleasure and avoiding pain without even consciously realizing what they are doing. Moreover, this self is also situated almost exclusively in the present and the immediate future. It is not a long-range planner and usually has no awareness of long-term self-interest. This self Freud identified as the id, a blind groping for pleasure.

The appeal to the hedonistic self most neatly resolves the difficulties about the difference between genuine and apparent self-interest without any reference to states of belief. The distinction between genuine and apparent self-interest depends on the distinction between what one believes is best (that is, maximizes self-interest) and what actually is best. By grounding self-interest in the hedonistic self, the psychological egoist bypasses this entire issue. Self-interest simply is whatever in the moment increases pleasure and reduces pain. There is simply no issue of "genuine" self-interest. The issue is simply whether something increases pleasure or not. Because there is no distinction between apparent pleasure and genuine pleasure, there is no distinction between apparent self-interest and genuine self-interest for the hedonistic self.

The difficulty with interpreting self-interest exclusively in hedonistic terms is that it makes it much less likely that psychological egoism is true. The claim that people act solely to increase pleasure and reduce pain seems to refute the facts. There are numerous cases in which people we know choose a course of action that at least in the short term causes them more pain and less pleasure (for example, training for a marathon instead of staying in bed in the morning and sleeping late), but they do so in order to achieve some goal or purpose that they have, which may ultimately be in the person's self-interest, but it is certainly not something which increases the immediate pleasure that the person experiences.

The Project-Bearing Self It is precisely difficulties such as these with the hedonistic concept of the self that have led many psychological egoists to revise their views of the self in such a way that the self is seen primarily as the *bearer of projects*. Self-interest then comes to be defined as that which promotes the individual's projects, and that which is contrary to self-interest is that which is detrimental to those projects. Psychological egoism then asserts that everyone acts in ways that they believe will promote (or maximize) their own projects.

As with the shift from exclusive egoism to predominant egoism, so too does the shift from hedonistic self-interest to project self-interest seem to be a move toward a more defensible but less interesting form of egoism. Once self-interest is seen in terms of projects, it is no longer as narrow, as blind, or as selfish as it was when it was interpreted in purely hedonistic terms. Project self-interest encompasses a wider range of possible motivations than hedonistic self-interest, including altruistic behavior, and thus seems more compatible with our experience of the range of people's motivations.

The flexibility of the concept of a project is at once both a strength and a weakness. It is a strength, as we have already seen, because it recognizes that human beings have a wider range of motivations than simple pleasure and pain. Yet this flexibility also threatens to be a liability if it becomes too great. Can *anything* count as an egoistic project? If so, then the notion of egoistic motivation is so broad as to be useless. Egoists—as Kavka has pointed out in *Hobbesian Moral and Political Theory*—must therefore place some limitations on the notion of what counts as a self-interest project. Some of these restrictions are negative, others positive. Clearly, it cannot be a project that is (a) self-destructive, (b) done for the sake of duty or some other moral motivation, or (c) done for the sake of others (that is, altruistic). Many other motivations, however, are acceptable because they do count as personal benefits, Kavka lists the following aims as self-directed: ". . . the agent's pleasure, pain, wealth, power, security, liberty, glory, possession of particular objects, fame, health, longevity, status, self-respect, self-development, self-assertion, reputation, honor, and affection" (42). Typically, projects done for any of these purposes will count as self-interested in the relevant, egoist's sense.

Noncausal versus Causal Egoism

When egoists claim that people act out of self-interest, there is an ambiguity in their claim. Do they mean that people always *choose* to act out of their own self-interest or that people *necessarily* act out of their own self-interest because they are determined to do so? The latter claim is a causal one about the sources of people's motivations, suggesting that people have no choice about whether they act in self-interested ways. Since we will consider the issue of causal determinism and human behavior in the next section, we will confine our discussion here to noncausal versions of egoism.

Support for Psychological Egoism

What evidence can be presented in support of the claim that people always act out of self-interest? Let us consider here three possible sources of support for the egoist's position: (a) the argument that people always derive pleasure or satisfaction from their actions, (b) the claim that we often deceive ourselves about our actual motives, and (c) the evidence of the social sciences.

The Pleasure Argument

Some psychological egoists advance an argument that initially may appear fairly strong. Everyone, they claim, derives pleasure (or satisfaction) from what they do; therefore, they conclude, their behavior is done for the sake of pleasure and is thus self-interested. I will call this *the pleasure argument.*

As soon as the argument is stated clearly, we can see the hole in it. It may be true that people feel pleasure in what they do, but that does not mean necessarily that they do it *in order to* experience that pleasure. Often during times of natural disasters, people perform genuinely heroic acts, saving other people at great risk to themselves. Presumably, when such rescues are successful, the heroes feel a deep sense of pleasure and satisfaction. But it is a big—and unwarranted—step from saying that to concluding that they performed the rescues *in order to* feel pleasure. Yet that is precisely what the psychological egoist claims.

Two other points should be noted about this argument. First, all too often people do not feel pleasure or satisfaction in what they do. The world certainly would be a happier place if this fact were not true, but unfortunately many people fail to find pleasure or satisfaction in at least some of what they do. Second, people may experience pleasure or satisfaction in performing altruistic actions. Far from counting against the altruistic character of such actions, this fact simply suggests that, at least in this regard, our world is well-constructed. How much less happy the world would be if altruistic behavior never carried any pleasure or satisfaction with it!

The Self-Deception Argument

The second source of support for psychological egoism is one with which most of us are familiar. We have all had the experience of initially believing that we are acting out of purely altruistic motives and subsequently, perhaps in the quietude of solitary reflection, realized that there were self-serving motives buried beneath the surface. It is much more acceptable in our society—and in most other societies as well—to cloak our selfish motives in the garb of altruism, which, moreover, is not simply a matter of concealing selfish motives from other people. There is a good reason for concealing them from ourselves as well. Insofar as our society defines a good person as one who acts altruistically, and insofar as all of us naturally want to think of ourselves as good people, we need to think of ourselves as having altruistic motives, even when we do not. Self-deception, so the psychological egoist claims, helps us to have a better opinion of ourselves.

There is undoubtedly an element of truth in this argument, perhaps even a large element. The difficulty with the argument is that there is no evidence to suggest that *all* apparently altruistic actions really have this structure below the surface. Moreover, this argument suggests that our apparent motives are not our real motives, that our genuine motives lie beneath the surface. If that were so, are these actions really free? Is the egoist saying that some unconscious force makes us act selfishly, even when we think we are acting altruistically? This question raises difficulties about free will and determinism that we will consider in the second part of this chapter.

Self-Interest, Altruism, and the Behavioral Social Sciences

It would be much easier to reach a decision about the validity of psychological egoism if the social sciences offered a single, conclusive picture of the motives of human behavior. Unfortunately, that is not the case. Although there is certainly no shortage of empirical research showing that human beings often act out of self-interest, a sufficient number of studies indicate that at least some people act morally or altruistically at least some of the time. Moreover, some theories *begin* with the premise that everyone acts out of self-interest. Yet such a starting point can hardly provide conclusive evidence that all behavior must be self-interested, for that belief is built into the starting point of the theory rather than arrived at through empirical investigation. In general, the sciences of human behavior do not provide a strong, unequivocal case to support exclusive psychological egoism.

Some of the most interesting evidence in this area has come from a relatively new area of study, *sociobiology*, a discipline that studies social behavior in light of genetics. Sociobiologists have found that altruistic behavior exists not only in human beings, but throughout the animal world. Animals often share food and take care of each other in ways that would count as altruistic if done by human beings. In some instances such as worker bees, the behavior is almost completely altruistic, done solely for the sake of the other with little or no concern for one's own interests. Most instances, however, are less extreme, involving a mixture of altruistic and self-interested behavior. Natural selection, so sociobiologists hypothesize, favors altruistic behavior in at least two situations: close kinship relationships and cooperative behavior in which all participants benefit (reciprocal altruism). The evidence of sociobiology suggests that exclusive psychological egoism is wrong. Behavior is *not* always self-interested. However, sociobiology is consistent with *predominant* psychological egoism, that is, with the claim that behavior is usually self-interested.

Indeed, in some instances—heroes, philanthropists, and rescuers of Jews in Nazi Germany provide three categories of examples—individuals not only have acted altruistically, but also have done so at great personal risk. All that is necessary empirically to defeat exclusive psychological egoism is one instance of someone who does not act exclusively in terms of self-interest, and there is no shortage of such examples. Predominant psychological egoism, on the other hand, is not as easily disproved empirically, since it simply maintains that people generally act out of self-interest. A few instances of altruistic behavior are not enough to undermine predominant psychological egoism.

The villagers of Le Chambon, who will be discussed in more detail in the chapter on virtue theory, provide a startling example of altruisic behavior. Le Chambon was a pacifist Huguenot village that was responsible for saving the lives of several thousand Jews from the Nazis. The villagers risked their lives on numerous occasions to hide Jews, often including children, who were being hunted by the Germans. In their own words, they were "ready to serve"; that is, they considered it their duty simply to help anyone in need. Their commitment was a purely altruistic one, done for the sake of those who were suffering.

Falsifiable versus Unfalsifiable Hypotheses

At this point in our story of the villagers of Le Chambon, many dedicated psychological egoists will ask, "But was their behavior *really* altruistic? Or did they really get something out of it for themselves, even if it was only a feeling of satisfaction about acting like a good person?" Indeed, one could question whether the villagers were being honest in their accounts of their own behavior or whether, even if they were honest, they might have been deceiving themselves about their own motives.

It is always possible to ask questions such as these about any example of apparently altruistic behavior. The interesting issue raised is whether any possible empirical example could undermine the psychological egoist's faith in egoism. Would the committed egoist doubt that the Dalai Lama, Mother Teresa, Bishop Desmond Tutu, or some other apparent saint was really altruistic? If so, we have to question whether psychological egoism is a genuine empirical belief or an unfalsifiable belief for such a person.

Karl Popper, one of the most influential figures in twentieth-century philosophy of science, was impressed by the apparent explanatory power of the unfalsifiable beliefs characteristic of Freudian, Marxist, and many religious frameworks. No matter what happened, these perspectives had an explanation for it. Consider psychoanalytic theory. If behavior exhibited overt sexual motivation, that showed that the Freudian theory was sound. If behavior did not show any signs of sexual motivation, then that simply showed that repression or sublimation was at work, again, illustrating that the theory was sound. Yet Popper became suspicious of such frameworks, for he quickly saw that there was *no* empirical evidence that could count against the theory. Such theories, or pseudo-theories, are what he calls **unfalsifiable hypotheses.** They appear to be grounded in empirical evidence, but in fact are not. For unfalsifiable hypotheses, there is no empirical instance that could in principle invalidate the hypothesis.

Is psychological egoism a doctrine that people accept or reject on the basis of the empirical evidence available to them, or is it a viewpoint that largely is accepted or rejected in advance of any empirical evidence? Is it, in other words, usually an unfalsifiable hypothesis? Rather than attempt to answer this question on a general level, reflect for yourself on whether your own acceptance or rejection of psychological egoism is based on empirical evidence or if it is unfalsifiable hypothesis for you.

Tautological Psychological Egoism

There is another way in which psychological egoism can appear to be an empirical claim but in actuality not be based in empirical evidence at all. Some people have claimed that all human behavior is self-interested because, after all, it all stems from our own motives. If we do something, so this line of thinking goes, we are doing it because we want to; our motives are our own, so we must be acting for ourselves. Mother Teresa, for example, is doing what she wants (that is, helping others) because she wants to do it; therefore, she is acting out her own interests and thus is acting egoistically. This type of argument appears to make an empirical claim about people's motives, but when we look at it more closely, we see in fact it is simply a matter of establishing the egoist's case by definition. Any motive that a person has is defined to be self-interested because it is the person's own motive. Following Bernard Gert, we shall call this **tautological egoism** because it is based on a tautology:

self-interest = any interest that the self has

There are two difficulties with this type of egoism. First, it tells us nothing about the world, nothing about actual people's real motivation. It simply tells us about how we have defined certain words. Second, the definition is in fact misleading since most people (including egoists) understand "self-interest" in a narrower, more specific way that is almost synonymous with "selfish." When tautological egoism is used as support for psychological egoism, it gives the appearance of providing empirical evidence when in fact it is simply establishing its case by definition of key terms.

The Relevance of the Altruism-Egoism Axis

Finally, we should note an expressed premise of the psychological egoists' discussion. They presuppose that the distinction between altruistic and egoistic actions is *the* relevant distinction for classifying behavior. But perhaps this distinction is not the case. I have several friends who are artists, for example, and their concern for art is the major motivating force in their lives. Whether decisions are altruistic or egoistic is of secondary importance to them. Similarly, several of my friends are avid sports fans, and their love of sports plays a major role in their lives. Their decisions often are based on this concern for sports, not on either altruism or egoism. Certainly, they could be classified along this axis, but to do so in their cases would neither be illuminating nor helpful. We can classify fruit, for example, as either quiet or noisy, but that does not guarantee that it will be very illuminating to discover that oranges are quiet. True, they are, but that is not the most important thing about them. Similarly, to say of given actions that they are either altruistic or egoistic is not always to pick out what is most salient about them. Finally, there are situations—in close friendships, for example—where the altruist/egoism dichotomy is just not very illuminating. Often in friendships it is not a question of acting in either one's self-interest or in one's friend's interest. Instead, we may be acting for the sake of the friendship itself, which is not reducible to either friend's interest.

So far, the evidence we have considered does not support exclusive psychological egoism, although much of it is consistent with predominant psychological egoism. Yet there is a whole range of arguments to consider that proceed from a quite different premise than any considered in this section: the premise that human behavior is causally determined. Since this notion raises distinct conceptual issues that touch not only on psychological egoism but also on certain versions of moral relativism and moral skepticism, we will consider this issue separately.

DETERMINISM AND FREEDOM

We have seen a recurring theme throughout the last three chapters. Psychological egoism, certain causal versions of descriptive ethical relativism, and even a few divine command theories of ethics that involve predestination all presuppose *determinism.* Psychological egoists say that we are causally determined to act solely in our own pleasure or self-interest. Some descriptive ethical relativists claim that our moral values are causally determined by our culture. Certain divine command theorists claim that our behavior is determined by God's foreknowledge. What all of these positions have in common is the conviction that human behavior is causally determined by certain types of factors and that human behavior is therefore not free.

Nor are there only these three versions of determinism. Various types of *psychological determinism* have achieved prominence in the twentieth century. Some followers of Freud have seen him as maintaining that human behavior is determined by *unconscious forces* in the human psyche. B. F. Skinner and his radical behaviorist followers maintain that human behavior is completely determined, primarily by positive and negative reinforcers in the environment. His *Beyond Freedom and Dignity* is a contemporary manifesto for radical behaviorists. A comparable claim on behalf of *genetics* has been central to sociobiology, which maintains that human behavior is determined by genetic factors. Edward Wilson's *On Human Nature* is the comparable manifesto for sociobiologists. What all these positions have in common is the belief that *human behavior is causally determined;* they differ only in their specification of which kinds of causes play the dominant role in shaping such behavior.

The Actor and the Spectator

Human behavior exhibits two faces, the face that is shown to the external world and the face that is turned in on itself. When we look at human behavior from the sidelines of life, as it were, we are viewing it as spectators. Often, the spectator's viewpoint sees human behavior in causal terms. Radical behaviorists, for example, look at human behavior and attempt to uncover the psychological reinforcers that shape that behavior. When behaviorists see people mindlessly feeding coins into slot machines in Las Vegas, they look for the intermittent reinforcers (the occasional small payoff, the infrequent large jackpot) which promote such behavior. When they do that, behaviorists are being spectators, looking at the external face of human behavior. All scientific studies of human behavior assume the stance of the spectator, the impartial observer. As spectators, such scientists continually are asking the question "What caused this behavior to happen?" They never ask whether the behavior was caused; it is simply taken for granted. The only question regards what particular factor caused it. The claim that human behavior is causally determined is not a conclusion that such scientific approaches reach; rather, it is the starting point from which they proceed.

Yet when we act, we are unable to assume the spectator's standpoint. We must necessarily assume the standpoint of the actor, and a central element in that standpoint is the assumption that we are free. Imagine, for a moment, that you are faced with a decision about which movie to see tonight. Even if you were a radical behaviorist, you could not help but use the language of choice, of freedom. You could hardly say, "Well, I'll go to the movie that is most positively reinforcing." How do you know which is most reinforcing? Even if you did know, you would find yourself saying that you are deciding to go to the most positively reinforcing one. Indeed, you hardly feel your body being moved toward the correct movie theater like a magnet moves a piece of iron around. From the viewpoint of the actor, you feel yourself make up your mind. You feel that you yourself decide what to do. The claim that human behavior is free is not the result of reflection on our behavior as actors; rather, it is the premise from which such reflection begins.

This, then, is the dilemma we face about freedom and determinism. From the viewpoint of disinterested scientific spectators, we have to assume that human behavior is causally determined. Yet from the viewpoint of people who act, we have to assume that we have freedom of choice. Moreover, we have to be both spectators and actors in life. There are times when we must all be spectators, observing the behavior of other people, trying to understand why they act the way they do. Yet we are also actors, and as such we have to make decisions about what we are going to do at any given moment. A hard core determinist, working long hours in the lab, still has to decide whether to order a pizza with pepperoni or mushrooms or both for dinner. The language of choice is as inescapable an element in the actor's standpoint as the language of causality is in the spectator's perspective.

Most of the issues surrounding the problem of freedom and determinism lie outside the scope of ethics itself. They usually are considered within the context of metaphysics and the philosophy of mind. There are, how-ever, at least two related issues which have a direct bearing on ethics: the transition from "is" to "ought" and the relationship between determinism and responsibility.

The Transition from "Is" to "Ought"

Although having these two quite different perspectives is a significant problem in itself (and, as we shall see in the next chapter, the German philosopher

Immanuel Kant had much to say about it), the greatest difficulties arise when the two standpoints are mixed. Where the spectator's viewpoint is *action-explaining*, the actor's perspective is *action-guiding*. A fallacy occurs when one tries to transfer information from one perspective to the other, taking a claim intended to explain behavior and using it to guide behavior. Recall the way in which this claim occurred in causal versions of ethical relativism. On a descriptive level, the causal ethical relativist claimed that people's behavior and values were causally determined by the culture in which they were raised. Yet the illicit move occurred when they attempted to shift from a descriptive level to a prescriptive one that says we ought to follow the values of our culture.

Egoists often attempt to make a similar move. Although psychological egoism is in itself a purely descriptive position, it is often in fact advanced within the context of discussions about normative theories. The alleged truth of psychological egoism is then offered as support for ethical egoism, that is, for the normative claim that everyone ought to act in his or her self-interest. Yet a moment's reflection reveals the peculiarity of such an argument. If exclusive psychological egoism were true, then what would be the point of telling people that they ought to act in their own self-interest? Exclusive psychological egoism states that people always in fact act in their own self-interest, and if true, there is little point in telling them that they ought to do so. (Of course, it might reduce the extent to which people condemn themselves and others for selfish behavior.) If exclusive psychological egoism were true, ethical egoism would be largely superfluous.

Over 250 years ago, a Scottish philosopher by the name of David Hume pointed to a suspicious move in moral discourse from descriptive statements to prescriptive claims. No set of purely factual or descriptive premises, Hume contended, could entail a normative conclusion. The reason is clear. A normative conclusion contains the word "ought" or its equivalent. But if all the premises are descriptive, none of them contains an "ought" statement. But since the conclusion of a valid deductive argument cannot contain anything that is not contained in the premises, the conclusion cannot contain an "ought" statement. Purely factual premises can yield only purely factual conclusions. According to Hume, one cannot derive an "ought" simply from an "is."

Freedom and Responsibility

There is a second problem that relates to causal versions of psychological egoism and to other versions of determinism as well. If determinism is true, then our traditional notion of moral responsibility must either be jettisoned or at least severely restructured. Typically, we tend not to hold people responsible if they are not free. If, for example, someone slips LSD into another person's coffee without that person's knowledge and the other person then drives erratically, we would not hold that other person responsible for the erratic driving in the same way we would if the LSD had not been slipped into the coffee. The reasoning behind this attitude is clear: we believe that the person is less free because of the influence of the drug and therefore less responsible. Of course, this theory changes if the person chooses to take LSD rather than being tricked into taking it unknowingly, for then we consider the taking of the drug to be a free act.

If our traditional notion of moral responsibility is undermined by determinism, then our traditional notions of blame, praise, reward, and punishment likewise are changed radically. Traditionally, praise and blame presuppose that the person being praised or blamed is free. We praise people's heroic deeds, for example, when we think they could have done otherwise. If we thought their heroism was not a matter of choice but rather one of simple causal necessity, we would be much more reluctant to praise it or reward it. Similarly, we tend not to blame or punish those who could not have acted differently. If we do punish, it is for a different reason: to correct behavior rather than because the punishment is merited. We may punish a dog that has misbehaved, not because we think the dog "merits" punishment, but because punishment is necessary to correct the behavior in the future. Yet with human beings, the situation is usually different. Although we may sometimes punish solely to change behavior, we usually believe that punishment is justified because the person knowingly and freely did something wrong. Thus we punish even in situations where we have no reason to believe that the person will commit the crime again.

If we give up the notion of freedom, we also give up our traditional notions of responsibility, praise, blame, and punishment. If determinism is true, we lose much of our basic moral vocabulary.

The Task of Becoming Free

In concentrating on whether human behavior is free or determined causally, philosophers have tended to view the question of freedom in rather dichotomous terms: either we are causally determined or else we are free. Scant attention is given to the possibility that we are partially free and partially unfree, yet there seems to be good reason for believing that this mixture is in fact the case. Moreover, there is good reason for believing that progress in life consists, at least in part, in moving from a state of bondage to one of freedom.

Consider an example. A classic behaviorist experiment can be performed in the classroom. Imagine, for the sake of our example, an introductory college ethics course in which the students wanted the instructor to spend less time talking about Immanuel Kant and more time discussing John Stuart Mill. Whenever Kant is mentioned, members of the class, without the instructor's knowledge of the plan, engage in behavior that the instructor experiences as negative. Students may begin to look out the window, to appear bored, to shuffle their feet, to squirm around in their chairs, to look confused, to ask irrelevant questions, and generally to convey the impression that nothing in Kant's philosophy is of interest or value to them. When John Stuart Mill is mentioned, on the other hand, the reaction is quite different. Students perk up, look intently at the instructor, smile, ask intelligent and relevant questions, exhibit an interest in knowing more about Mill's philosophy, and even ask about supplementary reading. If the principles of behaviorism are correct, within a short period of time the instructor should be talking much about Mill and virtually ignoring Kant. This example, so the behaviorist would argue, both illustrates and proves the behaviorist's claim that behavior is causally determined by environmental factors. Thus determinism has once again been vindicated—or so it would appear.

Yet the story need not end here, with the hapless instructor abandoning Kant for Mill. Let us imagine that the instructor discovers what the students are doing. At this juncture, two interesting developments may take place. First, realizing what the class has done, the instructor may compensate for its unbalanced influence by making a special effort to spend more time on Immanuel Kant, thereby consciously offsetting their impact. Yet there is a second, and even more important, step that the instructor can take. Realizing that any class's reactions to specific material may affect how much time an author is given in class, the instructor may ask whether he or she wants to be guided by such a principle. Once it is made explicit, it is unlikely that the instructor would adopt that principle of popularity as a sufficient criterion for determining which philosophers should be considered in an ethics course. The point here is that, *once we realize that we are causally influenced in a particular way, we are often free to choose to accept or reject that influence*. Instead of making us less free, knowledge of deterministic influences actually may liberate us from their domination.

To be sure, such a change is not always possible, and the task of changing is often a difficult and slow one. But the basic insights remain: we begin largely in a state of predetermined action, and one of the measures of progress in life is to become aware of the ways in which we have been determined in the past and consequently freely choose to shape our lives in the future.

Ethical Egoism

Ethical egoism purports to tell us how to live. It tells us that we should always act in our own self-interest. As such, it is a *consequentialist* theory; that is, it maintains that the rightness or wrongness of acts depends on their consequences. More specifically, it says that right actions are those that promote self-interest and wrong actions are those that detract from self-interest.

Is Ethical Egoism a *Moral* Theory at All?

The first striking thing about ethical egoism is that it does not seem to be an *ethical* theory at all. Whatever disagreements may exist among ethicians, one

Types of Ethical Egoism

Type of Ethical Egoism	*Main Thesis*
Personal Egoism	I am going to act in my own self-interest and everything else is irrelevant
Individual Ethical Egoism	Everyone ought to act in my self-interest
Universal Ethical Egoism	Each person ought to act in his or her own self-interest

thing that most of them are agreed upon is that morality is about overcoming our selfishness and living our lives with a positive concern for the well-being of other people for their own sake. Insofar as ethical egoism exhorts us to act in a purely self-interested way, it does not seem to be a moral theory at all—rather, it is what morality is attempting to overcome!

Ethical egoists have a number of replies to this charge, most of which consist in attempting to show that ethical egoism possesses enough of the formal characteristics—universalizability, consistency, and so on—of a moral theory to justify its inclusion in the domain of moral theories. We will not pursue this argument here, but rather concede the point and turn to the more important question: is ethical egoism a *good* moral theory, that is, an adequate or a sound one?

Types of Ethical Egoism

As usual, we need to draw some distinctions among various versions of the position we are discussing. Ethical egoism is no exception. At first glance, it appears straightforward enough: ethical egoism tells people that they ought to act in their own self-interest. As we look more closely, we see that this demand could be meant in several different ways.

The first point that needs to be clarified is whether the ethical egoists are saying (a) that people are going to act in their own self-interest and everything else is irrelevant; or (b) that each person ought to act in his or her own self-interest; or (c) that everyone ought to act in my self-interest. These viewpoints result in three distinct types of ethical egoism.

Let us look at each of these three positions.

Personal Egoism

Personal egoists maintain that they are going to act in their own self-interest and that anything else is irrelevant to them. They actually have no interest in telling other people how to act at all, and in this sense their position is hardly a moral theory at all. They are simply saying, "This is how *I* am going to act." There have been virtually no philosophical attempts to defend personal egoism since the mid-fifties, but this lack of defense does not mean that no one lives according to this position. Personal egoists are simply the selfish, egotistical persons whose only concern in life is to further their own self-interests. Although the position has virtually no merit as a theory, it still has its adherents in practice.

Individual Ethical Egoism

The difference between personal egoism, which is hardly an ethical theory at all, and individual ethical egoism is that the latter does make a claim about how other people ought to act. If I were an individual ethical egoist, I would claim (a) that I ought to act in my own self-interest and (b) that everyone else should also act in my self-interest. It is an ethical theory—even if ultimately it turns out not to be a good ethical theory—because it states how *everyone* ought to act.

Universal Ethical Egoism

Whereas individual ethical egoists think everyone ought to act in their own self-interest, universal ethical egoists think that each individual ought to act in his or her own self-interest. Each person, universal ethical egoists maintain, ought to be out for himself or herself.

The relationship between individual ethical egoism and universal egoism is an interesting one. At first glance, *individual ethical egoism* seems implausible. Why should everyone act in my self-interest? That's absurd! Yet, although universal ethical egoism initially seems to be the more reasonable position, we can see how one arrives at individual ethical egoism. Let us imagine that I am following the mandate of universal ethical egoism, looking out for my own self-interest and telling everyone else to look out for theirs. Is it then actually in my self-interest for you to act in your own self-interest? Would it not in fact be more in my self-interest—and hence more consistent for me—if I could convince you (and everyone else, for that matter) to do things that will benefit me? In fact, if I were an ethical egoist, would I not want everyone else to be altruists, especially to be altruistic toward me? Universal ethical egoism, in other words seems to lead to individual ethical egoism.

In his defense of universal ethical egoism, Jesse Kalin has suggested an intriguing way out of this difficulty. There is, he points out, one type of situation in which we act solely out of our own self-interest but simultaneously want everyone else to act in their own self-interest as well: games. In sports or chess or any other type of competitive game, I will be trying as hard as I can to win, but I also expect my competitors to do the same. Indeed, I *want* them to do so. Competitive games provide a notable example of situations in which it is not inconsistent for me to try to maximize my self-interest but also to will that you try to maximize your self-interest at the same time.

Maximizing and Non-Maximizing Versions

There is a second major distinction among types of ethical egoism, one which we have already encountered in our discussion of psychological egoism. We can distinguish between maximizing and non-maximizing versions of ethical egoism. The *maximizing version* of ethical egoism says that everyone should try to maximize self-interest. The *non-maximizing version* simply tells us that everyone should promote self-interest, leaving open the possibility of doing so in a way that also takes the interests of other people into account.

The most obvious difficulty with maximizing versions of ethical egoism is that they lead to a kind of ruthlessness in the pursuit of self-interest. If we must maximize our self-interest, the interests of other people virtually are excluded. Our own self-interest becomes our exclusive motive, which seems to permit—indeed, require—all sorts of behavior such as cheating, lying, exploitation, and the like.

Moreover, as game theorists have shown, the ruthless pursuit of self-interest often results in a comparative loss for everyone. Game theorists often appeal to what is known as the Prisoner's Dilemma. Typically the Prisoner's Dilemma provides an example of a situation in which two people are faced with a choice about whether to act in a self-interested way or altruistically, and the example shows that both come out ahead if both act altruistically. Peter Singer gives an interesting variation of this dilemma in *The Expanding Circle*. Imagine two early human hunters who are confronted with a sabertooth tiger. If the tiger chases them, the tiger will be able to chase only one of them but will have at least a 90 percent chance of catching and killing the one that is chased. If both stand their ground together, there is only a very small chance that the tiger could kill either of them. If both hunters are narrowly self-interested, they will both flee in order to save their own skin—and there is a fifty-fifty chance for each hunter of being caught and killed. If, on the other hand, both are altruistic and both stay to help the other hunter, then in fact both will benefit. In some situations, in other words, individuals actually derive more benefit by *not* being self-interested!

Much of the criticism that has been directed against ethical egoism has been aimed at its maximizing versions. Non-maximizing versions are much less susceptible to such criticism, but they are also less striking precisely because they are much more moderate than maximizing variants.

The Concept of the "Self" in "Self-Interest"

When the ethical egoist enjoins us to act in our own self-interest, we must stop and be sure that we understand what is meant by the "self" in "self-interest." There are at least two concepts of the self which could form the basis for the

The Self of Self-Interest

Type of Self	*Type of Egoism*	*Main Thesis*
Pleasure-Seeking	Hedonistic	Act in such a way as to promote our own pleasure
Calculating	Rational	Act in such a way as to promote our long-term self-interest

egoist's concept of self-interest: the hedonistic self and the rational self. Each of these yields a very different picture of egoism.

Hedonistic Egoism. If we see the self purely as a pleasure-seeker, then the injunction to promote self-interest will be a command to seek pleasure, to be a hedonist. This position suffers from all of the drawbacks of hedonism generally, including that there seems to be nothing morally admirable about it. Moreover, it is susceptible to what has been called the *hedonistic paradox*: often, we can best achieve pleasure by not directly aiming at it. Most contemporary ethical egoists are not hedonistic egoists.

Rational Egoism. When the ethical egoists speak of self-interest, the majority of them mean rational self-interest. The rational egoist urges us to reflect on future alternatives and choose those which will be most beneficial to us in the long-run. The rational egoist places no restrictions on what can count as legitimate self-interest (pleasure, power, fame, success, and so on) except presumably self-destructive, moral, and altruistic goals do not in principle qualify as being in one's self-interest.

Short-Term versus Long-Term Self-Interest

Egoists also draw a distinction between two concepts of self-interest that again depends on our conception of the self, but this time centers around the *temporal* dimensions of the self. Self-interest can be either short-term or long-term, depending on whether we are considering what is immediately beneficial to the self or what is beneficial over the long run. Since pleasure tends to be immediate and calculating tends to look to the future, this distinction often parallels the distinction between hedonistic and rational egoism.

It makes a crucial difference whether we adopt a short-term or a long-term view of self-interest. Actions such a lying, cheating, and exploitation might be permitted in terms of short-term self-interest but prohibited if we considered them within the context of long-term self-interest. Consider a simple example from business. If a person has a small retail business in a local neighborhood and deals with the same clientele year after year, it may well be in the shopkeeper's long-term self-interest to be scrupulously honest with customers, even though in particular cases there might be a short-term advantage to cheating some customers. Of course, if the same person had a business on a major interstate highway and had very few repeat customers, it might be in his or her self-interest to gouge them whenever possible, since they are unlikely to return or to otherwise negatively affect subsequent business from other people.

In recent years, this distinction between short-term self-interest and long-term self-interest has become a crucial one for American corporations. In a time of swift corporate takeovers and of relatively short tenures for CEOs, short-term self-interest increasingly has overshadowed long-term self-interest with many corporations, often to the detriment of stockholders, employees, and the country as a whole.

Act versus Rule Egoism

One final distinction remains to be drawn. Egoists claim to act in terms of self-interest, but it is important to consider how they go about making their decisions. Do they consider the consequences of each individual act in terms of its effect on their self-interest? If so, they are *act egoists*. If, on the other hand, they ask what general rules they should live by in order to promote their self-interest, they are *rule egoists*. As we shall see, there is a similar distinction to be drawn among act utilitarians and rule utilitarians, and we shall postpone a consideration of the merits of act consequentialism versus rule consequentialism until that chapter.

Support for Ethical Egoism

Ethical egoism has been a topic of hot debate among philosophers for several decades, and it has generated dozens of refutations and replies to such refutations. Yet one finds a curious gap in the philosophical literature when one looks for strong statements of the *initial* reasons for accepting ethical egoism. There is no shortage of arguments against objections to it, but it is as if ethical egoists tend to believe that the initial commitment to ethical egoism is so obvious as not to need justification. A further contributing factor may be the fact that some form of egoism is a prevalent premise in areas such as economics, which begin with the assumption that all persons are self-interested actors. Let us examine those arguments that are available.

The Appeal to Psychological Egoism

Proponents of ethical egoism sometimes appeal to psychological egoism in order to gain support for their own position, but the relationship between the two positions is more complex than one of simple support. As we have seen in the second part of this chapter, if psychological egoism were true, then ethical egoism would seem to be redundant. If people inevitably acted in their own self-interest, then there would be no need to urge them to do so. In fact, the very existence of ethical egoism seems to show that some ethical egoists believe psychological egoism is false. Otherwise there would be no need to urge people to act in this way.

The "Better World" Argument

Some ethical egoists advance an interesting argument in support of their position. They claim that if everyone behaved as ethical egoists, the world overall would be a better place. Many attempts to help other people, they suggest, are misguided and ineffective. Each person is best suited to promote his or her own self-interest, since no one else is more directly in a position to act in the situation than the agent is.

Although this argument may be appealing, it has two serious flaws. First, it makes an empirical claim—namely, that everyone will benefit more if all people act just in their own self-interest—that may well be false. It might well be true in a society composed solely of adults with roughly the same levels of skill and resources, but such a society has never existed. We live in a world with children and the elderly, with the infirm and disabled as well as the able-bodied, with the developmentally delayed as well as the mentally gifted, with the poor and starving as well as with the rich and well-fed. We live, in other words, in a world of radical differences, many of which are beyond an individual's control.

Second, even if the argument were sound, it is not primarily an argument for ethical egoism; rather, it is a rule utilitarian argument—we will discuss utilitarianism in detail in Chapter Six—in which the justification for acting as an ethical egoist is that it produces the greatest overall benefit for society as a whole, then presumably if it does *not* do so, we ought not to act in that manner.

The "Altruism Is Demeaning" Argument

The final argument that ethical egoists typically advance has its origins in Friedrich Nietzsche, a nineteenth-century German existentialist philosopher, and in this century is most strongly developed by Ayn Rand in *The Virtue of Selfishness*. Altruistic morality, Nietzsche argued, was demeaning because it was essentially a morality of the weak, a morality for slaves, for the herd, for those who were afraid to assert themselves. Altruism is for people who value themselves so little that they put other people ahead of their own selves. It is, moreover, a self-deceptive morality, for it takes a weakness (namely, failing to value oneself sufficiently) and turns it into a virtue (that is, altruism). It is, finally, self-serving in a deceptive way. The weak, Nietzsche claims, preach the gospel of altruism in order to gain control over the strong, to try to convince the strong to take care of the weak, to give up their power. Genuine morality, Nietzsche maintains, is about self-assertion and self-transcendence, ideas he discussed under the headings of the Overman (*Übermensch*) and the will-to-power. The morality of altruism is a morality of weakness and should be replaced by a morality of strength.

Ayn Rand, as we saw in the opening passage in this chapter, has developed a similar argument, claiming that altruism is about self-sacrifice. Altruistic morality maintains that one individual's interests—and sometimes even that person's life—ought to be sacrificed for another person. Such a morality does not value individuals and their full development. Ethical egoism, she argues, presents a far different picture of morality, one which affirms the absolute value of the individual and encourages all individuals actively to seek that which will promote their flourishing. It is the only moral position that genuinely values the individual.

The "It's Not so Different after All . . ." Argument

Finally, some ethical egoists advance an intriguing claim in support of their position. They argue that ethical egoism does not really result in such radically different behavior as its critics allege and that the egoist's perspective actually provides a unifying reason for meeting all the different obligations that we usually meet. For example, it is in our best interest, they argue, to tell the truth in the long run. People are more likely to trust us, which is to our advantage. We can gain more from a general policy of truthfulness than from one of deceit.

This argument depends on three crucial assumptions. First, it presupposes some nonexclusive version of egoism. Exclusive egoists who consider only their own self-interest and leave no moral room for the interests of other people are far less likely to act in ways that coincide with common sense morality or the requirements of other moral theories. Second, this argument takes for granted that we will consider the *long-term* consequences characteristic of rational egoism. Actions such as lying, cheating, or stealing may be justified in terms of short-term consequences but not for long-term self-interest. Finally, this argument is much more compatible with rule egoism than act egoism. The act egoist might find a particular case of lying or cheating to be justified, but a *rule* permitting that as a general policy hardly would further the egoist's self-interest. Thus the nonexclusive, rational rule egoist would probably act in most—although not all— situations the same way that most moral people would act.

The intriguing part of this argument is that it suggests that there are frequently very good self-interested reasons for being moral, reasons that all too often are overlooked by advocates of altruistically oriented accounts of morality. Seen in this light, ethical egoism can be interpreted in two different ways. On one hand, ethical egoists will argue that this shows that ethical egoism can replace other, competing accounts of morality and introduce into the moral life a single principle—self-interest—on which all moral decisions can be based. On the other hand, critics of ethical egoism can look at the same situation and argue instead that ethical egoism simply provides a second line of defense, as it were, for being moral. When all other reasons fail to convince people, we can often point to considerations of self-interest. In order to help decide which of these two approaches we should assume, let us now consider some of the major criticisms of ethical egoism.

Criticisms of Ethical Egoism

Several main lines of criticism of ethical egoism have crystallized in recent years. They center around four questions which critics pose to the ethical egoist.

- Does ethical egoism yield consistent advice about how we should act?
- Is ethical egoism a morality that its adherents can proclaim publicly?
- Can ethical egoists be good friends?
- Are ethical egoists morally insensitive?

Let us consider each of these issues.

Consistency

A number of critics of ethical egoism have argued that it is essentially flawed because it yields contradictory commands about how we should act. Brian Medlin, for example, has argued that in any given situation ethical egoists must seek to promote their own self-interest and yet at the same time, if they are universal ethical egoists, they must will that everyone else also act to promote their own self-interest. We have already seen the difficulty with this approach: often it is in my self-interest for other people to act against their own self-interest. If I am a salesperson, for example, it is usually in my best interest to have other people pay full price for my products, even though it is not generally in their best interest to do so. If I am an ethical egoist, I seem committed to ensure both that they pay full price and that they not pay full price. Ethical egoism, in other words, seems *inconsistent.*

We have already seen Jesse Kalin's reply to this objection. There is no more inconsistency in ethical egoism, he argues, than there is in a hard-fought game of chess in which each opponent wants to win but also wants the other person to play as good a game as possible. This reply is interesting, for it may provide consistency for the ethical egoists's argument, giving us a deeper insight into the egoist's world. Essentially, the world of the ethical egoist is a deeply competitive world in which each person is pitted against everyone else. It is hardly surprising that Kalin should appeal to examples from sports and other competitive activities. We will consider this issue further when we discuss friendship for the ethical egoist.

Public and Private Morality

We already have caught a glimpse of a second difficulty for ethical egoists. In order to promote their own self-interest, ethical egoists may well find it to their advantage to hide their moral beliefs, especially in a world that values altruism. If an egoistic politician were making a large donation to a hospital building fund because it was a good tax deduction and would look good in subsequent political campaigns, it would hardly be to the egoist's advantage to *say* so. Rather, it would be better to claim that it was being done out of a spirit of kindness and concern for the community.

Although this point might not be an ultimately decisive mark against ethical egoism, it does raise our level of moral suspicion. One of the hallmarks of moral theories since the Enlightenment is that they are essentially public in character. Indeed, some philosophers have argued even that it is precisely the public discussion of reasons which provides the most reliable procedure for guaranteeing their rationality. The reason is that genuine public discussion is the best way of insuring that everyone's interests will receive full and equal representation. Consequently, when we encounter a moral theory that is resistant to public exposure, we are naturally suspicious about whether everyone's interests do receive full and equal representation. A moment's reflection tells us that this suspicion is well-grounded. In fact, the egoist's own interests receive much more weight than everyone else's interests. James Rachels has argued that this dimension is the major flaw of ethical egoism: it gives unwarranted weight to one's own interests at the expense of everyone else's without any morally relevant reason for doing so, which is akin, Rachels suggests, to racism, for racism assigns a higher value to the interests of some people than others and does so on the basis of a characteristic (skin color) that has no moral relevance.

There is a second related issue about the private character of the ethical egoist's motivations. It is easy to imagine situations in which egoists must deceive other people about their motives, and such deception both raises serious moral issues in their own right and poses questions about how close the egoist can be to other people, especially non-egoists. Let us turn to the latter issue now.

Friendship

One of the more difficult issues for ethical egoism to surmount is friendship. Clearly ethical egoists can have acquaintances, and at least in some sense they can and do have friends. Yet it is unclear whether they can have the type of deep friendships that most of us value highly. Even defenders of egoism such as Kalin admit that friendship poses a problem for ethical egoism. Deep friendships are grounded in a mutual concern for the welfare of the other person for his or her own sake, and it would seem that ethical egoism precludes the having of such concern. Certainly egoists can have friends and can help their friends, but only insofar as having and helping them promotes the egoists's own self-interests.

Consider the qualities many of us value in friends. Close friends are people we can trust—trust with our secrets, trust with our feelings, trust with those parts of ourselves that are most vulnerable. Conversely, we respect, protect, and cherish those same qualities in our friends. Moreover, we trust our friends to be loyal to us, just as we are loyal to them. Just as we stick by them, even when things get rough, so we expect that they will stick by us. Yet is it realistic to expect ethical egoists to do the same? Egoists ask whether respecting trust, remaining loyal, and so on are in their own self-interest or not. In those instances in which it is in their self-interest to respect trust, they will; in those cases when it is not, they will not. Moreover, since it may not be in their self-interest to tell you so, they may lie and tell you that you can trust them when you can not. This is not, of course, to say that they will always lie. They will lie only when it is in their self-interest to do so. Similarly, they will remain loyal to their friends as long as it is in their self-interest to remain loyal. But they will lie to their friends and betray their friends when it is in their self-interest to do so—and perhaps the most peculiar thing about ethical egoism is that its adherents are *morally obligated* to do so when it is in their self-interest.

Is this picture of the ethical egoist as a friend too harsh? There are certainly mitigating factors. Truly enlightened nonexclusive rule egoists might realize that there is a big difference between short-term self-interest and long-term self-interest within the context of friendship. The behavior of such egoists might resemble the behavior of real friends, but even then there would be one crucial difference. Both might show concern for their friends, but the motives behind such concern would be quite different. Whereas genuine friends are concerned with their friends at least in part for their friends' own sake, genuine ethical egoists do not necessarily have any such reason to be concerned about their friends. The only motive that they must have is one of self-interest. They may be concerned about their friends, but only insofar as having such concern is in their own self-interest.

Moral Insensitivity

Although moral theories generally are evaluated on the basis of the *actions* that they specify, it is also possible to consider the *sensibility* that a moral theory encourages. Typically, an ethical egoist is sensitive to issues that many non-egoists overlook. For example, the ethical egoist is particularly sensitive to the self-deception that most of us engage in, especially when we are trying to think of ourselves as good people. Most of us, the egoist realizes, want to think of ourselves as good people; furthermore, we usually want others to think of us in the same way. This desire is essentially self-deceptive, for we cannot admit it to ourselves without acknowledging a motivation which is inconsistent with our desire to think of ourselves as good people. A genuinely good person does not do things in order to appear good, but rather because those things are the right thing to do.

Ethical egoists also tend to see individuals as largely, sometimes, completely, responsible for their own lives, and this viewpoint leads to a curious kind of moral insensitivity and unwillingness to help other people. There are at least two reasons for that unwillingness. First, ethical egoists are more likely than others to believe people are responsible for the misfortunes they encounter in life. Second, and this reason is in part a corollary of the first belief, they doubt that one person can really do anything effective to help another person. People have to help themselves, and in their eyes attempts at intervention usually create inappropriate dependency and cause more problems than they solve.

The issue, however, seems to go deeper than a simple unwillingness to help other people, although this point is by itself no small matter. On a more basic level, there seems to be something that blocks the egoist's compassionate *perception* of the suffering of other persons. Egoists would seem to show little compassion for the suffering of others, for genuine compassion has nothing to do with self-interest. Compassion is just a concern for other people for their own sake, and it is precisely this attitude which is beyond the ethical egoist's grasp. Yet to banish compassion from the ethical landscape is to impoverish our moral lives, to diminish ourselves and our humanity.

Consider three areas in which this issue of moral insensitivity manifests itself: world hunger, the suffering of animals, and our treatment of people with disabilities. World hunger certainly presents daunting problems on almost every level, but presumably the egoist's response is one of pure self-interest: starving people should only be helped only when it is in our own self-interest to do so. Yet the egoist's assumptions hardly seem applicable in this situation. Certainly it is difficult to reasonably believe that all those starving people (in Bangladesh, sub-Saharan Africa, and so on) have brought their fate on themselves. It may be the case that a few government, military, and business leaders have contributed to that fate, but it is a far cry from saying so to saying that the individual citizens are responsible for their plight. The egoist's other concerns about increasing dependency and the possible ineffectiveness of help are hardly conclusive either. Certainly there is some danger of creating dependency, but some dependency in human life is appropriate. Furthermore, aid can be given in ways that minimize or control the extent to which it creates such dependency. Nor is the concern about the ineffectiveness of help really convincing. Certainly such concern is legitimate, but the best way to deal with it is to find ways of helping effectively, not simply refusing to help. We are not limited to only two alternatives, ineffective help or no help at all.

The suffering of animals also presents problems for ethical egoists. Part of their view is that each person is responsible for presenting, pursuing, and protecting his or her own interests. It seems to follow that beings who cannot represent themselves have no standing, which has obvious implications for animals, which cannot represent their own interests to human beings because they cannot speak. Animals cannot take care of themselves in the same way that adult human beings can, and ethical egoism has no way of recognizing this fact except insofar as it fits into one's own self-interest.

Finally, consider the issue of our treatment of persons with disabilities that prevent them from having, presenting, or pursuing their own interests. Some of these cases might be quite severe and present deep moral problems for any ethical theory: people with advanced Alzheimer's disease, persons in possibly irreversible comas, individuals with profound mental retardation. Ethical egoists would attempt to help such persons only if it were in their self-interest to do so, and it is easy to imagine situations in which it would not be. Ethical egoism condones a moral callousness to the suffering of the disabled that conflicts with some of our deepest moral intuitions.

The Truth in Ethical Egoism

Ethical egoism is a disquieting moral doctrine. There are good reasons for concluding that it is wrong, perhaps even profoundly wrong, in its exclusive focus on self-interest and in the curious way in which it simply seems to miss the point of the moral life. But even if it is wrong, we can learn from it. There are at least two areas in which the ethical egoist has much to teach us.

First, ethical egoism shows that there are often good self-interested reasons for being moral. All too often, we see self-interest as being in sharp conflict with morality. However, in many situations there are good long-term self-interested reasons for doing the morally right thing. Honesty, for example, is often the best policy for self-interested, prudential reasons as well as for moral reasons. Self-interest and morality, in other words, often may coincide, and one of the things that we can learn from ethical egoism is that there are often good self-interested reasons for acting morally.

Second, ethical egoism may well in part be a reaction to a relative neglect in some ethical traditions of the proper role of self-love in the moral life. Insofar as many ethical theories demand a strict impartiality toward one's own self-interest, they perhaps undervalue the importance of one's own special interests, projects, and attachments in life. As we shall see in Chapter Ten, one of the strengths of Aristotle's virtue ethics is precisely its recognition of the fundamental importance of the virtue of self-love in the moral life. Yet Aristotle, in contrast to ethical egoists, was able to balance this belief with a genuine concern for the welfare of other people and a deep appreciation of the communal dimension of human existence.

Third, there is an important, if exaggerated, lesson we can learn from ethical egoism about personal responsibility. The ethical egoist sees each person as solely responsible for his or her own existence, as evidenced in speech from

Atlas Shrugged that opens this chapter. Once again, this view is extreme, but it may serve as a helpful corrective to everyday moral attitudes which tend to see individuals purely as victims of forces beyond their own control. The truth, as usual, is somewhere in between these two extremes.

The moral life, we have suggested, is characterized by a plurality of value. Different moral traditions are like the branches of the United States government, keeping each other in check, each balancing the influence and power of the other two. We see at least three ways in which ethical egoism serves this function in regard to other moral traditions. It pushes us to reflect on the ways in which our moral motives often coincide with self-interest, to question whether our moral outlook gives sufficient weight to legitimate self-interest, and to probe the extent two which we may be more responsible for our lives than we thought. Ethical egoism helps to keep us honest with ourselves.

BIBLIOGRAPHICAL ESSAY

One of the **classical sources** for a statement of psychological egoism is Thomas Hobbes's *Leviathan* edited by C. B. Macphearson (Harmondsworth, England: Penguin, 1968), originally published in 1651. For a contemporary reinterpretation of Hobbes which partially challenges the belief that he was a psychological egoist, see Gregory S. Kavka, *Hobbesian Moral and Political Theory* (Princeton N.J.: Princeton University Press, 1986), especially chapter two. Bernard Gert's "Hobbes and Psychological Egoism," in *Hobbes' Leviathan: Interpretation and Criticism,* edited by Bernard Baumrin (Belmont, Calif.: Wadsworth, 1969), pp. 107–26, introduced the term "tautological egoism"; Gert argues against reading Hobbes solely as a psychological egoist. For a vigorous defense of Hobbes's place in English philosophy, see David Gauthier, "Thomas Hobbes: Moral Theorist," in his *Moral Dealing. Contract, Ethics and Reason* (Ithaca, N.Y.: Cornell University Press, 1990), pp. 11–23. Also see F. S. McNeilly's "Egoism in Hobbes," *Philosophical Quarterly,* Vol. 16 (July, 1966), pp. 193–206. On empirical criteria for evaluating psychological egoism, see Michael Slote, "An Empirical Basis for Psychological Egoism," in *Egoism and Altruism,* edited by Ronald Milo (Belmont, Calif.: Wasdworth, 1973), pp. 100–07.

On **sociobiology and altruism,** see Edward O. Wilson's *On human Nature* (Cambridge Mass.: Harvard University Press, 1978), which is directed toward a nonscientific audience, and his *Sociobiology: A New Synthesis* (Cambridge Mass.: Harvard University Press, 1975), which provides a more technical statement of the issues. The literature generated by sociobiology is vast, but for two good anthologies of critical evaluations, see *The Sociobiology Debate,* edited by Arthur Caplan (New York: Harper and Row, 1978) and *Sociobiology Examined,* edited by Ashley Montagu (New York: Oxford University Press, 1980), and my own article,

"The Ambiguity and Limits of a Sociobiological Ethic," *International Philosophical quarterly*, Vol. XXIII, 1 (March, 1983), pp. 79–89. For a discussion of the relevance of sociobiology to egoism, see Peter Singer, *The Expanding Circle* (New York: New American Library, 1982) and Kavka, *Hobbesian Moral and Political Theory*, pp. 56 ff.

For a defense of the possibility of **altruism,** see Thomas Nagel, *The Possibility of Altruism* (Princeton N.J.: Princeton University Press, 1970). On the rationality of altruism, see Kristen R. Monroe, Michael C. Barton, and Ute Klingemann, "Altruism and the Theory of Rational Action: Rescuers of Jews in Nazi Europe," *Ethics*, Vol. 101 No. 1 (October, 1990), pp. 103–122, and Kristen Renwick Monroe, "John Donne's People: Explaining Differences between Rational Actors and Altruists through Cognitive Frameworks," *Journal of Politics*, Vol. 53 (May, 1991), pp. 394–433. For an overview of the psychological literature, see Dennis Krebs, "Psychological Approaches to Altruism: An Evaluation." *Ethics*, Vol. No. 3, (April, 1982), 447–58. For a further discussion of the villagers of Le Chambon, see the chapter on virtue ethics below and the bibliographical essay for that chapter. Also see the essays in the issue on altruism of *Social Philosophy & Policy*, Vol. 10, No. 1 (Winter, 1993).

For a **review of the literature on ethical egoism,** see Tibor Machan, "Recent Work on Ethical Egoism," *American Philosophical Quarterly*, Vol. 16, No. 1 (January, 1979), pp. 1–15. Alasdair MacIntyre's "Egoism and Altruism" in *The Encyclopedia of Philosophy*, edited by Paul Edwards (New York: Macmillan, 1967), Vol. 2, pp. 462–66, contains a perceptive overview of the work in this area. Also see Edward Regis, Jr., "What Is Ethical Egoism?" *Ethics*, Vol. 91 No. 1 (October, 1980), pp. 50–62, for a careful consideration of the various meanings of ethical egoism. There are two excellent anthologies of articles on ethical egoism: *Morality and Rational Self-Interest* edited by David Gauthier (Englewood Cliffs, N.J.: Prentice-Hall, 1970); and Ronald D. Milo's *Egoism and Altruism* (Belmont, Calif.: Wadsworth, 1973). For a review and analysis of attempts to reconcile egoism and traditional accounts of morality, see Gregory S. Kavka, "The Reconciliation Project," *Morality, Reason and Truth. New Essays on the Foundations of Ethics*, edited by David Copp and David Zimmerman (Totowa, N.J.: Rowman and Allanheld, 1984), pp. 297–319.

Among the **major critiques of ethical egoism** are C.D. Broad, "Egoism as a Theory of Human Motives," reprinted in *Egoism and Altruism*, edited by Ronald Milo (Belmont, California: Wadsworth, 1973), pp. 88–100; David Gauthier, "Morality and Advantage," *Philosophical Review*, Vol. 76 (1967), pp. 460–75, reprinted in his *Morality and Rational Self-Interest*, and his "The Impossibility of Rational Egoism," *The Journal of Philosophy*, Vol. 71 (1974), pp. 439–56, and his "The Incompleat Egoist," in his *Moral Dealing: Contract, Ethics, and Reason* (Ithaca N.Y.: Cornell University Press, 1990), pp. 234–73; James Rachels, "Two Arguments Against Ethical Egoism," *Philosophia*,

Vol. 4 (1974), pp. 297–314; Brian Medlin, "Ultimate Principles and Ethical Egoism," *Australasian Journal of Philosophy*, Vol. 35 (1978), pp. 111–18; Warren Quinn, "Egoism as an Ethical System," *Journal of Philosophy*, Vol. 71 (1974), pp. 456–72; Kurt Baier, *The Moral Point of View* (Ithaca N.Y.: Cornell University Press, 1958), and his "Ethical Egoism and Interpersonal Compatibility," *Philosophical Studies*, Vol. 24 (1973), pp. 357–68; and Richard Brandt, "Rationality, Egoism, and Morality," *Journal of Philosophy*, Vol 69 (1972), pp. 681–97. For an excellent collection of critical essays on self-interest from a wide range of disciplines, see *Beyond Self-Interest*, edited by Jane J. Mansbridge (Chicago: University of Chicago Press, 1990).

Among the significant **replies to these criticisms** are John Hospers, "Baier and Medlin on Ethical Egoism," *Philosophical Studies*, Vol. 12 (1961), pp. 10–16, and his *Human Conduct*, 2d ed. (New York: Harcourt Brace Jovanovich, 1982), chapter four; and Tibor Machan, "Was Rachels' Doctor Practicing Egoism?" *Philosophia*, Vol. 8 (1978), pp. 338–44.

Jesse Kalin's articles provide a **tightly argued defense of the ethical egoist's position.** See his "On Ethical Egoism," *American Philosophical Quarterly Monograph* Vol. 1 (1969), pp. 26–41; "Two Kinds of Moral Reasoning," *Canadian Journal of Philosophy*, Vol. 5 (1975), pp. 323–56; and "In Defense of Egoism," in *Morality and Rational Self-Interest*, edited by David Gauthier (Englewood Cliffs, N.J.: Prentice-Hall, 1970). The game metaphor in Kalin's argument is discussed in Sidney Trivus, "On Playing the Game," *The Personalist*, Vol. 59 (1978), pp. 82–84. Edward Regis, Jr., in "Ethical Egoism and Moral Responsibility,: *American Philosophical Quarterly*, Vol. 16 No. 1, (January 1979), pp. 45–52, defends a version of **non-maximizing ethical egoism** that escapes some of the standard criticisms that ethical egoism permits behavior that common sense morality would prohibit.

Much of the discussion of ethical egoism has appeared in a journal called *The Personalist* (which is now published under the name *Pacific Philosophical Quarterly*): Donald Emmons's "Refuting the Egoist," *The Personalist*, Vol. 50 (1969), pp. 309–19, elicited Nathaniel Branden's "Rational Egoism: A Reply to Professor Emmons," *The Personalist*, Vol. 51 (1970), pp. 196–211; and Emmons's "Rational Egoism: Random Observations," *The Personalist*, Vol. 52 (1971), pp. 95–98. Also see Erling Skorpen, "Ethical Egoism's Brief and Mistaken History," *Personalist*, Vol. 50 (Fall 1969) pp. 448–72; Frank J. Murphy, "Moore on Ethical Egoism," *Personalist*, Vol. 52 (1971), pp. 744–49; Robert Nozick, "On the Randian Argument," *The Personalist*, Vol. 52 (1971), pp. 282–304; John Hospers, "Rule Egoism," *The Personalist*, Vol. 54 (1973), pp. 391–95; D. J. Den Uyl, "Ethical Egoism and Gerwith's PCC," *The Personalist*, Vol. 56 (1975), pp. 432–47; William Dwyer, "Criticism of Egoism," *The Personalist*, Vol. 56 (1975), pp. 214–27; G. R. Carlson, "Egoism and Renewed Hostilities," *The Personalist*, Vol. 57 (1976), pp. 279–89; Donald Burrill, "The Rule-egoism Principle," *The Personalist* Vol. 57 (1976), pp. 408–

10; S. M. Sanders, "A Credible Form of Egoism?," *The Personalist* 57 (1976), 272–78; Theodore M. Benditt, "Egoism's Inconsistencies," *Personalist*, Vol. 57 (1976), pp. 43–50; S. M. Sanders, "Egoism's Concept of the Self," *The Personalist*, Vol. 58 (1977), pp. 59–67.

On the issue of **ethical egoism and moral sensitivity,** see Anthony Duff, "Psychopathy and Moral Understanding," *American Philosophical Quarterly*, Vol. 14 No. 3 (July 1977), pp. 189–200; Chong Kim Chong, "Ethical Egoism and the Moral Point of View," *Journal of Value Inquiry*, Vol. 26 No. 1 (1992), pp. 23–26; and Daniel Putnam, "Egoism and Virtue," *Journal of Value Inquiry*, Vol. 26 (1992), pp. 117–24. For general comments on the issue of moral sensitivity, see Larry May, "Insensitivity and Moral Responsibility," *Journal of Value Inquiry*, Vol. 26, No. 1 (1992), pp. 7–22. For a consideration of **egoism and friendship,** see R. D. Ashmore, Jr., "Friendship and the Problem of Egoism," *The Thomist*, Vol. 41 (1977), pp. 105–30. On the role of **altruism in friendship,** see Lawrence A. Blum, *Friendship, Altruism, and Morality* (London: Routledge and Kegan Paul, 1980) and Jeffrey Blustein, *Care and Commitment* (New York: Oxford University Press, 1991). For an argument that the dichotomous categories of altruism and self-interest do not fit friendship, see John Hardwig, "In Search of an Ethic of Interpersonal Relations," *Person to Person*, edited by George Graham and Hugh LaFollette (Philadelphia: Temple University Press, 1989), pp. 63–81.

Much contemporary work about ethical egoism is inspired by **libertarianism.** Ayn Rand's novels, such as *Atlas Shrugged* (New York: Penguin Books, 1985) and *The Fountainhead* (New York: New American Library, 1971), provide a powerful literary expression of the ethical egoist's standpoint; her explicit statement of the egoist's standpoint is found her *Virtue of Selfishness* (New York: Signet, 1964). For a libertarian approach that is particularly sensitive to the issue of **egoism and rights,** see Eric Mack, "How to Derive Ethical Egoism," *The Personalist*, Vol. 52 (1971), pp. 735–43; "Egoism and Rights," *The Personalist*, Vol. 54 (1973), pp. 5–33; and "Egoism and Rights Revisited," *The Personalist*, Vol. 58 (1977), pp. 282–88. Also see Tibor Machan, *Individuals and Their Rights* (LaSalle, Ill.: Open Court, 1989).

Citations. The quotation from Ayn Rand at the beginning of this chapter comes from her novel *Atlas Shrugged*, pp. 984, 993. The citation from Kavka is from his *Hobbesian Moral and Political Theory*, p. 66.

Discussion Questions

1. Recall statement 19 of the Ethical Inventory: "Everyone is just out for himself or herself."
   (a) What is the proper name for the theory that this statement exemplifies?

(b) What is the evidence in support of statement 19? What evidence can be offered against it? How would the egoist try to refute such evidence?
(c) Does the support for this argument ever rest on a tautology? Explain.
(d) Has your rating of this item changed after reading this chapter? If so, in what way? If your rating has not changed, are your reasons for your rating any different now than they were when you first responded to this statement?

2. Recall statement 20 of the Ethical Inventory: "Some people think they are genuinely concerned about the welfare of others, but they are just deceiving themselves."
   (a) Why is it difficult, if not impossible, to support this claim?
   (b) Has your rating of this item changed after reading this chapter? If so, in what way? If your rating has not changed, are your reasons for your rating any different now than they were when you first responded to this statement?

3. Recall your response to statement 21 in the Ethical Inventory: "People are not really free. They are just products of their environment, upbringing, and other factors."
   (a) What theory does this statement exemplify?
   (b) Has your rating of this item changed after reading this chapter? If so, in what way? If your rating has not changed, are your reasons for your rating any different now than they were when you first responded to this statement?

4. Recall statement 22 of the Ethical Inventory: "Everyone should watch out just for himself or herself."
   (a) What would the world be like if everyone followed this advice? Do you think the world would be a better place than it is now? Why or why not?
   (b) Has your rating of this item changed after reading this chapter? If so, in what way? If your rating has not changed, are your reasons for your rating any different now than they were when you first responded to this statement?

5. What is the most selfish act you can imagine? Why is it the most selfish one? If you found the act morally objectionable, what specifically was objectionable about it?

6. In his "Fable of the Bees," Bernard Mandeville (1670–1733) argues, perhaps in jest, that "private vices" produce "publick benefits." Can you think of a situation in which this works? If so, is it exceptional or can we make it the rule?

7. Is self-preservation a moral imperative or just a fact? Are there situations in which self-preservation is not the highest value? Is it selfish to prefer (saving) one's own life to that of others? From an evolutionary standpoint, is "survival of the fittest" selfish or selfless?
8. Is "enlightened self-interest" a contradiction in terms or is it really the basis for all action?
9. Do you have any friends or acquaintances who act like ethical egoists? Does this fact present any special problems or issues in your relationship with them? Can an ethical egoist be a good friend? Why or why not?
10. Ethical egoism maintains that you should act in your own self-interest. Give two or three examples of situations in which you think it would be wrong to act in the way that the ethical egoist recommends. Reflect on these situations. What—if anything—overrides the demands of self-interest for you? (There are a number of possible concerns which might be more important to you, including your religious beliefs, a sense of duty, love for other people, a sense of justice, and respect for other people's rights.)

CHAPTER 6

The Ethics of Consequences: Utilitarianism

Introduction

In the 1970s, Americans became increasingly aware of the carcinogenic effects of asbestos. Becoming aware of its cancer-causing consequences was no easy matter, for asbestos often does not cause cancer until twenty or more years after exposure to the asbestos dust. During World War II, a number of American factory and dock workers handled large quantities of asbestos that were needed for the war effort. In the 1960s, a disproportionately large percentage of them were coming down with lung cancer—and researchers began to realize that it was the result of their earlier exposure to asbestos.

By the time the harmful effects of asbestos exposure were discovered, it was being used widely throughout the country for insulation and brake linings and pads. Asbestos was in office buildings, schools, nursing homes, and private residences. Because of its harmful nature, it was difficult and costly to remove. Workers had to have special training and wear special protective clothing and breathing apparatuses before they could safely work with it. One of the questions we faced as a country was precisely what to do about this problem.

To answer this question, we had to look at the consequences of either leaving the asbestos in place (perhaps with an appropriate warning) or of removing it (at high cost). When we looked at the consequences, we had to add up the potential costs and benefits of the various courses of action in various types of situations. The clearest case was in elementary schools. Children exposed to asbestos might come down with lung cancer in their thirties. Requiring the removal of asbestos from elementary schools was a comparatively easy decision: whatever the costs of removing it, the potential damage was so great that few would disagree with regulations requiring its removal from schools. Should we also require its removal from all individual homes? Here the decision was more difficult, for the costs were higher proportionate to the benefits. For every elementary school in the country, there are probably hundreds of private residences insulated with asbestos. The work involved in removing asbestos from all those residences would be considerably more than the work required for the schools, and the enforcement task would be much greater as well. Moreover, the cost would presumably be borne by the individual residents or owners, who may be neither able nor willing to shoulder such a benefit. Whereas a young couple with children would probably be willing to do whatever is necessary to remove the asbestos from their home, a retired couple in their eighties on a fixed income would presumably be more reluctant to spend much money for this purpose. A utilitarian might well decide to leave this decision in each individual's hands.

Utilitarianism begins with one of the most important moral insights of modern times and couples it with a powerful metaphor which underlies our moral life. The insight is that consequences count; indeed, it goes one step further and claims that *only* consequences count, putting it in sharp contrast to Kant's moral philosophy, which—as we shall see in the next chapter—places almost exclusive emphasis on the intentions behind an action. Utilitarianism goes to the other extreme, maintaining that the morality of an action is to be determined solely through an assessment of its consequences. It is for this reason that we call utilitarianism a *consequentialist* moral doctrine; morality, for the utilitarian, is solely a matter of consequences. (Utilitarianism is not the only consequentialist doctrine we have seen. For example, ethical egoism is also consequentialist, but demands that we consider consequences only insofar as they affect our own individual well-being.) Utilitarianism demands that we consider the impact of the consequences on everyone affected by the matter under consideration. The morally right action, the one which we ought to perform, is the one that produces the greatest overall positive consequences for everyone.

Once utilitarians have claimed that morality is solely a matter of consequences, they have to address themselves to several questions. First, they need to specify *the yardstick* or criterion in terms of which consequences are measured. Typically, utilitarians claim that we ought to do whatever produces the greatest amount of utility. But then utility must be defined. Pleasure, happiness, and preference satisfaction are the three most common candidates for the definition of utility. Second, utilitarians need to indicate *how the consequences can be measured.* They need, in other words, to provide an account of how the yardstick can be applied, how utility can be measured. Third, utilitarians must address the question of how high their standards are, of *how much utility we must strive for.* How much, in other words, is enough utility? Although utilitarianism often has been stated in terms of maximizing utility, some have suggested recently that a less stringent and more attainable standard of expectations should be assumed. Fourth, utilitarians must indicate *what types of things are to be judged* in terms of their consequences. The three most common candidates here are acts, rules, and social policies. Finally, utilitarians must answer the question of *whom these are consequences for.* Clearly, they are not just the consequences for the individual agent—that would be ethical egoism. Do utilitarians take into account the consequences for all human beings or just for some subset, such as those in our own country? Do they take into account the consequences for future generations as well as the present one? Do they take into account the consequences for all sentient beings, animals as well as human beings? the natural environment as well as our constructed world? or just the human population?

Let us see how utilitarians have taken this basic insight about the moral significance of consequences and elaborated it into a formal theory of ethics.

Defining Utility

Utilitarians claim that the only thing that counts morally is whatever produces the greatest amount of utility, the greatest overall positive consequences. Yet what is the proper yardstick of utility? Historically, utilitarians have taken pleasure and happiness as the measure of consequences. More recent versions of utilitarianism have turned either to higher ("ideal") goods or to preferences as the measure of consequences. Each of these four yardsticks has its strengths and its limitations.

Bentham and Pleasure

Originally, utilitarianism became influential with the work of Jeremy Bentham (1748–1832), who defined utility in terms of pleasure and pain. According to Bentham, we should act in such a way as to *maximize pleasure and minimize pain.* This position is what is known as **hedonistic utilitarianism.** Notice that this approach is very different from straightforward hedonism, which recommends maximizing one's own pleasure and minimizing one's own pain. Hedonistic utilitarianism recommends maximizing the overall amount of pleasure and minimizing the overall amount of pain.

Mill and Happiness

Bentham's philosophy quickly came under attack as "the pig's philosophy" because of what seemed to be its crude emphasis on sensual, bodily pleasures. John Stuart Mill (1806–73), Bentham's godson, proposed a major reformulation

The liberal English philosopher John Stuart Mill (1806–73) was one of the most influential founders of utilitarianism.

of the utilitarian position by arguing that utility should be defined in terms of happiness rather than pleasure. Mill's standard seemed to be a definite advance over Bentham's, for it was based on a higher standard than mere pleasure. This position is called **eudaimonistic utilitarianism.** (The word "eudaimonistic" comes from the Greek word for happiness, *eudaimonia*). In order to see why this higher standard is the case, let us consider some of the differences between pleasure and happiness as the standard of utility.

Pleasure versus Happiness

The differences between pleasure and happiness are significant. We tend to think of pleasure as being primarily bodily or sensual in character. Eating, drinking, and having sex come immediately to mind as paradigm cases of pleasure. Happiness, on the other hand, is usually less immediately associated with the body. We initially might characterize it as belonging more to the mind or spirit than the body.

Secondly, pleasure generally seems to be of shorter duration than happiness, stemming from the nature of pleasure itself. Pleasure, at least in the eyes of many psychologists and philosophers, is the enjoyable feeling we experience when a state of deprivation is replaced by a state of satiation or fulfillment. In other words, pleasure is what we feel when we drink a nice cool glass of water when we are thirsty. This example gives us an insight into the reason why pleasures are short-lived. Once we are satiated, we no longer experience the object as pleasurable. Once we are no longer thirsty, drinking water becomes less pleasurable. Happiness, on the other hand, seems to lie in the realization of certain goals, hopes, or plans for one's life. Insofar as these goals are intrinsically rewarding ones, we do not tire of them in the same way that we may tire of certain pleasures.

Third, happiness may encompass both pleasure and pain. Indeed, we could easily imagine people saying that they have happy lives while still acknowledging painful moments. A good example is a woman giving birth to a long-hoped-for child. She may experience quite a bit of pain during and after the birth, but she may still feel happy. Conversely, we can imagine someone experiencing pleasure but not feeling happy. Think of a man who smokes crack, which directly stimulates the brain's pleasure center. He might take pleasure from it as he inhales deeply, but he could be feeling very unhappy with his life, career, or marriage.

Finally, there is more of an evaluative element in our notion of happiness than there is in our idea of pleasure. In reading the preceding example, many non-smokers might have been repulsed at the idea of taking pleasure in smoking cigarettes, especially in the morning. Yet this repulsion is not a reason for doubting that some smokers do find pleasure in it. We may want to distinguish between good and bad pleasures, between harmless and harmful ones, but we do not doubt that the bad pleasures are still pleasures. With happiness, on the other hand, we build in an evaluative component. We are likely to question whether someone is genuinely happy in a way that we do not question whether they genuinely are feeling pleasure.

The problem with weighing consequences is that it is much easier to weigh pleasure than happiness or ideal goods, yet pleasure is the least suitable standard. *The closer we move toward a suitable standard of utility, the less able we are to subject it to quantification.*

Moore and Higher Goods

Philosophers in the twentieth century were dissatisfied with Mill's standard of happiness. G. E. Moore, a prominent British philospher, proposed replacing happiness with a collection of ideal goods, such as freedom, knowledge, and justice. We should thus act, according to Moore, in such a way as to maximize these ideals; that is, we should act in such a way as to create the greatest possible amount of freedom, knowledge, justice, beauty, and so on. This approach usually is called **ideal utilitarianism**, since it takes these ideal values rather than happiness or pleasure as the measure of utility. One of the strengths of Moore's ideal utilitarianism is that it allows us to avoid giving equal weight to certain negative feelings and preferences, such as racist feelings, as we would give to other, morally more laudable feelings such as compassion and love.

Arrow and Preference Theory

The dominant version of utilitarianism today is preference utilitarianism. It is well represented by the work of K. J. Arrow and has been tremendously influential in economics and the social sciences. We will see below that one of the difficulties with some versions of utilitarianism centers around how utility is to be measured. How can pleasure, much less happiness or ideals such as justice, be given quantitative measure—and if they cannot, how can they usefully be compared? Arrow's suggestion is that various goods can only be ranked relative to one another; our *preferences* become the measure of utility. We can thus rank various goods on the basis of the extent to which they are objects of preferences. I will say more about this below.

The Measures of Utility

Type of Utilitarianism	*Standard of Utility*	*Number of Intrinsic Goods*	*Main Proponent*
Hedonistic	Pleasure	One	Bentham
Eudaimonistic	Happiness	One	Mill
Ideal	Justice, Freedom, etc.	Many	Moore
Preference	Preference	None	Arrow

These various versions of utilitarianism are summarized in the table on page 160.

No single candidate has emerged as the sole choice among philosophers for the standard of utility. The disagreement among philosophers over this issue seems to reflect a wider disagreement in our own society. If consequences count, we have still to decide upon what yardstick to use in measuring them. The attraction of preference theory in this context is that it permits this multiplicity of standards, all of which are expressed as preferences.

Indeed, there may be a distinct advantage to allowing a *multiplicity* of different types of factors to underlie utility. This type of pluralism is within a specific moral theory. Utilitarianism sometimes has been criticized for being too narrow, for reducing all our considerations in life to a single axis of utility, usually either pleasure or happiness. There is much to be said for a fuller, more supple theory which permits us to recognize that consequences need to be measured according to several yardsticks. The difficulty with such a move, however, is that it then makes utilitarianism a more complex doctrine, one which is more difficult to apply in practice. Furthermore, utilitarians who go in this direction then need to specify the relationship among the different kinds of yardsticks. When one alternative ranks high on the yardstick of happiness, for example, and another course of action is high on the scale of justice, which takes precedence? Finally, it threatens to rob utilitarianism of its chief advantage—namely, that it offers a clear method for calculating the morality of actions, rules, and social policies. Utilitarians who opt for a multiplicity of yardsticks must address themselves to questions such as these.

Applying the Measure

Once we accept a standard of utility, we are still faced with the task of specifying how that standard is to apply to the world in which we live, which is a thorny but crucial issue for utilitarians because one of the major attractions of utilitarianism is that it promises precision in the moral life. If it cannot deliver on this promise because it cannot be applied precisely, then it loses a significant factor for preferring it over competing moral theories.

The Scale Metaphor

One of the things that makes utilitarianism attractive is the root metaphor which underlies much of its language about measuring consequences. Utilitarianism is grounded in a root metaphor which has tremendous intuitive appeal to many of us: the metaphor of the scale. The very notion of weighing consequences presupposes that consequences are the kinds of things that can be placed on a scale. This metaphor pervades our everyday discourse about deciding among competing courses of action. Consider the types of things we often say.

- On *balance*, I'd rather go to the movies.
- When I *weigh* the alternatives, going to Hawaii looks best, even if it is hot at this time of year.
- Buying me an extra nice present *balanced* out the fact that they forgot to send it until a week after my birthday.
- Nothing can *outweigh* all the grief that the hit-and-run accident caused us.
- Only the death penalty can right the *scales* of justice.
- This is a *weighty* choice with *heavy* consequences.

Some of these scale metaphors have specifically monetary overtones, as though things were weighed in terms of their dollar value.

- I'm going to *pay him back* for all the grief he's given me over the years.
- How can I ever *repay* you for your kindness?
- That was a *costly* mistake.
- I'll be forever in your *debt*.

In these expressions, we see the way in which money metaphorically plays the role of the measure in terms of which consequences are assessed.

In order to weigh consequences, the utilitarian needs some kind of measure in terms of which utility is determined. We have examined various candidates for this yardstick: pleasure, happiness, ideals, and preferences. But we also need some way of marking off the units to be measured. Scales often are marked off in terms of ounces or grams. Yardsticks are usually marked off in terms of inches. How do we mark off units of utility? One of the ways of doing so is by assigning cardinal numbers (1, 2, 3, and so on) to pleasure or happiness, for example. In the following section, we will consider this approach by using the stipulative concepts of hedons and dolors. The other way is to assign things ordinal (1st, 2nd, 3rd, and so on) or co-ordinal rankings relative to one another, which is the approach that preference utilitarianism takes. Let us look at both.

Hedons and Dolors

Once they agree upon the kind of yardstick, utilitarians must arrive at some consensus about the way in which the individual units on the measuring stick are to be marked. Utilitarians sometimes refer to units of pleasure or happiness as **hedons** and units of displeasure, suffering, or unhappiness as **dolors.** (The word "hedon" comes from the Greek word for "pleasure," which is the same root from which "hedonism" comes. The word "dolor" comes from the Latin word "dolor," which means "pain.") Particular things, at least in textbook examples, are then often assigned some number. A good corned beef sandwich may, for example, be five hedons, while a pleasant vacation to the Bahamas may be 6,000 hedons. A visit to the dentist could be 100 dolors, and the death of a close friend several thousand dolors.

Such a system may at first sound artificial, but utilitarians would argue that this apparent artificiality is not a serious problem. While there may be no absolute scale in which going to the dentist is a 100, it may be the case that having a close friend die is roughly twenty or thirty times worse than going to the dentist. It is this relationship of relative suffering (or pleasure) that the utilitarian seeks to capture in assigning numerical values to various consequences. This is, the utilitarian further argues, something which we do quite naturally in our everyday lives. The utilitarian calculus is but a refinement and formalization of that everyday activity of assigning relative values to various occurrences, of ranking them in relation to each other according to the amount of pleasure or pain they yield. But as soon as cardinal utilitarians admit this system, they are on their way to becoming preference utilitarians.

The Decision Procedure

How do utilitarians go about deciding upon the moral worth of an action, granting that the consequences of an action can be specified in terms of hedons and dolors? They claim that, in any given situation, we must to the best of our ability (a) determine the consequences of the various courses of action open to us, (b) specify the hedons and dolors associated with each alternative, and then (c) perform that course of action that results in the greatest total amount of pleasure (that is, of hedons minus dolors). Imagine, for example, that you are a utilitarian in the process of deciding between two pieces of proposed legislation about medical aid for the elderly. There are three possibilities open to you: to vote for a bill to reduce medical aid, to vote in favor of a bill that would increase such aid, or to vote against both and thus effectively vote in favor of keeping things the same. Reducing medical benefits for the elderly may result in ten hedons apiece for 100 million people and 200 dolors for 20 million people, resulting in an overall utility of 3 billion dolors. Keeping benefits the same may result in twenty hedons apiece for 20 million people and three dolors for 100 million people, with a total overall utility of 100 million hedons. Finally, increasing benefits may result in ninety hedons apiece for 20 million people and twenty dolors for 100 million people, with a total overall utility of 200 million hedons. Thus from a utilitarian point of view, we would be obligated to keep the benefits the same, since the other two possible courses of action both have a lesser overall utility.

Preferences

Instead of assigning cardinal numerical values to various outcomes, it is possible to rank them in terms of the degree to which they are preferred by agents in the situation. It is important to see that this ranking is not saying the same thing as the language of hedons and dolors. Both are relative, but hedons and dolors can refer to units of pleasure/pain or happiness/unhappiness, while preference utilitarianism refers to choices or priorities. The course of action that maximizes preference satisfaction may not be the same course of action that yields the greatest overall amount of happiness.

In some ways, this approach is quite close to what we do in the democratic political arena. We attempt to determine preferences by having people vote. Perhaps the most significant difference here is that in elections and votes on ballot propositions, there is no way of indicating the strength of one's preference. There are only three alternatives in standard elections: an affirmative vote, a negative vote, or no vote at all. One cannot (at least legally) cast several votes in favor of the same proposition because one feels very strongly in favor of it; a very strong preference and a weak preference both are expressed with a single vote. But most utilitarians are willing to take the strength of preferences into consideration when deciding on which course of action is best.

How Much Utility is Enough?

One of the difficulties which utilitarians have faced centers around the question of how much utility we are obligated to produce. The usual answer has been that we ought to do whatever produces the greatest overall amount of utility. When we compare competing courses of action, we should choose the best one, the one which maximizes utility.

Optimizing Utilitarianism

It is easy to understand the initial plausibility of this answer. Imagine that we are considering whether to pass a particular piece of social legislation. We naturally consider how we can produce the greatest amount of good. If we are weighing the alternatives impartially, there is no attraction toward anything else, no pull toward doing less than the best. If some particular special interest group desired that we do less than the best, their wishes would be factored into the utilitarian equation along with everyone else's. There would, however, be no reason for giving them special weight. If we thought they deserved more weight, then presumably it would be for some reason that would be recognizable within the utilitarian framework. It is only when we have partial interests of our own that there is a desire to do less than the best.

Yet the picture changes rapidly when we consider what it would be like to be making decisions about our own personal lives in the same way. Here personal desires and wants have a much more prominent role. Yet traditional versions of utilitarianism seem to demand that we do the maximum, even in these more personal situations. The utilitarian always tries to produce the greatest overall amount of utility. This idea is in sharp contrast, for example, to Kantian ethics, which we shall discuss in detail in the next chapter. Kant's position states negatively that a particular action is morally forbidden, while the utilitarian tells us positively that we must choose the specific course of action that maximizes utility. Thus utilitarianism is an extremely demanding moral doctrine, since it demands that we sacrifice our own pleasure, happiness, or preference satisfaction for the greater good—that is, for social utility.

Supererogation

Philosophers have noted an interesting implication of the utilitarian view that we must always try to maximize utility. In many moral philosophies, it is often possible to act in a *supererogatory* fashion, that is, to go beyond the demands of duty and thus do something exceptionally meritorious. For the utilitarian, however, supererogation is impossible. One is always obligated to do the thing which yields the greatest amount of utility, which is precisely what constitutes duty. Thus there is nothing above the call of duty. For the utilitarian, there is no room for supererogatory actions, for duty is so demanding that there is nothing above it which is greater.

This exclusion of supererogation is a cause for concern among some philosophers, for they believe that a moral theory which has no room for supererogation must be mistaken in some important way. Our everyday moral intuitions tell us that sometimes people do something that is above the call of duty. But if utilitarianism is correct, then doing so is impossible. Duty always calls for the maximum, so it is impossible to do anything above its call.

Optimizing and Satisficing

These issues have led some philosophers to distinguish between two types of utilitarianism. We are already familiar with the first type, **optimizing utilitarianism,** which requires that we always try to maximize the amount of utility our actions produce. Because optimizing is open to the kind of objections outlined here, some utilitarians have been led to develop a less demanding standard, one which says that we may produce less than optimal consequences. **Satisficing utilitarianism** maintains that we should act in such a way as to produce a *sufficient* amount of utility, but it is not necessary to try to produce the maximal amount. All that is morally required is that we be "good enough."

The attraction of satisficing utilitarianism is clear: it makes utilitarianism a less demanding moral doctrine, thereby making goodness more attainable and re-establishing room for supererogatory actions. (We shall also see that it allows us to reply effectively to some recent criticisms of utilitarianism that center around integrity and moral alienation.) Yet the notion has its drawbacks as well. First, the notion of "good enough" is vague in a way that is not true of optimizing utilitarianism. Where, precisely, do we draw the line? Certainly we are able to work with vague notions, and recently have even developed a logic ("fuzzy logic") to deal more easily with them, but it was exactness in the moral domain that was one of utilitarianism's main attractions.

Second, satisficing utilitarianism seems to open the door to a kind of moral mediocrity. To draw a comparison from college, one could liken it to wanting to take the moral life on a pass-fail basis instead of taking it for a letter grade. Perhaps every age laments the disappearance of the expectation of excellence, but it is clear that satisficing utilitarianism would do little to encourage the pursuit of moral excellence. Paradoxically, however, it would recognize such excellence as excellence, since it would have generally lower moral expectations. Optimizing utilitarianism, on the other hand, threatens to eclipse the recognition of excellence because it expects it in every instance.

A Multiplicity of Distinctions

The distinction between optimizing and satisficing utilitarianism cuts across several other distinctions, including the ones we have already seen among hedonistic, eudaimonistic, ideal, and preference utilitarianism. Each of these four types of utilitarianism can be either optimizing or satisficing. Furthermore, as we shall see shortly, other distinctions can be drawn as well. Each distinction is independent of the others, so the number of possible types of utilitarianism increases accordingly. A chart later in this chapter will display all the possibilities. For the sake of simplicity and because it is the dominant version of utilitarianism, I shall often discuss utilitarianism as though it is equivalent to optimizing utilitarianism. Remember, however, that there is this other version of utilitarianism, satisficing utilitarianism, which avoids some of the problems associated with optimizing utilitarianism.

Consequences of What?

The utilitarian maintains that we ought to prefer whatever produces the greatest (or at least sufficient) overall utility, and this amount is determined by weighing the consequences. But the consequences *of what?* Utilitarians have given at least four different answers to this question, answers that are not necessarily mutually exclusive: acts, rules, motives, and practices.

Act Utilitarianism

The first and most common version of utilitarianism says that we should look at the consequences of each individual action when attempting to determine its moral worth. This position, which is called **act utilitarianism,** maintains that we should always perform that *action* that will maximize utility, producing the greatest overall utility. Act utilitarianism is a tremendously powerful doctrine. One of its main attractions is that it seems to allow us to avoid rule-worshipping, and to deal with exceptions on the merits of the individual case.

The Advantage of Focusing on Acts

One of the principal attractions of act utilitarianism is that it deals with individual decisions on a case-by-case basis. There is no such thing as an exception for the act utilitarian because every case is judged on its individual merits, which is in sharp contrast to a rule-oriented morality such as Kant's, which might well demand in some specific situation that we act in a way that would cause more harm than good. As we shall see in Chapter Seven, Kant held very strict views on lying. At times Kant seems to believe that we are *never* permitted to tell a lie, even if lying would result in saving innocent human life. The standard example is of the Gestapo asking if you have seen any Jews running away from them. If you know the location of any such Jews, and if you must follow a rule that prohibits ever telling a lie, then you must tell them the location of the fleeing Jews. The probable result is that innocent people will be killed, people who might otherwise have escaped from their captors.

An act utilitarian, on the other hand, would have no difficulty lying in that particular situation if lying would produce the greatest overall amount of utility. It is simply a matter of doing the calculations, which in this case seems relatively straightforward. Moreover, such an approach accords with our basic moral intuitions. Common sense morality tells us that it would at least be permissible to lie in such a situation—perhaps that it even would be required of us.

Despite its sensitivity to particular cases, or perhaps because of it, act utilitarianism is open to a number of objections. Let us briefly consider three of them: (1) it is too time-consuming to calculate the consequences of each individual action; (2) it is too difficult to predict the consequences of individual actions, especially the long-term consequences; and (3) act utilitarianism opens the door to abuses, especially to abuses of justice, because of its neglect of general moral rules.

Time to Calculate

Act utilitarians seem to be faced with quite a challenge. If they are going to weigh the consequences of each individual action they perform, they will probably spend a large and disproportionate portion of their life just calculating consequences! That, critics charge, hardly seems like the best way to spend one's time. Furthermore, there may well be situations in which there simply is not time to calculate. When we see an out-of-control cement truck careening toward a pedestrian about to cross the street, we can hardly stop to calculate the hedons and dolors before trying to pull the passerby to safety!

Act utilitarians have an answer to such criticisms. We can, they maintain, live most of our lives on the basis of *rules-of-thumb*, rules that summarize past experience in such situations. Indeed, many of our general moral rules in society are precisely of this type. They express our collective social wisdom about what generally produces the best consequences for everyone. Act utilitarians have no difficulty with generally following such rules, but they insist that we be clear about the moral status of those rules, which are not absolute; rather, they are simply convenient summaries of past evaluations of individual acts. If, in some particular situation, we have reason to question whether the rule-of-thumb will produce the best consequences, then it is entirely appropriate to call that rule-of-thumb into question in that instance. So an act utilitarian may accept the rule-of-thumb "Don't lie," but reconsider it in the Gestapo example.

Such an approach, act utilitarians maintain, gives them the best of both worlds: they are able to recognize the advantages of generally relying on rules in the moral life without being caught up in the rule-worship that seems to characterize those who consider such rules to be absolute.

The Limits of Prediction

Act utilitarians face a second difficulty, one which they share with other versions of utilitarianism but which may be more acute for act utilitarians. How accurately can we predict consequences, especially long-term consequences of individual actions? Think, for example, of deciding which college to attend. It is often a difficult decision that involves endless comparisons. Yet for many of us, the most influential factors—such as the individuals we met, the friends we developed, the people we fell in love with—were ones we could never have predicted.

Most act utilitarians are willing to agree with critics about the limits of our predictive powers, but they reframe that insight in such a way that it no longer counts against act utilitarianism. Our predictive powers are limited, they concede, but this unpredictability is a difficulty with life, not with act utilitarianism. The proper response to this limitation is not to reject act utilitarianism, but simply to recognize that limitation is part of the human condition. The best that we can do is to try to increase our ability to foresee consequences. It is unrealistic, however, to hope that we can eliminate uncertainty completely. The moral life contains an ineluctable element of uncertainty, which can be reduced but never eliminated.

It is impossible to imagine that we could live without some basic belief in the general predictability of the human as well as the natural world. If we turn on the shower in the morning, we expect the water to be there and to

Chaos and Predictability

A butterfly flutters its wings in Peking, and a month later as a result a severe storm drenches New York City.

In recent years, scientists have become increasingly interested in the problem of chaos. The impetus for much of the original thinking about this problem was weather forecasting. Scientists long have thought that, if they only had enough data and sufficient computing power, they could predict the weather. (The computer was first developed in hopes of providing sufficient computing power to predict weather). Recently, a number of scientists have argued that predicting weather is impossible. Systems such as the weather are so complex that some little factor in the initial conditions can have unforesseable consequences later in the process. Thus when a butterfly flaps its wings in China, this event eventually has an impact on a thunderstorm in New York. If our predictive powers are so limited in regard to comparatively simple systems such as the weather, how much more limited they must be in regard to human society, which is infinitely more complex!

This line of reasoning gains plausibility when we recall one of the major events of this decade: the collapse of communism. From the destruction of the Berlin Wall to the dissolution of the USSR, we have witnessed a series of events of truly major importance that virtually no one predicted. It is unsettling to realize how truly unforeseen this event was.

Friederich Nietzsche, a nineteenth-century German philosopher who influenced twentieth-century existentialism, once said that human beings need predictability—and if they do not have it, they will create the illusion that they do. We need to *believe* that events are predictable, even when there is evidence to the contrary.

be at the proper temperature—and it usually is. We do not expect that tomato juice will come out of the shower head, just as we do not expect that food will cook if we put it in the refrigerator. We would quickly go crazy if there were not a significant degree of predictability in the natural world. Similarly, in human affairs, we have general expectations about how people will behave. If we ask people questions, we generally expect that they will answer. If we give someone a million dollars, we generally expect that the person will be delighted about it. If a close friend dies, we expect to be sad. We could hardly act in the social world if we did not believe that there is a general predictability to human behavior. This predictability does not have to be complete. We can make mistakes in our predictions and be surprised; but the very idea of being surprised presupposes expectations. Predictability is necessary for living.

The Limits Imposed by Justice

Critics see a third difficulty with act utilitarianism, one which is potentially much more disturbing than the preceding two objections. Act utilitarianism, they charge, opens the door to potential abuse, to condoning—perhaps even requiring—acts that contradict our everyday moral intuitions, especially intuitions about justice.

Let us begin by considering a bizarre but real example. In Texas a few years ago, a woman had a clause in her will stipulating that she be buried in her red Ferrari after she died. Apparently it costs quite a bit of money to bury someone in a Ferrari. What would be wrong with disregarding that provision of the will and giving her a regular burial and using the money saved to do some good among the living? Clearly, one difficulty is that there are laws against such things. But imagine what would happen if we embellished the example a little bit. Imagine that the woman told only you about her will, and imagine that you promised her that it would be carried out. Imagine, finally, that you know the location of her earlier will, which is exactly the same except that it contains no proviso about being buried in the Ferrari. What would be wrong with burning the most recent will and substituting the earlier one, a will which would leave all her money to a worthy charitable organization?

The obvious answer to this question is that you promised the woman to do what she asked. Yet promise-keeping in itself has no value for act utilitarians; its value depends on the consequences of the particular promise. In this case, who would benefit from your keeping the promise? Clearly, the woman would not—she is already dead. Whatever benefit she might have derived from the thought of being buried occurred before her death. The institution of promising, including other people's confidence that their wishes will be honored after their deaths, would neither suffer nor benefit, since no one else knows her wishes in this matter. The numbers seem to come out clearly in favor of breaking the promise. Moreover, if the numbers do come out this way, then not only are we *permitted* to break the rules, because if we are optimizing utilitarians, we are *obligated* to break them.

Consider a second, more difficult example. Imagine that you are the police chief in a small town that has been terrorized for months by a child rapist. Imagine that you discover through some unusual act of circumstances that the rapist has died in a freak accident, but there is no way that you could convince the public that the person was indeed the rapist. The threat is past, but the public still lives in fear since you cannot convince them that the rapist is actually dead. Now imagine that you have arrested someone whom you could frame for the rapes, a hobo with tuberculosis who has only six months to live.

What would be wrong with framing him for the rapes? There would be no danger that the real rapist would be free to continue his rapes; you are certain the rapist is dead. The public would be reassured, feeling that their town was once again safe. The man being punished would have died soon anyway, and he might actually receive better medical care in jail than on the street. The act utilitarian would seem to be justified in convicting the man, even though he had not committed these crimes, because his conviction would result in the greatest overall utility.

Rule Utilitarianism

Examples like these last two are disturbing to utilitarians, for they seem to suggest that act utilitarianism is too open to abuse, too likely to justify actions that conflict with justice or other values that intuitively are accepted by common sense morality. Yet many think that utilitarianism still basically is correct in its emphasis on consequences and in its standard of utility. The problem, they conclude, lies in the fact that utilitarianism looks at the consequences of each individual act. Instead, we should look at the overall consequences of adopting a *rule* that everyone act in a particular way under certain types of circumstances. This approach is known as **rule utilitarianism**, which **claims that we ought to act in accordance with those rules that will produce the greatest overall amount of utility for society as a whole.**

Clearly rule utilitarianism has a much better chance of dealing with the types of examples described here than act utilitarianism does. It would be much more difficult to imagine how one could justify a *rule* that supports breaking promises to the dead or convicting innocent people of crimes. Such rules simply do not maximize utility. By insisting that we justify rules instead of individual acts, the rule utilitarian seems to avoid certain injustices contained in act utilitarianism.

Act utilitarians disagree. They maintain that rule utilitarians are caught on the horns of a dilemma. They must maintain either that their rules are without exceptions or else that their rules do have exceptions. If their rules are without exceptions, they they are rule-worshippers according to act utilitarians, for they say that we should follow the rule at any cost, even when it produces bad consequences. Act utilitarians would admit that we generally should keep our promises to the dead, but that it would simply be rule-worshipping to keep the promise about being buried in the Ferrari in the circumstances described. On the other hand, if rule utilitarians are willing to make exceptions in those cases when following the rule would produce bad consequences, then they are really covert act utilitarians. If, for example, they would be willing to break their promise to the dead in the Ferrari case, then they would really be thinking as an act utilitarian. They would be willing to admit that they can disregard the

	How much pleasure apiece?	*How many people?*	*Total*
Slaves	8 dolors	100	−800
Masters	2 hedons	900	+1,800

rule in any individual case when the overall utility clearly demands it. Thus, rule utilitarianism seems to collapse back into act utilitarianism.

Justice and Rule Utilitarianism

As we have seen, one of the principal concerns of critics of utilitarianism has centered around the possibility that act utilitarianism might require us to perform acts that clearly violate our common sense moral expectations about justice. Yet it does not seem that rule utilitarianism is entirely immune to such criticisms either. Imagine a society in which 10 percent of the population is enslaved but provided with many of the basic physical comforts of life such as good housing, nutritious food, and reasonable working hours. Imagine further that the slaves are given plenty of free entertainment (television, movies, music, and so on); much of which stresses the joys and rewards of being a good slave. As a result of this on-going indoctrination and the tolerable physical conditions, the slaves do not feel a tremendous amount of discontent about their state in life. The masters, on the other hand, feel great that they have slaves, and it makes their lives significantly happier. Let us say that living in accord with this rule about slavery causes the slaves generally to feel about eight units of displeasure (eight dolors) apiece in their condition. Let us say that the masters experience two units of pleasure, two hedons, apiece as a result of being masters and having slaves. Recall that the slaves comprise only 10 percent of the population. The picture we get is given in the table above.

Rule utilitarianism would seem to justify slavery under these conditions, but our clear moral belief is that slavery is unjust. There are two possible conclusions we could draw from this example. On the one hand, we could argue that since utilitarianism leads to morally unacceptable conclusions (in this instance, the justification of slavery), it is unacceptable.

The other possible conclusion involves the modification, rather than the rejection, of utilitarianism. We could imagine that some people might agree to such a societal arrangement if they knew in advance that they would be among the masters rather than the slaves. However, would anyone agree to it if they did not know which of the two classes they would be in? Some philosophers—John Rawls in *The Theory of Justice* (1971) is the most influential of these—have argued that we need to set up limits on the range of possible rules that could be adopted, limits that would be determined by considerations of justice, by consensual agreements, by human rights, and the like. Within these limits, utilitarian justifications of particular rules would be permitted, but no justification would be allowed that violated those limits. It is, then, debatable whether proponents of such positions would still count, or count themselves, as utilitarians. Some contemporary theorists who accept this view such as Samuel Scheffler continue to insist that they are consequentialists.

Motives and the Domain of Applicability

There is another aspect to this continuing controversy between act and rule utilitarians, centering around the role of motives and intentions in the moral life. Although there has been some attempt (discussed below) recently to develop an account of motive utilitarianism, utilitarianism has long been open to the objection that it ignores intentions and motives. Typically, philosophers give hypothetical examples. Imagine an assassin, motivated purely by resentment and envy, is trying to kill the president of a small Middle Eastern country during a public ceremony. The assassin's bullet misses the president but strikes a rock, causing oil to gush forth. The newly discovered oil proves to be a main source of revenue for the previously impoverished country, and soon the entire country prospers. Utilitarians would have to maintain that this act was good because the consequences were good. Yet this conclusion seems to contradict our basic moral intuition that the assassin's motives of resentment and envy should count in our evaluation of the action.

Examples of this problem do not need to be far-fetched. Consider the attempted military coup in Russia in 1991, in which old guard communists tried to take over the government from Gorbachev. The coup failed, and in the end reformist leaders, especially Boris Yeltsin, emerged as far more powerful than they had been before. Presuming that this result will eventually bring more utility than any alternative, do we want to say that the hard-liners' attempted coup was a good act? Clearly, it was not *intended* to strengthen Yeltsin's position. The fact that it had this consequence was purely accidental. Indeed, it was intended to produce exactly the opposite consequences. It seems as though our moral evaluation of that action should somehow take account of the intention behind the act.

It is here that the distinction between act and rule utilitarianism has a particular relevance. Although both act and rule utilitarianism ignore motives and intentions, it seems to be less of a problem for rule utilitarianism. When, for example, we want to assess the moral correctness of proposed governmental legislation, we may well wish to set aside any question of the intentions of the legislators. After all, good laws may be passed for the most venal of political motives, and bad legislation may be the outcome of quite good intentions. Instead, we can concentrate solely on the question of what *effects* the legislation may have on the people. When we make this shift, we are not necessarily denying that individual intentions are important on some level, but rather confining our attention to a level on which those intentions become largely irrelevant, which is particularly appropriate in the case of policy decisions by governments, corporations, or groups. In such cases there may be a diversity of different intentions which one may want to treat as essentially private matters when assessing the moral worth of the proposed law, policy, or action. Therefore, rule utilitarianism's neglect of intentions intuitively makes the most sense when we are assessing the moral worth of some large-scale policy proposed by an entity consisting of more than one individual.

Imagine again that the government is debating proposed legislation to change health care benefits for the elderly. We could examine the motives of the individual legislators and lobbyists who support or oppose the new bill, but this understanding might be of little help in determining whether the bill itself was a good one or not. We might discover, for example, that a large percentage of the people who either support or oppose the legislation are motivated by a concern with political advancement or financial gain. Some may be acting out of principle, but the number may be roughly evenly split between the two camps. Looking at these individual motivations, we may simply decide that such motivations are just a matter of personal concern. They may tell us whether Senator X is morally well-motivated in supporting this legislation, but they give us no insight into the question of whether the proposed law itself will prove to be a good or a bad one. Thus we may decide simply to set aside the question of individual intentions and turn to the law itself. Once we do so, one of the ways in which we may assess its moral worth is by looking at what results or consequences would follow from adopting the proposed law. We then assess these consequences in terms of some yardstick, for example, in terms of the amount of pleasure and pain they may cause, or in terms of the amount of happiness and unhappiness which could result from their adoption. This approach is roughly what the rule utilitarian seeks to do: to assess the moral worth of a policy or rule in terms of the consequences that it will probably have.

Practices

Some philosophers have gone a step further than rule utilitarians by suggesting that utilitarian considerations have relevance in justifying the existence of certain types of practices, even though utilitarianism may not provide a proper basis for deciding particular acts within that practice. One can consider this approach as being a type of rule utilitarianism, but it is important to notice that there is a significant difference between rules and practice. Rules are more specific than practices, and a practice may encompass numerous rules. Stamp collecting, for example, is a practice, and it contains many specific action-guiding rules about what types of stamps to buy, when to sell, and so on.

Practices include rules, but contain more as well. They often are embodied in specific institutions (philatelic societies) and in patterns of social interaction (such as stamp collectors' conventions) that go beyond any specific set of rules.

John Rawls, a contemporary philosopher whose *Theory of Justice* is one of the most influential works in recent ethics, has suggested that we may justify the *practice* of punishment as a whole through utilitarian arguments. A society without institutions and practices of punishment would produce less overall utility than one that contained such institutions and practices. Rawls avoids the problems raised by utilitarian justifications of specific acts of punishment by arguing that specific punishments be determined, not on utilitarian grounds, but rather on the basis of retributive considerations. The specific punishment would depend on the severity of the offense, not the utility of imposing the punishment. Specific individuals, in other words, would be punished because they deserved it, not because of the consequences produced by punishing them.

The merit of a suggestion like Rawls's is that it allows us to combine both utilitarian and Kantian insights. Utilitarian reasoning justifies the existence of the institution of punishment, while Kantian considerations of desert and retribution determine the nature and severity of specific acts of punishment.

Motive Utilitarianism

We have already seen that motives and intentions are largely irrelevant to mainstream utilitarianism, which is a problem especially for act utilitarianism. Recently, some philosophers have suggested that it is also possible to take a utilitarian approach to questions of motive and character traits. They argue that, from a utilitarian perspective, society as a whole benefits from encouraging the development of certain motives or traits. A society that encourages the development of compassion as a valued character trait may well be one which produces a greater overall amount of happiness than one which places a comparable emphasis on competitiveness instead. Even specific actions can in part be evaluated in light of their motives and their impact on character. Mistreatment of animals may be objectionable to a motive utilitarian because it encourages the formation of motives which, at least when generalized, would not produce the greatest utility for society.

The advantage of this approach is that it speaks to what has been a nagging problem for utilitarians: the neglect of intentions and motives. But this approach need not be considered incompatible with traditional versions of act or rule utilitarianism. Instead, one can treat motive utilitarianism as supplemental to those other more dominant traditions. Motive utilitarianism will be particularly relevant in situations in which our principal concern is with the long-lasting effects of specific acts or rules on the formation of character.

Consequences of What?

Type of Utilitarianism	*Consequences of What?*	*Main Principle*
Act	Each Act	Perform the act that will produce the greatest overall amount of utility
Rule	Rules	Follow the rule that will produce the greatest overall amount of utility
Practice	Practices	Support those practices that produce the greatest amount of utility
Motive	Motives/Traits	Act on the motive that will produce the greatest utility

Overview

When we summarize these various positions, we get the chart above.

CONSEQUENCES FOR WHOM?

Utilitarianism is a type of consequentialism. It makes moral judgments on the basis of consequences. However, we need to ask: consequences for whom? Initially, that would seem to be a rather straightforward question with an equally straightforward answer: for people. Few things, though, are that easy. Let us examine three areas in which there is some controversy about who should count in determining consequences. The first of these relates to non-humans. To what extent, if at all, should the suffering of animals count in our calculations of utility? Second, are all human beings included in our calculations of utility, or should subgroups (such as our nation or our family) be given special weight? Third, to what extent should we take into account the consequences for future generations? Let us look at each of these issues.

The Suffering of Animals

Utilitarianism, at least in some of its principal forms, is dedicated to the reduction of suffering. Certainly human beings suffer, but suffering does not appear to be limited to human beings. Animals suffer, even if their suffering is not exactly the same type as ours. What weight, if any, should utilitarians give to animal suffering?

Pets

Clearly many of us, whether utilitarians or not, accord at least some value to the suffering of our pets. In fact, some of us will even go to great lengths, in terms of time as well as money, to reserve or restore the well-being of a pet. Although some of this effort may be a selfish concern for our own well-being if we were to lose the pet, in at least some of the cases there is no reason to doubt that it is also a concern for the animal itself. We *care* about our pets, and consequently their suffering counts. Yet the difficulty for a utilitarian is that this concern for a pet apparently violates the impartiality of the utilitarian outlook. From an impartial moral point of view, the suffering of one dog does not count any more than the same amount of suffering of any other dog. The only relevant difference is that in the case of pets, we need to add the suffering of their owners (and others who care about them) when the pets are in distress. There is a legitimate element in the utilitarian calculus, but it should be recognized that this element has nothing directly to do with the suffering of animals.

Painless Killing

It is also not clear that a utilitarian perspective prevents the killing of animals as long as it is done in a way that does not cause them suffering. Take raising mink for their fur as an example. If the mink are bred and raised in conditions of comfort (a very large, enclosed area instead of individual cages) and if they are killed painlessly without feeling fear in advance, then it would seem that there is little a utilitarian could find objectionable in terms of suffering. We should realize, of course, that actual conditions rarely correspond to this example.

The Borders of Our Group

In theory, utilitarianism maintains that we be impartially concerned with overall utility. There is nothing in the theory to suggest that we draw a line at national borders or at some other point. Indeed, the history of utilitarian thought is quite interesting in this respect. It flourished in Britain precisely during the period of the Empire, and was particularly influential in shaping—and being shaped by—Britain's rule of India. This fact reveals the potentially non-democratic side of utilitarianism and suggests the importance of our answer to the question "Who decides what the utility is?" The British were quite willing to rule India for the sake of the greatest utility—as long as they were the ones who decided what the utility was.

Today, the situation is not quite the same. Many of us, especially those of us in affluent countries, often seem to draw the boundaries of utility at the customs booth. Yet there are few good arguments to justify this article, except the claim that the citizens of a country are in the best position to decide what is best for that country. Yet we are faced with vast social and economic inequalities between countries, and there is little in utilitarianism to justify being concerned only with the welfare of one's own country.

Future Generations

The interests of future generations present a perplexing problem. On one hand, they do not yet exist—and, depending on our actions, they might never exist. Yet they are affected by the consequences of our actions, just as we (although presumably to a lesser extent, given differences in technological effectiveness) have been affected by our ancestors' actions. When utilitarians compute consequences, should they take into account the consequences for future generations, people who are as yet unborn? If so, to what extent? These remain vexing questions, not only for utilitarians, but for many other moral philosophers as well.

Issues in Utilitarianism

We have begun to develop a fairly comprehensive picture of utilitarian ethical theory in the preceding pages, but there remain a number of key issues that need to be discussed if we are to complete our understanding of utilitarianism and evaluate its strengths and weaknesses. We will focus on four of those issues here: (1) the difficulties of reasoning about matters of life and death; (2) the role of emotions in the utilitarian view of the moral life; (3) the limits of personal responsibility; and (4) the place of personal integrity in the utilitarian's world.

Weighing Matters of Life and Death

We are sometimes hesitant about utilitarianism because it seems to weigh everything, even human life. Some things, many of us want to argue, cannot be put on the utilitarian scale. Kant, for example, clearly maintained that human beings were priceless; they could not be assigned a monetary value in the way that mere physical objects could be. Indeed, as we shall see in the next chapter, this issue was for Kant one of the principal differences between people and things: things have a price tag, but people do not. Yet to put human life into the utilitarian balance seems to come perilously close to placing a price tag on it.

The Asbestos Example

At the beginning of this chapter, we discussed the example of removing asbestos from buildings. Some of you may have felt that human life is too precious to put into the balance, that any price is worth paying in order to save people's lives. Yet this belief is open to two rejoinders. First, sometimes we simply do not have an unlimited amount of funds; sometimes we have to make choices that result in letting some people die. But there is a second reply that is possible as well: even though we say that human life is priceless, we do not really act that way. Let me give an example.

The Speed Limit Example

During the energy crisis of the 1970s, a national speed limit of 55 MPH was instituted in order to conserve gasoline. One of the side effects of this change was that hundreds of lives a year were saved and thousands of traffic injuries were averted. Let us imagine that additional deaths and injuries could be avoided if we reduced the speed limit even further. At what point do we draw the line? At what point do we say that even if it means that a certain number of people will die or be injured in automobile accidents, we still want to keep the speed limit from being lowered?

My suspicion is that virtually all of us would draw the line at some point, even if it is considerably lower than the present limit. (Many actually would like the limit higher, and many drive as though it were.) My point here is not to argue in favor of any particular speed limit, but rather to illustrate that most of us in fact are willing at some point to put human lives into the equation. Notice, too, that these may be innocent lives; there is no guarantee that those killed or injured in traffic accidents are necessarily the ones at fault. We should not be too quick to judge utilitarians harshly solely because they are willing to put human lives into the equation. Most of us are willing to do the same, even if we are reluctant to admit it.

The Role of Emotions in the Utilitarian Moral Life

Recently, some philosophers have criticized utilitarianism because of the role—or lack of a role—that it gives to emotions in the moral life. There are two aspects of it that merit our attention here. The first relates to the question of whether we ought to accord more weight to some emotions than others; the second issue centers around the nature of our relationship to our own emotions in utilitarianism. The latter issue, as we shall see, leads directly into the question of personal integrity.

Which Emotions Are Given Weight?

Utilitarianism obviously gives moral weight to the emotions. If, for example, I am contemplating stealing some money from a friend, one of the things that I would have to take into account as a utilitarian is the suffering that my friend would undergo at the loss of the money and the possibility of even greater suffering if he discovered that it had been stolen by a friend. I would also, of course, have to take into account my own feelings, possibly quite positive ones with a high hedonic value, if I were to succeed in stealing the money. Let us assume that my friend would have only negligibly negative feelings at having the money stolen and only slightly more negative feelings if he discovered that I were the thief. In addition, assume that I would certainly get great pleasure and happiness from successfully taking the money. Under these conditions, it would appear—all other things being equal, which they never are in real life—

that my feelings could tip the balance in favor of committing the theft. What the utilitarian seems unable to do is to distinguish between what we could call good and bad feelings, or, more precisely, morally justified and morally unjustified emotions.

Examples of this problem need not be as far-fetched as the preceding one was. Consider the problem of racism in our own society. Certainly there are many courses of action—such as genuine integration of schools—which would at least initially bring about intensely negative feelings on the part of a large segment of the population. It is easy to imagine, if we were for the moment to grant the utilitarian premise that feelings can be placed on some hedonic scale, that integration would cause more negative feeling in the oppressors than it would cause positive feeling in the oppressed. Yet is this reason, again assuming other things to be equal, sufficient for not seeking to eliminate racism from the society? (This example, of course, does not even touch on the question of *who* weighs these feelings. One suspects that it would be much easier for a white person to sympathetically weigh the amount of fear and displeasure that white people experience at the thought of integration, while presumably an African-American would be much more sensitive to the pain suffered by other African-Americans. It is far from evident that there is a neutral standpoint here.)

The difficulty that the utilitarian faces is obvious: if all feelings are of equal value, and if all that distinguishes them is their valence (negative or positive), quantity (how many people experience the feeling), and intensity (how strong the feeling is for each), then morally good and justifiable feelings will have no greater weight than morally evil and unjustifiable feelings of the same sign, quantity, and intensity. Yet we want to say—or at least our everyday moral intuitions suggest—that some types of feelings should be given greater weight than others.

The utilitarian seems at first to have an answer to this dilemma, but it is just the appearance of an answer. It seems that one could differentiate among various emotions on the basis of their overall social utility. Altruistic feelings, for example, may have a greater social utility than discriminatory feelings. It may thus be beneficial from a utilitarian point of view to encourage courses of action that promote the development of altruistic feelings and reduce discriminatory feelings. Yet this approach will hardly do, for it really just deals with the question of the feelings that result from particular courses of action, not the feelings that might provide reasons for such actions. We could imagine, in the integration case, for example, that the results might not bring about a greater amount of altruistic feelings. It could produce more bad feelings than good, but it might still be the right thing to do if we think that some of the negative feelings it produces are unjustified.

Thus the first problem with the utilitarian account of the emotions is that it fails to provide any adequate way of discriminating between justified and unjustified feelings, between good and bad emotions, and is committed to giving both the same weight in its utilitarian calculations.

My Relation to My Own Emotions and Convictions

The second major problem with the utilitarian account of the relationship between morality and the emotions centers around the question of how I am related to my own emotions, deeply held beliefs, and reasoned commitments. Bernard Williams develops this objection in some detail, and here I shall only summarize the main elements of this argument.

Imagine the following kind of case, one of the type that Williams describes. A chemist—call him Harold—with a wife and children is out of work. He and his family are beginning to suffer significantly as a result of his unemployment. During the past few years, he has become increasingly convinced that all war, but especially chemical and biological warfare, is immoral. He is offered a job by an old friend as a chemist in a firm developing and producing chemical warfare weapons. Furthermore, he is told by his old friend that if he does not take the job, it will in all probability be given to a younger chemist he knows who is both a better chemist and quite committed to the development of such weapons. The moral quandary which he faces is this: he is morally opposed to war and does not want to participate in developing weapons of war. His deepest moral commitments tell him not to take the job. However, he knows that if he takes the job, he will fulfill his obligations to his family and, at the same time, he will not be doing anything that will result in chemical warfare being more advanced than if he refused the job. Indeed, if he turns the job down, then he will probably be helping the chemical warfare industry, since his position will be filled by someone better and more enthusiastic than he is. Thus the problem this example initially poses for us is this: what weight should Harold give to his own strong feelings against the morality of chemical warfare?

The standard utilitarian answer to this question certainly recognizes Harold's commitments, but only in a limited way. Clearly these deeply held feelings and beliefs are one of the factors that Harold must take into consideration, but no special consideration must be given to the fact that they are *his* emotions and beliefs. He must also take into consideration everyone else's emotions and beliefs, and these presumably must be given equal weight. Indeed, in this situation Harold might even be obliged to give less weight to his own feelings and convictions. After all, his own feelings are probably the ones over which he has greatest control, so he may be obliged to try to change them to positive feelings about warfare. One thing is clear: his emotions do not deserve special weight simply by virtue of the fact that they are *his* emotions. Indeed, the utilitarian might well want to argue that the very essence of morality is impartiality. In not giving special weight to his own feelings, Harold simply is assuming the moral point of view. To be moral is to be impartial.

Yet critics such as Williams have suggested that there is still a serious problem here, namely, that utilitarian morality sometimes demands that a person give up his or her most deeply held feelings and convictions. So, if it is precisely these kinds of things that make life worth living for an individual, then utilitarian morality may demand that the individual give up his or her very reason for existing. Something is seriously wrong, Williams argues, if morality makes this kind of demand on an individual.

The reason utilitarianism falls short of the mark here is that it fails to recognize any special relationship between the agent and his or her own feelings and deeply held beliefs, failing also to recognize that these are one's own in some unique way. When the utilitarian contemplates the consequences of an action (including the feelings it may create), there is nothing significant about the fact that some of the consequences may be one's own in a special fashion. All feelings and commitments are taken into account simply as a group, summed up, and then the "bottom line" dictates the decision one should make.

The Limits of Personal Responsibility

In another intriguing example, Bernard Williams presents us with the following situation in which we must make a moral choice.

> Jim finds himself in the central square of a small South American town. Tied up against the wall are a row of twenty Indians, most terrified, a few defiant, in front of them several armed men in uniform. A heavy man in a sweat-stained khaki shirt turns out to be the captain in charge and, after a good deal of questioning of Jim which establishes that he got there by accident while on a botanical expedition, explains that the Indians are a random group of the inhabitants who, after recent acts of protest against the government, are just about to be killed to remind other possible protesters of the advantages of not protesting. However, since Jim is an honored visitor from another land, the captain is happy to offer him a guest's privilege of killing one of the Indians himself. If Jim accepts, then as a special mark of the occasion, the other Indians will be let off. Of course, if Jim refuses, then there is no special occasion, and Pedro here will do what he was about to do when Jim arrived, and kill them all. Jim, with some desperate recollection of schoolboy fiction, wonders whether if he got hold of a gun, he could hold the captain, Pedro, and the rest of the soldiers to threat, but it is quite clear from the set-up that nothing of that kind is going to work: any attempt at that sort of thing will mean that all the Indians will be killed, and himself. The men against the wall, and the other villagers, understand the situation, and are obviously begging him to accept. What should he do?

The utilitarian, Williams maintains, has a clear and easy answer to this question. Within the utilitarian perspective, there is no question that Jim should shoot the one prisoner so that the others could go free. It is not only the right thing to do, it is the *obviously* right thing to do. When we add up the hedons and dolors in even the most cursory way, we see clearly that the alternative that will produce the greatest overall amount of utility is for Jim to pull the trigger. Nineteen lives would be saved. Everyone wants him to do it.

The question that Williams raises in regard to this example is an important one. He does not deny that shooting the one villager may be the best alternative, but he points out that in the utilitarian perspective Jim cannot attach any special weight to the fact that *he* is the one who pulls the trigger. Jim is equally responsible for the deeds that he does directly and the deeds performed by others which he could have prevented. Jim is responsible for Pedro's killing the twenty prisoners because he could have prevented it himself by killing one of the prisoners, which, William contends, is a confused notion of personal responsibility. We bear a special relationship to, and responsibility for, our own actions that utilitarianism fails to capture.

The example that Williams gives is far-fetched, but there is no shortage of real-life cases that illustrate the same point. All you need is a situation in which you can prevent a larger evil by committing a smaller evil yourself. Recall the riots in Los Angeles in 1992, which were triggered by the acquittal of the police officers charged with beating Rodney King in Los Angeles. Imagine that—and we are making *no* claim that this result was the actual situation—that in the second trial the jury came to know three things: (1) that, on the basis of videotapes not shown on television, the officers were not using excessive force; (2) that, if they failed to convict any of the officers, there would be devastating riots; (3) that, although innocent in the present case, these officers had in the past mistreated suspects and had not been prosecuted; and (4) that if the officers were acquitted, even worse riots would occur. Could jurors decide to convict the police officers, even though they were innocent of the actual charges, in order to prevent the suffering and destruction that would occur if they were acquitted? Does utilitarianism open the door to this scenario as a possibility, if the calculation of consequences indicates that such a conviction would produce the greatest overall utility?

Integrity and Impartiality

There are two final characteristics of utilitarianism that it is particularly important to note here. First, utilitarians are not allowed to give any special weight to the fact that certain consequences may affect them personally. The popular image of utilitarians is often of people who are just concerned with achieving their own selfish aims and who then view everything else simply as a means to the attainment of those ends. Yet the picture we get of utilitarians from an ethical standpoint is quite different. Utilitarians are not allowed to give any special weight to the fact that some negative consequences will affect them quite personally. If, for example, we have a utilitarian legislator who will personally suffer if there is not an increase in medical benefits for the aged, the utilitarian legislator will still be required to vote against such an increase if that increase would yield a lesser total utility than the alternatives. If, to take a second example, we have a utilitarian gourmet who is contemplating either having dinner at Chez Panisse, an expensive restaurant in Berkeley, or donating the money that would have been spent on the dinner to a charity devoted to relieving hunger in the world, it is clear from the utilitarian standpoint that there is only one morally right alternative: to give the money to help reduce hunger. Even though dinner at Chez Panisse may yield one hundred hedons for the gourmet, the same amount of money may well bring ten hedons for thirty people. Thus utilitarians apparently cannot give special weight to the fact that certain pleasures or displeasures are their own; they must be weighed just like everyone else's hedons and dolors.

When we hear on the news that a concert pianist was involved in an auto accident in which his hands were crushed, or when we hear that a famous painter has gone blind, or that a well-known baseball pitcher has suffered irreparable damage to his pitching arm, we are especially moved. Our heart goes out to such people, because we realize the way in which such an accident strikes at the very heart of who they are as persons. Indeed, we want to say that certain projects, commitments, and desires are closer than others to a person's sense of their own identity, their idea of who they are. Those closest to the person's sense of their own identity comprise what we shall call that person's **fundamental projects.**

The issue about fundamental projects becomes even more vivid if we recall Williams's example of Jim in the South American town. The way that Williams sets up the example, we are asked to imagine what Jim (a hypothetical character) would do. But let us change the example a bit. Imagine two different scenarios. First, instead of Jim, imagine a person whose whole life was devoted to peace and nonviolence. Mother Teresa or Martin Luther King, Jr., come to mind as obvious examples. What should they do? Second, imagine that a mercenary soldier, for whom killing is a casual activity, arrives in the village instead of Jim. What should the soldier do? Most of us would give quite different answers to these questions, depending on whether the visitor was someone like Mother Teresa, Dr. King, or the mercenary. The reason for our different answers is precisely the issue of fundamental projects. To kill anyone would run counter to the whole sense of what Mother Teresa's or Dr. King's lives are about. It would not, however, contradict the mercenary's life at all (except perhaps in the fact that he is not being paid for it). Utilitarianism seems to give insufficient recognition to this difference in fundamental projects.

Living the Utilitarian Life

When we are considering so many arguments for and against utilitarianism and drawing so many distinctions between various types of utilitarianism, it is easy to lose sight of what it means to live life as a utilitarian. Yet utilitarianism is a moral theory that was meant to be lived, and a consideration of what it would look like in practice can provide us with a good way of drawing together some of our conclusions about it.

Two insights guide the utilitarian's life. The first of these is that *consequences count.* Consequently, *utilitarians will always want to know what actual effects their choices will have for real people* (and perhaps other sentient beings as well.) They continually direct their attention to the basic facts of the moral life, facts about who will be hurt and who will be made happy as a result of a particular decision. It may be very difficult at times to predict what the actual consequences of a particular decision will really be, but utilitarians are committed to trying to make such predictions as accurately as possible. The fact that they are not able to make such predictions accurately indicates that there is an unavoidable element of luck in the moral life. The presence of luck is a problem with the moral life, but not an objection to utilitarianism as a moral theory.

Second, *utilitarians want the world to be a better place for everyone.* It is a benevolent moral doctrine; that is, it wishes people well and seeks to increase the amount of well-being in the world. Indeed, the whole point of morality for utilitarians is that it produces a better, ultimately happier world. Ethical reflection is not something pursued in abstraction from the real pain and suffering of the world around us. The point of ethics is to help reduce that pain and suffering. Morality should make the world a better place for everyone.

Despite these strengths, many find that utilitarianism does not provide the whole story of the moral life. One of the dangers that many utilitarians—especially act utilitarians—face is that their principles might require actions that violate the rights of small groups of individuals. Act utilitarianism alone cannot provide sufficient guarantees against the possibility of such abuse. There are two ways to respond to this difficulty. On the one hand, some philosophers have opted for some version of rule utilitarianism, which seems less susceptible to such difficulties. Others have suggested that *there must be a moral "floor" or minimum below which we cannot go,* even if utilitarian considerations seem to demand that we do so. To live only by utilitarian considerations, especially act-utilitarian ones, is to open the door to possible abuses of the minority when such injustices yield high benefits for the majority. Ethical theories that emphasize the importance of human rights seem to offer a standard of value in the moral life that escapes from these dangers. Chapter Eight of this book is devoted to rights-based moral theories.

Another difficulty plagues utilitarian accounts of ethics. Most *utilitarians ignore the importance of intentions.* Although there are certainly plenty of circumstances in which intentions do not matter, there are times—especially in personal relationships—when they are of crucial importance. This dimension of the moral life has been almost completely ignored by utilitarians because of their exclusive focus on consequences. Three quite different approaches to morality help to understand this dimension of the moral life better than utilitarians alone have been able to do. First, Kantian accounts of morality, as we shall see in the next chapter, emphasize the importance of intentions in the moral life, especially the importance of acting from a motive of duty. Kantians see something morally admirable about acting for the sake of duty that utilitarians are unable to recognize. Second, some critics of morality have argued—as we shall see in Chapter Nine—that all major moral theories fail to provide an adequate account of our moral motivations. Such theories, critics such as Michael Stocker argue, produce a kind of motivational schizophrenia, a deep and pervasive split between our actual motives and the legitimate reasons within any particular moral theory. Such criticisms can be answered, I shall argue, only by a moral theory that focuses primarily on character, which as we shall see in Chapter Ten, is precisely the kind of theory that Aristotle offers.

Bibliographical Essay

The **classic texts** for utilitarianism are those of Jeremy Bentham, John Stuart Mill, and Henry Sidgwick. Among **Bentham's** works, see, in particular, Bentham's *A Fragment on Government,* edited by J. H. Burns and H. L. A. Hart (London: Athline Press, 1977) and his *The Introduction to the Principles of Morals and Legislation,* edited by J. H. Burns and H. L. A. Hart (London: Athline Press, 1970). (These are also available in other, less expensive editions.) For excellent introductions to Bentham's moral and political thought, see John Dinwiddy, *Bentham* (Oxford: Oxford University Press, 1989) and Ross Harrison, *Bentham* (London: Routledge and Kegan Paul, 1984). Also see David Lyons, *In the Interest of the Governed* (Oxford: Clarendon Press, 1973) and H. L. A. Hart, *Essays on Bentham: Jurisprudence and Political Theory* (Oxford: Clarendon Press, 1982).

Many of **John Stuart Mill's** works are relevant, especially his *Utilitarianism* and *On Liberty.* These are available in various editions, including several that also contain critical essays. See John Stuart Mill, *Utilitarianism: Text with Critical Essays,* edited by Samuel Gorovitz (Indianapolis, Ind.: Bobbs-Merrill, 1971); Mill's *Utilitarianism: Text and Criticism,* edited by James M. Smith and Ernest Sosa (Belmont, California: Wadsworth, 1969); and *On Liberty: Annotated Text, Sources and Background,* edited by David Spitz (New York: Norton, 1975). For an excellent selection of Mill's writings on ethics, see *Mill's Ethical Writings,* edited by J. B. Schneewind (New York: Collier, 1965). Among the best books on Mill's philosophy are Fred Berger's *Happiness, Justice, and*

Freedom: The Moral and Political Philosophy of John Stuart Mill (Berkeley: University of California Press, 1984).

Book IV of **Henry Sidgwick's** *The Methods of Ethics*, 7th edition (Indianapolis, Ind.: Hackett Publishing Company, 1981) is also a classic source of utilitarian thought. For a fine introduction to Sidgwick's thought and times, see J. B. Schneewind, *Sidgwick's Ethics and Victorian Moral Philosophy* (Oxford: Clarendon Press, 1977).

Richard Brandt introduced **the distinction between act and rule utilitarianism** in his *Ethical Theory* (Englewood Cliffs, N.J.: Prentice Hall, 1959). On this distinction, also see A. C. Ewing, "What Would Happen if Everyone Acted Like Me?" *Philosophy*, Vol. 28 (1953), pp. 16–29 and A. K. Stout's "But Suppose Everybody Did the Same?" *Australasian Journal of Philosophy*, Vol. 32, pp. 1–29. On the tendencies toward *rule* utilitarianism in Mill's work, see J. O. Urmson, "The Interpretation of the Philosophy of J. S. Mill," *Philosophical Quarterly*, Vol. 3 (1953), pp. 33–39 and Henry West, "Mill's Moral Conservatism," *Midwest Studies in Philosophy*, Vol. 1 (1976), pp. 71–80.

Several of the editions of Mill's *Utilitarianism* and *On Liberty* contain excellent collections of **critical essays.** In addition to these anthologies, see *The Limits of Utilitarianism*, edited by Harlan B. Miller and William H. Williams (Minneapolis: University of Minnesota Press, 1982) as well as the collection of essays in the *Canadian Journal of Philosophy*, supplementary volume 5 (1979). One of the more recent books that often provides a good starting-point for studying utilitarianism is *Utilitarianism: For and Against* (Cambridge: Cambridge University Press, 1973), which contains an explication and defense of act utilitarianism by J. J. C. Smart and an interesting critique by Bernard Williams. The essay by Williams has been one of the most influential in raising the issue of moral alienation. One of the most nuanced and powerful replies to Williams and others on this issue is Peter Railton's "Alienation, Consequentialism, and the Demands of Morality," *Philosophy and Public Affairs*, Vol. 13, No. 2 (Spring, 1984), pp. 134–71. This essay, along with a number of other important pieces, has been reprinted in an excellent anthology edited by Samuel Scheffler, *Consequentialism and Its Critics* (Oxford: Oxford University Press, 1988); also see David O. Brink, "Utilitarian Morality and the Personal Point of View," *Journal of Philosophy*, Vol. 83 (1986), pp. 417–38. The anthology that Bernard Williams and Amartya Sen edited, *Utilitarianism and Beyond* (Cambridge: Cambridge University Press, 1982), contains a number of perceptive articles. For a helpful anthology of essays on the place of rights in utilitarian moral theory, see *Utility and Rights*, edited by R. G. Frey (Minneapolis: University of Minnesota Press, 1984) and Richard B. Brandt, *Morality, Utilitarianism, and Rights* (New York: Cambridge University Press, 1992).

Anthony Quinton's *Utilitarian Ethics* (New York: St. Martin's Press, 1973) provides a helpful overview of classical utilitarian thought. Also see David Lyons, *Forms and Limits of Utilitarianism* (Oxford: Clarendon Press, 1965) and D. H. Hodgson's *Consequences of Utilitarianism* (Oxford: Clarendon Press, 1967). For a very perceptive discussion of **well-being** in relationship to utilitarianism, see James Griffin, *Well-Being: Its Meaning, Measurement and Moral Importance* (Oxford: Clarendon, 1986).

The discussion of utilitarianism often takes place within the context of a contrast with Kantian and other deontological accounts of morality. John Rawls' "Two Concepts of Rules," *Philosophical Review*, Vol. 64 (1955), pp. 3–22 is an important attempt to reconcile partially these two traditions. Samuel Scheffler's *The Rejection of Consequentialism* (Oxford: Clarendon Press, 1982) provides a provocative rethinking of some of these issues, as does Michael Slote's *Common-Sense Morality and Consequentialism* (London: Routledge and Kegan Paul, 1985), which contains an extended discussion of satisficing consequentialism.

Citations. The example of Jim is found in Bernard Williams, "A Critique of Utilitarianism," *Utilitarianism: For and Against* (Cambridge: Cambridge University Press, 1973), pp. 98–99. The butterfly example comes from James Gleick, *Chaos: Making a New Science* (New York: Viking, 1987).

Discussion Questions

1. Recall your response to statement 24 ("When I am trying to decide what is the right thing to do, I look at the consequences of the various alternatives open to me.") in the Ethical Inventory.
   (a) What moral theory does this statement illustrate?
   (b) Has your rating of this item changed after reading this chapter? If so, in what way? If your rating has not changed, are your reasons for your rating any different now than they were when your first responded to this statement?
2. Recall statement 25 in the Ethical Inventory ("The right thing to do is whatever is best for everyone") and your response to it.
   (a) In what types of cases, if any, are we not justified in doing what will produce the greatest overall amount of good? Be specific.
   (b) Has your rating of this item changed after reading this chapter? If so, in what way? If your rating has not changed, are your reasons for your rating any different now than they were when you first responded to this statement?

3. Recall statements 28 and 29 in the Ethical Inventory about whether pleasure or happiness is the most important thing in life.
   (a) If you agreed with statement 28, what arguments do you now see could be advanced against your position? How would you reply to these arguments?
   (b) Have your ratings of these items changed after reading this chapter? If so, in what way? If your ratings have not changed, are your reasons for your ratings any different now than they were when you first responded to this statement?
   (c) If you hold that neither pleasure nor happiness is of intrinsic value, what is? Explain.

4. Take a contemporary social issue, such as kidney transplants, that involves the allocation of scarce resources and discuss the ways in which various types of utilitarians would recommend that we deal with it. How would their recommendations differ from the recommendations of ethical egoists? Which of these traditions do you find more convincing? Why? If you do not agree with either, what are your reasons for disagreement?

5. In recent decades, Americans have been reconsidering their treatment of those with physical handicaps or disabilities in a number of different areas of life, including education and sports. Imagine that a proposal has been put to your local school board to institute a limited sports program for physically impaired students. The projected cost of running such a program would be approximately four times as much per student as is spent on the regular sports programs, although the number of students is much lower. How would a sophisticated utilitarian deal with this proposal?

6. Ben Franklin (1706–1790) said "Honesty is the best policy." Is this adage true (as Franklin thought) only on utilitarian grounds? Or do we need some other justification for it? When, if ever, do you think honesty is *not* the best policy? Give an example.

7. The Pentagon often uses "cost/benefit analysis" to evaluate (proposed) new weapons systems. Is this strategy utilitarian? If so, is it moral, immoral, or amoral? Why?

8. Human life, the philosopher Immanuel Kant tells us, is priceless. However, we often seem to put a price tag on human life. Is it always wrong? Why or why not? If it is ever morally permissible to do so, when is it allowed? Why? If we do not put a price tag on human life, how do we deal with (a) the allocation of scarce medical resources in which we have the money to save only some of the people, and (b) jury awards in wrongful death suits?

9. Imagine that you are a utilitarian who has 10 million dollars to spend on health care for infants. Which would be better—spending it on extensive prenatal care or high technology neonatal intensive care units? In order to answer this question, what further questions would you have to ask about each alternative? Would you agree with the utilitarian solution to this question?

C H A P T E R 7

The Ethics of Duty: Immanuel Kant

Introduction: Duty in the Life of Edmund G. Ross

After Abraham Lincoln's assassination, Andrew Johnson succeeded to the presidency, pursuing Lincoln's policy of reconciliation and rebuilding in the South. Radical Republicans, disliking Johnson personally and committed to pursuing a much more punitive policy toward southern states, barely had the two-thirds majority necessary consistently to override presidential vetoes. With the appointment of Edmund G. Ross, long an ardent opponent of Johnson and his policies, to finish out the Senate term of the deceased Jim Lane (a Johnson supporter), it looked as though the Radical Republicans would at last have their solid two-thirds majority, enabling them not only to override vetoes but also even to impeach the president.

The bill of impeachment was passed by the House early in 1868 and went quickly to the Senate for a vote on Johnson's removal from office. Public sentiment was strongly against Johnson, and especially strong in Kansas, Ross's home state. He knew well that he would probably destroy his political career and any further opportunities for success in public life if he failed to vote against Johnson. He opposed Johnson's policies and disliked him personally. Yet despite his feelings and in the face of intense pressure and threats to his life and reputation, Ross took seriously his oath "to do impartial justice." His was the deciding vote on the floor of the Senate, and his decision was clear: Andrew Johnson did not deserve to be removed from office. To remove him for what were essentially partisan political considerations would be equivalent to degrading the presidency itself and turning the United States *de facto* into a purely congressional government.

Ross was never elected to political office again. When he returned to his native Kansas, he was shunned by his former friends and sentenced to a life of isolation and relative poverty. Ross anticipated this rejection, yet he voted the way in which he did because he believed it was the right thing to do. He did it despite the personal consequences, and he did it despite his personal feelings about Johnson and his policies. This conviction is what Kant means by *acting for the sake of duty*, doing something because it is the right thing to do. If any moral philosopher is able to truly appreciate Edmund Ross's decision, it is Immanuel Kant.

In this chapter, we shall look closely at Kant's moral philosophy, beginning with a consideration of his understanding of the role of duty in the moral life. His ethical theory rests on three central insights. The first two of these insights state the conditions for a morally good act:

- an action has moral worth if it is done for the sake of duty;
- an action is morally correct if its maxim can be willed as a universal law.

Actions which have both moral worth and moral correctness are morally good actions. In addition to these two insights, Kant develops a third claim about the way in which we ought to act in order to respect both ourselves and other people: we should always treat humanity, whether in ourselves or other people, always as an end in itself and never merely as a means to an end.

These are the three pillars on which Kant's ethics rests: duty, universalizability, and respect. Let us consider each of these three insights in turn.

THE ETHICS OF DUTY

One of the morally admirable characteristics of Edmund Ross's decision is that he not only did the right thing, but he also did it for the right reason. Ross did not act for any self-centered motives. Indeed, if Ross had been an ethical egoist, he would have acted quite differently. There were plenty of factors pushing him in the other direction. He did not like Johnson, he disagreed with Johnson's policies, his political career would be ruined by a vote in Johnson's favor, and even his family's fortunes would be affected adversely. The only reason for voting against removing Johnson from office was that it was the right thing to do.

Contrast this actual case with a hypothetical variant. Imagine that the same events were unfolding today, but that Ross's motivation was somewhat different. Imagine that he was tired of politics, feeling that his political career had reached a dead end. Imagine, further, that he saw the crucial vote on Johnson as an excellent career possibility. By skillfully manipulating the media,

Perhaps more than any other philosopher, Immanuel Kant (1724–1804) emphasized the importance of duty in the moral life.

he could focus attention on himself and the agony of his decision. Media coverage would increase dramatically. A best-selling book, talk shows, the lecture circuit, and perhaps even a miniseries beckon in the future. "Integrity," our hypothetical Ross says to himself, "is a big thing with the voters today. If I vote against removing Johnson from office, I might even have a good chance at the presidency myself in a few years." Buoyed by these prospects, our imaginary Ross casts his vote against removing the President from office.

Acting for the Sake of Duty

Which action, Kant would ask, do we think is morally the better action? Both actions, in terms of their external characteristics and results (at least in regard to the president), are the same. Both are in conformity with duty in the sense that the external behavior conforms to the requirements of duty. Yet clearly, most of us would agree that the action in the real-life case is better than the one in our hypothetical example because it was done for the right reason. One of Kant's key insights is that an act's moral worth depends on the reason for which it is done. It is not enough that an act conform to duty; it must also be done for the sake of duty. It must be done out of a concern for what is morally right, not out of some self-serving motive, which is precisely what makes the real-life case better than the imaginary one. The act is done just because it is the right thing to do; in other words, it is done for the sake of duty.

Duty and Self-Interest: The Grocer Example

In the *Groundwork of a Metaphysics of Morals*, a short work in which he presents the underpinnings of his moral philosophy, Kant himself offers examples of acting for the sake of duty. These examples give us some insight into why Kant attaches such moral importance to the motive of duty. Kant's first example is of a grocer dealing with inexperienced customers. While it is often in a merchant's self-interest to be honest, it is not always so. If we imagine a neighborhood grocery store in which the grocer knows almost all of the customers, and if those customers are long-term patrons and if they know one another, and if there is a competitive grocery store nearby, then it is clearly in the grocer's self-interest to be honest. The grocer depends on repeat business, and if the grocer cheats even a few of the regular customers, they will probably tell others and the grocer's business will be seriously hurt. Self-interest and simple prudence dictate honesty as the best policy in such cases.

However, this result is not always the case. Imagine someone who runs a gift shop in a toll plaza on an interstate highway. The customers rarely return, they virtually never know one another, and there is usually no immediate competition. In situations such as these, if there is little scrutiny by consumer groups or police, there is little reason for the shopkeeper to be honest out of self-interest. Indeed, self-interest may well dictate overpricing items and selling shoddy products that will not stand up to any extended use. There are, in other words, plenty of situations in which the motive of self-interest cannot be counted on to require the right action. In situations such as these, if we are not acting for the sake of duty, we will not perform the morally correct action.

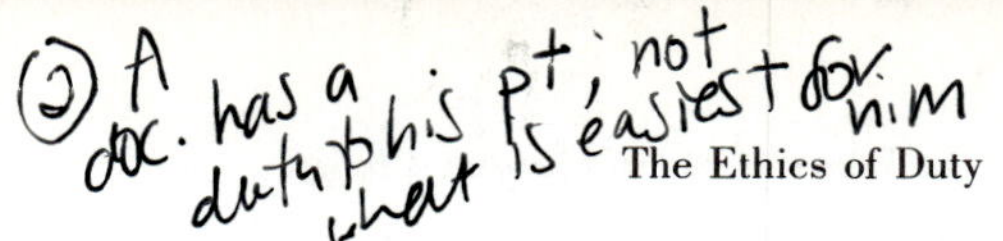

Kant's example is intended to show that self-interest is not a sufficient motive to guarantee the moral rightness of our actions. It also serves to illuminate Kant's differences from the ethical egoist. Obviously, they disagree on what gives an action moral worth. Whereas the ethical egoist takes self-interest as the standard, Kant focuses on duty. However, Kant's example here challenges a second aspect of the egoist's position. Egoists often claim that the world will be a better place if everyone acts in terms of his or her own self-interest. Yet both the grocer and the gift shop examples show that there are common circumstances in which ethical egoism is unlikely to be true.

Duty and Utility: The Suicide Example

The second example which Kant offers is of the person who refuses the temptation to commit suicide even though his life is wretched, filled with disappointments and misery. When such a refusal is motivated by duty, it has moral worth in Kant's eyes. It would not have moral worth, however, if the refusal were motivated by other considerations, such as a squeamishness about the actual act of killing oneself or a mere desire or inclination to live.

Kant's views on suicide provide an interesting contrast with utilitarians. Kant condemns all suicides, but contemporary Kantians are often less rigid in their reasoning about the issue. In a perceptive essay on "Self-Regarding Suicide," Thomas Hill, Jr., a contemporary Kantian philosopher at the University of North Carolina, develops a sensitive and insightful analysis of suicide that still manages to preserve a number of Kant's essential insights in a modified and more nuanced form. Hill does not suggest condemning suicide and does not even claim that suicide is always irrational. He recognizes that there is a range of cases in which suicide, although sad, is not necessarily morally objectionable. He does, however, argue that there are certain types of suicides that show that the individual in question does not value life "as a rational, autonomous agent for its own sake." Those who commit suicide from motives of self-abasement, for example, see themselves as unworthy of continued life, as not even meriting the punishment of continued existence. Except in the most extreme cases, such judgments are unwarranted and are inconsistent with the fundamental self-respect that all human beings should have.

Utilitarian reasoning about suicide takes a quite different tack. Not surprisingly, it is a matter of weighing consequences. The motive is of virtually no importance. Good utilitarians must imagine what the course of the world would be like if they killed themselves and what the course of the world would be like if they continued to live. Which of these alternatives produces the greater alternative? A sensitive utilitarian such as Richard Brandt, a contemporary utilitarian whose work has long shown a deep awareness of the psychological complexity of the moral life, points out quite rightly that the people contemplating suicide must be very wary of letting depression and other factors distort their judgment as they attempt to weigh such factors. Nonetheless, it is clear that the utilitarian might permit—indeed, even require—suicide under circumstances and for reasons that no Kantian could accept.

Duty and Inclination: The Sympathy Example

The final example that Kant offers is the most controversial. He is concerned with the moral worth of actions done in order to help another person when the motive is one of sympathy or some other feeling such as compassion. He contrasts two types of people who help others. One the one hand, "there are spirits of so sympathetic a temper that, without any further motive of vanity or self-interest, they find an inner pleasure in spreading happiness around them and can take delight in the contentment of others as their own work." The actions of such people, Kant argues, have no moral worth, because they are done out of inclination or feeling instead of being done for the sake of duty. On the other hand, imagine a quite different case.

> Suppose then that the mind of this friend of man were overclouded by sorrows of his own which extinguished all sympathy with the fate of others, but that he still had power to help those in distress, though no longer stirred by the need of others because sufficiently occupied with his own; and suppose that, when no longer moved by any inclination, he tears himself out of this deadly insensibility and does the action without any inclination for the sake of duty alone; then for the first time his action has its genuine moral worth. Still further: if nature had implanted little sympathy in this or that man's heart; if (being in other respects an honest fellow) he were cold in temperament and indifferent to the sufferings of others—perhaps because, being endowed with the special gift of patience and robust endurance in his own sufferings, he assumed the like in others or even demanded it; if such a man (who would in truth not be the worst product of nature) were not exactly fashioned by her to be a philanthropist, would he not still find in himself a source from which he might draw a worth far higher than any that a good-natured temperament can have? Assuredly he would. It is precisely in this that the worth of character begins to show—a moral worth and beyond all comparison the highest—namely, that he does good, not from inclination, but from duty.

This claim is strong and perhaps even startling. The person who helps other people from a sense of duty without any feeling of care or compassion or sympathy is morally superior to the person who performs the same actions while motivated by altruistic feelings. Yet Kant's point here, whether we agree with it or not, is clear: there is something *morally* valuable in the actions of a person who, despite feelings to the contrary, does something because it is the right thing to do. We may like the person who does the same thing spontaneously out of a feeling of compassion or pity, but there is nothing morally praiseworthy in such a person's intentions.

Criticisms of an Ethics of Duty

It is hardly surprising that Kant has been criticized for his strong emphasis on the importance of duty. Let us consider three of the ways in which his position has been questioned.

Moral Minimalism

The first possible objection to Kant's emphasis on duty is that it seems to imply a kind of moral minimalism, that is, an undue emphasis on only doing what is morally required in a given situation. Genuinely altruistic acts, according to critic Lawrence Blum in *Friendship, Altruism and Morality* (1980), go beyond the moral minimum. Yet such an objection, as Marcia Baron has pointed out, rests on a misunderstanding. Both morally required and morally *recommended* acts may be done for the sake of duty. Kant's emphasis on duty in this context focuses solely on duty as the motivation for actions; it is not restricted to acts necessitated by duty. Whether the act be morally required or merely morally recommended, the crucial thing is that it is performed for the sake of duty and because it is the morally good thing to do.

Moral Alienation

There is a second, more serious and more complex charge that has been leveled against Kant's emphasis on duty. Several critics of Kant's ethics have argued that his exclusive emphasis on duty as the sole motive of moral action leads to moral alienation. Although this objection is discussed in Chapter Nine in a more general form as an objection against all ethical theories, it will be helpful here to consider some aspects of the specifically Kantian version of the problem.

Recall the example of the man who had no "sympathy for the fate of others," but helped them solely out of a motivation of duty. Why is it wrong—or at least without moral worth—to help other people simply because you *care* about them? Indeed, as we shall see in Chapter Eleven, feminist approaches to ethics often take care as the center of the moral life. One of Kant's answers clearly falls short of the mark. Emotions, he claims, are fickle and a moral life based on emotions would lack the reliability of one based on reason. Yet this response presupposes a questionable view of both emotions and reason. Some basic moral emotions such as caring, especially if strengthened through moral education, can be quite reliable. Indeed, they often may provide a stronger motivation than reason. Finally, reason may be less reliable than Kant thinks. There is no shortage of examples in which reasons have been offered for morally suspect actions.

There is, however, a deeper source for Kant's mistrust of the emotions. Essentially, Kant sees the moral agent as composed of reason and will—emotions are not part of the composition of the moral agent as such. There are complex reasons for this attitude that relate to Kant's views on freedom and causality, but we need not concern ourselves with those here. Suffice it to say that Kant saw the human person as deeply divided between reason, freedom, and duty, on one hand, and irrationality, causality, and emotion on the other. Emotions were a threat to the autonomy of the moral agent for Kant, rather than an enhancement of it.

Emotions, as we shall see in Chapter Nine, need not be thought of in Kant's terms. They play an important role in our moral perceptions, usually have subtle cognitive structures, and are to some extent subject to choice. They play an especially important role in the ethics of personal relationships, an area that Kant neglected. Moreover, as we shall see in Chapter Ten when we discuss the ethics of character, there are other, more robust conceptions of the moral agent than Kant's. These fuller accounts of the moral agent recognize that our emotions are an essential part of who we are as moral agents.

Duty and "Just Following Orders"

The final objection to Kant's emphasis on duty does not come primarily from professional philosophers. Instead, it rests on a deep misunderstanding of Kant's philosophy that is rarely found among professional philosophers. It is, however, a misconception that is sometimes found in popular ideas about Kant. Sometimes Kant's conception of duty is misinterpreted as implying that acting for the sake of duty is somehow equivalent to an unthinking obedience to authority, to just following orders. Indeed, Adolf Eichmann even appealed explicitly to Kant's notion of duty in his defense of his actions at Auschwitz, claiming that he was just "doing his duty." Indeed, when first arrested, Eichmann told his police interrogators that throughout his life he tried to follow Kant's philosophy, especially obeying Kant's Categorical Imperative. When asked what he understood the Categorical Imperative to be, he replied that earlier in his life

> I had known the Categorical Imperative . . . , but it was in a nutshell, in a summarized form. I suppose it could be summarized as, "Be loyal to the laws, be a disciplined person, live an orderly life, do not come into conflict with laws"—that more or less was the whole essence of that law for the use of the little man.

Yet it is clear from even the most cursory reading of Kant that his notion of duty is *not* equivalent to following orders, unthinkingly obeying the law, and so on. But if duty is not just following orders, how do we determine what our duty is? Let us now turn to Kant's answer to this question.

Universalizability and the Categorical Imperative

The second principal insight of Kant's ethics centers around the universality of genuine morality. Before looking at some of the more technical ways in which Kant sought to formulate this claim, let us see if we can grasp the basic intuition behind it. Then we can examine Kant's strictly philosophical formulations of this insight and see whether his formulations adequately capture the insight.

What's Fair for One Is Fair for All

One of our basic intuitions in the moral life centers around the belief that what is fair for one is fair for all. If I am allowed to run traffic lights whenever I want to, then everyone else should be allowed to do so as well. There would be something wrong, something *unfair*, about allowing me to disobey traffic signals whenever I choose while demanding that everyone else treat them as binding. Part of Kant's insight into morality is that it is equally applicable to everyone.

But, you may want to say, do we not in fact sometimes allow people in our own society to disobey traffic signals? Ambulance drivers, police officers, and others in emergency situations are permitted to go through red lights, although they must do so with proper caution. Is Kant's ethics so rigid that it does not permit this kind of exception? No, of course not. But his commitment to moral fairness demands that we justify this exception in a particular way. Anyone driving an ambulance during a medical emergency is permitted to disobey traffic signals, although with proper caution. The exception depends on the person's role as an ambulance driver and is applicable to anyone who occupies that role. We will consider the issue of exceptions in more detail below.

Imperatives

Categorical and Hypothetical Imperatives

Kant calls his basic moral principle the Categorical Imperative. It is an *imperative* because it tells us to do something, giving us a command; it is *categorical* because it is unconditional. The opposite of a categorical imperative would be a conditional or *hypothetical imperative*, such as "If you want to get to UCLA, take the 405 freeway." The corresponding categorical imperative would be "Take the 405 freeway." However, even though this command has the form of a categorical imperative, it is clear that it does not apply to everyone all the time. We would hardly want to tell everyone to take the 405 freeway all the time. Is there, in fact, any command or imperative that we would want to issue to everyone and tell them to follow it at all times?

The Categorical Imperative

Kant believes that there is such an imperative, and one version of it that he gives is as follows:

- Always act in such a way that you can will that the maxim behind your action can be willed as a universal law.

A **maxim** for Kant is the subjective rule that a person has in mind when performing an action. The test for a maxim, then, is whether people consistently could will that everyone adopt this maxim as a guide in their actions. Then it would pass the test of universalizability.

The Example of Lying

Kant gives several examples of how this Categorical Imperative might be applied, and the most powerful and defensible one relates to lying. If people tell a lie, what they are doing in effect is saying that it is permissible to deceive another person for personal gain of some kind. This implicit maxim is behind their action. Yet imagine what would happen if we willed that everyone adopt it as a maxim. Think of the things in our society which depend on believing what another person says. When we sign a check, we are giving our word that we have the funds to cover it; when we sign a contract, we are promising to abide by the terms of that agreement; when we make a date to meet a friend for dinner, we are saying that we will show up at the appointed time; when I write these pages, I am saying implicitly that what I write is true and worthy of your belief. But imagine if we were to adopt the maxim that people can lie whenever they think it is to their benefit to do so. If we will that everyone adopt such a maxim, then we undermine the very possibility of gaining an advantage from our own lying—for if this maxim were universally accepted, no one would believe what anyone else said or promised, for they would know that it could easily be a lie. We cannot consistently will that everyone lie or make false promises whenever it is to their personal advantage to do so, for it would undermine the credibility of our own lies and thus negate their effectiveness. Thus this maxim cannot be willed as a universal law.

Consistency

Notice that this example is not really an argument about consequences, although it may appear that way at first. Kant is not saying that if we start to tell lies, other people will follow suit, clearly with negative results. (As we saw in the previous chapter, a utilitarian might make this argument.) Rather, he is saying that if we imagine the consequences, we cannot will consistently that everyone adopt this maxim, giving us an insight into what lies behind lying: when we tell a lie, we make an exception of ourselves. We say that the rules that apply to everyone else should not, at least in this case, apply to us. But, and here is the crucial part, we are not willing to admit this exception. For our lie to work, it depends on having other people believe us—and thus on their not knowing that we are lying. Consequently, we simultaneously have to affirm two contradictory propositions: that people should tell the truth and that I should be allowed to lie. The first is necessary for my lie to be believed, the second necessary to permit me to tell it. Yet these two propositions are inconsistent and thus cannot be willed together.

Another way of making this same point is that, in lying, I have to will that other people not lie. If I were to will that everyone lie, then no one would believe anyone. In order for my lie to be believed, I have to will that people generally believe that we should tell the truth. My lying depends on a general expectation of truthfulness that would be undermined if I willed my maxim as a universal law.

Impartiality and Fairness

Behind Kant's argument here is a further insight, one which we already have begun to consider: what is fair for one is fair for all. If a law applies to one person, it should apply equally to all. In this sense, we must treat everyone impartially. If it is wrong for other people to lie, it is also wrong for me to do so. I cannot give myself special treatment.

Indeed, our everyday morality often reflects Kant's insight here. We should be morally suspicious of ourselves when we find that we are making an exception of ourselves. If, for example, I say to myself that cheating on an exam is bad, but just this one time it is OK for me to cheat, then I am making an exception of myself. A good rule-of-thumb for the moral life is to be suspicious whenever we start making an exception of ourselves. We cannot be certain in advance that what we are doing is morally wrong, but we can be sure that it merits further moral scrutiny.

Thus, while there are tremendous difficulties surrounding the articulation and application of Kant's Categorical Imperative, I think he is correct in his basic insight that we cannot arbitrarily make an exception of ourselves. Yet this insight raises a further question: can we ever make an exception?

Exceptions

Our last remark raises a more general question, one which often has been asked of Kant's ethics: can it deal adequately with exceptions? The classic example involves lying to the Nazis. If you are sheltering Jews during World War II, and the Gestapo comes to your door and asks whether you are hiding any Jews, are you (if you are a Kantian) obligated to tell the Gestapo where the Jews are? Before answering this question, let us look at an easier example.

The Speeding Car

Imagine that you are driving in the country with a friend who suddenly becomes gravely ill. You do not know for sure what has happened, but you suspect a heart attack. It is clear that he needs medical attention immediately, but the area is so deserted that there is not even a telephone between your location and the hospital. The hospital is ten miles away; seven minutes later you pull up to the Emergency entrance.

Were you justified in speeding? I think a Kantian could easily say "yes." True, you were making an exception of yourself, but presumably this exception is one that we would be willing to grant to anyone in the same emergency situation. Anyone, with a critically ill passenger in the car and under the other requisite conditions, is permitted to speed in order to bring the passenger to the hospital for medical attention. If we were to formulate the maxim behind this action, it might be something like this: A person is justified in breaking minor laws (such as traffic regulations) in order to save a person from death or grievous physical harm when there is no other feasible alternative and when proper concern for the safety of other persons is shown. We could consistently will this maxim as a universal law. We in fact have countless such exceptions in our society, and no one finds them inconsistent. Despite what Kant thought, universalizability need not exclude exceptions.

The Gestapo Example

The more interesting and difficult case comes when we imagine the Gestapo example described above. Would you be justified in lying to the Gestapo, telling them that you did not know the location of any Jews? What would the maxim behind your action be? Initially, we might say that the maxim is something like the example below.

- A person is justified in lying to the Gestapo if it will result in preventing them from killing innocent people.

Yet we would hardly want to tie our maxim so closely to the Gestapo in particular. What makes us single them out? Presumably we would also find it justifiable to protect innocent people from, say, the death squads in Argentina, the Ton Ton Macoute in Haiti, Pol Pot's secret police in Cambodia, and perhaps even certain branches of the KGB in Russia or the CIA here. Yet not all the groups in this list are the same. Some are official government agencies; others, such as the death squads, are not.

It is easier to develop a defensible maxim that applies to self-appointed groups such as the death squads in Argentina. It could be formulated as follows.

- It is permissible to lie to self-appointed vigilante groups in order to protect the life or well-being of an innocent person from those groups.

We could imagine willing such a maxim as a universal law without inconsistency, for we could say that such groups have no right to that information in the first place and that, if they did receive the information, they would commit a serious evil. Yet it is more difficult to formulate a maxim that would cover the Gestapo example, because the Gestapo at that time was a legally sanctioned part of the German government. Here the maxim is more questionable.

- It is permissible to lie to legitimate government authorities in order to protect an innocent person's life or well-being from those authorities.

The difficulty with this maxim centers around the question of who decides whether someone is an innocent person. Generally, this decision is one that we accord to the judiciary; yet in this case, the individual is taking over a function that usually is reserved to governmental authorities. It seems that we open the door to abuse, and perhaps even anarchy, if we allow individuals to take such responsibility on their own shoulders at will. Yet it also seems to open the door to oppression and totalitarianism if we never allow individuals to assume such responsibility, for there will be cases (and the Gestapo example is surely one such case) in which lying will be the morally right thing to do. Thus we see the issue coming into clearer focus. We must formulate a maxim that describes the conditions under which individuals are allowed to take this responsibility onto their own shoulders.

- It is permissible to lie to government authorities in order to protect an innocent person's life or well-being from those authorities when those authorities have clearly shown a pattern of abuse of their authority.

Even this maxim would need further refinement, but we can begin to see the way in which we would go about dealing with exceptions within the context of Kant's ethics.

Formulating Maxims

The preceding discussion of exceptions is important for two reasons. First, it shows that Kant's approach to ethics may be less rigid than it is sometimes portrayed as being. Second, it begins to focus our attention on the importance of maxims in the moral life. Let us turn to a closer consideration of this issue.

A **maxim** is a *subjective rule according to which we determine behavior*. There are all sorts of possible rules that we may have as maxims. Consider a few examples, most of which are stated in the form of imperatives.

- Never do anything that hurts other people's feelings if you can avoid it.
- Always be loyal to your friends.
- Never act in a way that would make your parents ashamed of you.
- Never do anything that you would be unwilling to acknowledge publicly in the *New York Times*.
- Always watch out for number one.
- Winning isn't the most important thing—it's the only thing!

These are all maxims that people in fact live by, subjective rules that they have which help them to decide in particular instances how they ought to behave.

In stressing that we always have a maxim underlying our actions, Kant is emphasizing the way in which every action is tied into a subjective network of reasons that motivate us as well as to an objective system of moral rules. The maxim is the link which connects the subjective reasons behind our actions to the system of reasons that comprises an ethical standpoint. The test of universalizability determines whether those subjective reasons fit within the objective system of reasons.

Relevant Act Descriptions

In formulating a maxim, we must pay attention to the *way* in which we describe the act. "Exerting two pounds of pressure on a metal lever," "pulling a trigger," "shooting a person," and "killing a guard in order to rob a bank" may all describe the same act. We need to be sure that we choose the relevant act descriptions which are potentially morally suspect in order to test whether they pass the test of universalizability.

Sufficient Generality

In addition to choosing the relevant act descriptions, we should formulate maxims with a sufficient level of generality. "Shooting Bill Smith" is specific; "shooting armed robbers who are threatening to kill innocent bystanders" is more general because it refers to types of people rather than specific individuals.

From Maxims to Categorical Imperatives

For Kant, the measure of a maxim is whether it survives the test of being translated from a maxim into a categorical imperative, that is, into a maxim that would be universally binding on everyone. Thus the maxim has a threefold relationship: (1) to the motivating reasons of the agent; (2) to the act itself; and (3) to a universal system of reasons. The test of universalizability, which we will now consider, determines whether the maxim is consistent with the universal demands of reason.

The Test of Universalizability

Recall Kant's formulation of the Categorical Imperative that we cited above.

- Always act is such a way that you can will that the maxim behind your action can be willed as a universal law.

We can now appreciate the way in which the test of universalizability measures the morality of our actions. Actions begin with motivating reasons which prompt us to act in a particular way. Latent in those motivating reasons is the maxim which guides our action. In order to develop this process, we need to formulate the maxim, following certain guidelines about the relevant act description and sufficient generality. Then we need to determine whether this maxim is one which it would be possible for everyone to accept consistently and rationally. If it is, then the action is morally permissible.

This test of universalizability can appear mechanical and far removed from the concerns of everyday life, but it is not intended to be so. What Kant saw most powerfully was that morality consists in doing what *any* rational being would do in the situation, which involves setting aside our own personal preferences and potential gains in order to do the right thing. The test of universalizability, whatever its apparent artificiality may be, is intended to help us see which of our actions are ones that any rational being would willingly acknowledge as his or her own.

RESPECT AND USING PEOPLE

An Introductory Example

Imagine the following situation. A shy, unattractive guy named Harold is living in the college dorm. He has virtually no friends and seems too timid to seek them out. His roommates spend little time with him, and he spends most of his time studying, presumably because he has nothing better to do. Things remain unchanged for the first year-and-a-half that Harold is at college. Then suddenly, within a single week, two things happen that greatly affect his popularity. First, his father gives him a new sports car for his birthday—probably the most impressive car on campus. Second, his sister, who is enrolled at a nearby women's college, comes to visit. There is general agreement that she is probably the most beautiful creature on the face of the earth. Suddenly Harold's popularity soars. He is invited to countless parties, although the invitations usually contain a request to bring along his sister. Invitations to go out to movies or bars abound, especially from guys with no transportation of their own. He quickly develops an extensive set of friends, a remarkably high percentage of whom lack either a car or a girlfriend or both.

At the risk of sounding cynical, we could reasonably assume that at least some of Harold's new-found friends are using him. They are not really interested in Harold as a person or presumably they would have made overtures of friendship long ago. Rather, they are interested in Harold only insofar as he can loan them his car, give them rides, or introduce them to his sister. Many of us would want to say that there is something wrong with using people in this way. Certainly Kant would say so. Indeed, one of the most important contributions that he made to ethics was his discussion of respect for other persons and his injunction that we not use other persons as mere means to our own ends. Let us look more closely at what he meant and why there is something morally objectionable about behaving in this way.

Kant's Imperative about Respect

In the *Groundwork of a Metaphysics of Morals,* Kant presents the following formulation of the categorical imperative.

- Act in such a way that you always treat humanity, whether in your own person or in the person of any other, never simply as a means, but always at the same time as an end.

Let us look more closely at what Kant says here. There are several things that we should note about Kant's exact language.

First, notice that Kant says that we should always treat humanity, whether in ourselves or in anyone else, as an end in itself and never merely as a means to an end. Kant's directive prescribes an attitude of respect toward ourselves as well as toward other people. We will consider the issue of self-respect later in this chapter.

Second, notice that Kant's imperative tells us how to act, not how to feel. This idea is particularly relevant in understanding respect, for we need to ask whether respect is just a way of acting or whether it also involves feeling a particular way.

Third, note that Kant says that we ought never to use humanity merely or only as a means, but that we should also at the same time treat people as ends in themselves, seeming to imply that some element of using people as a means to an end is permissible; what is prohibited is *only* using them as a means. We will consider this factor in more detail below.

What Does It Mean to Use Other Persons Merely as Means?

In our opening example, we saw a relatively clear-cut case of a person being used as a means. It could be made even more indisputable if we imagined that Steve, one of Harold's roommates, constantly belittled and criticized Harold until he found out about the car and the sister. Then Steve pretended to be Harold's best friend, although still continuing to belittle him behind his back. Finally, when Harold's car crashes and his sister decides to go to school in Australia, Steve drops his friendship with Harold. In such a case, most of us would say without hesitation that Steve was using Harold and that he was wrong to do so.

Yet many examples in life are not nearly as clear-cut, and in order to decide on the more difficult cases, we need to have a clearer notion of what it means to use a person as a mere means—and then to understand what is wrong with doing so. Let us start with our initial example before considering some of the harder cases. Why would we be inclined to say that Harold's friends were using him? There are several possibilities. First, Harold's friends were deceiving him insofar as they pretended to have friendly feelings toward him when in actuality they did not have those feelings. Second, his friends might have profited at Harold's expense insofar as they gained use of his car and introductions to his sister which they might not otherwise have had. Moreover, Harold might have done favors for them which he would not have done if he had known their true feelings. Third, they undermined Harold's opportunity to make informed choices insofar as some of Harold's choices were based on inaccurate information about his apparent friends' feelings and intentions. Whereas Harold would, for example, be inclined to loan his car to someone he considered to be a genuine friend, he would not want to loan it to someone who disliked him. If someone were pretending to be his friend, Harold's choice would be skewed because of this false information. Fourth, we might object to this situation because it violates the rules of friendship. There are special obligations, one could argue, that pertain to being a friend, and Harold's so-called friends failed to live up to those obligations. Finally, we might object that when Harold eventually discovered the truth (that is, that his apparent friends were really only interested in his car and his sister, not him), he was hurt by it.

The Syphilis Experiments

Now let us consider some additional examples which at least on the surface appear to be examples of using other people and see if they exhibit the same characteristics that our first example did. In the 1930s in America, some doctors and government officials were interested in doing research on the long-term effects of syphilis on men. By this time, they knew that syphilis generally could be cured by administering penicillin, which meant that it was more difficult to do long-term studies, since once a case was found, it could usually be cured rather easily. It was decided to take a group of black men who were already diagnosed as having syphilis, not tell them that they had the disease, not treat them, and follow the development of the disease in them until they died. They became the unwitting subjects in a medical research project that cost them their lives.

What do we find objectionable in this example? Certainly, we object to the fact that men were allowed to die when they could have been treated, easily and cheaply, in a way that would have prevented their death from that particular illness. In other words, we object to the easily avoidable pain, suffering, and death that resulted from this course of action. Second, we object to the fact that the men were deceived. They should have been informed of their condition. Third, because they were not told what was actually going on, they were not given any choice about their participation in this experiment. Thus it is not simply the deception, but also the fact that the deception serves to undermine the conditions of a meaningful choice, that makes this case so objectionable.

Moreover, we would probably object to it even if it did not result in avoidable suffering and death for the participants. Imagine scientists doing a medical research project in which they were testing the efficacy of a drug that they already knew had no harmful side effects. Suppose, furthermore, that the condition it treats was not life-threatening or painful. Most of us would still maintain that it would be wrong to administer this drug, without their knowledge or consent, to patients who were hospitalized for some other reason and then observe the effects of the drug. Our intuition here is that people have a right to know and to make up their own minds, and that we have an obligation to respect this right even if no direct harmful consequences result from ignoring it.

Factory Closings

Consider a less controversial and less clear-cut example: industrial plant closings. There has been a long-standing national debate over the issue of whether factory owners should be required to inform employees of a potential plant closing by a given number of weeks or months before the plant actually is closed. Owners generally oppose such a requirement, because once workers know that their plant is going to close, absenteeism and quitting increase dramatically as workers look for steadier employment elsewhere. (Moreover, their competition immediately knows that the plant is closing, possibly putting them at a further competitive disadvantage.) Consequently, efficiency and productivity decrease.

On the other hand, workers support such requirements about advance notification because, they argue, it allows them to look for alternative employment over a longer period of time, thus increasing the possibility of a smooth transition to another job. They further contend that when the owners know of a plant closing and do not notify the workers, they are using the workers to their own ends without regard for the welfare of the workers themselves. They keep the truth from the workers because it might otherwise adversely affect their profits.

Again, we see some common elements emerging here. The first relates to avoidable harm. By informing the employees in a timely manner, the company might reduce the amount of harm the employees experience. At the same time, this decision may increase the cost to the company. Second, we again find if not deception at least the withholding of important information. Third, we see why that information is important: it affects the choices that the workers may make. In many cases, they would have made different choices if they had known that the plant was closing soon. Indeed, from the company's point of view, one of the reasons for not telling them is precisely to prevent them from making those choices. Finally, we see that the employees—or at least some of the employees—are hurt by them.

Firing Long-Time Employees

Consider another example that relates to employment. In a wide variety of areas of the American workforce, there has been a tremendous amount of change in recent decades, especially with the introduction of computers and other sophisticated equipment in the workplace. All too often, we find employees who have served a company faithfully for years, sometimes at great personal sacrifice, no longer able to keep up with changing times—or, in some cases, not even given the chance to do so, which of course, raises the issue of using persons. Companies that fire such employees often are criticized for using their employees and when they are no longer useful to them, discarding them. While this attitude may be appropriate to have toward tools (to use them and discard them), it is not a proper way of treating persons.

Precisely what is objectionable in this practice? It may not involve deception, but it certainly seems to involve a change in messages. Employees might have been hired under one set of guidelines with the tacit assumption that those guidelines would continue to remain in effect indefinitely; yet, perhaps under new management, those guidelines might change significantly. Certainly two of the moral issues here are how far one is justified in making such changes and whether employers who make those changes are also obligated to provide employees with the realistic opportunity to conform to the new standards. Our underlying intuition, whether valid or not, is that employers owe employees something, especially employees who have in the past met the employers' expectations.

The Elements of Respect

Respect, Feeling, and Action

From the preceding examples, we begin to get a picture of what Kant means by respect. It is, first and foremost, an attitude that manifests itself in action. To respect someone is to act in particular ways toward that person (and to refrain from acting in particular ways). Although Kant occasionally refers to it as a feeling, the emotive aspect of respect is clearly of secondary importance. Respect is, first and foremost, a way of acting.

What kind of action does respect require of us? Kant is clearer on the kinds of action respect prohibits than what it requires. Most fundamentally, respect demands that we do not take away the conditions of moral agency or autonomy from other people. Central to Kant's understanding of autonomy is the ability to make up one's own mind on the basis of the relevant information. In several of our examples above, using people involved (1) not allowing them access to information relevant to their own decisions or (2) not allowing them to act on the basis of such information. Kant's views on punishment, which we have not discussed here, reflect this same view. For Kant, it would be insulting and a mark of disrespect if we did *not* punish a criminal. In punishing someone, we treat them as responsible, full-fledged moral agents. To do less is to show a lack of respect for them.

Respect also involves recognizing the unique value of each individual and the fact that each person is priceless. In the *Groundwork*, Kant makes an interesting remark about price. If something has a relative value, Kant says, then it has a price. If it has a price, it can be replaced by something else of equivalent value. If it has an absolute value, it has dignity and is not for sale.

It is also irreplaceable. We can, I think, take this insight as a cue and say that what sets human beings apart from everything else on earth is that human beings do not have a price, are not for sale; rather, they have an absolute value, are unique, and cannot be substituted one for the other.

What Is Worthy of Respect

Respect is directed only toward persons, and even then it is related to only one aspect of persons: their rationality. What we respect in other people, according to Kant, is their ability to reason and, on the basis of their reason, to choose to act in particular ways. Proper respect always is directed toward reason and will. Because there is a sense in which everyone possesses rationality to the same degree (although they may not exercise it to the same degree), respect is something that we owe everyone in equal measure simply because they are human beings. Respect of this type is not dependent on a person's unique accomplishments, but only on his or her rationality.

Respecting Animals

This attitude has important implications both for how we treat other people and for how we treat animals. Precisely because it is reason and will that are the proper objects of respect, we cannot properly respect animals in themselves, for (at least according to Kant) animals have neither reason nor will. Animals have feelings, but in themselves those are not a proper object of respect for Kant. We have an indirect duty to respect animals, not because of the animal's feelings, but because of the effects that lack of respect toward animals would have on us and our behavior.

Respecting Feelings

Kant's attitude toward animals gives us an insight into the limits of his view of respect toward human beings. While we respect reason and will in human beings, we apparently have no direct duty to respect their feelings. Thus Kant's notion of respect is curiously lacking in affective components in both subject and object. The subject, the person having the respect, is primarily the acting subject, not the feeling subject; the object of respect in the other person is primarily reason and will, not feeling.

Self-Respect

Kant's categorical imperative about respect not only enjoins us to respect other people, but also to "respect humanity" in ourselves as well. Thomas Hill, whose article on self-regarding suicide we discussed earlier in this chapter, has developed the most insightful and stimulating account of Kant's ideas on self-respect. In a 1973 article entitled "Servility and Self-Respect," Hill argues that it is sometimes a moral failing to fail to respect oneself. He develops three examples: the Uncle Tom, the self-deprecator, and the deferential wife. The third of these types has, by far, generated the most interest and response. Let us look at his analysis of this type of case.

The Deferential Wife

Consider Hill's description of the deferential wife. As you read his account, ask yourself what—if anything—you find morally objectionable in the attitude of the deferential wife.

> This is a woman who is utterly devoted to serving her husband. She buys the clothes he prefers, invites the guests he wants to entertain, and makes love whenever he is in the mood. She willingly moves to a new city in order for him to have a more attractive job, counting her own friendships and geographical preferences insignificant by comparison. She loves her husband, but her conduct is not simply an expression of love. She is happy, but she does not subordinate herself as a means to happiness. She does not simply defer to her husband in certain spheres as a trade-off for his deference in other spheres. On the contrary, she tends not to form her own interests, values, and ideals; and, when she does, she counts them as less important than her husband's. She readily responds to appeals from Women's Liberation that she agrees that women are mentally and physically equal, if not superior, to men. She just believes that the proper role for a woman is to serve her family. As a matter of fact, much of her happiness derives from her belief that she fulfills this role very well. No one is trampling on her rights, she says; for she is quite glad, and proud, to serve her husband as she does.

The deferential wife has not been coerced into this role, and she is not unaware of alternative ways of understanding the role of a wife. Nor is she unhappy. What, then, is morally objectionable about this type of case?

Hill argues that the deferential wife fails to understand and appreciate her own moral rights. Part of this failure of understanding is that she does not know when she is entitled to waive her rights and when she is not. The deferential wife seems to waive her rights—especially her right to being treated as an autonomous agent—in situations where such waivers are not justified. There is a close analogy here between how we treat ourselves and how we treat other people. For example, we do not have the right to kill another person, even if that person consents to being killed, because no one has the right to give up his or her life in this way. Similarly, we do not have the right to treat ourselves in certain fundamentally disrespectful ways, even if we consent to doing so.

THE KANTIAN HERITAGE

We can see that Kant had a number of valuable insights into the moral life, insights that are not only still valid today, but which helped shape today's moral consciousness. Yet we can also see that Kant went too far with several of those insights, mistaking them for the entire story of the moral life when in fact they offer only part of the story. Let us briefly summarize what Kant got right, and then look at where he went wrong.

What Kant Helped Us to See Clearly

The Admirability of Acting from Duty

Despite many recent criticisms of Kant on this point, I think we have to agree with him that there is something morally admirable about people who do the right thing, even when they do not feel like doing it, because it is the right thing to do, because it is their duty. Morality is sometimes a struggle, and those with the courage to go beyond narrow self-interest and do what is right for its own sake are deserving of our admiration. Edmund Ross did the right thing, not because he would gain from it, not because he liked Andrew Johnson or his policies, but because it was the right thing to do. Even knowing that he would suffer as a result, he judged the case against Johnson fairly. That is admirable.

The Evenhandedness of Morality

The second element in the moral life which Kant undoubtedly got right is the evenhandedness of duty, his insight that from a moral standpoint we are all to be treated in the same way. This idea is stated most powerfully as a negative injunction to ourselves: we are not permitted to make an exception of the laws of morality just in order to benefit ourselves or those about whom we care. The essence of this standard of morality is that it applies to everybody equally.

Respecting Other Persons

Without a doubt, one of Kant's key insights into the moral life was his insistence that we treat other people as ends-in-themselves, that we respect them as autonomous beings capable of reasoning and of making choices based on the results of that reasoning. This idea has been, I think, an absolutely central insight in ethics, and its impact on our understanding of the moral life has been profound. Largely because of Kant, we are able today to see the ways in which persons deserve respect for their right to think and act for themselves.

Where Kant Missed the Mark

The Neglect of Moral Integration

Kant was correct in emphasizing the admirability of acting for the sake of duty, but he emphasized this aspect so strongly that he missed something more important and often more admirable: the quest for moral integration and for overcoming the split between duty and inclination. There is certainly something admirable about people who do the right thing even though they want to do something else, but I think our moral goal should be to move toward that state where morality and inclination coincide whenever possible. As we shall see in Chapter Ten, Aristotle's distinction between the temperate person and the continent person offers a framework within which we can better understand this goal. At present, suffice it to say that our highest moral ideal should contain some idea of reconciling duty and inclination, healing the split between reason and emotion.

The Role of Emotions in the Moral Life

Closely connected with Kant's neglect of moral integration is his exclusion of the emotions from any positive role in the moral life. Emotions, for Kant, are like forces that sweep over us, threatening to overwhelm our commitment to the good and to distort our vision of what is right. Even when emotions push us in the right direction, they are still untrustworthy, for they are fickle as the wind, constantly changing direction. Indeed, even phrases such as "push us in the right direction" give us a clear indication that emotions are not part of the self; they are external to who we are as persons. For Kant, our identity as persons—at least, as moral agents—is composed almost entirely of reason and will. Emotions are not seen as an essential part of who we are as persons.

This exclusion of emotions from a positive role in the moral life has serious and undesirable consequences. First, as suggested above, it militates against the possibility of moral integration, against overcoming (or at least minimizing) the tension between reason and emotion, between duty and inclination. Second, it makes the moral life myopic, for often it is only through emotion that we can see suffering that otherwise would be hidden. Our emotions help us to perceive the world; they do not just block perception. Third, often in the moral life what is needed most is an emotional response, which is precisely what Kant seems least equipped to give. Often, we cannot do anything to help a person in pain, but we can *care* and feel *compassion* for their suffering. Kant's ethics has little room for such emotive responses.

The Place of Consequences in the Moral Life

Kant wanted, for good reasons, to insulate the moral life from the vicissitudes of everyday life. If the moral worth of our actions depended on consequences, it would make morality a matter of chance, of luck. Yet in his attempt to insulate moral worth from chance, Kant seems to have gone too far. He provided us with part of the story, an important part for assessing the moral worth of the agent's intention, but he mistook a part for the whole story. As we saw in the previous chapter, consequences do count. It is to Kant's credit that he saw that they were not the only thing that counted, but he failed to provide an adequate account of their full role in the moral life.

Bibliographical Essay

Probably the most influential of **Kant's works in ethics** is his *Groundwork of a Metaphysics of Morals;* H. J. Paton has done an excellent translation and commentary, published as *The Moral Law* (London: Hutchinson University Press, 1948). Robert Paul Wolff edited a helpful volume containing the *Groundwork* and a number of classic critical essays in his *Kant: Foundations of the Metaphysics of Morals. Text and Critical Essays* (Indianapolis: Bobbs-Merrill, 1969). Wolff's own commentary on the *Groundwork* is published as *The Autonomy of Reason* (New York: Harper Torchbooks, 1973). W. D. Ross's *Kant's Ethical Theory* (Oxford: Clarendon Press, 1964) and most of Bruce Aune's *Kant's Theory of Morals* (Princeton, N.J.: Princeton University Press, 1979) also provide excellent commentaries on the *Groundwork.* Most recently, Thomas E. Hill's *Dignity and Practical Reason in Kant's Moral Theory* (Ithaca, N.Y.: Cornell University Press, 1992) offers an insightful analysis of many of the main themes in the *Groundwork.* H. B. Acton's *Kant's Moral Philosophy* (London: Macmillan, 1970) provides a good, short introduction to Kant's ethics.

The *Groundwork* is just what its title implies: a groundwork or foundation for later work in ethics. Kant completed it with two works: his *Metaphysical Elements of Justice,* translated by John Ladd (Indianapolis: Bobbs-Merrill, 1965) and his *Doctrine of Virtue,* translated by Mary Gregor (Philadelphia: University of Pennsylvania Press, 1964). The general place of ethics in Kant's large philosophy is developed in his *Critique of Practical Reason,* translated by Lewis White Beck (Indianapolis: Bobbs-Merrill, 1956). See Lewis White Beck's *A Commentary on Kant's 'Critique of Practical Reason'* (Chicago: University of Chicago Press, 1960) for a thorough introduction to this important work of Kant's. His views on a number of ethical issues also are found in his *Lectures on Ethics,* translated by Louis Infield (New York: Harper and Row, 1961), the often neglected *Anthropology from a Pragmatic Point of View* (The Hague: Martinus Nijhoff, 1974) in an excellent translation by Mary Gregor, and his *Religion within the Limits of Reason Alone,* translated by Theodore M. Green and Hoyt H. Hudson (New York: Harper and Row, 1960), with a superb introductory essay on Kant's ethics and religion by John Silber. His moral philosophy is rounded out by his political writings, which have been translated and edited in a helpful anthology by Hans Reiss as *Kant's Political Writings* (Cambridge: Cambridge University Press, 1977).

There are many **contemporary followers of Kant.** Perhaps the most influential philosopher who works, broadly speaking, within the Kantian tradition is **John Rawls,** especially his *Theory of Justice* (Cambridge: Harvard University Press, 1971). Some of the most interesting and sensitive work in the Kantian tradition includes **Thomas E. Hill, Jr.**'s essays, especially "Servility and Self-Respect," reprinted in his *Autonomy and Self-Respect* (Cambridge: Cambridge University Press, 1991) and his *Dignity and Practical Reason in Kant's Moral Theory* (Ithaca, N.Y.: Cornell University Press, 1992); **Onora O'Neill's** numerous essays collected in her *Constructions of Reason* (Cambridge: Cambridge University Press, 1989) as well as her earlier work, *Acting on Principle* (New York: Columbia University Press, 1975, published under the name of Onora Nell), which addresses the question of how Kant's categorical imperative actually can be applied to specific actions; and **Barbara Herman**'s essays, "On the Value of Acting from the Motive of Duty," *Philosophical Review*, Vol. 90 (1981), pp. 358–382; "The Practice of Moral Judgment," *The Journal of Philosophy*, Vol. 82, No. 8 (August, 1985), pp. 414–36; "Integrity and Impartiality," *The Monist*, Vol. 66, No. 2 (April, 1983), pp. 234–50; "Obligation and Performance: A Kantian Account of Moral Conflict," *Identity, Character, and Morality*, edited by Owen Flanagan and Amélie Oksenberg Rorty (Cambridge: MIT Press, 1990), pp. 311–38; and her "Agency, Attachment, and Difference," *Ethics*, Vol. 101, No. 4 (July, 1991), pp. 775–97. Also, see the defense of Kant in **Stephen Darwall**'s *Impartial Reason* (Ithaca, N.Y.: Cornell University Press, 1983) and in his "Kantian Practical Reason Defended," *Ethics*, Vol. 96, No. 1 (October, 1985), pp. 89–99.

For a skilled defense of Kant's emphasis on **duty,** see Barbara Herman's article "On the Value of Acting from the Motive of Duty," cited above; Marcia Baron, "On the Alleged Repugnance of Acting from Duty," *The Journal of Philosophy*, Vol. 81 (1984), pp. 179–219; and Onora O'Neill's "Kant After Virtue," in her *Constructions of Reason*, cited above. On Kant's interest in the **virtues,** see Robert Louden's "Kant's Virtue Ethics," *Philosophy*, Vol. 61 (1986), pp. 473–89. On Kant's notion of **respect,** see especially Stephen Darwall's, "Two Kinds of Respect," *Ethics*, Vol. 88, No. 1 (October, 1977), pp. 36–49. On some of the difficulties surrounding the issue of **using persons as a mere means,** see especially Nancy (Ann) Davis' "Using Persons and Common Sense," *Ethics*, Vol. 94, No. 3 (April, 1984), pp. 387–406.

The contrasting views of **suicide** are to be found in Thomas E. Hill, Jr., "Self-Regarding Suicide: A Modified Kantian View," in his *Autonomy and Self-Respect* (Cambridge: Cambridge University Press, 1991), pp. 85–103, and Richard B. Brandt, "The Morality and Rationality of Suicide," in his *Morality, Utilitarianism, and Rights* (Cambridge: Cambridge University Press, 1992), pp. 315–35. For an excellent collection of philosophical essays on the morality of suicide which includes Brandt's piece, see *Suicide: Right or Wrong?*, edited by John Donnelly (Buffalo, New York: Prometheus Books, 1990).

Citations. The example of Edmund Ross is drawn from chapter six of John F. Kennedy's *Profiles in Courage* (New York: Harper and Row, 1955). Kant's example of the man "overclouded by sorrows," comes from Paton's translation of the *Groundwork, The Moral Law,* p. 64. The discussion of Eichmann's view on Kant comes from A. Zvie Bar-On, "Measuring Responsibility," *The Philosophical Forum,* Vol. XVI, Nos. 1–2 (Fall-Winter), 1984–85) pp. 95–109. Hill's description of the deferential wife is found in his "Servility and Self-Respect," *Autonomy and Self-Respect,* pp. 5–6.

Discussion Questions

1. Recall your response in the Ethical Inventory to statement 27 ("If someone tries to do the right thing but it works out badly, that person still deserves moral credit for trying") and your rating of statement 30 ("It is important to do the right thing *for the right reason.*")
   (a) How important are intentions in the moral life? Should moral credit depend solely on intentions? Why or why not?
   (b) Have your ratings of these items changed after reading this chapter? If so, in what way? If your ratings have not changed, are your reasons for your ratings any different now than they were when you first responded to this statement?
2. Recall your response to statement 32 in the Ethical Inventory: "What is fair for one is fair for all."
   (a) Has your rating of this item changed after reading this chapter? If so, in what way? If your rating has not changed, are your reasons for your rating any different now than they were when you first responded to this statement?
   (b) When, if ever, should exceptions be made to moral rules? How does your answer to this question compare with your rating of statement 26?
3. What was your initial response to statement 33 that "People should always be treated with respect?"
   (a) What does it mean to treat someone with respect? Does respecting people mean being nice to them? Explain. When, if ever, are you justified in not respecting someone? Explain.
   (b) Has your rating of this item changed after reading this chapter? If so, in what way? If your rating has not changed, are your

reasons for your rating any different now than they were when you first responded to this statement?

4. Recall your rating of statement 34: "We should never use other people merely as a means to our own goals."
   (a) What does it mean to use someone merely as a means? Do you think this is a common attitude in our society?
   (b) Has your rating of this item changed after reading this chapter? If so, in what way? If your rating has not changed, are your reasons for your rating any different now than they were when you first responded to this statement?

5. Kant says that it is never right to tell a lie, even to save a life. Is it always right to tell the truth, even if it hurts or destroys someone else? What matters more, the life of an individual or the majesty of the moral law?

6. Why should you tell your sexual partner(s) that you have (or are at risk for) AIDS? Why not conceal this information for as long as possible? What would Kant say that you should do? Why?

7. Is a "conscientious Nazi" who does his duty for duty's sake obeying the categorical imperative or parodying it? Explain the reasons for your answer. Give an example of a contemporary equivalent of the "conscientious Nazi."

8. Use Kant's notion of a maxim to show what, if anything, is wrong with cheating on the final exam in a course that you do not like and from which you feel you will not benefit. How would Kant's approach to this kind of example differ from the approaches of the ethical egoist and the utilitarian? Which comes closest to your own position on the issue?

9. Drawing on your own experience, give a clear-cut example of a case in which one person is using another person merely as a means; then give an equally clear-cut example of a case in which a person is respecting another person as an end-in-him/herself. Is it possible to live a life in which you do not use other people merely as a means? Why or why not?

10. In the movie *The Color Purple*, the issue of self-respect plays a central role. Indeed, one of the central themes of the movie is Celie's movement from servility to self-respect. How would you assess each of the major characters in terms of self-respect? What role does fighting (and violence) play in the formation and destruction of self-respect? What role do loving relationships play in the strengthening of self-respect?

CHAPTER 8

The Ethics of Rights: Contemporary Theories

When the founders of the United States stated in the Declaration of Independence that certain rights were inalienable, they were at the forefront of a moral movement that continues to exert a profound impact on American society today. Indeed, at the same time as the Americans were implementing the notion of rights as one of the cornerstones of our democracy, the French also were developing their own equivalent to our Declaration of Independence, their Declaration of the Rights of Man and Citizen. Thus two of the most influential political documents of the modern age take the notion of rights as the central concept upon which their political organizations are built.

Nor does the interest in rights remain restricted to the seventeenth and eighteenth centuries. The second half of this century has witnessed a major resurgence of interest in the notion of human rights. In our own country, issues of rights play a central role in our political life. The civil rights movement from the sixties onward has had a profound impact on American society—and, as its name implies, it took *rights* as the cornerstone upon which the rebuilding of our society was to be based. More recently, issues about the rights of women and disadvantaged minorities, especially in the workplace, have been matters of national debate. The controversy over abortion often has been posed as a conflict of rights—the woman's right to privacy pitted against the fetus's right to life. With increasing medical advancement, we now are discussing whether persons have a right to die. Powerful groups in America still strongly champion the right to bear arms. Every year in our neighborhood, there is a gay rights parade. Discussions about using animals in research and testing often are phrased in terms of animal rights. The language of rights, in other words, has become the *lingua franca*, the common language, in terms of which we discuss our domestic political lives.

Nor has talk about rights been confined to domestic issues. Human rights increasingly became a concern in American foreign policy in the last two decades. Our policy toward the Soviet Union, for example, was shaped profoundly by what we perceived as its neglect of human rights. In our dealings with Latin American countries, we have shown a steady, even if selective, concern with their internal human rights policies.

Nor are appeals to rights limited solely to American foreign policy. The controversy in the Middle East often is framed as a conflict between Israel's right to secure borders and the Palestinians' right to a homeland. Eastern European countries talk of their right to self-determination. Shortly after its founding, the United Nations approved its Universal Declaration of Human Rights, encompassing and going beyond our own Bill of Rights. Interestingly, we have never ratified this broader declaration of human rights.

Nor, finally, is rights talk confined to the strictly political realm. We talk of fishing rights, of mineral exploration rights, of patent rights, and of many other rights that regulate our commercial interactions. This book is protected by a copyright.

Discourse about rights, in other words, is pervasive in our society. We often see our relationships with one another in terms of rights, and occasionally even see animals and the natural environment in those terms. *The language of rights has proved to be the most powerful language for a moral change in the twentieth century.* In this chapter, we shall look at a number of issues which lie at the heart of contemporary rights theory: theories about where rights come from, the various types of rights, how we determine what rights we have, and how we deal with conflicts of rights.

RIGHTS: SOME INITIAL DISTINCTIONS

Rights, Entitlements, Claims, Duties, and Responsibilities

Rights express a certain kind of relationship between two parties, the *right-holders* and the *right-observers*. Rights thus have two faces, depending on whether they are viewed from the perspective of the holder of the right or from the standpoint of those with whom the right-holder is interacting.

From the standpoint of the right-holder, a right is a permission to act (Nozick), an *entitlement* "to act, to exist, to enjoy, to demand" (McCloskey). The right-holder is entitled to *claim* whatever is covered or guaranteed by the right (Feinberg). When Rosa Parks refused to ride in the back of the bus in Montgomery in 1954, she was claiming that she had a right to sit wherever

The work of John Locke (1632–1704) on human rights had a profound effect on the American Declaration of Independence.

there was a vacant seat. She was entitled to choose where she wanted to sit without regard to its being among white passengers.

From the standpoint of the right-observers, the right usually imposes a correlative *duty* or *obligation* upon them. That duty may be either negative (to refrain from interfering with the right-holder's exercise of the right) or positive (to assist in the successful exercise of the right), depending on the nature and scope of the right.

Finally, and perhaps most controversially, to have a right may entail certain *responsibilities* on the part of the right-holder about how that right is to be exercised. I may, for example, have a right to drink alcohol at a party, but

I may have certain corresponding responsibilities about arranging for a designated driver, not damaging my health, and so on.

Let us examine some of the distinctions that this brief description of rights suggests, beginning with the difference between negative and positive rights.

Negative and Positive Rights

If the duty is simply negative, we need only refrain from interfering with the right-holder's exercise of the right. If the duty is a positive one, we are obligated to take positive steps to insure that the right is respected. As such, a right (a) gives me a permission and (b) obligates others to respect that permission or entitlement.

For example, I have a right to free speech. That gives me permission (within certain limits) to say whatever I want, and it obligates other people (within certain limits) to refrain from interfering with my speech. The right of free speech is one of a group of rights that we will call *negative rights* or *rights of non-interference*. Characteristically, these rights prevent other people from interfering with the actions (such as speech or religion) protected by them. Other rights enunciated at the beginning of our Constitution have a similar structure. The rights to life, liberty, property, and the pursuit of happiness are all construed largely as rights of non-interference. The right to life, for example, prevents other people from killing us. It does not, however, obligate them to do anything positive to assist me in living or to extend my life.

Some rights, however, do more than prevent other people from interfering with us. Some rights impose an obligation on other people to do something positive for us. Contracts often embody such rights. If you have a rental agreement with your landlord for your apartment, your landlord is not only obligated to refrain from interfering with some of your actions (such as your right of free association), but also is positively obligated to do certain things for you (such as provide heat, adequate locks on doors, and so on). Our society currently is involved in a debate about whether, and to what extent, we have certain rights to minimum income and basic health care. These differ from rights of non-interference in an important way. If the right to basic health care were simply a right of non-interference, then it would state that no one was allowed to prevent us from obtaining basic health care. If, however, there is a positive right to basic health care, then someone—presumably the state—is obligated to provide us with such care, even if we are unable to pay for it. Following common usage, we shall call these *positive rights*, because they obligate others to do something positive for the right-holder.

The term "positive rights" may be misleading in two senses. First, please note that sometimes the term "positive rights" is used in another way to designate those rights which a society in fact *posits* or recognizes. This usage will be discussed below, but unless specifically noted, we will not be using the term

Negative and Positive Rights

	Examples	*Obligations toward the Right-Holder*
Negative	Life, Liberty, Property, Pursuit of Happiness	Avoid interfering with life, expressions of liberty, holding property, and pursuing happiness
Positive	Basic Subsistence, Basic Health Care	Provide minimal subsistence needs of food, shelter, and clothing; provide basic health care

in that sense in this chapter. Second, although philosophers typically talk about negative and positive rights, it is not really the rights that are positive or negative; rather it is the *obligations* that the rights entail for right-observers. Negative rights entail only negative obligations of non-interference; positive rights entail positive obligations on the part of the right-observer to do something to assist in the right-holder's exercise of the right.

Who is obligated in the case of positive rights? In some instances, these rights obligate some specific individual, such as the landlord, to provide a particular good; in other cases such as the health care example, they obligate the state to provide the service. The state must then decide how to apportion this obligation to particular individuals; in the health care example, the state presumably would contract with some individuals to provide the service. The financial cost would be borne equitably by taxpayers. In other cases, the burden is distributed in a random fashion. We have a right to trial by a jury of our peers; the state then determines by lot which particular individuals are obligated to serve on juries at any specific time. The most controversial cases of rights in our society often involve instances in which the burden seems to be distributed in an inequitable way to certain individuals or groups. Affirmative action policies sometimes are seen as imposing an unfair burden on the individual majority job candidates who would otherwise have been selected if affirmative action policies were not in place.

We will be considering several of these specific rights later in this chapter, but it is worth noting here that there is at least one philosophical position—libertarianism—that maintains that there are *only* negative rights. Indeed, many libertarians claim that there is only one right, the negative *right to liberty* which obligates other people to refrain from interfering with the exercise of a person's liberty.

Classifications of Strength

Absolute Rights

Rights also can be classified according to their strength. The strongest right is an *absolute* right. There are at least two ways in which we can understand the qualifier "absolute." On one hand, an absolute right may be one which cannot be overridden by any other *types* of considerations (such as utility or expediency) that do not involve rights. Ronald Dworkin captured this idea well when he said that rights are like "trump cards," that is, they overrule any other types of considerations. The right to life, for example, may be an absolute right. It cannot justifiably be overridden by considerations of expediency or even utilitarian calculations. We are not justified in killing an innocent street person to gain body parts for transplants, even if doing so might yield greater social utility. There may be a number of rights that are absolute in this sense.

On the other hand, there is a stronger sense of an absolute right, one which cannot be overridden by anything else at all, *including other rights*. If there are absolute rights in this latter sense, then it would seem that there can only be one such right. Otherwise, unless there were some guarantee that such rights could not conflict, we would be at a stalemate if a conflict between two such absolute rights occurred. If, for example, a pregnant woman's right to choose an abortion and a fetus's right to life are both absolute, what do we do? If one right takes precedence over the other, then that other right is not absolute and can be overridden under certain conditions. If neither can take precedence, then we have no basis for deciding what the proper course of action is.

Prima Facie *Rights*

Some philosophers have suggested that most, perhaps even all, rights are *prima facie* rights. The phrase "*prima facie*" is a Latin one that means "at first glance." To hold that a right is a *prima facie* right is to say that, at first glance, it appears to be applicable but to acknowledge that, upon closer scrutiny, we may decide that other considerations outweigh it. To call a right "*prima facie*" is not to say that it is merely apparent. It acknowledges that it is a real right but leaves open the question of whether it is applicable and overriding in a particular situation. A *prima facie* right is a *presumptive* right, one which we initially presume to be relevant but must subject to further scrutiny. Gregory Vlastos, in his article "Justice and Equality," has argued that *all* rights are *prima facie* rights, subject in principle to being outweighed by other considerations.

Scalar

Instead of thinking of rights as either absolute or non-absolute, we can think of their strength as scalar, as a matter of degree. This perspective is compatible with treating them as *prima facie*. Rather than call a right "absolute," we could say that it initially appears to be so strong that we cannot imagine some other right overriding it. The right not to be tortured would be a strong candidate for such a position. Other rights may be strong, but at least not presumptively as strong as the right not to be tortured. Even the right to life seems to be less strong than the right not to be tortured. We can imagine situations in which the state, given due process, is allowed to kill people (for example, capital punishment), but we have a much more difficult time finding a case in which the state (or anyone else, for that matter) is permitted, even with due process, to torture someone. Other rights are less strong. For example, we have a right to private property, which is a strong right, but we recognize that it can be overridden by other rights and other types of considerations. The right of eminent domain allows the state to override an individual's right to ownership of a particular piece of property, given fair compensation. Similarly, if an individual is lost and starving in a remote forest area, that person may break into an unattended cabin for food and shelter. (Presumably the person would be obligated at a later date to repair damage and replace goods taken.) The right to life, at least in this type of case, overrides the right to property. Other rights may be presumptively quite weak. Increasingly in our society, the right to smoke is seen as presumptively weak in comparison with other people's right to a healthful environment. Thus we might get an initial scale which looks like this one.

RIGHTS: A MATTER OF DEGREE

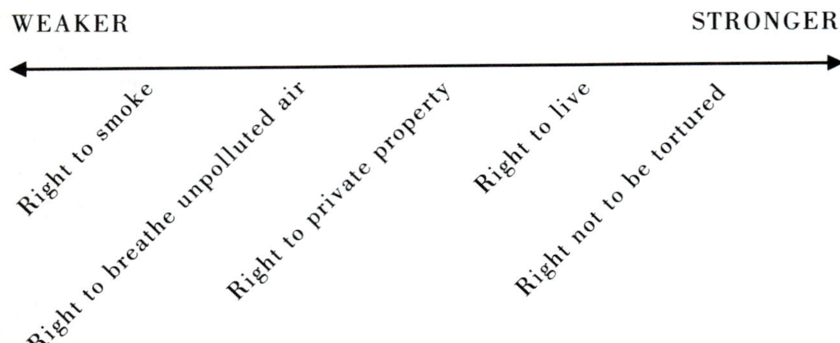

The advantage of this way of looking at rights is that it avoids making claims about rights so absolute that there is little room for dialogue and negotiation.

Types of Rights

In addition to classifying rights in terms of negative/positive and in terms of strength, philosophers also distinguish among several different and sometimes overlapping types of rights: natural rights, moral rights, legal rights, and positive rights. In addition, they and others often refer to welfare rights and to human rights.

Natural Rights

Some rights, such as the right to life, allegedly belong to us simply by virtue of the fact that we are human beings. They are *natural rights*, rights that are ours by nature. The third part of this chapter is devoted to a discussion of these rights.

Moral Rights

Some rights come to us, not by nature, but by virtue of acceptance of a particular ethical system, such as egoism or Kantianism or utilitarianism. Acknowledgment of these rights is dependent on acceptance of the ethical system from which they derive. In the fourth section of this chapter, we shall examine some attempted derivations of moral rights within Kantian and utilitarian frameworks.

Legal Rights

Many of the rights we enjoy are dependent upon our legal system. The right to protection from unlawful search and seizure is, for example, a right spelled out in our Bill of Rights and further articulated through laws, statutes, and court decisions. These rights are no longer in force when one is beyond the jurisdiction of the legal system within which they are articulated.

Legal rights may overlap with natural rights and moral rights insofar as legal rights embody natural or moral rights. The natural right to liberty may be embodied in specific legal rights that protect such activities as public speaking or publishing. If the legal right is abolished, the natural right remains. Legal rights also may guarantee things that go beyond natural or moral rights. For example, we now have a legal right to a smoke-free environment on all commercial domestic flights in the United States, but no one would want to maintain that it is a *natural* right.

Positive Rights

This meaning of positive rights is quite different from the one given above. Positive rights, in this context, are those rights which are in fact guaranteed by our society, through its laws and other institutions. It includes legal rights. A major school of jurisprudence, *legal positivism*, maintains that the only rights we have are those that are explicitly guaranteed (posited) by our legal system.

Unless otherwise noted, when there term "positive rights" is used in the rest of this chapter, it will be meant in the earlier sense that contrasted with negative rights. We will *not* be using the term here in the sense that legal positivism uses it. You should be aware that other books may use the term in this second sense.

Welfare Rights/Rights to Well-Being

The terms "welfare rights" and "rights to well-being" are of relatively recent vintage, and often refer to those positive rights to subsistence (food, shelter, clothing), health care, and education. The notion of welfare rights usually is grounded in some account of basic human needs. Some philosophers claim that welfare rights are a subdivision of natural rights.

Human Rights

The term "human rights" is defined less clearly than some of the preceding notions, but the dominant usage today seems to be roughly equivalent to the idea of natural rights. Within the context of American foreign policy, human rights usually refers to certain fundamental natural rights such as freedom of religion, freedom from torture, and freedom to emigrate. It usually does not refer to positive welfare rights such as the right to health care.

THE JUSTIFICATION OF NATURAL RIGHTS

In the last sixty years, we have seen several tragic situations in which the issue of human rights has arisen in a particularly perplexing and disturbing way. Think of the atrocities of the Third Reich against Jews, Gypsies, homosexuals, Poles, and others, all of whom the Germans attempted either to exterminate or to enslave—in large measure through actions that were first approved by German legislatures. Recall the situation of African-Americans before the civil rights movement, when they were systematically and legally discriminated against. Think of the conditions under which blacks and people of mixed racial backgrounds live in South Africa—until recently, under the sanction of the laws which supported apartheid. All three of these situations share a common characteristic: they all involve *legally sanctioned* mistreatment of particular groups of people.

The fact that this mistreatment generally did not involve violating laws raises important questions for a philosophy of human rights. Do people have rights even when such rights are denied by their country's laws? Defenders of human rights have argued that the various persecuted groups mentioned above did have rights which their governments failed to recognize. Yet if they did have rights, then these rights must have some foundation that is independent of the particular governments and societies that recognize (or fail to recognize) them. Many theorists have tried to establish a foundation for human rights that is so secure that it justifies claiming that people have certain fundamental rights even if their government and society fail to acknowledge those rights. They see those rights as belonging to people simply by virtue of their nature. Such rights are **natural rights.** Those in this tradition offer different accounts of the foundation of natural rights. Some see their foundation as self-evident, some claim they are grounded in God's will or the natural law, while others see rights as based in some characteristic of the person, such as the ability to choose. However, they all agree that at least some rights belong to us simply by virtue of the fact that we are human beings and thus possess a human nature.

Broadly speaking, there have been four main approaches to establishing and justifying natural rights: (1) the appeal to self-evidence, (2) the appeal to a divine sanction or guarantee, (3) the appeal to a natural law, and (4) the appeal to human nature. These are not mutually exclusive and are sometimes combined to reinforce one another. Let us examine each of these approaches.

Self-Evidence

When the authors of the Declaration of Independence declared that it was "self-evident" that we possessed certain inalienable rights such as the rights to life, liberty, and the pursuit of happiness, they were articulating an approach to rights that is still prevalent today. Even such a staunch defender of rights as Ronald Dworkin simply takes the *existence* of rights for granted in his *Taking Rights Seriously*, dismissing those who question their existence as outside of "orthodox political theory" (p. 184). Similarly, Robert Nozick, whose *Anarchy, State, and Utopia* (1974) is one of the most influential defenses of rights theory among contemporary philosophers, takes the existence of rights to be self-evident. This *appeal to self-evidence* is an understandable one, for some things appear so obvious to some of us that it is hard to understand how anyone could question them. The United Nations Universal Declaration of Human Rights (1948) similarly offers no arguments in support of its long list of human rights, but instead simply seems to take their existence for granted as obvious to all.

The difficulty with this claim to self-evidence is that, even if it is true, it is usually unhelpful. The controversial cases are the ones that we need help with, and it is these cases that are *not* self-evident to a significant number of people. Indeed, with the advantage of hindsight, we wonder how some of the founders of our country could have held the right to liberty to be self-evident and yet approved of slavery.

There is a further disadvantage to appeals to self-evidence. Most of the controversy about rights centers around the question of precisely *which* rights are justified. If we can begin with something more specific, more determinate than an appeal to self-evidence, then we are more likely to be able to shed light on the issue of which specific rights count as natural rights. As we shall see, the appeal to human nature offers a brighter prospect in this regard.

Excursus on Natural Law Ethics

Throughout history, the appeal to natural law was not limited to natural rights. It also served to provide a powerful justification for other aspects of the moral code as well. Indeed, in certain traditions (such as Roman Catholicism) it continues today. The Catholic Church's prohibition of birth control, for example, is grounded in a view of the natural order that maintains that the sexual act is oriented naturally toward procreation and that anything which thwarts that purpose is immoral. Similar objections have been advanced against homosexuality.

Philosophically, one of the most interesting things about this tradition is that it bridges the fact/value dichotomy, the gap between "is" and "ought." Because the natural order of things is created by God, it is fundamentally good. Thus to call something "natural" is to attach a normative as well as a descriptive label to it. It says that something is good, not simply that it is.

Divine Foundations

Some of the earliest formulations of strong doctrines of natural rights saw them as being founded in God—indeed, the framers of our Constitution thought that it was self-evident that "all men . . . are endowed by their Creator with certain inalienable rights." Similarly, John Locke, whose *Two Treatises on Government* is among the major formative documents in modern political theory, saw God as the ultimate source and foundation of human rights.

We already have alluded to one of the benefits of claiming a divine foundation for rights: initially, appeals to rights often were advanced by citizens against the Crown, which claimed divine sanction for itself. In order to put some limitations on the rights of kings, justification of the rights of citizens must have at least as strong a foundation—hence the need to justify rights as divinely sanctioned. Anything less would have failed to override the right of monarchs to do whatever they wanted to their subjects. A divine foundation for human rights offers the strongest imaginable basis for claims of natural rights insofar as there is (by definition) no stronger power imaginable than God to guarantee those rights.

One of the other attractive aspects of this tradition, in addition to the power associated with a divine foundation for human rights, is that it places rights firmly in the basic structure of the moral universe. Since rights come from God, they are part of the deep structure of the world rather than merely superficial phenomena.

This foundation is quite powerful for many theists, but it suffers from drawbacks for believers and unbelievers alike. The issue for non-theists, whether they be atheists or agnostics, is obvious: since they do not believe in God, they will not be convinced to take human rights more seriously because those rights are alleged to be founded in God's will. Yet theists have difficulties with this proposed foundation for human rights as well. Many people believe in God without claiming to know God's mind. Even if rights came from God, how are we to know *which* rights God ordained? Indeed, it is not even clear that God, or the divine, speaks the language of rights in many traditions. One is hard-pressed to find references to rights in the New Testament or in the work of Confucius or in many Native American religious traditions, to name but a few. It is not that these traditions are opposed to human rights; rather, it is simply historically their message was not presented in terms of rights at all. One can deduce certain conclusions about rights from their original beliefs, but those implications are in a language foreign to the original.

Natural Law

It is a small step from claims about the divine foundation of human rights to attempts to base human rights in some notion of natural law. The natural order, at least insofar as it is uncorrupted by evil, was created by God. Consequently, there is an important (if limited) sense in which the natural is necessarily good. Anything that comes from an all-good source (that is, God) must be good insofar as it is true to its origins. Furthermore, in many religious traditions, the natural order is oriented toward a final purpose or goal, union with the divine, which is necessarily good. Once the goodness of the natural order is established in this way, it is a short step to claiming that people are entitled (that is, have a right) to whatever fulfills the natural order.

Appeals to natural law do not have to have a theistic foundation, but those which dispense with any theistic underpinnings encounter a difficulty not present for theistic theories of natural law and rights. The theistic approach to natural rights is based on a notion of the natural order as fundamentally good (because it comes from, and is oriented toward, the divine). Non-theistic approaches to natural law need some way of establishing that the natural order is fundamentally good. Without this foundation, there is no basis for reaching a normative conclusion about the rights without committing the naturalistic fallacy. (Recall that the *naturalistic fallacy* involves illicitly drawing a normative conclusion about what ought to be from a set of purely descriptive premises about what is the case). Certain versions of naturalism in ethics attempt to avoid this difficulty by adding an additional premise to such arguments, asserting that the natural order is in some fundamental way good.

Human Nature

In the last few decades, many arguments in support of rights as primary have not depended on appeals to self-evidence, God, or a notion of natural law with a theistic underpinning; rather, they have focused on the way in which some fundamental characteristic, or group of characteristics, of human nature (and perhaps some of the nature of other types of beings as well) entails the recognition of their rights. Most of these characteristics, which we shall call **rights-conferring properties,** are ones we think of as distinctively human: the ability to reason, the capability of making free choices, the ability to have interests and to make plans, and the capability of being autonomous. Some, such as the ability to have desires or the ability to suffer, are characteristics that humans share with other beings in the natural world. These arguments move from the existence of such a property to a conclusion about the existence of a corresponding right.

Arguments for natural rights that appeal to human nature usually involve the following steps.

- Establish that some characteristic of human nature, such as the ability to make free choices, is a **rights-conferring property,** or a property that is:
  (a) essential to human life; and
  (b) either good or morally neutral.
- Establish that certain **empirical conditions,** such as the absence of physical constraints, are necessary for the existence or the exercise of that characteristic.
- Conclude that people have a right to those empirical conditions

These steps, however, are often only the first part of such arguments. As we have seen, to say that someone has a right is only half of the story; we also have to specify what obligations these rights establish for other people. Here there is a significant difference between negative rights and positive rights. The final step in arguments for *negative* rights is to:

- Conclude that people have a **duty not to interfere** with the pursuit of those empirical conditions.

The final step in arguments for *positive* rights is to:

- Conclude that people (the state, society, or some other specified party) have a **duty to provide** those empirical conditions.

These are quite different. Let us look more closely at each of these steps.

Determining Rights-Conferring Properties

Clearly, not all characteristics of human nature are rights-conferring properties. Two criteria most frequently are used together to determine which properties qualify as rights-conferring ones. The first criterion is: *the more essential a property is to being human, the stronger it will be as a rights-conferring property.* Some things are just not important enough. Human beings possess the ability to spit, but few would want to argue that we therefore have a right to spit. Our humanity would not be diminished by the restrictions on our freedom to spit. A good test of whether a property is essential to being human is to ask whether restricting it would diminish our humanity. Restricting expressions of religious beliefs commonly is accepted as something which diminished our humanity, as are attempts to restrict freedom of expression.

Second, *rights-conferring properties are limited to those characteristics which are morally good or morally neutral.* One can present strong arguments that human beings are by nature aggressive and violent. Yet even if one grants the soundness of such arguments, few would want to conclude that we have a *right* to be aggressive and violent. It is this covertly normative criterion which explains how such arguments seem to move from an essentially *descriptive* premise stating a characteristic of human beings to a fundamentally *normative* conclusion about a right that human beings have. The normative element is buried in the selection of characteristics which legitimately count as rights-conferring properties.

Several candidates have been advanced for rights-conferring properties. Among the most important of these are:

- the fact of being born a human being
- rationality, the ability to think
- autonomy, the ability to make free choices
- sentience, the ability to feel and suffer
- the ability to be a "self" or person
- the ability to have projects and plans

Some of these, such as rationality or the ability to be a self, are applicable only to human beings. Others, like the ability to suffer, are characteristics that human beings share with other kinds of beings, especially animals. These open the door to a notion of animal rights.

Rights-Conferring Properties and Indicators

There may be a difference between a rights-conferring property and the indicators that tell us a being possesses that property, which is the case with a characteristic like brain wave activity, used sometimes as an indication of whether a being is able to think. If the ability to think is a rights-conferring property, then brain wave activity may be an indicator of its presence. We do not have rights because of brain wave activity. We have them because of the ability to think, and we determine whether a particular being has this ability or not by examining (among other things) brain wave activity.

One of the continuing controversies among rights theorists is trying to specify the rights-conferring properties and indicators in such a way that they are neither too broad nor too narrow. If they are too broad, they will include beings (for example, animals) that some people may not consider to be proper rights-holders; if they are too narrow, they will exclude beings (for example, newborn infants or severely mentally retarded human beings) who should be rights-holders. Some criteria, such as sentience, threaten to be too broad; some, such as the ability to make free choices, seem to be too narrow.

Determining the Conditions Necessary to the Exercise of Rights-Conferring Properties

Once we agree upon a rights-conferring property, the next step in the argument is to determine the conditions necessary to the existence of that property. Typically, the rights-conferring property will be an *ability* such as the ability to make informed choices or the ability to think. The next step in the argument is to show that certain conditions are necessary to the development or exercise of that ability. Consider our ability to make free choices. If we are to exercise this ability, certain conditions must be met. We must not, for example, be physically constrained. We cannot execute many free choices if we are physically tied up! It also requires information. We can hardly execute our ability to be free if we do not have any information on which to base our choices.

An Example: Gewirth on Human Rights

All of this is rather abstract. Let us look at a particular example of this kind of argument, one advanced by Alan Gewirth in his book *Reason and Morality* (1978). It is one of the most tightly-knit and sustained arguments for a notion of fundamental human rights that has been published in recent years.

Gewirth begins with a simple fact about human beings: they act voluntarily for purposes or ends. Human action is, in other words, (at least sometimes) both free and purposive. Human well-being, according to Gewirth, consists in having the conditions necessary for performing purposive acts. Some of these conditions may be physical (absence of physical restraint), while others may be less tangible (education or self-esteem). Thus freedom and well-being are necessary to human existence. Because they are necessary, we have a right to them. Gewirth puts it this way.

> Since the agent regards as necessary goods the freedom and well-being that constitute the generic features of his successful action, he logically must also hold that he has rights to these generic features and he implicitly makes a corresponding rights-claim.

To deny that we have a right to freedom and well-being would, in Gewirth's eyes, be equivalent to denying that we must have freedom and well-being. But to deny that we must have freedom and well-being, Gewirth argues, is clearly mistaken. Whenever we claim to be doing anything for a freely chosen purpose, we are implicitly claiming that we must have the conditions necessary for free, purposive actions. Thus we necessarily are committed to believing that human beings must have freedom and well-being. If they must have freedom and well-being, then—according to Gewirth—they have a *right* to freedom and well-being.

The questionable part of Gewirth's argument is that he seems to move from a *fact* about human beings (namely, that they are purposive) to a claim about their *rights*. Critics, such as Alasdair MacIntyre in his book *After Virtue*, have argued that Gewirth's argument is doomed to fail. From the mere fact that human beings *need* something, nothing follows about their having a *right* to that thing. Rights, MacIntyre maintains, are simply "moral fictions" that claim an objectivity that they do not in fact possess. We cannot derive a right merely from a need.

There is, however, another way of reading Gewirth's argument that avoids MacIntyre's objection. Far from deriving a right from a need, Gewirth is advancing a *transcendental argument* in support of certain rights. Typically, transcendental arguments are arguments that claim to establish the conditions necessary to explain some undeniable fact. In our discussion of freedom and determinism, we encountered a typical transcendental argument: if we are to make sense out of making any choices at all, then we must posit freedom. Furthermore, we have to assume that we make *some* choices, even if it is only the choice about whether to accept this argument as good or not. Thus a transcendental argument takes an undeniable fact and articulates the conditions necessary to it.

Gewirth's argument can be read as a transcendental argument of this type. The undeniable fact is that we are free and purposive beings. If people deny this fact, they are engaging in free and purposive activity. It would be deeply inconsistent and irrational to say that we are free and purposive beings and at the same time to deny that we have a right to be such. Implicitly claiming a right to be free and purposive is a condition of the possibility of being free and purposive. We are not dealing with some peripheral human need (such as the desire for a color TV) or incidental characteristic (such as liking soccer), but rather with the core conditions of being human. Being free and purposive beings is at the very heart of being human, and it would be deeply irrational to deny that we have a right to be the kind of being that we most fundamentally are.

A Concluding Question

The value of MacIntyre's objection to Gewirth's position is that it focuses our attention on one of the central questions in the development of a theory of human rights: what human characteristics—whether these be abilities, needs, or whatever—justify claims about human rights.

We can, of course, avoid—or at least postpone—MacIntyre's objection by introducing a premise claiming that we have a right to whatever we need, but such a premise is clearly not true as it stands. Drug addicts may need cocaine, but this fact hardly established that they have a right to it. I may need a new computer, but it is not clear that there is any interesting sense in which I have a *right* to one. If there is any defensible premise that links needs and rights in the desired way, it is clearly much more restricted in scope than a general claim that we have a right to whatever we need.

The central question which remains here is whether we have a right to anything simply by virtue of the fact that we are human beings—and if we do have such a right, precisely to what does it entitle us?

Who Has Rights?

As we have seen, there is considerable controversy about the criteria for judging whether a being possesses rights or not: sentience, rationality, free will, and the ability to have projects and interests were just a few of the candidates for the principal rights-conferring property. Our answer to this question has important implications for our position on what kinds of beings have rights. There is little controversy about acknowledging that adult human beings with normal capabilities possess rights; indeed, they are the paradigm case of right-holders. If anyone is capable of possessing rights, it is such adult human beings. There are, however, borderline cases even in this area. Many of them are found at the beginning or end of life. Fetuses, babies born with only a brain stem but no higher functions, people in apparently irreversible comas, and the elderly who have lost all sense of personal identity all provide difficult cases that often are filled with moral anguish.

Let us briefly consider three areas in which the issue of rights emerges in provocative and puzzling ways: the rights of future generations, the rights of animals, and the rights of other beings in the environment, such as trees.

The Rights of Future Generations

Generally, we think of rights as belonging only to *existing* individuals. Even in the controversy about the rights of the fetus, most opponents of abortion argue that the fetus is already a person, not just that it is a future, potential person. Yet future generations are more remote, more indeterminate than fetuses. Although we know that, barring some major disaster of global proportions, there will be future generations, we have absolutely no idea of who they will be. It seems odd, in light of most of our criteria, to think that non-existent beings have rights. It is doubly odd if one further recognizes that if we treat the environment and one another sufficiently badly, there may be no future generations whose rights could be violated.

Despite these logical difficulties, there is a strong intuition in everyday morality that we owe something—at least a minimally habitable world environment—to future generations; and if we owe it to them, then they would seem to have a right to it. There is, it would seem, an underlying metaphor here that is quite powerful. Parents have duties to their children, and those children have rights vis-à-vis their parents. It is this metaphor which underlies our intuitions that unborn generations have rights, yet the logical constraints of the language of rights makes it extremely difficult, perhaps impossible, to give a coherent account of what it would mean to say that future generations have rights.

Animals and Rights

The case of animals presents an increasingly intriguing challenge for rights theorists. The arguments usually turn on two issues: (a) what properties are necessary for the possession of a right? and (b) do animals in fact possess those necessary properties? The candidates for rights-conferring properties are precisely the ones that we would expect at this point: rationality, free will, interests and projects, and sentience. Since we already have surveyed the issues surrounding rights-conferring properties, we shall concentrate here on whether animals possess any or all of these properties.

Sentience, the ability to feel pleasure and pain, is the characteristic that almost everyone agrees animals possess. Unfortunately for animal rights advocates, it is also the weakest candidate for being a rights-conferring characteristic. If the ability to feel pleasure and pain is sufficient condition for having rights, then a number of different kinds of beings—presumably including fetuses—have rights. Some philosophers, such as Joel Feinberg, have maintained that animals do in fact have *interests*, and this characteristic is one that distinguishes them from mere things. One can act on behalf of an animal, for the sake of that animal, but it is impossible to act on behalf of a mere thing because there is no "behalf" or "sake" for which to act. It is meaningful to talk about what is good for an animal in a way that would no make sense for rocks. One of the attractions of this view is that it would allow us then to categorize the level of complexity of interests and perhaps work out a thesis about the proportionality of rights to interests.

Although there is relatively little prospect of showing that animals (with the possible exception of cats!) have *free will* in any interesting sense, proponents of animal rights point out that free will is too demanding a criterion for rights. Infants, adults in comas, and so on, would all fail the test. *Rationality* is a more promising candidate, but it suffers from some of the same drawbacks that the free will criterion possesses: it threatens to exclude certain classes of human beings to whom we usually would want to accord rights. If we take *language* as a typical rights indicator, then research into possible language use by dolphins, whales, and chimps becomes morally relevant.

If we acknowledge that animals have rights, then we have the further question of what rights they have. Most proponents of animal rights argue that they possess the right to live and the right to be free from unnecessary pain. Some maintain that these animal rights are as strong as human rights; others acknowledge that animals have rights, but see those rights as less strong than the rights of human beings. The difficulty with this position, which seems to be a reasonable one, is that it then raises the question of whether an animal's right can *ever* override a human being's right—and if it cannot, then it seems pointless to attribute rights to animals.

Do Trees Have Standing?

The final question to be mentioned here is whether the environment has rights. This claim is the least plausible, for the environment possesses none of the candidates for rights-conferring properties that we have discussed here. Yet our negative answer to this question does tell us something important about ourselves and the nature of the world in which we live.

Religious traditions often have been in the forefront of the movement which has attributed something like rights to the natural environment, although it is not clear that the language of rights provides the most appropriate idiom. Native Americans often have sacred places which they respect and which they treat as if those places had rights. Similarly, a number of religions have certain sacred animals that possess something like rights. There is a corresponding tradition in Christianity that sees human beings as stewards of creation, guardians of the natural world who are charged with preserving that world.

One of the insights that emerges from the contrast with religious beliefs is that our modern concept of the natural environment is shaped largely by the influence of natural science. We perceive nature differently because of science—in particular, we perceive it as oddly lifeless and lacking in integrity. Imagine what it would be like if our only interaction with human beings were as medical doctors. Human beings would then be just biological systems showing certain disorders that need to be corrected. If we approached human beings solely as doctors (or biologists, for that matter), we would never arrive at the concept of a person and thus never come to an understanding that human beings have rights. Analogously, as we approach the natural world from a scientific or technological standpoint, we are unable even to see the ways in which the natural environment may have rights or an integrity of its own.

Finally, we should note two additional issues that are intertwined with the question of whether the environment can have rights. First, we may indeed have a moral relationship to our environment, but perhaps it is not best understood in terms of rights. The language of rights may simply be too confrontational, too individualistic, to capture the proper relationship of harmony between human beings and the natural world. Second, we should be aware that the rights of future generations also are intertwined with these issues insofar as future generations may have rights *to* the environment. When we abuse the environment, we may be violating the rights of future generations to its resources.

MORAL RIGHTS

Contemporary philosophers are divided over the issue of whether rights are primary and overriding of all other types of considerations (including other types of moral factors), or whether rights are secondary and other moral considerations can override them. Whereas advocates of a notion of natural rights usually fall into the former camp, defenders of a notion of rights as principally *moral* rights generally belong to the latter group. They maintain that rights are secondary to, and derivative of, other moral considerations—and that, consequently, rights may be overridden by those other moral considerations. On the other hand, Kantians often argue that rights are simply correlatives of duties. Within a utilitarian tradition, the existence and enforcement of rights are seen as dependent on considerations of utility. Within a contractarian tradition, rights emerge as dependent on a specific (although largely implicit) social contract and without justification outside of the community constituted by that contract. Rights do not come first in any of these traditions.

In the Western intellectual tradition, the notion of natural human rights has been subjected to a sustained critique since Bentham that gradually has made the notion of natural rights peripheral in our own day. The notion of rights has remained, but it has generally become a derivative or secondary ethical concept, dependent on something else (for example, utility or duty) for its validity.

Utilitarian Arguments for Rights

Ever since the time of Bentham, utilitarians have been suspicious of approaches to ethics that begin with rights as primary, which is not because they are against rights *per se*, but rather because they feel that rights—like everything else—are only justified to the extent that they maximize utility. Thus for most utilitarians, rights can be overridden if they conflict with other stronger considerations of utility. This understanding of rights is in sharp contrast to the position of strong rights theorists like Ronald Dworkin, who maintains in *Taking Rights Seriously* that consideration of utility can never outweigh basic rights.

This issue has far-reaching practical implications. Consider the following example. Imagine a situation in which a very small tribe of Native Americans through a treaty owns an area of land which, although initially thought to be worthless, in fact contains valuable mineral resources essential to national security. Imagine, furthermore, that the land which has a sacred meaning for the indigenous people, and the sacred character of the place precludes activities such as mining. A strong rights theorist would maintain that the Native Americans have a right to their own land and a right to use it as they see fit, no matter how much benefit would accrue to the larger society as a whole if mining were permitted on the land. Utilitarians, on the other hand, would weigh all the possible consequences of either allowing the land to remain a sacred place or to use it for mining and choose the alternative that maximized utility—and that alternative may well be the one which deprives the Native Americans of their rights.

This example is not to deny, of course, that utilitarians can be defenders, even strong defenders, of human rights. It is merely to say that they defend such rights *only* insofar as observing such rights maximizes utility. A utilitarian may, for example, be a strong defender of the rights of the disabled, but will do so only insofar as the rights maximize the benefits to society as a whole. A strong rights theorist, on the other hand, would defend such rights even if they failed to maximize utility for society overall.

Kant, Rights, and Duties

There have been two distinctively Kantian approaches to the issue of rights. The first, and more traditional, has been to see rights in terms of the obligations they impose on others. The other approach has been to explore the link between rights and respect. Let us briefly consider both of these approaches.

Rights and Obligations

In Kant and other deontological (duty-based) approaches to ethics, rights are simply the correlates of duties. It is duty or obligation which comes first, and rights follow from duties. I have a duty, for example, to keep my promises, and as a result of this duty those to whom I make a promise have a right to hold me to it. Duties ground rights, not vice versa. For deontological approaches to ethics, it is possible to reduce—and thus, in principle, to eliminate—all statements about rights to statements about duties. Yet duty is a broader category than rights, for we may have some duties (including what Kant calls imperfect duties) that do not give any particular person a right in relation to us. We may have a duty to give to the poor, but that does not entitle any specific poor person to claim a right to some of our money. In addition to such imperfect duties, Kant sometimes claims that we have duties to ourselves—but it hardly makes sense to claim that we have a right that we can claim against ourselves.

The dispute between deontologists and strong rights theorists is in part a matter of emphasis. Whereas deontologists see the fundamental question of the moral life to be "What ought I to do," strong rights theorists focus principally on the question "What do I have a right to do?" Whereas for the deontologists morality is about obligations to others, for the rights theorist it is about rights for oneself and others. Whereas one will concentrate on fulfilling duty, the other will be concerned primarily with defending claims about rights.

Rights and Respect

There is another aspect of Kant's moral philosophy that is tied more closely to the issue of rights. One version of the categorical imperative is to "respect humanity, whether in others or in oneself." To respect humanity, some contemporary Kantians have suggested, is to respect their rights as autonomous, rational beings. The most fundamental right of human beings within this tradition is precisely to exercise their nature as autonomous, rational beings, that is, as beings able freely to give the law of reason to themselves.

Notice that Kantians hold that we have this duty to ourselves as well as to other people. In an influential article entitled "Servility and Self-Respect," Thomas Hill, Jr., has argued that failure to respect *one's own* rights is a moral failing. He discusses hypothetical examples of the self-deprecator, the Uncle Tom, and the deferential wife. "The moral defect in each case," Hill argues, "is a failure to understand and acknowledge one's own moral rights." We have a duty to respect our own rights as well as the rights of others.

Nowheresville

The connection between rights and respect has also been stressed by Joel Feinberg. Although not working in an explicitly Kantian tradition, Feinberg presents a compelling case that rights are necessary for respect. In his article on "The Nature and Value of Rights," Feinberg begins with a thought experiment. He asks us to imagine a world called Nowheresville which is like our own except that no one has any rights. He is even willing to imagine that it is a world which is morally as good as possible in other respects. People are benevolent, compassionate, and sympathetic—it is just that they do not have rights and cannot make rights claims.

What if anything, would be missing from Nowheresville that is morally significant? Feinberg maintains that *respect* would be absent from such a world. In Nowheresville, no one would be *claiming* anything on the basis of rights, even if they were treated grossly unfairly. People who were denied fair trials, for example, would not protest by claiming that they had a right to be treated fairly. Individuals who were discriminated on the basis of their race or gender would not claim the right to equal treatment. It is precisely this absence of claiming that undermines respect at least in Feinberg's eyes.

> . . . it is claiming that gives rights their special moral significance. This feature of rights is connected in a way with the customary rhetoric about what it is to be a human being. Having rights enables us to

> "stand up like men," to look others in the eye, and to feel in some fundamental way the equal of anyone. To think of oneself as the holder of rights is not to be unduly but properly proud, to have that minimal self-respect that is necessary to be worthy of the love and esteem of others. Indeed, respect for persons (this is an intriguing idea) may simply be respect for their rights, so that there cannot be the one without the other; and what is called "human dignity" may simply be the recognizable capacity to assert claims. To respect a person, then, or to think of him as possessed of human dignity, simply *is* to think of him as a potential maker of claims.

To Feinberg, both self-respect and respect for other people depend on having the notion of rights. Without it, our moral world is impoverished.

Nowheresville is not simply an interesting thought experiment. There have been many societies that did not have a notion of rights. If we look at ancient Greek society, we find no mention of rights in the modern sense of that term. Aristotle does not talk about rights, and there is not even a word in classical Greek that adequately conveys our modern notion of rights. Nor do we find any concept of rights in traditional Confucian Chinese society. Do we want to say that these societies are morally deficient because they lack this notion of rights?

Rights by Agreement

Rights also play a prominent role in contractarian approaches to ethics, that is, approaches which see morality as grounded in an implicit contract freely and rationally entered into by all the members of society. Basic human rights express the minimal entitlements that are built into the social contract.

This grounding for rights is particularly interesting in light of the fact that many have criticized the rights tradition for being too individualistic and even for being anti-communitarian. Yet the contractarian way of understanding rights seems to avoid, or at least minimize, this difficulty by seeing rights as establishing the moral minimums necessary to the existence and flourishing of any moral community.

A Pluralistic Approach to Rights

Although there is obviously disagreement among deontologists, utilitarians, and contractarians about the proper justification of rights, there is also wide-ranging agreement that rights do play an important role in the moral life. *Rights establish minimum standards for our interactions with other people, a moral "floor" below which we do not want to sink in our interactions with one another.* We should not let the disagreements among these various traditions, important as they are, overshadow the significant extent to which they agree that rights do establish minimum requirements in our dealings with other people. Rights occupy a crucial place in the moral universe.

We can integrate the various approaches to the issue of rights that strong rights theorists and deontologists, utilitarians, and contractarians take. Strong rights theorists say that we have certain rights simply by virtue of the fact that we are human beings—all human beings have these rights and, at least initially, have them to the same degree. In addition, certain rights are recognized by those who accept a particular philosophical theory, such as utilitarianism or Kant's ethics. What we are finding is that, at least in regard to certain basic rights, there is widespread agreement among different traditions. Yet such agreement is of little help unless it can be translated into a consensus on specific rights. Let us turn to a specific consideration of what rights we have.

WHAT RIGHTS DO WE HAVE?

Our discussion of rights has been rather general until this point. Now we need to turn to an even more difficult question. Granting that we do have rights, *which* rights do we have? Perhaps the clearest way of approaching this issue is by refining and expanding our earlier distinction between negative and positive rights.

Negative Rights: Rights to Non-Interference

Negative rights, as we have already indicated, are misnamed: it is not really the rights which are negative, but rather the corresponding obligations imposed on the rights-observers. In the case of so-called negative rights, right-observers are obligated only to refrain from interfering with the right-holder's exercise of the right. Traditionally in American political thought, there have been three main rights to non-interference. Interestingly, the French Declaration of the Rights of Man and Citizen contains three rights as well, but only one is the same as the United States Declaration of Independence. For the French, the three main rights are liberty, fraternity, and equality.

The Right to Liberty

Virtually all philosophers believe that we have a *right to liberty*, that is, a right to pursue the projects and goals of our choice as long as doing so does not impinge on the rights of others. Everyone else is obliged to observe our right to liberty by not interfering with our actions unless our actions interfere with their own rights to liberty. We all have a right, in other words, to the highest degree of liberty consistent with an equal degree of liberty for all.

Virtually all political movements in America are committed to the importance of the right to liberty, and it is one of the cornerstones of American democracy. However, there is at least one political philosophy and movement—libertarianism, at least in what James Sterba has called its "Spencerian" tradition—which takes it as the *only* right we have. All other rights are derivative from, and thus cannot override or contradict, the right to liberty. Libertarians in this tradition are opposed strongly to any but the most unavoidable governmental restrictions. The strength and exclusivity of their commitment to liberty cuts across traditional categories of liberal and conservative. They are as opposed to governmental regulation of big business as they are to governmental regulation of pornography. The sole value that they seek to preserve and enhance is the individual's right to liberty.

The Right to Life

Talk about rights usually arises out of a context of political repression, and repressive regimes throughout history have threatened to kill those who challenged them. Minimally, the right to life asserts that other people are not entitled to kill us. Generally, this right is relatively uncontroversial, but there are at least four areas in which contention still exists.

First, although there is widespread agreement throughout the world that the state does not have the right to kill people as a form of punishment, a few countries—including the United States and some Middle Eastern countries—still claim that *capital punishment* is justified and therefore continue to practice it. A very few countries, again including the United States, further maintain that the state has the right to kill adolescents or adults for their actions undertaken when they were adolescents.

Second, the right to life is invoked most often today in regard to the issue of *abortion*. The claim is imply that the fetus has a right to life and, consequently, no one is entitled to kill it except possibly under certain very narrowly defined circumstances such as when the continuation of a pregnancy poses a direct threat to the pregnant woman's life. Usually there is little disagreement among the disputing parties about the validity of the right to life; rather, the disagreement centers around two other related issues. First, does the fetus have a right to life in the same way that adults generally are recognized as having a right to life? This debate usually focuses on whether the fetus is a person or not. However, for those (such as animal rights proponents) who hold that rights are not restricted to human beings, it would seem that even if the fetus were not a person, it could have rights to some degree. Second, if the fetus does have a right to life, can it be overridden by the rights of the pregnant woman? Since *Roe v. Wade*, the primary *constitutional* ground for abortion has been the pregnant woman's right to privacy, which is seen as overriding any interest the state may have at least during the first trimester of pregnancy and, with qualifications, during the second trimester as well. Among the other arguments that have been advanced in support of a woman's right to choose to have an abortion is the claim that everyone owns their own bodies and thus has a right to control their own bodies. This aspect will be discussed in more detail when we consider the right to property.

Third, some people—usually strong pacifists—maintain that *the right to life is absolute*, and that consequently no one has the right to take the life of another human being. Some of the most influential moral leaders of our time, including Gandhi and Martin Luther King, Jr., have espoused this belief and lived by it.

Fourth, animal rights activists and others claim that *the right to life is not restricted to human beings*. Animals, they argue, have a right to live and we do not have the right either to kill them or to make them suffer.

There is a common thread running through all four of these cases, one which suggests a deep and pervasive respect for the right to life in all its forms. Insofar as this respect is based on a conviction that all living beings have a right to live and thrive, it suggests a powerful version of the right to life that cuts across traditional political boundaries. Except for the fact that it neglects the rights of animals, the doctrine of the "seamless garment" developed by the American Catholic Bishops incorporates this deep respect for the right to life and forges a strong link between opposition to abortion and opposition to war. Respect for the right to life, they maintain, ought to be pervasive, not selectively applied only in certain types of cases.

Finally, there is a cluster of issues centering around the *end* of life that is a continuing area of moral discussion. Do people have the right to end their own lives voluntarily? Do others, especially physicians who have taken the Hippocratic oath, have the right to assist terminally ill people in voluntarily bringing about their own death? As contemporary medicine continues to improve its ability to keep people alive even when they cannot live a minimally satisfying life, this issue will become increasingly important. So, too, will the issue of how we define "life." Is life simply a matter of continued breathing, or is it more than that?

The Right to Property

The right to property lies at the heart of Western political thought since the time of John Locke. The English jurist William Blackstone exemplifies this tradition in his *Commentaries on the Laws of England*, one of the most influential documents in the development of American legal thought. He describes the right to property in the following terms.

> The third absolute right, [after life and liberty] inherent in every Englishman, is that of property: which consists in the free use, enjoyment and disposal of all his acquisitions, without any control or diminution, save only by the laws of the land. . . . So great moreover is the regard of the law for private property that it will not authorize the least violation of it; no, not even for the general good of the whole community.

Do We Own Our Own Bodies?

One of the more interesting arguments advanced in support of a woman's right to choose an abortion has centered around property rights: a woman owns her own body and thus is entitled to do with it (including with the fetus, which is part of it) as she pleases.

This argument seems to involve two controversial principles. First, is *ownership* the best way of understanding our relationship to our own bodies? True, no one else owns them. But does the idea of ownership really capture the way in which we are related to our own bodies? If we own something, we can usually sell it—but that is hardly true about our bodies. Moreover, to own something implies a relationship of detachability, if not distance: what I own is separate from me. But it seems more accurate to think of my own body as part of me.

Second, even if we do own something, it is not clear—despite the tradition of Locke and Blackstone—that we can do whatever we want with what we own. Do we, for example, have a right to mutilate ourselves simply because our bodies are our own? If we own a priceless and irreplaceable work of art, do we have a right to do whatever we want with it—including scratching it up or destroying it—simply because we own it?

This discussion is not, of course, to deny we have a right to abortion, but simply to question whether the argument from ownership is a good one or not.

Clearly rejecting any utilitarian attempts to limit property rights on the basis of overall utility, Blackstone takes the right to property as absolute and unlimited. Indeed, there seem to be no constraints placed on people's use of their own property. The right to property became the paradigm or model on which all other rights are understood.

Those—including some libertarians in the Lockean tradition—who take the rights to life and property as basic also are committed deeply to the right to liberty, but for somewhat different reasons. For these Lockeans, the right to liberty is necessary in order to provide the necessary freedom to exercise the rights to life and property. In fact, the right to liberty may be redundant in this tradition, since to say that we have rights to life and property is to claim the freedom necessary to pursue these rights. As Sterba put it, for "Lockean libertarians, liberty is the ultimate political ideal because liberty just is the absence of constraints in the exercise of people's fundamental rights."

The Right to Equality

During recent decades in America, the right to equality has been a central consideration in our political and social life. From the civil rights movement of the 1960s through the movement for women's rights in the 1970s into the most recent legislation of the 1990s about the rights of Americans with disabilities, there has been a common theme of equal treatment and equal opportunity. It is a fundamental conviction of American society, even if we fail to live up to it in every instance, that we all have a right to be treated the same.

The right to equality has an unusual logical status, for it is almost a "meta-right," that is a right which guarantees how we hold other rights. It guarantees that we all have *the same* rights, that some persons are not accorded an unfair or unjust advantage over others. For this reason, the right to equality is related closely to the idea of justice. To treat people justly is to treat them equally, not to give some unfair advantage over others.

The right to equality has aspects of both negative and positive rights. It clearly imposes a negative obligation not unjustly to deprive certain people of opportunities on the basis of their race, sex, and so on. In this way, the right to equality would prevent racial discrimination in regard to applicants for college or professional schools. However, it often goes further. If we need to provide people with equal *opportunity*, then this need may require positive action on our part to insure that such opportunity is present. At what point is equal opportunity provided? Consider the issue of minority admission to medical schools. Is equal opportunity guaranteed simply by not discriminating against minority applicants? What if societal conditions usually provide minorities with far fewer opportunities to compete equally earlier in life? Are we then providing genuinely equal opportunity to minority applicants to medical school merely by not discriminating against them at this relatively late point in the process? Considerations such as these have led some to conclude that the right to equal treatment entails positive obligations to provide opportunities to overcome previous discrimination.

Positive Rights: Rights to Well-Being

Do our rights end with negative rights? Are we only entitled to claim noninterference from other people, or do we have a right in some instances to expect something *positive* from them? If we do have positive rights, who is thereby obligated?

There have been two distinct approaches to the issue of positive rights, and these yield very different pictures of the place of positive rights in the moral landscape. On one hand, there are those who have maintained that, in addition to negative rights, we also have certain positive rights, suggesting a twofold division of rights into negative and positive rights, a division embodied in the organization of this chapter. This approach has been reinforced by critics of positive rights. In denying the existence of positive rights, libertarians and others have accepted the twofold division of rights into negative and positive rights and simply argued that one of the two categories is empty. There is, however, a second approach to the issue of positive rights which suggests that *all* rights have both positive and negative aspects. The right to life, for example, would contain both a negative element that forbids others to kill us and a positive element that entitles us at least to the bare minimum necessary to life, such as food, clothing, shelter, and safety.

Rights to Well-Being

The second half of the twentieth century has witnessed a growing conviction that human beings have more than negative rights, that they have positive rights to the conditions necessary to their well-being. Not only, for example, do they have a right to life that entails that other people ought not to kill them, but they also have a right to life that entitles them to the kind of physical security necessary to human flourishing. The state thereby is obligated to provide such security. Similarly, the right to life entails a right to the basic conditions necessary to life: a right to employment and other goods necessary to subsist as a human being. This area of rights theory is the murkiest, for it seems to open the door to an almost endless expansion of rights.

Positive Rights and Correlative Obligations

Rights theorists who both (a) support strong positive rights to well-being and (b) see rights as entailing correlative positive duties on the part of rights-observers are faced with a significant challenge. These two beliefs together seem to create what Rodney Peffer in his "A Defense to Rights to Well-Being" has called "the problem of near innumerable positive obligations." The difficulty is clear. If we have extensive rights to well-being, and if people have positive duties to do things to fulfill those rights to well-being, then everyone will be saddled with countless duties to perform actions that would insure that everyone else's rights to well-being were met.

When faced with a dilemma of this kind, we have three options: we can choose to deny either the first or the second horn of the dilemma or we can try to go between the horns of the dilemma. Each of these first two possibilities has been tried. Some philosophers (including most libertarians) have denied that we have positive rights, and this approach is certainly one way of eliminating the problem. Others, such as McCloskey, have denied that rights entail corresponding duties. Peffer argues in this direction as well, denying that certain classes of positive rights entail corresponding positive obligations. So far, no one seems to have succeeded in going through the horns of the dilemma. Yet there does seem to be a way to compromise, namely, to admit that positive rights entail obligations, but that these obligations are shouldered by the group as a whole (usually, the nation), not by each individual separately.

Positive Rights: Social Contract Rights

The notion of *social contract rights* fills an important gap in our picture of rights. In discussing rights, it is important to distinguish between (a) rights to which *any* human being is entitled and (b) rights which belong to people who live in a particular society at a particular time. The former are natural rights that belong to people simply by virtue of being human, while the latter belong to those who have them by virtue of their participation in a particular social contract. Whereas a right to freedom of the press may be part of the social contract in many contemporary Western societies, it would hardly be meaningful to speak of such a right as part of the social contract in societies that have no written language. Similarly, rights to health care presuppose a specific social contract, institutions, and practices that are not found in all societies.

One of the clearest examples of a social contract right in our own society is found in the rights of the disabled. During the past two decades, the rights of disabled students have become established firmly in our society with federal legislation requiring equality of educational opportunity. In 1990, the Americans with Disabilities Act extended this protection to disabled persons at all stages of life. It "bars discrimination against the physically and mentally disabled in public accommodations, private employment, and government services, and . . . also requires most businesses, transportation systems, public accommodations, and telecommunications systems to make changes in their plants and equipment to facilitate access for the handicapped" (Kavka, p. 262). The law raises important issues that bear on the controversy between utilitarian approaches to rights and the approaches of strong rights theorists. For a utilitarian, the rights of the disabled (or anyone else, for that matter) are to be guaranteed only to the extent that doing so maximizes overall utility. Yet the clear message of the Americans with Disabilities Act is that these rights are to be respected, even if doing so does not maximize utility in the narrow sense.

The strongest argument in support of establishing such a right as part of our social contract centers around the role of work in the creation and maintenance of self-respect. Beginning with a Rawlsian premise that self-respect is a vital primary good and the conviction that distributive justice prescribes "easing the plight of society's less fortunate members" (p. 272), Gregory Kavka has argued that in modern societies such as our own in which the work ethic is central, self-respect is achieved primarily through the recognition that comes from workplace achievements. Given that the handicapped are less likely to be able to achieve appropriate workplace recognition without enabling legislation, it is important to insure equality of opportunity for them whenever possible.

The Limits of Rights Talk

In recent years there has been a significant increase in criticism of rights-based approaches to morality. Let us consider three strains of that criticism: the claim, stemming from Bentham, that talk about rights is just "nonsense on stilts"; the argument that rights talk places too great an emphasis on individualism and is therefore inimical to the building of genuine community; and the claim that appeals to rights have no place in intimate relationships such as families or close friendships.

"Nonsense on Stilts"

When Jeremy Bentham argued that talk about human rights was just "nonsense on stilts," he was articulating an attitude toward rights that is still held today. In *After Virtue*, Alasdair MacIntyre pursues the same line of argument, claiming—as we saw in our discussion of MacIntyre's critique of Gewirth—that they are "moral fictions which . . . purport to provide us with an objective and impersonal criterion, but they do not." MacIntyre does not deny that a given society may *decide* to establish certain rights for members of that society, but his point is that rights do not *exist* prior to, or independently of, such decisions. Moreover, the very notion of rights is a social one, embedded in the fabric of particular societies, and invented to further the ideal of autonomy. It is far from universal. There is not even a word for "rights" in any classical European language until the fourteenth century; in Asian languages, it was not until several centuries later that a word for "a right" was introduced. Rights, MacIntyre is suggesting, are social inventions that claim an objectivity and independence that they do not in fact possess. One of the most flagrant examples of such covert inventiveness is the UN Declaration of Human Rights, which contains such rights as the right to "periodic holidays with pay" and the right "to enjoy the arts." Such statements of rights, MacIntyre implies, lack any justification and contain a spurious claim to objectivity.

There is certainly some truth in criticisms such as these, but it is not the whole truth about rights. If there is such a thing as a right to "periodic holidays with pay," it is hardly a universal right of all human beings that has existed throughout all time. It may be a good idea to institute such a right in industrial and post-industrial societies, but it is "nonsense on stilts" to think that such a right has always *existed* in some sense. But critics such as MacIntyre go too far, mistaking sound criticisms of certain rights for good reasons to reject all rights. There is a much stronger case for maintaining that people have a right to life, even when their society fails to recognize it, than there is for claiming that they have a right to paid holidays. There are a few rights that are truly basic in the sense that it is impossible for us to imagine how a society flagrantly could disregard them and still be a humane and moral society. There are other rights—basic human rights—that are understood more appropriately as being the result of decisions, and these we have described as social contract rights. MacIntyre's criticisms are sound insofar as they are limited to social contract rights that claim to be basic human rights.

Rights, Community, and Individualism

To see the world in terms of rights, it is often argued, is to see human beings as isolated, autonomous individuals who interact with one another essentially as strangers. Although there are certainly circumstances when that way of seeing the world is appropriate, to see the world exclusively in terms of rights stresses individualism at the expense of community. Let us consider some of the reasons in support of this criticism.

The Autonomous Right-Holder

Consider, first of all, the image of the right-holder that underlies much of modern thinking about rights. Essentially, the bearers of rights are isolated individuals who make claims against other individuals or groups. The basic claim of the right-holder is, "*I* have a right. . . ." Indeed, one finds very little talk in the literature of rights about the rights of groups or any association above the individual level. This assertion is hardly surprising in that the classic texts about human rights, including those by Hobbes, Locke, and Rousseau, all tend to depict the original state of nature as composed of separate individuals, often in a relationship of conflict with one another. Although occasional mention is made of, for example, the family, there is no real notion of the rights of a family as distinct from the rights of the individuals comprising it. Rights are essentially individualistic.

The Right to Liberty

The heavy emphasis on the right to liberty as one of the most important of human rights further emphasizes the individualism characteristic of modern approaches to rights. The right to liberty generally depicts each individual as being entitled to pursue projects and plans as he or she sees fit as long as those plans and projects do not interfere with other people's right to liberty. Each person is seen as an island, and the purpose of the right to liberty is to insure that no one imposes any undue expectations or restrictions on the goals he or she wishes to pursue.

The Right to Privacy

In the American tradition, the right to privacy has come to assume an importance not found in other countries, which has intensified the emphasis on the isolated individual. Interestingly, the right to privacy is not mentioned explicitly in the Constitution, and it initially found its way—as Mary Ann Glendon tells us in *Rights*

Talk—into constitutional law as a *family* right to privacy that protected a married couple's right to choose to use contraceptives. In *Eisenstadt v. Baird* in 1972, the Supreme Court ruled that decisions about bearing or conceiving children were a matter of individual rights and thus not subject to governmental intrusions. This decision paved the way for *Roe v. Wade* a year later, which grounded a woman's right to choose an abortion in her right to privacy. At this point, the right firmly was established as an exclusively individual right that did not necessitate consent from, or even consultation with, anyone else in the family. The individualism characteristic of this approach emerged most clearly in a 1992 California State Supreme Court that ruled in favor of a minor's right to have an abortion without notifying her parents. The right to privacy became almost an absolute moral right that eclipsed other morally relevant concerns in a situation.

The point of these criticisms is not to suggest that these rights ought to be abolished, nor is it to suggest that individualism is a bad thing. Rather, it suggests that an *exclusive* emphasis on rights has a distorting effect on our vision of the moral life. We certainly have rights to liberty, to privacy, and the like; but if those are the only things that we find salient in the moral landscape, we will have a distorted and incomplete picture of the moral life. It will be distorted, seeing people as isolated individuals when they are more than that; it will be incomplete because it fails to see the bonds that hold us together, the relationships of caring, concern, and love that give richness to our personal lives.

Rights and Close Relationships

Recall the California State Supreme Court decision guaranteeing a minor's right to obtain an abortion without parental notification or consent. Without disagreeing with the decision itself, we certainly can ask whether the establishment of such a right addresses the most morally relevant aspects of the situation. Think of the questions that one might want to ask about such a situation. What is the relationship between the pregnant girl and her parents like? Would her parents oppose the abortion if they knew? Why? Would they support her choice, even if they disagreed with it? What impact will the decision have on the relationship between her and her parents? Will the secrecy of the decision estrange her from her parents? Was she already estranged from them? What would it take for this decision to be a genuinely positive one? These are the questions which largely are neglected as long as we focus solely on the question of whether the girl has the *right* to make the decision without informing her parents.

There is something odd, critics of rights-based moralities argue, about seeing close relationships primarily in terms of rights. In close family relationships, friendships, and relationships of love, rights are usually irrelevant unless something has gone seriously wrong. In the parental notification case, for example, it is difficult to imagine that the plaintiff finds herself in a family characterized by good communication and a mutual respect for differences. It is only necessary to appeal to the right to privacy when all else has failed.

It is easy to understand why appeals to rights seem out of place in close relationships. Rights, as we have seen, establish the moral *minimum* appropriate to our interactions with other people, and yet intimate relationships are precisely those that are characterized by a concern for the other person which makes the moral minimum either irrelevant or at least much less morally relevant than other considerations such as compassion, care, or love. There is simply more to such relationships than rights, and to see close relationships exclusively in terms of rights is either to miss or distort much of what is morally significant in them. When someone genuinely cares for another's welfare for the sake of that other person, then questions about moral minimums are usually not in the forefront. Rather, the morally relevant questions are about what is best for the other person and what is best for the relationship. Usually, it is only when relationships begin to break down that appeals to rights come to the fore.

Some of the most interesting work on the connection between rights and relationships has come from the research of Carol Gilligan. She has argued that the rights orientation is a typically male approach to the moral life that is in sharp contrast with the relationship-oriented approach that usually characterizes females' understanding of the moral life. This controversy is discussed in detail in the chapter on the Ethics of Diversity, and we shall postpone an extended discussion of this issue until then. Suffice it to note here that feminists have been split on the value of rights talk. On one hand, there is a tradition in feminist thought—exemplified by Gilligan's work—that sees rights talk as typically male approach to the moral life. Those who work in this tradition have been critical of approaches to the moral life that takes rights as central because they feel that such a focus obscures the importance of caring and compassion in the moral life. On the other hand, some feminists have been wary of such a line of reasoning. They have advanced at least two points. First, even within traditional contexts such as the family, it is important to have a strong notion of rights. To ignore rights is to open the door to various kinds of abuse—abuse that they feel often is found in the family. Even the most conservative statistics on the prevalence of child abuse and spousal rape within the family attest to the fact that abuses of rights occur far too frequently within families. Second, they argue that many of the advances women have gained in this century have been based precisely on appeals to rights. To eschew appeals to rights would be to give up valuable moral ground and to retreat from genuine equality.

The Role of Rights in the Moral Life

Rights play a crucial role in the moral life, for they define the moral minimum below which we cannot sink in our relations with other people. Basic human rights establish the "floor" for our relations with any other human being whatsoever, the minimal requirements for our treatment of any person at all. It is crucial to the flourishing of the moral life that we have and respect such a set of basic requirements for our interactions with other human beings. Far from being a threat to moral community, rights in fact establish the minimal conditions for the flourishing of a moral community.

We can understand the role of rights in the moral life in terms of some of our earlier metaphors. If we return to our "checks-and-balances" metaphor, we can see that rights provide a constant check against possible abuses of human dignity, against any attempts to treat people with less respect than they deserve as human beings and as members of a particular moral community. If we were to recast this insight in terms of the nutritional metaphor in Chapter One, we could say that rights are like the minimal daily requirements given for various vitamins and minerals. Health agencies attempt to specify how much we minimally must have of particular nutrients in order to have a healthy life, but which hardly tells us what a wonderful dinner would taste like. Similarly, rights tell us what the minimal daily requirements are for living together—but they hardly tell us what a happy and flourishing community would be like.

Finally, if we were to place this discussion of rights theories within the context of our pluralistic approach in this book, we would see that the appeal to rights is but one among several standards of value. Recall the baseball analogy. Being a good hitter is one of the standards we generally employ in judging who the best baseball player is. It is not, however, the only standard. In some instances (such as pitchers), it may not even be the most important standard. Similarly, rights provide us with an important standard in the moral life, but not the only standard. They are not the whole story of the moral life, and in some instances they are not even the most important part of the story. Rights are about what we minimally owe one another, but often—especially in relationships with people we care about on a personal level—rights are not the morally most salient aspect of the situation because the relationship involves much more than the minimum. The moral life is often about doing more than the minimum, and we must turn to other moral theories—especially virtue ethics—to shed light on those additional elements.

Bibliographical Essay

The **classical source** for discussions of rights is John Locke's *Two Treatises on Government* (New York: New American Library, 1965). For a collection of critical essays on the *Treatises*, see *John Locke's Two Treatises of Government: New Interpretations*, edited by Edward J. Harpham (Lawrence, Kans.: University of Kansas Press, 1992); for critical essays on various aspects of Locke's political philosophy, see *John Locke: Critical Assessments*, edited by Richard Ashcraft (London: Routledge, 1991). Also see A. John Simmons, *The Lockean Theory of Rights* (Princeton, N.J.: Princeton University Press, 1992). For a communitarian critique of Locke, see Thomas L. Pangle, *The Spirit of Modern Republicanism: The Moral Vision of the American Founders and the Philosophy of Locke* (Chicago: University of Chicago Press, 1988).

Several excellent **anthologies** contain a number of the most influential philosophical articles on rights in recent years. A.I. Melden's *Human Rights* (Belmont Calif.: Wadsworth, 1970) contains excerpts from the Virginia Declaration of Rights, the Declaration of Independence, the Declaration of the Rights of Man and Citizen, and the UN Universal Declaration of Rights as well as standard articles by MacDonald, Hart, Vlastos, Wasserstrom, and Morris. David Lyons's *Rights* (Belmont Calif.: Wadsworth, 1979) contains the Hart and Wasserstrom articles and pieces by Rawls, Dworkin, Hill, Nozick, Feinberg, and Lyons himself. Jeremy Waldon's *Theories of Rights* (New York: Oxford University Press, 1984) contains papers by MacDonald, Vlastos, Hart, Gewirth, Lyons, Scanlon, Dworkin, Mackie, and Raz. Also see *Human Rights*, edited by Ellen Paul, Fred Miller, and Jeffrey Paul (Oxford: Blackwell, 1984), which originally was published as Vol. 1, No. 2 of *Social Philosophy & Policy;* other issues of this journal dealing with rights include reassessing civil rights (Vol. 8, No. 2); and economic rights (Vol. 9, No. 1). Also see the special of *Ethics*, Vol. 92, No. 1 (October, 1981) devoted to rights. For an excellent collection of articles on contemporary moral issues that center on questions of rights, see Patricia Werhane, A.R. Gini, and David T. Ozar, *Philosophical Issues in Human Rights* (New York: Random House, 1986).

Two of the most influential **libertarian approaches to rights** are Robert Nozick, *Anarchy, State, and Utopia* (New York: Basic Books, 1974) and Ronald Dworkin, *Taking Rights Seriously* (Cambridge Mass.: Harvard University Press, 1977). Tibor Machan's *Individuals and Their Rights* (LaSalle, Ill.: Open Court, 1989) contains a detailed libertarian defense of the primacy of human rights.

The treatment of rights in John Rawls's *A Theory of Justice* (Cambridge Mass.: Harvard University Press, 1971) also has been quite influential. Some of the most important work in this area has been done by Joel Feinberg, whose essays on this topic are collected in his *Rights, Justice, and the Bounds of Liberty* (Princeton N.J.: Princeton University Press, 1980). Alan Gewirth first fully presented his account of human rights in his *Reason and Morality* (Chicago: University of Chicago Press, 1978) and elaborated them further in *Human Rights: Essays on Justification and Applications* (Chicago: University of Chicago Press, 1982). For a careful overview of the conceptual distinctions involved in thinking about rights, see Alan White, *Rights* (Oxford: Clarendon Press, 1984). Judith Jarvis Thomson has developed a comprehensive account of rights in her *Rights, Restitution, and Risk: Essays in Moral Theory*, edited by William Parent

(Cambridge, Mass.: Harvard University Press, 1986) and *The Realm of Rights* (Cambridge, Mass.: Harvard University Press, 1990).

There have been several extended **surveys of the philosophical literature on rights:** Rex Martin and James W. Nickel, "Bibliography on the Nature and Foundations of Rights, 1947–1977," *Political Theory,* Vol. 6 (1978), pp. 395–413; Martin and Nickel, "Recent Work on the Concept of Rights," *American Philosophical Quarterly,* Vol. 17 (1980), 165–80; Tibor R. Machan, "Some Recent Work in Human Rights Theory," *American Philosophical Quarterly,* Vol. 17 (1980), 103–16.

Important discussions of the relationship between **rights and utilitarianism** can be found in David Lyons's "Utility and Rights," *Nomos XXIV: Ethics, Economics and the Law* (New York: New York University Press, 1982), and Alan Gewirth's response to Lyons, "Can Utilitarianism Justify Any Moral Rights?," *Human Rights* (Chicago: University of Chicago Press, 1982). More recently, Russell Hardin's "The Utilitarian Logic of Liberalism," *Ethics,* Vol. 97, No. 1 (October, 1986), pp. 47–74, presents a utilitarian justification of rights; Arthur Kuflik's "The Utilitarian Logic of Inalienable Rights," *Ethics,* Vol. 97, No. 1 (October, 1986), pp. 75–87, criticizes Hardin and pursues an alternative consequentialist path to the justification of inalienable rights. Hardin's position is developed further in his *Morality within the Limits of Reason* (Chicago: University of Chicago Press, 1988), especially chapters three and four. Richard B. Brandt's *Morality, Utilitarianism, and Rights* (Cambridge: Cambridge University Press, 1992) contains two of his most important essays on the place of rights in utilitarianism, "The Concept of a Moral Right and Its Function" and "Utilitarianism and Moral Rights."

For a provocative contemporary **critique of the appeals to rights,** see Mary Ann Glendon's *Rights Talk. The Impoverishment of Political Discourse* (New York: Free Press, 1991); chapter three contains a fascinating history of the development of the right to privacy which forms the basis for my treatment of that topic here. The connection between appeals to rights and individualism is discussed in critical detail in C.B. Macpherson, *The Political Theory of Possessive Individualism: Hobbes to Locke* (Oxford: Clarendon Press, 1962). More recently, Joseph Raz has pursued this line of criticism in his "Against Rights-Based Morality," reprinted in Waldron's *Theories of Rights.* Robert Louden's "Rights Infatuation and the Impoverishment of Moral Theory," *Journal of Value Inquiry,* Vol. 17, No. 2 (1983), pp. 87–102, argues strongly against the tendency to see the moral life solely in terms of rights. For a much more positive evaluation of this connection, see George Kateb's "Democratic Individuality and the Meaning of Rights," in *Liberalism and the Moral Life,* edited by Nancy L. Rosenblum (Cambridge: Harvard University Press, 1989), pp. 183–206.

For a consideration of the issue of **animal rights,** see the anthology edited by Tom Regan and Peter Singer, *Animal Rights and Human Obligations* (Englewood Cliffs, N.J.: Prentice-Hall, 1976). Also Regan's *All that Dwell*

Therein: Essays on Animal Rights and Environmental Ethics (Berkeley: University of California Press, 1982) and Singer's *Animal Liberation* (London: Cape, 1976).

For the case in favor of **economic welfare rights,** see especially Henry Shue's *Basic Rights. Subsistence, Affluence, and U.S. Foreign Policy* (Princeton, N.J.: Princeton University Press, 1980). For a strong defense of welfare rights, see Rodney Peffer, "A Defense to Rights to Well-Being," *Philosophy and Public Affairs,* Vol. 8, No. 1 (Fall, 1978), pp. 65–87. Also see, most recently, the issue of *Social Philosophy & Policy,* Vol. 9, No. 1 (Winter, 1992), devoted to economic rights. Included in this volume is Gregory S. Kavka's "Disability and the Right to Work," one of the very few philosophical pieces on the **rights of the disabled.**

The link between **rights and respect** is developed most forcefully in Joel Feinberg's "The Nature and Value of Rights," reprinted in his *Rights, Justice, and the Bounds of Liberty* (Princeton, N.J.: Princeton University Press, 1980), pp. 143–58. It also plays a key role in Thomas Hill's "Servility and Self-Respect"; that essay and his later reflections on it, "Self-Respect Reconsidered," are reprinted in his *Autonomy and Self-Respect* (Cambridge: Cambridge University Press, 1991), pp. 4–18 and 19–24.

A.I. Melden's *Rights and Persons* (Berkeley: University of California Press, 1980) contains sensitive and nuanced discussion of the issue of **rights and the family.** His more recent *Rights in Moral Lives* (Berkeley: University of California Press, 1988) provides a perceptive historical overview of rights theory, including a very illuminating chapter on Mill and human rights and a provocative discussion of animal rights. Loren E. Lomasky's *Persons, Rights, and the Moral Community* (New York: Oxford University Press, 1987) develops a libertarian concept of rights that attempts to be sensitive to issues of community and individual projects. For a perceptive Kantian approach to this issue, see Onora O'Neill's "Children's Rights and Children's Lives," *Ethics,* Vol. 98, No. 3 (April, 1988), pp. 445–63, reprinted in her *Constructions of Reason* (Cambridge: Cambridge University Press, 1989), pp. 187–205. Also see Susan Moller Okin, *Justice, Gender, and the Family* (New York: Basic Books, 1989) and John Hardwig, "Should Women Think in Terms of Rights?" *Ethics,* Vol. 94, No. 3 (April, 1984), pp. 441–55.

For a thorough **history of the concept of natural rights,** see Richard Tuck, *Natural Rights Theories: Their Origin and Development* Cambridge: Cambridge University Press, 1979). For a philosophically sophisticated discussion of the **United Nations' Universal Declaration of Human Rights,** see James W. Nickel, *Making Sense of Human Rights* (Berkeley: University of California Press, 1987). On the specifically **American tradition of rights,** see the essays in *The Constitution of Rights. Human Dignity and American Values,* edited by Michael J. Meyer and W.A. Parent (Ithaca N.Y.: Cornell University Press, 1992).

Citations. The quotation from Alan Gewirth comes from his *Reason and Morality,* p. 63. Feinberg's description of the value of rights is found in "The Nature and Value of Rights," reprinted in Lyons, *Rights,* p. 87. The quotation from Blackstone is found in Mary Ann Glendon's *Rights Talk,* p. 18. Sterba's comment on Lockean libertarians is found in his *How to Make People Just,* p. 11. The quotes from Kavka on rights of the disabled are from his "Disability and the Right to Work," *Social Philosophy & Policy,* Vol. 9, No. 1 (Winter, 1992) pp. 262 and 272.

Discussion Questions

1. Recall your responses to statement 35 ("Morality is basically a matter of respecting people's rights") and statement 40 ("In personal relationships, rights usually are very important").
   (a) In light of your study of other moral theories, have your ratings of these items changed after reading this chapter? If so, in what way? If your ratings have not changed, are your reasons for your ratings any different now that they were when you first responded to this statement?
   (b) Are there any moral situations in which rights are not of primary importance? If so, describe one situation. What moral factor in the situation is more important that rights?
2. Recall your rating of statement 36: "Some rights are absolute."
   (a) If you agreed with this statement, *which* rights do you think are absolute? Why?
   (b) Has your rating of this item changed after reading this chapter? If so, in what way? If your rating has not changed, are your reasons for your rating any different now than they were when you first responded to this statement?
3. Recall your rating of statement 37: "I have a right to do whatever I want as long as it does not impinge on other people's rights."
   (a) What philosophical/political position does this best represent?
   (b) Has your rating of this item changed after reading this chapter? If so, in what way? If your rating has not changed, are your reasons for your rating any different now than they were when you first responded to this statement?
   (c) If you disagree with this claim, what other moral restrictions apply to people's behavior? Explain.
4. Recall your response to statement 38: "People have a right to health care, even if they cannot afford to pay for it."

(a) Do people have any positive rights to welfare? If so, who is obligated to see that these rights are met? How are such rights determined?
(b) Has your rating of this item changed after reading this chapter? If so, in what way? If your rating has not changed, are your reasons for your rating any different now than they were when you first responded to this statement?

5. Recall your response to statement 39: "Animals have rights."
   (a) Do animals have rights? If so, what are those rights? Do all animals have them? How are such rights determined?
   (b) Does the environment have rights? If so, what are those rights? How are they justified?
   (c) Has your rating of this item changed after reading this chapter? If so, in what way? If your rating has not changed, are your reasons for your rating any different now than they were when you first responded to this statement?
6. In his book *If I Were a Rich Man Could I Buy a Pancreas?* (Bloomington: Ind. University Press, 1992), Arthur L. Caplan has discussed a troubling new problem. In recent years in countries where it is not illegal, poor people have begun to sell some of their own body parts such as eyes or kidneys to rich people in need of a transplant. Do people own their own bodies? If they do, are they entitled to sell parts of them if they wish to do so? Why or why not?
7. Recently, a number of American firms have changed their employee health benefits in such a way that the coverage of AIDS and HIV-infected employees has been eliminated or severely curtailed. Critics of such changes have protested that it is a violation of the rights of those employees. Defenders of the policies often have cited utilitarian grounds for their decisions or, in some cases, what might be called corporate-egoist grounds (that is, what will produce the best consequences for my company). Do such changes violate the affected employees' rights? If so, which right(s) in particular? Why or why not?
8. The NBC television series "Reasonable Doubt" contains an unusual character: a female assistant district attorney who is deaf (presumably since early childhood) and has severe difficulty speaking. She has an interpreter, presumably paid for by the state, to translate what other people say into sign language and to translate her sign language into the spoken word. To what extent should governments be obligated to provide equal access to everyone, including those who are physically impaired? What limits, if any, should apply to the government's obligation to provide equal access? Do private

employers have the same obligations? Talk with someone who has some type of physical handicap. How do they view this issue? What are their reactions to your views?

9. Do I have a right to smoke cigarettes in public? Why or why not? In arriving at an answer to this question, what kinds of factors is it legitimate to consider on each side of the question? Do different philosophical traditions typically present different answers to this question? Explain. (For further information, see Robert E. Goodin, *No Smoking: The Ethical Issues* [Chicago: University of Chicago Press, 1989].)
10. The United States Constitution does not mention (let alone, guarantee) its citizens the right to privacy. Nevertheless, Americans consider privacy to be a basic human right. How would you defend this concept? (Hint: Examine Supreme Court cases on the subject, such as *Griswold vs. Connecticut* [1965] or the writings of Justice William O. Douglas. The classic article is by Warren and Brandeis in Harvard Law Review [1890]). What rights override the right to privacy? When?
11. The movie *Gandhi* presents interesting issues about the relationship between rights and ethical relativism. Are rights relative to whatever the majority—or, in the case of the British in India, the minority who held the majority of political power—believes, or are there basic human rights that no political regime legitimately can override? Why or why not? Do laws such as those requiring that people of one nationality carry special identification violate their rights? Again, why or why not?

CHAPTER 9

Interlude: Theories Against Theories—Recent Developments

Introduction

During the last two decades, our traditional understanding of ethical theory has come under attack on several fronts. Reflecting a growing awareness of the importance of personal relationships in the moral life, a number of philosophers have raised serious doubts about *the demand for impartiality* that lies at the heart of much of modern moral philosophy. Other philosophers have expressed serious reservations about *the ideals of moral goodness* implicit in mainstream moral theories. Finally, some philosophers—recognizing the importance of literature and other forms of discourse in the moral life—have voiced doubts about *the emphasis on the role of arguments* in ethics. These are trans-theoretical issues, that is, they arise as a problem in several of the moral theories we have considered, not just one.

There are several reasons for considering these issues at this juncture. First, they may speak to some of the reservations and objections that you, the reader, already have. They thereby may help to develop further your own criticisms of ethical theory. Second, these objections help to sharpen the theories themselves, for the theories must be refined in order to meet the objections. Far from undermining the value of the theories we have already studied, these objections make them more valuable. Third, these criticisms provide the background against which some of the recent developments in virtue ethics and feminist ethics will be considered in the next two chapters. Finally, these objections point to the importance of a pluralistic approach to moral theories, for it is precisely such an approach that allows us to appreciate and respond to these objections more effectively.

IMPARTIALITY AND PARTICULARITY

Much of modern moral philosophy—whether in the tradition of utilitarianism, deontology, egoism, or rights theory—essentially is concerned with providing a set of rules to guide our interactions with strangers. The principal focus of its concern has been on how we should act toward people considered simply as moral agents. Scant attention was paid to the question of whether we stood in any special relationship to other people, such as a spouse, family member, lover, or close friend. This approach was entirely consistent with the impartiality usually associated with the moral point of view. Insofar as the moral point of view was necessarily impartial, it seemed to demand that we set aside particular relationships we have with other people and treat them impartially in regard to moral matters. To do anything less would be to show a kind of moral favoritism that would be unacceptable to most ethicists.

In the past two decades, philosophers increasingly have become interested in the ethics of personal relationships. In part, this interest in personal relationships seems to have been motivated by an increasing awareness of the extent to which our personal relationships are constitutive of our identity. Who I am as a person is shaped deeply by my relationships to the people who are closest to me, my family and good friends. As philosophers began to look more closely at the moral dimensions of personal relationships, they discovered that traditional moral theories did not fit, or apply to, the domain of personal relationships nearly as well as they fit the everyday world of impersonal relationships. Upon reflection, we can see that this result is hardly surprising. If an automobile is designed to function well in hot and dry desert conditions, we would hardly expect it to function well in extremely cold and wet conditions without modification. A Hummer—the Jeep-like vehicle that American forces used in the Gulf War—is designed well for the desert, but it may be too poorly insulated to serve well in the Antarctic without substantial changes. Similarly, if ethics were designed principally to govern our interactions with strangers, it is hardly surprising if it is less illuminating when dealing with intimates.

When they attempt to apply traditional moral theories to the ethics of personal relationships, philosophers have found two distinct areas in which revisions may be necessary. The first of these relates to motivation, the second to our behavior. Let us examine each of these in turn.

Particularity and Moral Motivation

An Initial Example: Visiting a Sick Friend

Imagine that you were in the hospital, waiting after a long series of tests to find out whether you have cancer. It is summer, and many of your friends are away on vacation. There are few visitors, and your anxiety makes your loneliness even worse. Then one of your best friends comes to visit, and you feel really happy to see him. You tell him how much his visit means to you, and he replies like a perfect Kantian or rule utilitarian: "Of course I would come to visit you," he says. "I would do the same for anyone who was a good friend of mine." Imagine further that your friend then goes on, as a good Kantian, to say that it is the duty of any person to visit close friends in the hospital and that he is just doing his duty. Or imagine that he is a good act utilitarian and concludes that visiting you in the hospital would produce the greatest overall amount of good. Indeed, the friend might even be an ethical egoist who has concluded that visiting you in the hospital would best contribute to his overall self-interests.

How would you feel when you heard this reason? I know what my feelings would be. I would want to feel that my friend was visiting me because he or she cared about *me*, not because it was a duty to be performed toward anyone who was a good friend or because it produced the greatest overall utility. I would not like to feel that I was just the conclusion of a moral syllogism, but that I was genuinely cared about. Something seems to be lacking in my friend's motivation if that friend is acting solely out of a concern for duty or overall utility rather than a concern for me. While such a motivation may be appropriate for a hospital chaplain and some other stranger charged with being concerned with other people's welfare, it does not seem appropriate or sufficient for a friend. Between friends, we expect a directness of concern that makes duty irrelevant.

Moral Schizophrenia

A number of philosophers have addressed themselves to examples such as the one I have just given and attempted to isolate precisely what is wrong with the friend's motivation in such a case. In an influential article entitled "The Schizophrenia of Modern Moral Theories," Michael Stocker has argued that there is a deep split at the motivational heart of most modern moral theories, a split that he calls *moral schizophrenia*. This split is between our moral *motives* and the *reasons* that are acceptable within a moral theory.

Stocker's argument begins with an important premise. He assumes that there should be a "harmony of the spirit," a harmony between our reasons and our motives. We should be able, he contends, to value those things which motivate us most strongly and we should be motivated by those things we value most highly. Yet most ethical systems fail to permit, much less encourage, such harmony. Often what motivates us is a direct concern for friends, family, and others to whom we are close. Such direct feelings of friendship, love, and concern generally are not valued in themselves by ethical theories. Rather, such theories give value to duty, to optimizing consequences, and so on. Friendship, love, and direct caring for another person have only a secondary or instrumental value insofar as they contribute to duty, optimizing consequences, and so on. What these theories value and permit as legitimate reasons is not what motivates us. We are alienated from our own selves, from our deepest personal motivations, because morality seems to demand that we respond to strictly moral reasons deriving from a theory, rather than from particular motives and feelings that have no specifically moral dimension to them. The result is a deep split between particularistic motives of attachment and universal reasons that are essentially impartial. Insofar as morality demands that we set aside our particularistic motives in favor of universal and impartial reasons, and insofar as these particularistic motives are central to who we are as persons, morality seems to demand that we set aside key elements of our personal identity. Morality seems to require that we substitute a theoretical, impersonal reason for our own more individual, more personal motives.

Motivational Pluralism

Several points need to be made in reply to this argument. First, an ethics which seeks a convergence of duty and desire, one which promotes an ideal of striving to desire the good, is preferable to an ethics which perpetuates this split and sees nothing problematic about it. As we shall see in Chapter Ten, this idea is precisely what Aristotle's ethics of character—especially in his description of the temperate individual—attempts to achieve. The temperate person is the individual whose desires are rightly ordered toward the good. Continence, which presupposes a deep split between duty and inclination, is only acceptable when an individual cannot achieve temperance. Moral health, to return to the metaphor we introduced in Chapter One, involves a healing of the split between duty and desire whenever possible.

Second, there are times when motives of particularity fail us. When this failure happens, it is good to have more impartial motives available as a motivational backup. Let us return to our hospital example to make this point more concrete. It is preferable to have friends come to visit you in the hospital because they are concerned about *you*, because they want to comfort *you*, rather than to have them come out of a sense of duty. Yet what if their concern for you does not lead to visiting you in the hospital? (For example, they may have developed a strong aversion to hospitals because of painful childhood experiences.) It may well be preferable that they visit you out of a sense of duty than not at all. Furthermore, it may well be preferable that they strive to reach a point where visiting friends in the hospital would be a natural and spontaneous way of expressing their caring—but until they reach that point, duty will have to serve as sufficient motivation. Duty need not be external. Indeed, a primary goal of moral education is to develop the appropriate moral motivations as *internal* motivations such that we desire the good.

Third, it is reasonable to distinguish between different *motivational domains*, that is, different spheres of existence in which different kinds of motives are appropriate. It is appropriate that I visit my friends in the hospital because of a direct caring about them as individuals. Here my motivation is personal and *particularistic*, and there is certainly nothing wrong with such a motivation in that kind of situation. It is also appropriate, if I am a hospital chaplain or occupy some similar role, that I visit people in the hospital who are complete strangers. Visiting such individuals is part of my role as chaplain, and my motivation is bound up intimately with my role. We can call this *role-based motivation*. Finally, I may visit strangers in the hospital out of a general sense that I should help people in need when I am able to do so. Here a more particularistic motivation is neither appropriate nor even possible. I am concerned with such individuals simply because they too are human beings. This understanding is the universal domain in which traditional accounts of moral reasons are most appropriate. Thus we get a threefold division of domains and their corresponding motivations.

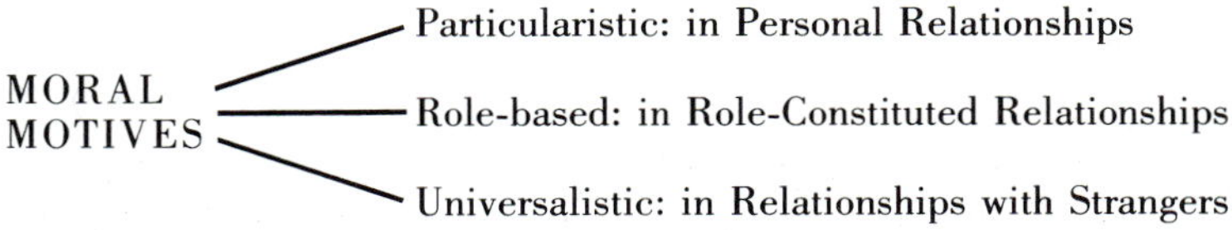

Different types of motivation are appropriate to different types of situations. The impartial, universalistic motivation that traditional moral theories espouse is most appropriate in the domain of our interactions with strangers. Other more specific motivations are dependent on specific roles. For example, as a teacher, I have a particular kind of concern for my students which is at least partially constituted by the role I have chosen. This role-based concern motivates me to act for the benefit of my students in ways that I would not act for people in general. Finally, my personal attachments motivate me to act for the sake of people I love and care about in ways that go beyond the ways in which I would act for either strangers or students. Different types of moral motivation are appropriate to different moral domains.

Still, recognizing motivations pluralism leaves an important issue unresolved. Granting that it is appropriate to have different kinds of motivations in different spheres of life, is it appropriate or permissible to treat people differently on the basis of personal attachments? We now turn from the question of motives to the question of behavior.

Particularity and Impartial Treatment

Godwin's Choice

In his *Enquiry Concerning Political Justice* (1793), the English political philosopher William Godwin poses an interesting dilemma. Imagine a burning building in which two people are trapped: the Archbishop of Cambray and his chambermaid. You are able to rescue only one of them, not both. Imagine, furthermore, that the chambermaid is your mother. Imagine, finally, that you have good reason to believe that the Archbishop of Cambray will do many great things that will benefit a large number of people and that your mother will do much less to benefit humanity than will the Archbishop. Which of the two should you choose to save?

Godwin's dilemma is an interesting one because it brings into focus two important questions about the role of particularity in the moral life. The first question relates to *motivation*. Why should I save that person? (Godwin's answer is clear: because the Archbishop would produce more benefit for humanity.) The second question is about *behavior*. Which one should I save? (Again, Godwin's answer is clear: the Archbishop.) Let us begin by considering the second question.

Special Considerations

When, if ever, are we entitled to give special consideration to friends, relatives, and others to whom we have especially close attachments? Several points need to be made in response to this question.

First, this issue is a matter in which cultural and moral pluralism come into play. We find cultural and moral traditions which value deep personal attachments highly, especially those of kinship, but we also find venerable cultural and moral traditions which place a high value on detachment and impartiality. We have seen examples of both in Chapter Three. On the one hand, the Navajo place a high value on relationships of attachment, and there are often significant differences between the way in which they treat strangers (especially non-Navajo) and the way in which they treat persons to whom they are related. On the other hand, Buddhists long have maintained a tradition of detachment and impartial compassion for the suffering of all. Indeed, for the Buddhist, moral and spiritual progress consists in part of overcoming attachments. For many of us, the Buddhist's ability to respond in a caring fashion to everyone is an admirable trait. As we shall see at the beginning of the next chapter, this trait is not limited to Buddhists alone. The French Huguenot village of Le Chambon provides a startling example of an entire village's ability to respond to the suffering of complete strangers.

Second, as we saw in Chapter Eight, there is a long tradition in Western moral and political philosophy that sees human rights as providing the limits on partiality. According to this tradition, we may show special consideration to those we care about *as long as we do not violate the rights of others in the process*. Indeed, when we reflect on Godwin's example, we can see that it might be quite legitimate to save one's mother rather than the Archbishop. Presumably they both have an equal right to be saved simply as human beings. Furthermore, my mother has, if anything, a stronger right than the Archbishop to be saved *by me* because I stand in a special relationship of responsibility to her that I do not have with the Archbishop.

Third, we should note Godwin's example in part because it mixes two different domains, the public and the private. The question would be much different if we had to choose between saving the Archbishop of Cambray or the Archbishop of Canterbury. Similarly, it would be quite different if we had to choose between saving our father or our mother. In either of those cases, both parties would have an equal right to be saved. What makes Godwin's example interesting is that it mixes two worlds and forces us to decide which of those two worlds is the more important. Here once again a pluralistic account of morality is relevant. Both worlds are important, and it is certainly reasonable sometimes to choose the personal world over the public world.

Fourth, some philosophers have suggested that personal relationships are incompatible with the impartiality traditionally associated with the moral point of view. Lynne McFall, for example, in her excellent article "Integrity" argues that "impartiality is incompatible with friendship and love." Yet this incompatibility is not necessarily the case. We may well be impartial *within* our personal relationships, just as we may be impartial *within* our public relationships. Parents may well try to treat their children equally, avoiding favoritism for one child over the others. Similarly, employers may treat their employees equally, not giving some unfair advantages or privileges over the others. The moral concerns that guide our personal relationships overlap those that guide our public relationships. The difficult issue is whether we must be impartial *between* personal relationships and public relationships. When employers hire their own children, may they extend special privileges to their children that they do not extend to other employees? Again, the rights perspective sheds light on the situation. It may be morally permissible—although not necessarily wise—to show special consideration to one's children if doing so does not violate the rights of one's other employees.

Finally, our analysis of Godwin's example in terms of a conflict between two distinct moral domains, the personal and the public, helps shed light on a difficulty raised by Bernard Williams. In "Persons, Character, and Morality," Williams presents a case similar to Godwin's, where a man must choose between saving his wife or a stranger. Presuming that the man saves his wife for some impartial moral reason, Williams wonders whether he would not have "one reason too many." In other words, if the man justified saving his wife on rule-utilitarian grounds—overall utility is maximized if family members are concerned first and foremost with the welfare of their immediate family—then his wife might well find his motivation wanting. She might well want her husband to save her because he loved her. However, when we see the way in which examples such as these involve mixing two domains, the public and the private, then we can see the answer to Williams's difficulty. The husband's rule-utilitarian considerations are relevant in the public domain, whereas his love and concern for his wife are appropriate within the private realm.

Pluralism, Particularity, and Impartiality

If we adopt the pluralistic account of moral values sketched in this book, there is a way of resolving the tension between particularity and impartiality. There is no single moral end or goal toward which we all strive, although certain moral values such as respect for persons and concern for consequences establish the limits within which we can choose our goals. Within these permissible limits, different lives may be characterized by quite different but—morally speaking—equally legitimate ends. These are expressions of our particularity, and they may vary from one individual to another. The moral life is characterized by both values of particularity and impartial values. Martin Benjamin, a philosopher at Michigan State University whose *Splitting the Difference* (1990) presents a compelling account of moral compromise, suggests a nautical metaphor to capture the back-and-forth movement between partial and impartial values. When we are sailing into the wind, we can never go straight ahead. We have to tack back and forth. So, too, in the moral life. Forward progress is made through tacking back and forth between the partial and the impartial viewpoints. Either one without the other would be impoverished. If we had only impersonal, impartial values, we would be moral automata suffering from the kind of alienation to which contemporary critics have pointed. If we had only particular, partial values, we hardly would be participating in the *moral* life. The tension between these two standpoints is what constitutes the moral life of the concrete individual. We shall examine this idea in more detail in Chapter Eleven when we discuss the ethics of diversity.

Moral Saints

"I don't know whether there are any moral saints," Susan Wolf—a philosopher who specializes in ethics at Johns Hopkins University—tells us in the opening sentences of her article "Moral Saints," but "if there are, I am glad that neither I nor those about whom I care most are among them." With these words, Wolf initiated a challenge, not just to a specific conception of morality, but to the place of morality within an individual's life as a whole. "Moral ideals," she goes on to claim, "do not, and need not, make the best personal ideals." In fact, a moral saint may well be a bore!

What makes this claim startling is that we have long assumed, not only that it is good to be good, but also that the better you are (morally speaking), the better person (in general) you are. Wolf is questioning this belief saying that if we really acted out these moral theories, the actual results would not be very desirable. We would be cardboard figures, lacking in individuality and interest. And this result, she claims, is not just a problem with some specific conception of morality, such as the Kantian or utilitarian, but a feature of morality as a whole. Morality, if taken seriously, leads to boring, uninteresting persons who lack a wide range of different interests and involvements, hopes and projects.

The Argument Against Saints

The general argument that leads to this kind of critique of saints is outlined easily. First, one needs to have *a moral theory that has a single dominant principle or value.* I shall refer to this theory as a monistic morality and shall call the claim that morality has some single, dominant value or principle the **monism thesis.** There is no shortage of these: divine command theories make God's word that principle; ethical egoism makes acting for one's own benefit the dominant principle; for Kant, the categorical imperative and its concomitant emphasis on duty form the primary value; utilitarians see maximizing utility as their principal value. Second, one needs a claim that *moral concerns override non-moral concerns* whenever the two conflict. I shall call this claim the **overridingness thesis.** Again, this argument is common to all the moral theories we have considered so far. God's command to Abraham is probably the most dramatic, but the egoist, the Kantian, and the utilitarian all agree that moral concerns override non-moral concerns.

These two theses alone do not quite suffice to produce the kind of dull, boring, single-minded moral saint that Wolf criticizes. We could imagine a monistic morality that always overrides non-moral concerns when these conflict, still leaving plenty of room for individuality *if* there were large portions of an individual's life which were untouched by moral concerns. Thus what this argument needs is some way of establishing that *in virtually any given situation for any given individual, moral concerns will be relevant.* I will refer to this belief as the **relevance thesis.** There are at least two ways of establishing this thesis. First, one might advance arguments to *enlarge* the moral ballpark, showing that it includes virtually everything. For example, if the moral ballpark is defined as including anything that affects suffering or well-being, then very little is excluded. What I order for breakfast tomorrow would become a moral concern, for I might have a shorter life if I had my first choice (French toast and thick-sliced bacon), which, in turn, might bring suffering to those who love me. Second, one might *intensify* what is within the moral ballpark in ways that draw everyone into the park. Think of the problem of world hunger. It is an intense problem that we should all be concerned with it, and concerned with it until it is solved. Because of its intensity, it affects the smallest choices we make. Do I buy the latest novel by my favorite author in hard cover as soon as it comes out, or do I wait and check it out from the library when it is available and send the money I save to a famine relief organization such as Oxfam? (The same choice, incidentally, would also be relevant to environmental concerns.) In fact, arguments of this type seem to have much merit. There are a number of intense moral problems in our world, and it seems unlikely that they will disappear in the foreseeable future. World hunger is certainly one of these, but here are others as well. Racism, torture, child abuse, and environmental destruction are but a few of the more important ones. It is sad, but establishing the relevance thesis is not difficult.

Thus we see the premises of the moral saints argument: morality is monistic; moral concerns are overriding; and moral concerns are virtually always relevant. Given these premises, we get the conclusion that morality leads to living a life that is dominated by a single (impersonal) principle to the exclusion of all personal interests, plans, hopes, and involvements. If one *really* follows the dictates of morality, then there is no room for these qualities of individuality. We now reach the next stage in the argument, which is to show that *having these qualities of individuality (personal interests, plans, hopes, and involvements) is highly desirable.* I will refer to this belief as the **individuality thesis.** Most of us would agree with this thesis, since we tend to value highly those things which comprise our individuality. If morality precludes individuality, and if individuality is highly desirable, then it seems that something is wrong with morality.

Defending Morality and Moral Saints

Several things need to be said about this argument. The first one is a point we have already made about some of the other arguments considered in this chapter as well: even if the argument ultimately does not turn out to be sound, we gain genuine insight into our own beliefs from trying to figure out what is wrong with it. I think that is particularly true about the moral saints argument. Even if it is unsound, we can learn a tremendous amount from it, for it forces us to rethink some of our basic convictions about moral goodness.

Second, the moral saints argument in fact is not limited particularly to morality. It points to a problem that may belong to any monistic, overriding belief system. Consider the person—let us call that person the Capitalist Saint—

who acts on the principle of trying to maximize profit in every situation. Virtually all the criticisms that Wolf levels against the moral saint could be seen as equally damaging to the capitalist saint. Individuality would be obliterated by the profit motive. Nothing would be undertaken if it did not contribute to profit. Similarly individuality is lost with the Communist Saint, who follows communist principles in all situations—at least until August, 1991, when communism began to collapse. My point is that the moral saints argument may have little to do with morality as such, rather, it may be an argument against living one's life solely on the basis of *any* monistic theory. But then the value of the moral saints argument is that it forces us to ask whether we can develop an account of morality that does not lead to a monistic theory. It is precisely this goal which ethical pluralism seeks to accomplish.

Third, while one way of replying to the moral saints argument is to attack the monistic character of theory, another avenue that is open is to reconsider the overridingness thesis. Several philosophers, including Philippa Foot, have gone in this direction, arguing that there are circumstances in which non-moral concerns override moral ones. Concerns of courtesy may override moral demands of strict honesty and lead us to tell people in social situations that they look nice when they in fact do not.

Fourth, the relevance thesis is also open to challenge. One of the more interesting areas challenged recently has been in utilitarianism. As we saw, utilitarianism usually is seen as requiring that we perform the action that produces the *most* good and the *greatest* amount of utility. Recall our distinction between optimizing utilitarianism and satisficing utilitarianism. Whereas optimizing refers to doing the best, satisficing refers to doing enough. Satisficing utilitarianism would require simply that we do enough, not the most, to satisfy our moral demands. While some have claimed that this approach just opens the door for moral mediocrity, such a criticism has force only if there is just one kind of moral value. Within a pluralistic context, satisficing utilitarianism may be supplemented by several other types of moral value.

Fifth, when we look at real saints, whether moral saints or religious saints, we see that they in fact are not always open to the objections based on the moral saints argument. In fact, they are clearly individuals with rich and varied interests who often experience a deep joy in everyday existence. If we look at the lives of people like Mahatma Gandhi, Albert Schweitzer, Mother Teresa, or Martin Luther King, Jr., we do not see cardboard figures. We see robust, complex individuals who are far more than the extension of some theory, which in turn, suggests an important truth: *the road to moral sainthood is not along the path of moral theory*. We do not achieve moral excellence by slavishly following a theory, no matter how good the theory is. In the next chapter, which deals with the ethics of character, we will see that there is another, more promising path.

One of the most profound moral leaders of the twentieth century, Gandhi (1869–1948) preached a doctrine of nonviolence.

Saints and Narcissists

Three additional issues that relate to moral saints remain to be considered. First, genuine moral saints should be distinguished from what I shall call moral narcissists. Moral saints respond with goodness to the moral challenges which surround them, and the focus of their concern is with those who are suffering. Mother Teresa, for example, sees the suffering of the homeless in Calcutta, and she is moved by their suffering to do whatever she can to alleviate it. Her concern is with *their* suffering, not with herself.

Moral narcissists often may behave in ways that externally resemble the behavior of the moral saint, but the focus of their concern is quite different. Moral narcissists want to be thought of, and seen as, good people, and the point of their actions is not to alleviate the suffering of others but rather to be thought of, by others as well as by themselves, as good persons. The focus of their concern in themselves, which is why we call them narcissists.

Incidentally, I suspect that there is a profound difference between the way we *experience* a moral saint and how we experience a moral narcissist. When we are in the presence of a moral saint, we tend to feel *elevated.* We feel a mixture of respect and admiration, which in some cases is strong enough to be called "awe." On the other hand, when we encounter a moral narcissist, we are much more likely to feel *put down.* Narcissists are concerned primarily with establishing their own moral superiority, and the corollary of their superiority is our inferiority. Whereas the moral saint's goodness carries with it an invitation to join in his or her good deeds with a common goal, the moral narcissist hardly can issue such an invitation, for it would simply be competition.

Flawed Saints

Finally, we should note that saints—whether moral or religious—may be flawed. Indeed, in most cases they are. Mahatma Gandhi was hardly an ideal husband, and certainly had his shortcoming in this role. Recent revelations by Ralph Abernathy suggest flaws in Martin Luther King, Jr.'s character, especially in regard to extramarital affairs. Similarly, if we look at someone like Arthur Schindler, whose courage and cleverness served him well in saving the lives of hundreds of Polish Jews in World War II, we see a flawed hero, who passionately loved liquor and women as well as goodness.

This is, I think, simply the human condition, but we should be wary of a danger here. Just because a hero is flawed, we do not have to give up our devotion to that for which he or she stands. We are all human.

Saints and Moral Pluralism

Wolf's arguments against moral saints may not support fully the conclusions that Wolf wants to draw, but they do provide strong support for our pluralistic approach to the moral life. Indeed, reflection on her arguments—and especially on the monism thesis—helps us to see the several senses in which pluralism has a place in the moral life.

Intra-Theoretic Moral Pluralism

First, recall the way in which Wolf depicted the moral saint's behavior as following from some single moral principle, whether Kantian or utilitarian. Yet our investigations have suggested that this picture is not accurate of most moral theories. Most moral theories can be understood as presenting a plurality of moral values, despite the fact that there is no shortage of defenders of monistic interpretations of each theory. Utilitarianism, for example, contains a number of possible standards of value (pleasure, happiness, ideals, preferences). Even Kant offers several standards (acting for the sake of duty, universalizability, and respect). Although Kant believed these were only different ways of saying the same thing, contemporary Kantians such as Thomas Hill in his article "Kantian Pluralism" have suggested that there may be a plurality of moral standards within Kant's ethics. Both utilitarianism and Kant offer examples of the first type of moral pluralism, what I shall call *intra-theoretic moral pluralism*, that is, a pluralism of moral values within a single theory. If a theory is intra-theoretically pluralistic, then there is much less danger of the cardboard figure of moral perfection that Wolf discusses. If a theory contains several important moral values, then there is a wider variety of ways in which individuals may realize them and strike a balance among them.

Inter-Theoretic Moral Pluralism

There is a second type of moral pluralism, *inter-theoretic pluralism*, which underlies the approach of this book and which was discussed in detail in Chapter Three. It suggests that different moral theories and traditions shed light on the moral life and that we can learn from them all. None of them is absolutely and exclusively right, but they all help us to understand better how we can lead a morally good life. If inter-theoretic pluralism is true, then there would be even more diversity in the realm of moral perfection than would be the case if only intra-theoretic pluralism were true.

Robust Value Pluralism

There is a third area in which pluralism is important, namely, a pluralism in the balance between moral and non-moral values. The overridingness thesis is opposed most directly to this kind of pluralism, for that thesis claims that moral concerns always take precedence over non-moral ones. The alleged boring quality of the moral saint follows not simply from the monism thesis, but also from the fact that (in Wolf's presentation) moral concerns crowd out all other non-moral values. Yet in a robustly pluralistic approach, we would recognize that non-moral values have an important place in our lives. The moral domain need not wipe out completely the non-moral realm.

Moral Discourse

Many philosophers believe that ethics—and philosophy is general—is concerned solely with the analysis of arguments. James Rachels, who is one of the more influential figures in contemporary ethics, states a position on the role of argument that is representative of the standard view.

> Philosophy without argument would be a lifeless existence. What good would it be to produce a theory without reasons for thinking it correct? And of what interest is the rejection of a theory without good reasons for thinking it incorrect? *A philosophical theory is exactly as good as the arguments that support it.* (Italics added.)

But increasingly philosophers are beginning to doubt that a theory is simply as good as the arguments that support it. Let us look at the sources of their discontent with argument as the sole form of moral discourse and examine the ways in which it points to a more pluralistic account of moral discourse.

Insofar as ethical reflection is equated simply with the process of moral argumentation—presenting arguments, considering objections, and offering replies—there is a danger that a number of important aspects of the moral life will be neglected. We will consider two principal areas of neglect here:

- the neglect of moral perception;
- the neglect of the place of moral beliefs in the narrative of an individual's life.

In addition to this twofold neglect, there is another liability associated with the equation of moral reflection with argument.

- The combative character of argument, which threatens to cloud the process of moral reflection.

Let us consider each of these issues in turn.

The Neglect of Moral Perception

The first problem with this exclusive emphasis on moral argument, and the concomitant concern with moral problems, is that it neglects the role of perception in the moral life. This neglect can be particularly unfortunate, for often much of the important work in morally assessing a situation is done before the argument stage. Think of the startling discrepancy in our own history between our theoretical commitment to equality and the reality of inequality in our everyday lives. While expressing a clear constitutional commitment to equality, the United States permitted slavery for decades and legally sanctioned segregation for over a century. In part, such discrepancies are maintained precisely through an inability or unwillingness to *perceive* inequality as inequality.

Similarly, think of such problems as poverty, homelessness, sexual abuse of children, cruelty toward the aged, and the suffering of animals. These problems exist, at least in part, because we manage not to *see* them. We turn a blind eye toward the poor and homeless, perpetrators do not see their abuse as abuse but as love, the aged are blamed for being old, animal suffering is hidden away from us in farms and slaughter houses. The very recognition of a moral problem as a *moral* problem involves a change in perception. Think of the role that Dickens played in shaping our perceptions of the suffering of children which, prior to him often was simply not *seen.* As we concentrate primarily on arguments about specific moral problems, we often neglect the cultivation of our moral perceptions.

Perception plays a crucial role, not only in the identification of moral issues, but also in their solution. Consider those cases in which you unthinkingly hurt someone else—for example, not bothering to keep in touch with a close friend who values your friendship. Imagine that you do not mean to hurt your friend in any way, you just do not really think about the effects of not writing. Here perception is important not only in identifying what has gone wrong, but also in rectifying the situation. In order to repair the relationship, you may well have to show your friend that you *see* what harm your failure to write has done to the relationship.

The Embeddedness of Moral Beliefs in Narratives

Insofar as we see moral philosophy mainly as a matter of argument, we usually are concerned with the way in which a particular moral belief is connected with a body of other beliefs (that is, a moral theory) or with the way in which a particular moral principle is applied to a specific moral problem. For example, would a belief in the priceless character of human life be compatible with a utilitarian moral theory? Or, to take an example of the second type of concern, would suicide ever be justified from a rule utilitarian perspective? The former concern is with the *internal consistency* of a moral theory, while the latter concern is directed primarily toward the *applicability* of a moral theory.

Both of these types of questions are important moral issues, but they are not the *only* important moral issues that should be considered in ethics. We also must consider the ways in which moral beliefs are related to the narrative structure of an individual's life. In other words, we must articulate how particular moral beliefs fit in with who we are as persons, with our individual moral identity. Let us consider three ways in which the embeddedness of moral beliefs in individuals' lives manifests itself.

The Place of Moral Beliefs in an Individual's Life

Often, our acceptance or rejection of a particular moral belief depends on how that belief fits in with our other convictions, commitments, and projects in life.

In those instances in which the new belief does not disturb the existing configuration of our beliefs, commitments, and goals, it is comparatively easy to accept. However, in those instances in which the new belief does not fit easily into the existing configuration, we may have to revise some of our existing beliefs and practices or else reject the new belief. In the most extreme cases, the new belief may demand an almost complete revision of our old beliefs. Such a revision is analogous to a conversion experience insofar as it involves deep adjustments in our basic commitments.

Consider two examples of beliefs that for many people would deeply upset the constellation of their present beliefs, commitments, and projects. First, for many of us a strong doctrine of nonviolence would threaten to upset a number of our other beliefs and commitments about self-defense, retribution, defending basic values, and so on. If we were to accept nonviolence, we would have to revise significantly a number of our other beliefs and practices. Moral discourse must address itself not only to the theoretical justification of such a doctrine, but also to the question of its place in our lives. How would evil be punished in the world if we could never respond to transgressions with violence? How would we be able to defend those we love, including our children, from threatened violence if we cannot resist with force? Similar questions could be raised about a strong belief in animal rights. If we accept that animals have rights, what does that do to our other beliefs about eating meat, wearing leather, and keeping pets? What effect does this have on our view of the importance of human suffering? Is the suffering of human beings less important if we acknowledge the importance of the suffering of animals? These are not simply questions about the justification of a theory, but about how a belief fits into an individual's life.

Moral discourse needs to address itself to issues such as these. Insofar as we see moral discourse as confined solely to moral argumentation, we will find it difficult to articulate the place of a new moral belief in the structure of an individual's life. On the other hand, insofar as we recognize other forms of moral discourse—such as stories in novels and movies, biographies and autobiographies, and dialogues—as also valuable, we will have a much richer range of discourse for understanding the moral life. We shall discuss these other forms of moral discourse in more detail below.

The Relationship between Argument and Arguer

Moral beliefs not only need to be evaluated in relation to the larger body of beliefs that constitutes a moral theory but also need to be understood in relation to the structure of an individual's life. Once we recognize this relationship, we can understand the relevance in the moral life of some types of considerations that usually are seen as fallacious.

Consider the *ad hominem* fallacy. In the traditional model, an argument is considered on its own merits, quite independently of any concerns about the person who advanced the argument. Indeed, to raise questions about the argument's author is to risk committing an *ad hominem* fallacy. Yet consider for a moment the difference in force that the same pro-choice argument would have if advanced by the president of the National Organization of Women, a fundamentalist Christian mother of four children (two of whom are adopted), or a Catholic priest. Similarly, think of the difference in force between arguments critical of an oppressed group (fill in whatever group you want: gays, African-Americans, and so on), depending on whether they are advanced by members of that group or staunch opponents of it. If arguments were completely independent of the persons who advance them, it would be quite difficult to explain the different force the same argument has when it comes from different people. On the other hand, if we recognize that moral beliefs are embedded in the narrative structures of individual lives as well as being parts of a theory, then these types of considerations have a relevance. Such considerations speak to the question of how a particular belief fits into the structure of an individual's life.

When we place this issue within the context of a pluralistic approach to moral value, this dual valence of moral beliefs becomes clearer. As we pointed out in Chapter Three, some moral theorists (such as emotivists) maintained that moral values were purely subjective. Although they seriously misunderstood the nature of the subjective (and especially the emotive), and although they mistakenly claimed that moral values were *only* subjective, such theorists were partially correct. Moral value is partially subjective, which is captured partially in the relationship between the argument and the arguer.

The Relation between Argument and Audience

Not only are moral values subjective, but they are also—as we saw in Chapter Three—intersubjective. Similarly, just as moral arguments may not be fully detachable from their authors, so too, may they not be fully detachable from their specific audiences. As long as we are addressing purely rational agents, there are no significant differences among audiences. However, once we acknowledge that we are talking to individual persons when we advance arguments, then there are significant differences among audiences—and this fact, too, opens up a place for rhetoric as the art of communicating with specific audiences. Once again, the issue turns on the way in which moral beliefs are related to individual lives as well as to larger theories. As long as one considers only the relation of a moral belief to a larger moral theory, it is unnecessary to consider possible differences in audiences. As soon as one admits that there is another dimension to the discussion of moral beliefs, namely, the way in which they relate to the larger fabric of an individual's (or group's or society's) life, then the question of audience assumes an importance it previously had lacked.

The Combative Nature of Argument

The final area in which the discontent with argument manifests itself centers around the root metaphor which underlies much of our talk about argument: *argument is war*. This adversarial metaphor essentially casts discourse as competition, attack, defense, and so on. Think about the way in which it is reflected in our everyday speech. We *attack opponents*, trying to *overcome* them before they *score a victory* against us. If we are lucky, we can *demolish* their positions, *destroying* their arguments, *tearing apart* their theories. We should *fortify* our positions to protect against *counter-attacks*.

What, if anything, is wrong with this approach? Certainly, proponents of this view of philosophizing maintain that it sharpens our philosophical beliefs, putting them to the test of critical examination, weeding out those that lack merit, sharpening up those that pass the test. And, undoubtedly, this point is true but, it is not completely true, nor is it the complete truth. Two types of objections have been raised against this set of metaphors.

The first type of objection is largely practical. If we adopt this model of philosophizing, we run the danger that the best debater, not the best theory, will win. Furthermore, once we become engaged in the process of debate, we may become more interested in winning than in discovering the truth. It is all too easy for us to become more interested in defending than in learning. When we do listen, it is in order to refute our opponents more effectively, not to learn from them. The practice of philosophizing as argument, in other words, does not necessarily lead to the truth.

The second type of objection centers around the view of the world into which this metaphor fits. The metaphor of argument as war is part of a larger picture of life as combative, competitive, a struggle for victory and dominance. Although it is still the dominant metaphor in our society, many—especially feminists—have found it morally repugnant. They contrast it sharply to a view of life as (at least potentially) cooperative and harmonious. In this alternative view of life, cooperation is valued over conflict. We are engaged in a shared search for the truth, not a contest to see who finds it first.

With a shift in root metaphors from war to cooperation, we also encounter a shift in forms of discourse. Whereas debate and argument were the paradigmatic forms of discourse in the traditional view, conversation and dialogue emerge as the primary models in this alternative view. There are no winners in a conversation—or, perhaps more accurately, there are no losers. It is an activity we engage in together, and we all benefit from one another's insights. In the argument model, other people's insights are threats to us; in the conversation model, those insights enrich us all. Moral conversation, whether as a dialogue between two people or as an internal dialogue, is an attempt to find the truth, not to vanquish the opponent.

A Pluralistic Account of Moral Discourse

The preceding considerations suggest that we must revise and expand our conception of moral discourse. Whereas moral discourse often has been confined to the analysis of arguments, we now see that a moral pluralistic account of moral discourse is in order. Let us consider several possible forms that moral discourse may take.

Argument

As we have seen, argument is important in moral discourse—of that, there is little doubt. It is particularly important in articulating the place of a moral belief in the larger whole of a moral theory. However, it is not the *only* important kind of moral talk nor, in certain circumstances, is it even the most important. Argument serves well to articulate the internal logical relationships within a theory, but we need other types of discourse to bring other dimensions of the moral life into clearer focus. Three deserve special mention here: literature, autobiography, and dialogue.

Literature

As we have already noted above, one of the most challenging tasks of the moral life is learning to *see* things more clearly. The more finely textured our moral perceptions are, the more well-grounded our moral judgments can be. It is here that literature plays a crucial role, for literature maps out the moral landscape in a detail beyond the reach of moral theory. In the process, it teaches us to see, sometimes differently, sometimes more clearly and finely. Moreover, it helps us to see, not only from our own perspective, but also from the perspective of other persons.

Autobiography

Moral reflection often is directed toward better discerning our own motives, at seeing the moral direction of our own lives more clearly, and at understanding the place of a moral belief within the larger structure of our life as a whole. When we are looking at other people's lives, literature allows us to achieve these goals more fully than argumentative discourse. However, when we turn to consider our own lives, our goal is to understand how a particular event or action fits within the moral story of our own life. At this point, our reflection becomes primarily autobiographical.

There is a long tradition of moral autobiography in the West. Augustine's *Confessions* is one of the earliest and most powerful examples in this tradition, and in it Augustine attempts to make sense of his life within an explicitly moral and religious framework. There are numerous examples of this same genre in the twentieth century. Albert Schweitzer's *Out of My Life and Thought*, Gandhi's *Autobiography*, Maya Angelou's *I Know Why the Caged Bird Sings*, Dorothy Day's *The Long Loneliness*, Alice Kohler's *An Unknown Woman*, and *The Autobiography of Malcolm X* are all examples of moral autobiographies, that is, attempts to write the story of one's life in terms of the moral commitments at the heart of one's identity. What all of these works have in common is that they seek to establish a moral sense to one's life and to see particular events within the larger context of this moral sense.

Dialogue

Finally, we should note that moral discourse is often something that we undertake with other persons in a shared quest for moral understanding. Whereas argument may be the preferred form of discourse when we are trying to convince someone else of our point of view, dialogue is more appropriate when we are engaged in a common voyage of moral discovery. This tradition is venerable in philosophy, stemming in the West directly from Plato's early dialogues that suggest that philosophy is essentially a conversation. The dialogical approach to moral discourse emphasizes the way in which moral reflection is a shared, dynamic enterprise characterized by mutuality. Far from emphasizing immutable moral truths, this approach sees ethical discourse as an on-going interpersonal process of looking for moral solutions through dialogue.

The Value of Methodological Pluralism

A pluralistic approach to moral discourse thus recognizes not only that there are several different kinds of moral values, but also acknowledges that there are several different ways of talking about those kinds of values. Argument provides one such way, but a full account of moral discourse must recognize the legitimacy of literary, autobiographical, and dialogical discourse as well.

Reshaping Ethical Theory

What implications do these criticisms have for our understanding of moral theory? They suggest that monistic theories of moral value are subject to strong objections, objections which largely are avoided when we turn to a more pluralistic account. An adequate moral theory must possess some characteristics that traditional versions of divine command theories, ethical egoism, Kantian deontology, rights theory, and utilitarianism lack. These include a greater degree of integration of the personal element in the moral life, at least a partial healing of the split between moral reasons and moral motives, a view of moral perfection which is more robust and pluralistic than traditional theories yield, and an account of moral discourse that encompasses more than argument. As we shall see in the next two chapters, recent developments in moral theory hold great promise of meeting these challenges.

Bibliographical Essay

One of the **key essays** to raise doubts about ethical theories as such was G.E.M. Anscombe's "Modern Moral Philosophy," originally published in 1958 and reprinted in her *Ethics, Religion and Politics* (Minneapolis: University of Minnesota Press, 1981). In the next two years, Philippa Foot's "Moral Arguments" (1958) and "Moral Beliefs" (1959) continued this attack on traditional moral theory; these essays are reprinted in her *Virtues and Vices* (Berkeley: University of California Press, 1978). More recently, Michael Stocker's "The Schizophrenia of Modern Ethical Theories," *The Journal of Philosophy*, Vol. 73 (1976), pp. 453–66, has set the stage for the discussion of this issue, along with Bernard Williams's essays, especially his critique of utilitarianism in *Utilitarianism: For and Against* (New York: Cambridge University Press, 1973); his essay on "Morality and the Emotions" in *Problems of the Self* (New York: Cambridge University Press, 1973); and "Persons, Character, and Morality," "Moral Luck," and "Utilitarianism and Moral Self-Indulgence" in *Moral Luck* (New York: Cambridge University Press, 1981). Stocker's most recent position on these issues is found in his *Plural and Conflicting Values* (Oxford: Clarendon Press, 1990); Williams's most recent work is *Ethics and the Limits of Philosophy* (Cambridge Mass.: Harvard University Press, 1985). A rather different perspective on the impossibility of moral theory appears in the eloquent opening chapter of MacIntyre's *After Virtue*, 2d ed. (Notre Dame, Ind.: University of Notre Dame Press, 1984) as well as his introduction to *Revisions*, edited by Stanley Hauerwas and Alasdair MacIntyre (Notre Dame Ind.: University of Notre Dame Press, 1983).

Stanley Clarke and Evan Simpson have edited a good anthology of recent works on this topic in *Anti-Theory in Ethics and Moral Conservatism* (Albany: State University of New York Press, 1989); it also contains a very good bibliographical essay.

For an account of the ways in which **different types of moral theories may be appropriate to different contexts,** see Virginia Held, *Rights and Goods: Justifying Social Action.* (New York: Free Press, 1984), esp. chapter four, "Moral Theory and Moral Experience." Michael Walzer makes a similar suggestion in his *Spheres of Justice* (New York: Basic Books, 1983). Dorothy Emmet sketches out an account of the perspectival character of moral theories in *The Moral Prism* (New York: St. Martin's, 1979). Stephen Toulmin's *The Place of Reason in Ethics* (Chicago: University of Chicago Press, 1986) argues against the universality of ethical principles and in favor of the case-by-case approach to moral problems that characterized the casuistical tradition.

For discussions of some general issues about **the relation between moral theory and moral experience,** which has come under intensive scrutiny in recent years, see especially Edmund Pincoffs, "Quandary Ethics," *Revisions*, pp. 92–112, and his *Quandaries and Virtues: Against Reductivism in Ethics* (Lawrence, Kans.: University of Kansas Press, 1986), esp. part one; Cora Diamond, "Anything but Argument?," *Philosophical Investigations*, Vol. 5 (January, 1982), pp. 23–41: Annette Baier, "Theory and Reflective Practices" and "Doing Without Moral Theory," *Postures of the Mind* (Minneapolis: Minnesota University Press, 1985), pp. 207–45; J.B. Schneewind, "Moral Knowledge and Moral Principles," *Revisions*, edited by Stanley Hauerwas and Alasdair MacIntyre (Notre Dame: University of Notre Dame Press, 1983), pp. 113–26: Amélie Okesenberg Rorty, *Mind in Action: Essays in the Philosophy of Mind* (Boston: Beacon Press, 1988) esp. chap. fourteen, "Three Myths of Moral Theory." For a strong defense of moral theory in light of such criticisms, see Robert B. Louden, *Morality and Moral Theory* (New York: Oxford University Press, 1992).

The importance of **moral vision** is stressed by Iris Murdoch, "The Idea of Perfection," *The Sovereignty of Good* (London: Routledge and Kegan Paul, 1970), esp. pp. 17 ff.; also see Murdoch's "Vision and Choice in Morality," *Proceedings of the Aristotelian Society*, Supplementary Volume XXX (1956), pp. 32–58. Among those deeply influenced by Murdoch, see especially the work of Lawrence Blum, including his "Iris Murdoch and the Domain of the Moral" *Philosophical Studies*, Vol. 50 (1986), pp. 343–67, and his "Moral Perception and Particularity" *Ethics*, Vol. 101, No. 4 (July, 1991), pp. 701–25. Working from a quite different background, Michael DePaul also makes a persuasive case for the role of perception in the moral life in his "Argument and Perception," *The Journal of Philosophy*, Vol. 85, No. 10 (1988), pp. 552–65. Perception is also an important theme in the work of John Kekes; see especially chapter nine of his *The Examined Life* (University Park Pa.: Pennsylvania State University Press, 1988) and his "Moral Imagination, Freedom, and the Humanities," *American Philosophical Quarterly*, Vol. 28, No. 2 (April, 1991), pp. 101–11. One of the major issues in the discussion of the nature of moral vision is that of moral realism; for an introductory discussion of the questions surrounding this issue, see David McNaughton's *Moral Vision* (Oxford: Basil Blackwell, 1988).

For illuminating comments on the general "thinness" of modern conceptions of the moral agent, see Alasdair MacIntyre, "How Moral Agents Became Ghosts," *Sythese*, Vol. 53 (1982), pp. 295–312.

The issue of **impartiality and particularity** has received much attention of late. As usual, much of it begins with the work of Bernard Williams; see especially his "Persons, Character, and Morality" *Moral Luck* (New York:

Cambridge University Press, 1981), pp. 1–19. Most recently, the Symposium on Impartiality and Ethical Theory in *Ethics*, Vol. 101, No. 4 (July, 1991) includes excellent essays by Lawrence Blum on "Moral Perception and Particularity," by Adrian Piper on "Impartiality, Compassion, and Modal Imagination," by Marcia Baron on "Impartiality and Friendship," and by Marilyn Friedman of "The Practice of Partiality," which provides a helpful refinement of our notion of partiality itself; Barbara Herman provides a subtle and tightly woven defense of Kantian impartiality in "Agency, Detachment, and Difference." In addition to Herman, some of the most able defenders of impartiality include Stephen Darwall, whose *Impartial Reason* (Ithaca N.Y.: Cornell University Press, 1983) is one of the best articulations of a Kantian view of moral reasoning; Derek Parfit, who argues in *Reasons and Persons* (Oxford: Clarendon Press, 1984) that ethics should be more impersonal; and, most recently, Shelly Kagan's *The Limits of Morality* (Oxford: Clarendon Press, 1989) offers a penetrating discussion of this issue. Robert Adams provides an excellent discussion of the issues surrounding Parfit's claims about impersonality in his review, "Should Ethics Be More Impersonal?" *Philosophical Review*, Vol. 98, No. 4 (October, 1989), pp. 439–84. Also see the work of Thomas Nagel, especially his *The View from Nowhere* (New York: Oxford University Press, 1988) and *Equality and Partiality* (New York: Oxford University Press, 1991).

The emphasis on impartiality has led to a neglect of some traditional virtues. Loyality is one of the most interesting of these. On this issue, see Philip Pettit's "The Paradox of Loyalty," *American Philosophical Quarterly*, Vol. 25, No. 2 (April, 1988), pp. 163–71, and especially George P. Fletcher, *Loyalty: An Essay on the Morality of Relationships* (New York: Oxford University Press, 1993).

On **the relationship between ethics and literature,** see especially the following two symposia: "Symposium on Morality and Literature" in *Ethics*, Vol. 98, No. 2 (January, 1988); "Literature and/as Moral Philosophy" in *New Literary History*, Vol. XV, No. 1 (Autumn, 1983); on the moral power of stories, also see Robert Coles, *The Call of Stories: Teaching and the Moral Imagination* (Boston: Houghton Mifflin, 1989); also see the wonderfully rich analyses in Martha Craven Nussbaum's *The Fragility of Goodness* (Cambridge: Cambridge University Press, 1986) and the conceptual framework elaborated by Richard Wollheim in his *The Thread of Life* (Cambridge: Harvard University Press, 1984). Wayne C. Booth's *The Company We Keep. An Ethics of Fiction* (Berkeley: University of California Press, 1988) offers an exceptionally insightful discussion of the rhetoric of moral theories. Richard Eldridge traces the unfolding of Kantian moral themes in Conrad, Wordsworth, Coleridge, and Jane Austen in his *On Moral Personhood. Philosophy, Literature, Criticism, and Self-Understanding* (Chicago: University of Chicago Press, 1989).

Several philosophers have discussed the issue of **the place of the emotions in the moral life.** Bernard Williams's "Morality and the Emotions,"

Problems of the Self (Cambridge: Cambridge University Press, 1973), pp. 207–29, is an excellent starting point. I have dealt with this issue in more depth in relation to Kant in "On the Purity of Our Moral Motives," *The Monist*, Vol. 66, No. 2 (April, 1983), pp. 251–67, as has Nancy Sherman more recently in "The Place of Emotions in Kantian Morality" in *Identity, Character, and Morality*, edited by Owen Flanagan and Amélie Okesenberg Rorty (Cambridge: MIT Press, 1990), pp. 149–71. Justin Oakley's *Morality and the Emotions* (London: Routledge, 1992) offers a strong defense of the positive role that the emotions play in the moral life. Among recent works that stress **the cognitive dimension of emotions,** see especially Ronald de Sousa, *The Rationality of Emotion* (Cambridge: MIT Press, 1987); Patricia S. Greenspan, *Emotions and Reasons: An Inquiry into Emotional Justification* (New York: Routledge, 1988); Jerome Neu, *Emotion, Thought and Therapy* (Berkeley: University of California Press, 1977); Gabriele Taylor, *Pride, Guilt and Shame: Emotions of Self-Assessment* (Oxford: Clarendon, 1985); and Martha Craven Nussbaum's *Love's Knowledge* (New York: Oxford University Press, 1990). In *Wise Choices, Apt Feelings* (Cambridge Mass.: Harvard University Press, 1990), Alan Gibbard articulates a theory of normative judgment in which emotions play a highly significant role.

The literature on **moral saints** is growing quickly. In addition to Susan Wolf's "Moral Saints," *The Journal of Philosophy*, Vol. 79, No. 8 (August, 1982), pp. 419–39, and Robert Adams's rejoinder, "Saints, *The Journal of Philosophy*, Vol. 81, No. 7 (July, 1984), pp. 392–401, see Pincoff's "A Defense of Perfectionism" and "Ideals of Virtue and Moral Obligation: Gandhi," both of which are in his *Quandaries and Virtues* (Lawrence, Kans.: University of Kansas Press, 1986) and Robert Louden's "Can We Be Too Moral?" *Ethics*, Vol. 98 No. 2 (January, 1988), pp. 361–78. For an excellent analysis of the issue of moral perfectibility in political theory, see Virginia Lewis Muller's *The Idea Of Perfectibility* (Latham, Md.: University Press of America, 1985). Two recent philosophical works direct themselves to issues about the relationship between moral goodness and individuality: Owen Flanagan's *Varieties of Moral Personality* (Cambridge: Harvard University Press, 1991) and John Kekes's *Facing Evil* (Princeton N.J.: Princeton University Press, 1990). Both Edith Wyschogrod's *Saints and Postmodernism: Revisioning Moral Philosophy* (Chicago: University of Chicago Press, 1990) and Robert Inchausti's *The Ignorant Perfection of Ordinary People* (Albany: State University of New York Press, 1991) contain detailed discussions of specific figures. Lawrence Blum's "Moral Exemplars," *Midwest Studies in Philosophy*, Vol. XIII (1988), pp. 196–221, contains excellent discussions of specific figures, including Schindler, and a penetrating consideration of the question of flawed exemplars. For an excellent biography of Oscar Schindler's life, see Thomas Keneally, *Schindler's List*. (New York: Simon and Schuster, 1983).

Comparatively little work has been done on **metaphors of discourse.**

See the excellent discussion of argument as war in George Lackoff and Mark Johnson's *Metaphors We Live By* (Chicago: University of Chicago Press, 1981) and the discussion by Janice Moulton of "A Paradgm for Philosophy: The Adversary Method" in *Discovering Reality: Feminist Perspectives on Epistemology, Metaphysics, Methodology, and Philosophy of Science*, edited by Sandra Harding and Merril B. Hintikka (Dordrecht, Netherlands: Reidel, 1983), pp. 149–64.

The importance of **dialogue** is emphasized by Hans-Georg Gadamer in his *Truth and Method* (New York: Seabury, 1975); the idea of conversation, and the conditions necessary for genuine conversations, is developed by Jurgen Habermas, especially in his *Moral Consciousness and Communicative Action* (Cambridge: MIT Press, 1990) and in his exchanges with Gadamer. Some helpful essays on this theme are gathered together in Michael Kelly's anthology *Hermeneutics and Critical Theory in Ethics and Politics* (Cambridge: MIT Press, 1990). For a well-argued defense of dialogue that is couched in the language of contemporary Anglo-American philosophy, see Bruce Ackerman, "Why Dialogue?" *The Journal of Philosophy*, Vol. 86, No. 1 (January, 1989), pp. 5–22.

Citations. The quotation about impartiality and friendship is from Lynne McFall in her article, "Integrity," reprinted in *Ethics and Personality*, edited by John Deigh (Chicago: University of Chicago Press, 1992), p. 90; the quotation from James Rachels about argument is from *The Right Thing to Do* (New York: Random House: 1989), p. 33.

Discussion Questions

1. Recall your rating of statement 41 in the Ethical Inventory: "We should always strive to do what is best, not just the moral minimum."
   (a) What are the advantages of an ethical theory that stresses the moral minimum? What are its disadvantages?
   (b) Has your rating of this item changed after reading this chapter? If so, in what way? If your rating has not changed, are your reasons for your rating any different now than they were when you first responded to this statement?

2. Recall your response to statement 42: "Morality applies to friends in just the same way that it applies to strangers."
   (a) When, if ever, are we justified in applying different moral standards to our dealings with our friends?
   (b) Has your rating of this item changed after reading this chapter? If so, in what way? If your rating has not changed, are your

reasons for your rating any different now than they were when you first responded to this statement?

3. The movie *Gandhi* certainly gives us a vivid portrait of a saint. How does this picture of a moral saint compare to what Susan Wolf tells us about moral saints? Do Wolf's criticisms of saints as dull, boring, and unwilling to offend other people apply to Gandhi? Why or why not?
4. Can a person be saintly in one way yet sinful in another? If so, what does that prove? Give at least one real-life example.
5. In your own experience, what has been the most significant factor in bringing about moral change in yourself and the people you know? Can reading a book about ethics (or attending a class) make you a better person? If so, how? If not, what will?
6. Does everyone have a "fundamental project" in life? Can people have more than one fundamental project? Do some people just drift? How would you characterize the fundamental project(s) in your life?
7. Critics of the impartiality of moral theories have argued that it leads to moral alienation. At one point in the movie *Gandhi*, Gandhi tells his wife that she must either clean the toilets (a task in Indian society reserved exclusively for the Untouchables) or else leave. Was Gandhi right to take such a strong stand with her? Is this example one of moral alienation?
8. Begin your own attempt at writing a moral biography. What were some of the ideas and events that had a profound moral impact on your sense of self? Describe an instance of moral change. What prompted the change? How did you change? In what other ways could you have responded to the event that promoted the change? Why did you change in the way in which you did and not in some other way? How did the change affect your other moral beliefs? Was the change a morally positive one? Why?

C H A P T E R 10

THE ETHICS OF CHARACTER: ARISTOTLE AND OUR CONTEMPORARIES

The Village of Le Chambon

The first big Nazi raid on the village of Le Chambon came in the summer of 1942. The villagers already had been warned about what would happen to them if they tried to hide Jews from the Nazis, and it was no surprise when squads of police descended on the village looking for the hundreds of Jews that were in fact hidden in the village and the surrounding countryside. The police vans were followed by a group of buses, ready to cart away the prisoners.

The villagers had prepared well. None of the Jews that had hidden were found for several days. Philip Hallie tells us what happened next.

> Later in the week they captured an Austrian Jew named Steckler—he had made the mistake of going to a pharmacy without all of his papers. The police put him—their only prisoner—in one of the big buses. As he sat there, the villagers started gathering around the periphery of the square. The son of Andre Trocmé [the village pastor], Jean-Pierre, walked up to the window of the bus at which Steckler sat and gave him his last piece of rationed (imitation) chocolate. This started the closing of the circle of villagers. They brought their most precious foodstuffs and put them through the window into Steckler's arms. Soon the quiet little man had a pile of gifts around him about as high as he sat in the seat.
>
> When the buses left with their one Jew the villagers sang a song of affection and farewell to him. A few days later he came back—he

> was only half-Jewish, and at this time he was legally classified as non-Jewish. He was pulling a cart with the presents on it as he came into the square. When the villagers gathered happily around him, smiling and nodding in their restrained Huguenot way, he wanted to give them back their gifts. They would not take them, precious as those foodstuffs were to them. Steckler wept. This is the story of the first big *rafle* or raid upon Le Chambon-sur-Lignon.

From then until the end of the war, the villagers of Le Chambon were responsible for saving the lives of thousands of innocent Jews, especially children.

When we look at the villagers of Le Chambon, we are not only struck by what they *did*, but also by who they *were*. We are struck by what *good people* they were. Their goodness did not seem to stem from any Kantian test of universality or utilitarian calculus of consequences. It came from the heart, from who they were as persons. They did not follow some elaborate set of rules, but rather responded spontaneously to the suffering of those around them. It is, first and foremost, a goodness of *character*. As we shall now see, there is an entire tradition in ethics that takes character as the central focus of ethics. Let us look at that tradition more closely.

From the Ethics of Action to the Ethics of Character

Asking a Different Question

In our discussions of Kant and of utilitarianism, we looked at two different answers to the question of how we should *act*. Kant and the utilitarians answer this question in quite different ways. For Kant, the answer depends largely on our *intention*: always act for the sake of duty, that is, because it is the right thing to do. Moreover, act in such a way that the maxim behind your act can be willed as a universal law. The utilitarians gave a very different answer to this question. For them, the rightness or wrongness of actions depended on *consequences* instead of intentions. The right action was the action that produced the greatest overall amount of happiness or pleasure. Yet what both the Kantians and the utilitarians have in common is that they see ethics as being an answer to the question "What ought I to *do?*"

Aristotle approaches ethics in quite a different way. For him, ethics is concerned primarily with answering the question "What kind of *person* should I be?" Ethics concentrates on *character* rather than action. Thus it is that Aristotle is interested principally in *virtues* and *vices*, that is, in those strengths and weaknesses of character that either promote or impede human flourishing.

The contrast between act-oriented approaches to morality (including both utilitarianism and Kantianism) and character-oriented approaches (especially

Aristotle) raises some important philosophical questions about how these two approaches relate to one another and whether one of them is preferable to the other. Before pursuing these questions, consider an analogy between this controversy and our American criminal justice system.

A Judicial Analogy

In order to insure justice, we as a country established a criminal justice system that has two distinct dimensions to it. First, it is a system of *laws*, of rules for acceptable behavior. Indeed, our system of laws has become increasingly well-articulated, detailed, and complex. As we discover loopholes in the present laws, we add new laws in the hope of closing the gaps. Yet, at the same time, there is a second element which we have built into this process: *people*. We leave the application of these rules to the good judgment of various people, especially the judge and jury. Both judge and jury have to use their own judgment in determining how these rules are to be applied. They temper the laws, applying them (at least in the best cases) with fairness, compassion, insight, and wisdom. The application is not automatic; human judgment has to enter into the process. Indeed, in order to insure that the judgment will be as unbiased as possible, we have a number of people on the jury, not just one. In order to insure that the judge is unbiased, we try to remove the selection process as much as possible from partisan politics and not make judges dependent on politics for their continued tenure. In order to insure that the rules are paid sufficient attention, we expect that the judge will be well versed in the law. The appeals process helps to guarantee that the rulings of those judges who ignore the relevant law will be overturned.

What we can learn from this example? We see that as a country we have decided to rely on both laws and people, both principles and persons. We have built that dual reliance into our system of justice. We put our money on laws, on our ability to develop a system of rules to determine what is acceptable or unacceptable behavior—but only up to a point. We also place our faith in people, in individuals who will have the good judgment to know how to apply the laws. Neither can exist without the other. Without laws, judges and juries would be free to decide arbitrarily about cases, and no one would have firm guidelines for behavior. Yet without judges and juries, the laws could never be applied fairly. Their judgment, their insight, and their wisdom are necessary to interpret and apply those rules. As a country, we have shown the good judgment to depend on both laws and people.

Persons and Principles

Ethics is similar to the law in this respect: it needs both principles and persons. Both the Kantians and the utilitarians articulate principles that shed vital light on the moral life, and they are not to be ignored. Yet the application of those principles depends on people of good judgment and character, and it is precisely this element which virtue ethics hopes to provide. It is in this sense that virtue ethics offers the context within which both deontological and consequentialist moral considerations can be embraced. This is not to say that virtue ethics reconciles these two approaches within a single unified theory, but rather that it offers a way of understanding how we as moral persons can contain the creative tension that comes from the conflict between these two traditions.

Moreover, we obviously are not suggesting that there is no correlation between character and actions. Particular character traits lead to specific kinds of actions. A courageous person manifests his or her courage in courageous acts. Indeed, the acts often are our best clues to what the person's character is really like.

Nevertheless, there is good reason for giving virtue ethics a limited kind of priority over act-oriented approaches. We already have seen one sense in which virtue ethics has that priority: it embraces both Kantian and utilitarian approaches. Yet there is another way in which virtue ethics seems to be, if not prior, at least more desirable than deontological or utilitarian approaches. In order to show how, let us go back to Kant.

The Continent and the Temperate Persons

In Kant's moral philosophy, when there is a conflict between duty and inclination, between what you ought to do and what you feel like doing, duty always is supposed to conquer inclination. However, there is relatively little concern on Kant's part to heal the rift between duty and inclination, between reason and emotion. Rather, he simply urges us to follow the path of duty and reason, eschewing inclination and emotion. The alternative is to suggest that we try to overcome this dichotomy, that we attempt to reconcile what we ought to do and what we feel like doing.

Here Aristotle is particularly insightful. He draws a distinction between two different types of persons, the temperate and the continent persons (EN, Book VII). Temperate people are individuals who do what is right *because they want to do so.* The continent person also does what is right, but does not really *want* to do so. Let me offer an example in regard to eating. My wife is a temperate person: she eats in moderation, and naturally chooses healthful foods as the mainstays of her diet. She actually seems to enjoy celery and carrot sticks. Her eyes light up at the thought of raw broccoli. I, on the other hand, am at best a continent person in this regard. I may eat salads, fish, and whole grains, but there is not a day that passes that I do not *want* rich Brie cheese, red meat, and cheesecake. I may not always eat these things, but I certainly want them. I think, at least in regard to food, my wife has the better life.

As we have seen in the previous chapter, the Kantian moral person seems in greater danger of being the continent rather than the temperate person, which is a serious drawback in Kant's ethics. For Kant, moral actions do not have to come from the heart, only from the head. Yet our moral ideal should be one of *striving* to have our actions come from both head and heart, from both reason and feeling. Moreover, part of that process of reconciling reason and emotion will involve educating the emotions, something that has been all too often ignored in the past.

A similar problem arises with utilitarianism. Motives count for relatively little among most utilitarians, and emotions occupy a strange place in the utilitarian calculus. Although emotions certainly count for the utilitarian, the difficulty is that everyone's emotions count equally. Indeed, if any emotions are to be given less weight, it is the agent's own feelings, for these are at least somewhat under his control. Thus utilitarianism also tends to promote this split between the reasoning part of the self and the emotional side.

All other things being equal, an ethics which seeks to heal this split is preferable to one which perpetuates it. One of the most striking characteristics of the villagers of Le Chambon was that they risked their own lives to save the Jews, not from any externally imposed sense of duty, but because they wanted to do so. They responded from the heart. However, we are not always able to do so. Temperate people have rightly ordered appetites, and for them act-oriented moralities that emphasize the importance of rules usually will be of secondary importance. Intemperate people, on the other hand, do not have rightly ordered desires, at least in the areas in which they are intemperate. For them, it is important to have rules that govern and control their actions. Thus act-oriented moralities that provide rules of behavior properly will have a more prominent place in the lives of intemperate persons.

Character and Human Flourishing

One of the principal attractions of Aristotle's ethics is the way in which it encourages human flourishing. Indeed, Aristotle's ethics is concerned largely with the question of what promotes human happiness or flourishing, about what leads to a fuller and happier human life. (The Greek word for happiness that Aristotle uses, *eudaimonia*, can also be translated as "flourishing" or "well-being.") Virtues and vices are understood precisely within this context. **Virtues** are those strengths or excellences of character that promote human flourishing, while **vices** are those weaknesses of character that impede flourishing. Courage, for example, is a virtue because we have to be able to face and overcome our fears if we are to achieve our goals in life. Yet what, exactly, is human flourishing?

Aristotle (384–322 BC), who is shown here with his pupil Alexander the Great, emphasized the strong connection between ethics and politics.

Aristotle on Human Flourishing

Flourishing and Function

The notion of human flourishing or happiness is a notoriously slippery one, but Aristotle's approach is helpful, even if ultimately incomplete. Two lines of argument run through his approach to determining what counts as human flourishing. On one hand, flourishing is understood in a *functional* context. A hammer, for example, is a good hammer if it does what it was designed to do well—if it hammers nails well. A guitar is a good guitar if it is capable of making good music. Aristotle expresses it this way in Book Two of the *Nichomachean Ethics:*

> . . . every virtue causes its possessors to be in a good state [or disposition] and to perform their functions well; the virtue of eyes, e.g., makes the eyes and their functioning excellent, because it makes us see well; and similarly, the virtue of a horse makes the horse excellent, and thereby good at galloping, at carrying its rider and at standing steady in the face of the enemy. If this is true in every case, then the virtue of a human being will likewise be the state [or habit or disposition] that makes a human being good and makes him perform his function well.

Notice, however, that these are objects designed to meet a particular human purpose, such as hammering nails or making music. Human beings do not have an obvious function in the same unproblematic way that hammers and guitars have functions.

(Of course, within certain religious contexts, human beings do have an obvious function or purpose, and this purpose is ordained by God. Within such a worldview, virtues have a much more obvious justification: they are those strengths of character necessary for us to fulfill God's plan for us. But such a view presupposes that (a) we have been given a purpose by a divine being and (b) we can know what that purpose is.)

Flourishing and Uniqueness

On the other hand, Aristotle sometimes understands flourishing in terms of the exercise of *unique properties*. Consider a plum tree. Its unique characteristic is that it bears fruit (plums). Consequently, a good plum tree will be one that produces plums well. In a similar way, there is a unique characteristic that sets human beings apart from other kinds of beings: the ability to reason or think. Consequently, a good human being will be one who reasons well. Human flourishing is thus defined in terms of reasoning or thinking—for Aristotle, ultimately in terms of the contemplative life.

Two Conceptions of Flourishing

When flourishing is approached through an analysis of function, Aristotle tends to emphasize the way in which happiness is related to practical wisdom. People of practical wisdom, Aristotle tells us in the *Nicomachean Ethics*, are persons who can deliberate well about what is good for their lives as a whole, not just what is good for some part of it or what is expedient. Such individuals often find that flourishing has a deep social and political element to it. According to this conception of flourishing, human beings are profoundly social by nature and participation in the common life of the city-state, the *polis*, is an essential part of any happy life. Happiness or flourishing would be impossible without community. We can call this *the political conception of happiness*, but it is important to recognize that the word "political" does not carry negative connotations for the Greeks of Aristotle's time. For the Greeks, the political realm encompasses virtually everything that is concerned with forging a common life together.

There is a second conception of flourishing in Aristotle's thought which exists in uneasy tension with the first. This theory of flourishing derives from the uniqueness argument. According to this account, flourishing essentially consists in contemplation of the good. Leisure is a necessary presupposition of such a view, for there must be some way of creating the time necessary for contemplation. This theory is *the contemplative conception of happiness*. Whereas the political conception of happiness sees happiness as residing at least partially in activity, the contemplative account of happiness stresses the way in which happiness is found through a withdrawal from the world of everyday affairs.

A Pluralistic Approach to Happiness

Aristotle's own writings suggest that he vacillates between these two accounts of happiness, and scholars have been divided about which represents his true view or whether the two accounts can be reconciled. If we were to extend our pluralistic approach to this issue in Aristotle's philosophy, we could say that happiness itself can be understood pluralistically. Happiness in general may be seen as the satisfaction that comes with achieving one's most important goals in life, but we can recognize that there is a wide range of variability in acceptable goals. Some of these goals may be located firmly within the social realm, while others may be principally contemplative. Yet we also can recognize that there are some minimal restraints imposed on these goals by both our social and our intellectual natures. Just as we cannot find happiness in complete isolation from other people, so we could hardly find it without some significant reflection on the goals for which we choose to strive. Both elements are necessary to some minimal extent, but there is a wide range of variability in the relative weight we give to one over the other.

Assessing Aristotle's Account of Flourishing

Anti-Reductionism

There is much to be said in favor of Aristotle's account of human flourishing, not the least of which is that it is anti-reductionistic. Aristotle does not try to reduce human existence to a single common lowest denominator, which is in stark contrast to theories that reduce human beings to some single factor such as genetics (as sociobiology does) or economics (as both some Marxists and some capitalists try to do) or environment (as strict behaviorism does) that human beings have in common with other types of living beings. Aristotle sees human beings as unique among other living things and does not try to downplay or ignore that aspect of human beings that makes them unique.

Holism

However, Aristotle does at times seem to go almost to the other extreme, looking as it were only for the *highest* common denominator. Because thinking is what makes human beings unique, he treats it as the *only* thing which does so. As a result, at times he has a more intellectualistic and contemplative notion of human nature and of virtue than is warranted. His mistake in reasoning is a simple one, as we can see from another example. My computer has a number of fancy gadgets, including a CD-ROM drive that holds six disks. The CD-ROM drive makes it unique, yet its excellence lies in the *totality* of its functions, not just in the CD-ROM drive. Similarly with human beings: their excellence lies in the totality of their functions and powers (including the ability to feel), not just in their ability to think. Aristotle, by sometimes overemphasizing the role of thinking in his conception of human flourishing, was not sufficiently *holistic* in his approach. I stress this aspect because all too often the positive role of emotions and feelings in the moral life is denied or neglected, a danger to which Aristotle sometimes, but not always, succumbs.

Ethics for the Nobility

There is yet another drawback to Aristotle's account of the virtues, one which it shares with most other ancient and, to a lesser extent, medieval and modern accounts. It is an ethics for the ruling class, for privileged, free, adult Greek males whose main interests were domestic politics, war, and leisure. Such an ethics completely excluded women and most foreigners, many of whom were treated as slaves or as less than full moral persons. Yet the life that this privileged class enjoyed depended in large measure on the support of these excluded groups. Greek leisure, which Aristotle saw as a prerequisite to philosophy, is based on these inequalities.

What are we to say about this aspect of Aristotle's ethics? Clearly, in important respects, Aristotle was on the right track. Just as clearly, we see that his vision at times was clouded or distorted, in part because of the era in which he lived. We can learn from Aristotle's account of flourishing, but we can hardly take it as the final word.

Contemporary Accounts of Flourishing

Contemporary thinkers—psychologists, economists, and other social scientists as well as philosophers—have continued Aristotle's task of understanding human flourishing. Broadly speaking, their approaches fall into two categories, depending on where they locate the primary impediments to human flourishing. For those who see the main barriers to human flourishing as being *external* to any particular individual, their account of a flourishing life usually will stress external, *social* factors. For those who see the main obstacles to human flourishing as *internal* to the individual, flourishing usually is depicted primarily in internal, *psychological* terms.

External Approaches

The external or social approach to human flourishing covers a wide range of different kinds of factors that affect human well-being. Some are obvious: many people believe that economic factors, for example, play a significant role in determining human flourishing. Here flourishing or well-being can be described in terms of such objective factors as standard of living. Those who achieve a certain level of economic well-being are said to be flourishing, while those who fall beyond the minimum level are seen as not flourishing.

Other types of external factors may be less immediately obvious to most of us. Think, for example, of the relationship between architecture and human flourishing. The ways in which we structure our living and working environments both reflect and affect our interactions with other people. Workplaces with no common areas for employees encourage an isolation and separation from co-workers not found as readily in working environments that stress interaction. Homes in which all the chairs face the television reflect a different conception of happiness than homes in which the chairs all face one another.

Historically, utopian thinkers often have provided us with possible models of a social life that encourages human flourishing. Many such models presuppose that people will be happy (that is, will flourish) if certain material and social conditions can be met. Many versions of both Marxist and capitalist social theories share this presupposition.

Once flourishing is specified in terms of external conditions, we have a clear path to increasing the amount or degree of flourishing in society. We merely have to increase the external conditions necessary to flourishing, whether these be specified in terms of income, health care, or some other objective factor.

Internal Approaches

Many theorists have linked human flourishing primarily with some *internal* state. Virtually all spiritual approaches to human well-being, for example, see flourishing primarily as a state of the soul that is largely (perhaps even entirely) independent of external conditions. Similarly, many psychological accounts of flourishing emphasize the internal factors within the individual's psyche that affects well-being. Some psychological approaches like Freud's or Jung's see the path to flourishing as *intra*psychic in which the crucial question concerns the balance among competing psychological factors. Other psychological approaches have looked even more directly at the question of human flourishing, especially at factors which affect peak experiences. The work of Abraham Maslow has been particularly influential in this area.

What is common to most of these internal approaches is the shared presupposition that we are often our worst enemy, preventing ourselves from having the very satisfactions we value so highly. We sabotage ourselves without even realizing what we are doing. The road to happiness primarily involves overcoming internal barriers to flourishing, which is often a matter of spiritual discipline or psychological health. In this tradition, flourishing is primarily a state of mind rather than a state of matter.

The Structure of Virtues

We already have talked much about virtues without really defining what we, or Aristotle, mean by the term. Let us remedy that situation.

The Definition of Virtue

Virtue, Aristotle tells us, is (1) a habit or disposition of the soul, (2) involving both feeling and action, (3) to seek the mean in all things relative to us, (4) where the mean is defined through reason as the prudent man would define it (*Nichomachean Ethics*, II, 6). Virtue leads, as we already have seen, to happiness or human flourishing. Each of these elements in Aristotle's definition is important, so let us pause to examine each part of the definition.

Habits of the Soul

Aristotle tells us that virtue is a *hexis*, a disposition or habit. We are not born with virtues. They are not natural or inborn; rather they are acquired, often through practice. Moral education for Aristotle thus focuses around the development of a person's fundamental character, what Aristotle calls "soul."

Feeling and Action

Virtue, for Aristotle, is not simply a matter of *acting* in a particular way; it is also a question of *feeling* certain ways. Virtue includes emotion as well as action. The compassionate person not only acts in certain ways that help alleviate the suffering of others, but also has certain kinds of feelings toward their suffering.

The inclusion of feeling in the definition of virtue is important to our concerns here, for as we saw in the previous chapter, the exclusion of emotions from the moral life (or at least their devaluation) leads to significant problems for Kantian, utilitarian, and egoistic moral theories. Aristotle's account of the moral life in terms of virtue, with its emphasis on the emotive or affective character of virtue, allows us to set aside this objection.

Seeking the Mean Relative to Ourselves

A virtue, Aristotle tells us, involves finding the mean between the two extremes of excess and deficiency. Courage, for example, is that middle ground between cowardice (too little) and foolhardiness (too much).

In virtues that contain several elements, there might be several associated vices, depending on which of the elements are in excess and which are deficient. Courage, when we examine it more closely, has at least two components: fear and confidence. We can err in regard to either factor: we may have too much or too little fear, or we may have too much or too little confidence in ourselves.

Aristotle himself suggests that this tripartite framework may not always be applicable. The example he gives is murder. There is, he tells us, no mean in regard to murder. It is just an extreme. Yet I think Aristotle is confused on this matter, for murder is neither a virtue nor a vice. It is an *action,* not a quality of character. Indeed, probably the relevant quality of character would be something like respect for life, which is a virtue that can have extremes. On one hand, there are those with too little respect for life. They kill and injure others with no regard for the pain and suffering they are inflicting. On the other hand, there are those who would never knowingly even step on an ant. One could argue that they have an excessive respect for life. Unfortunately, our society is plagued much more by the former than the latter.

Defining the Mean Through Reason and the Prudent Person

Interestingly, Aristotle gives two ways for determining what the mean is: through reason and through observing the prudent person. This duality reflects precisely the point made earlier in this chapter through the judicial analogy: we need both principles and persons for the moral life. Rather than choosing one or the other, Aristotle chooses both, seeing them as complementary.

Virtues and Spheres of Existence

One of the common criticisms of Aristotle's list of the virtues is that it is arbitrary. Certainly it is culturally bound, shaped by the values of ancient Athens. Yet there are some universal elements, and Aristotle provides a good hint about how these can be established. There are, he suggests, certain spheres of existence which all of us have to encounter. We all have to develop an attitude toward the accomplishments and successes of other people: envy, admiration, or belittling are some of the possible attitudes. We all have to develop an attitude toward the offenses and hurts that others inflict on us. Some people will be resentful and revengeful, others forgiving, yet others will be doormats. Correlatively, we have to develop an attitude toward *our own* offenses to other people. Again, there is a wide range of possibilities, ranging from being indifferent to being overly guilty. Somewhere in the middle is the proper attitude of remorse and reparation.

Sphere of Existence	*Deficiency*	*Mean*	*Excess*
Attitude toward self	Servility Self-Deprecation	Proper Self-Love Proper Pride Self-Respect	Arrogance Conceit Egoism Narcissism Vanity
Attitude toward offenses of others	Ignoring them Being a doormant	Anger Forgiveness Understanding	Revenge Grudge Resentment
Attitude toward good deeds of others	Suspicion Envy Ignoring them	Gratitude Admiration	Overindebtedness
Attitude toward our own offenses	Indifference Remorselessness Downplaying	Agent regret Remorse Making amends Learning from them Self-forgiveness	Toxic guilt Scrupulosity Shame
Attitude toward our own good deeds	Belittling Disappointment	Sense of accomplishment Humility	Self-Righteousness
Attitude toward the suffering of others	Callousness	Compassion	Pity "Bleeding Heart"
Attitude toward the achievements of others	Self-satisfaction Complacency Competition	Admiration Emulation	Envy
Attitude toward death and danger	Cowardice	Courage	Foolhardiness
Attitude toward our own desires	Anhedonia	Temperance Moderation	Lust Gluttony
Attitude toward our friends	Indifference	Loyalty	Obsequiousness
Attitude toward other people	Exploitation	Respect	Deferentiality

Notice, too, that the emphasis here is not on individual actions, but on character, which manifests itself in habits of perception and behavior. Take courage as an example. Aristotle's question is not whether this or that particular action is courageous. Rather, he asks what a life without courage, or without courage in a particular range of situations, would be like. The focus is not on specific acts, but rather on the patterns that reveal a person's character.

There are a variety of ways in which we might summarize these various spheres of existence. The preceding page shows one which I have developed, amending a similar outline by Martha Nussbaum.

Thus Aristotle tells us that virtue is the disposition of the soul through reasoning to find the mean in all things relative to us. The mean is that middle ground between two extremes, the extremes of excess (having too much of something) and deficiency (having too little of something). The mean is described differently, depending on the particular sphere of existence in which we are seeking the mean. Certain spheres of existence are found in almost all cultures.

Executive and Substantive Virtues

Virtues, Aristotle tells us, are those strengths of character that promote human flourishing. Some of those strengths, later commentators have suggested, are strengths of the will. *Perseverance* in the face of a difficult and lengthy task is a virtue of the will, what some have called an **executive virtue.** So, too, is *courage,* the ability to act in the face of one's fears. These virtues of the will are largely independent of moral goodness. One can just as easily persevere in a life of crime as a life of goodness; the bank robber may exhibit as much courage as the FBI agent who tries to capture him. Other virtues are related more closely to moral goodness, and we will call these **substantive virtues.** *Compassion* is clearly a substantive virtue, for it is tied directly to a concern for moral goodness in a way that perseverance and courage are not.

Let us turn now to consider some specific virtues and their associated vices.

COURAGE

The Everyday Need for Courage

Think about the people you know who are afraid of something. Do you know anyone who is afraid to ask someone out on a date for fear of rejection? Do you know anyone who is afraid of saying something dumb and looking stupid—and consequently does not ask questions in class? Or is afraid to disagree with friends and consequently says whatever the friends want to hear? Do you know anyone who got into trouble but was afraid to ask for help from family or friends?

Do you know anyone who is afraid to end a bad relationship because they are afraid of being alone? Do you know anyone who was afraid to "just say 'no' " to something they did not want to do because their friends would think less of them?

Think about those people. All of them are faced with something they fear, and the challenge is for them to overcome that fear. When Aristotle suggests that virtues are necessary to human flourishing, it is easy to see how courage would contribute to human flourishing, especially if we think of courage as facing and overcoming our fears. *If we are unable to overcome those fears, we often will be unable to obtain or accomplish some of the most important things in life.* Take, for example, the person who is afraid to ask anyone out on a date. He will probably be lonely and feel unfulfilled. Or consider the person who is afraid to speak out in front of other people and especially to disagree with others. He will be unable to hold certain kinds of jobs that require leadership, and he probably will not be able to be a loyal friend. He certainly would not be able to defend his friends against the criticisms of others, since he is afraid to speak out in disagreement. Moreover, it would be difficult for such a person to have close friends, for others would find it hard to get to know him. If he lacks the courage to disagree, then he will always present a pleasant and compliant face to others and thus they will never know his true feelings. He has to have the courage to stand up for himself or else he will never be able to be a good friend.

Courage, in other words, is a virtue of everyday life that involves facing and overcoming our fears.

The Elements of Courage

Fear and Danger

You may have been surprised by the preceding examples of courage, for we most often think of courage in a military context or in situations of great objective danger.

Let us begin by considering that to which courage is a response and to what sphere of experience it belongs. At least two candidates immediately present themselves. Courage can be seen as a response either to *danger* or to *fear*. It is important to distinguish between danger and fear, for one is objective and the other is subjective. **Danger** refers to *objectively* specifiable characteristics of a situation or object that threaten our safety or security in some way. A burning building is dangerous because, if we are trapped in it, we will be incinerated by the fire or killed indirectly through asphyxiation. Similarly, driving a car at high speeds on icy pavement is dangerous because the car easily could go out of control, resulting in possible injuries or death. **Fear,** on the other hand, is a *subjective* reaction that we have to certain objects or events. Certainly some of the things I fear may be objectively dangerous. I may, for example, be afraid of driving very fast on icy roads. However, there are also many people who are afraid of things or events that are not in fact dangerous. Many people are afraid of snakes, even when they know that they are harmless. Some people are afraid of flying on airplanes, even when they know that the flight is probably safer than the drive to the airport. Other people are afraid of things that most of us never even notice. One friend of mine, for example, is very afraid of birds, even though in fact the birds she encounters (sparrows, robins, and so on) are not actually dangerous at all.

This distinction becomes useful in understanding courage, for we get two different conceptions of courage, depending on whether we see courage as a response to fear or to danger. If courage is a response to danger, then those who overcome their fears of things that are not actually dangerous will not count as courageous. Moreover, if courage is a response to objectively specifiable dangers, then a response to such things as psychological dangers will not count as courage. Finally, if courage is a response to danger, then those who do not have the good sense to be afraid of dangerous things will be counted as courageous. On the other hand, if courage is seen as overcoming fear rather than danger, it opens the door to admitting these three types of cases as legitimate instances of courage.

The underlying issue here is interesting, for what is really at issue is the question of *rightly ordered fears*. People who have the courage to go on picnics despite a deathly fear of squirrels may be courageous, but their courage does not exist within a context of rightly ordered fears. Their fears are not proportionate to the actual risk present in the situation. Similarly, the person who does not feel fear when thrown into a pit full of poisonous snakes does not have rightly ordered fears either, for that is a genuinely dangerous situation in which fear is an appropriate response. Paradigmatic or model cases of courage occur within a context of rightly ordered fears.

Confidence and Risk

Not only do we need to have rightly ordered fears to be fully courageous, but we also must have an appropriate level of confidence in our own ability. Self-confidence is grounded in our perception of risk, our own measure of our ability to deal with a specific type of challenge or task. The assessment of risk is based on two factors: the objective danger and our own level of ability to deal with that kind of danger. Thus the level of risk depends in part on our level of ability. It is much riskier for me to drive in a Grand Prix auto race than it would be for a professional driver, for the professional presumably would have a much higher level of ability. The lower one's level of ability, all other things being equal, the riskier it becomes.

Courage, in its fullest sense, rests on (a) *rightly ordered fears* and (b) on *accurate assessment of risk*, of one's ability to meet the specific kind of challenge presented. Differing levels of ability may make one person's action courageous, while another person's identical action simply would be an everyday non-courageous action. Imagine flying on an airplane when the pilot suddenly has a heart attack. I have no idea of how to fly a plane, and for me to take over the controls and follow radio instructions on how to land the plane would be courageous. For my friend Norm, who can fly virtually anything with a semblance of two wings, to land the plane would be "a piece of cake" and require no courage on his part.

The Extremes

Aristotle suggests that courage is the mean between two extremes. One of these extremes is initially quite clear: *cowardice*. The cowardly person is the person with a deficiency of courage, with too little courage. There are two ways of being cowardly: a person may have (1) too much fear or (2) too little self-confidence. We might call having too much fear *timidity*, since the word "timidity" comes from the Latin word *timere*, which means "to fear." On the other hand, one can have too much courage, which is the other extreme. Aristotle suggests that there are two ways in which too much courage can occur. First, an individual may have too much confidence in his own ability, and such a person Aristotle calls *rash* or *foolhardy*. Second, a person can have too little fear. (Aristotle says that we lack a name for such a person, just as we lack names for many other virtues and vices.) In a sense, this example is the opposite of the one about the person who was afraid of harmless birds. Such people are not afraid of things of which they *should* be afraid.

Proper Ends

Thus courage involves at least two elements: *proper confidence* and *rightly ordered fears*. Yet proper confidence and proper fear are not the only two elements necessary to courage. We can imagine a scene in which someone is standing outside of a burning building, wailing, "My baby is trapped inside!" A passerby realizes what is happening and courageously rushes into the building and saves the infant. We would, without hesitation, call this brave or courageous. But what if the person had been standing outside the building, wailing, "I left my hamburger inside!" If someone were to rush inside to rescue the hamburger, we—or at least I—would be inclined to say that he was a fool. The hamburger was not worth the risk, and it would have been easy to buy another one for a few dollars. This example suggests another element to courage: *good judgment*. We need to balance the risk against the possible gains and be sure that the possible gains are worth those risks. In the case of the trapped baby, they clearly are; in the case of the hamburger, they are not. Consequently, courage involves three elements: rightly ordered fears, proper confidence, and good value judgments about ends.

Some Difficult Cases

If courage involves rightly ordered fears, proper self-confidence, and good value judgments about ends, we are left with some perplexing cases that do not quite fit into the standard model. I will briefly describe two.

The Mountain Climber

What do we want to say about the mountain climber who has both rightly ordered fears and proper self-confidence? It is the climber's judgment about ends that seems suspect. A climber who completes a challenging climb in order to save someone's life is clearly courageous. Our problem is with the one who does the same climb simply in order to get to the top. Does this feat show good value judgments about the ends being sought?

Clearly, if the point of mountain climbing is to get to the top, it is silly. Why not just take a helicopter? (Even better, why not just stay home?) Yet it seems that, for people who regularly climb, the point is continually to reconquer their own fear. They need to climb for the self-knowledge it gives them. Yet I still would hesitate to see climbing as a full-fledged case of courage, for it does not seem to be in the service of particularly high ends.

It is also important to ask what kind of character a person develops when courage is that individual's central virtue. The world then is seen in terms of potential challenges, occasions to prove one's courage. Such opportunities are sought out, perhaps even created. Other virtues, such as compromise or compassion, may well recede into the background to the extent that they conflict with proving one's courage.

The Terminally Ill

Another set of difficult cases centers around those with terminal illnesses. What about their courage? What is their goal? The thing about their courage is not *that* they face death and the possibility of dying painfully, but *how* they do so. It is not that they do so fearlessly. Indeed, fear seems quite appropriate in such a situation. Rather, it is how they manage to impress a meaning on their suffering that is most significant for our understanding of courage.

Courage and Gender

Aristotle is unabashed about it: women cannot be courageous in the fullest sense. Aristotle's model of courage is the warrior who intrepidly faces the possibility of death in war. Since women are not allowed to fight in wars, they cannot be brave. If they do succeed in performing brave acts, they will usually be acts that traditionally have been confined to male roles.

Nor is this view restricted to Aristotle or ancient Greece. Consider our own society—where, incidentally, women still had not been allowed in active combat roles as of 1992. On rare occasions, women's courage in traditional male roles is recognized and valued. For example, Major Rhonda Cornum's courage as an Iraqi prisoner of war during the Gulf War was certainly given wide publicity and praise. A flight surgeon, pilot, paratrooper, and biochemistry PhD, Cornum was captured when her helicopter was shot down in the Iraqi desert. With two broken arms, a badly injured knee, a shoulder shattered from a bullet wound, and a bad infection, Cornum's only regret was that she was not able to swallow her wedding ring before her captors got it. Yet she is the exception. In general, two points stand out. First, the courage of women usually is under-recognized and undervalued in our society. Second, courage is seen as much more integral to male identity than it is to female identity in our society. Let us briefly examine both of these issues.

The Under-Recognition of Women's Courage

Women are no less courageous than men, but on the whole the ways in which they exhibit their courage are less likely to be recognized and values as courageous than are the ways in which men exhibit their courage.

Sometimes women exhibit a degree of courage in the face of physical dangers that is comparable to their male counterparts, but it often goes unnoticed. Consider the courage of both the Native Americans and the European pioneers in North America. The courage of the Native American men and the pioneer men who fought each other generally is accepted and valued—even though many of us have profound doubts about the morality of the goal of colonization. Yet the courage of both Native American and pioneer *women* largely is unrecognized and undervalued, despite the great dangers and hardships that they faced.

Women also faced dangers unique to them, most notably childbirth. Prior to the development of modern antiseptic procedures and childbirth techniques, the danger of death was high, the chances of great suffering even higher. Yet women facing such danger intrepidly rarely were recognized for their bravery.

Not all dangers are purely physical. Consider those who have been abused sexually as children and confront their pain—and often their abusers—in order to heal. Most of the victims of such abuse are women. (We are, however, discovering a greater percentage of men were sexually abused than we previously had realized.) The courage they show in facing their greatest fears and overcoming them is remarkable, but we are more likely to recognize the courage of soldiers as the genuine article than we are to acknowledge the courage of individuals who overcome this type of fear.

Finally, consider the courage that some girls show in the passage from adolescence to adulthood. In *Meeting at the Crossroads: Women's Psychology and Girls' Development* (1992), Lyn Mikel Brown and Carol Gilligan have suggested that girls face a developmental challenge requiring great courage as they begin to move into womanhood. Brown and Gilligan found that the transition from girlhood to womanhood was one in which girls typically found themselves increasingly interpersonally isolated, emotionally disconnected, and intellectually uncertain about the truth of their own experience. It took great courage for them to refuse to give up the sense of connectedness that they had developed in girlhood, for them to insist—often against prevailing social expectations—on retaining and enhancing their relationships with other people. So, too, did it take great courage—what Annie Rogers refers to as "ordinary courage"—to remain true to their own experience and to speak out on behalf of that experience.

Courage and Gender Roles

Courage is tied to the issue of gender in a second way as well in our society. Our society, whether rightly or wrongly, tends to see courage as much more integral to a masculine identity than to a feminine identity. If a man is not courageous, he is much more open to the charge of being less of a man than a woman is open to the corresponding charge if she is not courageous. Failing to be courageous usually is not seen as detracting from her femininity (except possibly in the area of defending her children) to the same extent that it is perceived as detracting from a man's masculinity.

Most of us, myself included, would be highly skeptical about this restriction of courage to men. But it raises important philosophical questions about the role of gender in ethics and the ideals toward which we are striving. We shall return to this issue in Chapter Eleven in our discussion of the ethics of diversity.

COMPASSION

Responding to the Suffering of Others

One of the striking things about the villagers of Le Chambon was their ability and willingness to respond spontaneously and wholeheartedly to the plight of the Jews who came to their doors. It is precisely this responsiveness to suffering which is at the heart of compassion. Even the etymology of the word "compassion" highlights this element of compassion. It comes from the Latin words for "with" and "feel" or "suffer" or "endure." To experience compassion for someone is, at least to a limited extent or in some metaphorical fashion, to share their suffering with them. Yet the etymology only takes us part of the way, for compassion is more than simply "feeling with"; it also involves a disposition to respond to the other's suffering in a caring way that seeks to alleviate that suffering or to comfort those who are experiencing it. Let us look at both aspects of compassion: feeling and acting.

Compassion and Emotion

Compassion begins in *feeling*, in our affective relationship to the world. The compassionate person is not some type of utilitarian computer that infers or deduces the suffering that others are experiencing; rather, the compassionate person suffers with the other person to some extent. This dimension of compassion is *heart-wrenching*. I remember watching my father in a hospital room fighting for his life after major surgery, and my heart poured out to him. Similarly, the villagers of Le Chambon responded to the Jews who came to their door by opening their hearts as well as their homes. At other times, we may experience compassion less intensely, but the basic affective response to the suffering of another person is the same.

There are at least two reasons why this affective dimension of compassion is so important. First, without compassion we often will fail to *recognize* the suffering of others as suffering. The compassionate person has, as it were, the emotional radar to detect suffering that would otherwise not be noticed as suffering. The Nazis did not perceive the suffering of the Jews as suffering, but rather simply as what they deserved. Often, precisely in order to be able to treat other people inhumanely or to prevent our own lives from being disturbed by the suffering of others, we shut ourselves off emotionally from perceiving the suffering of other people as suffering. Think, for example, of how many of us shut out the suffering of the homeless or the aged or those with AIDS. We do not let ourselves *feel* anything for these people, for such feelings may disturb our lives.

Second, those who are suffering often need precisely this affective dimension of compassion, need the *feeling* of being cared about. A woman who had been saved through the village of Le Chambon commented on the difference between the experience of those who were saved through Le Chambon and those who were saved by fleeing to another country. "If today we are not bitter people like most survivors," she wrote, "it can only be due to the fact that we met people like the people of Le Chambon, who showed to us simply that life can be different, that there are people who care, that people can live together, and even risk their own lives for their fellow man."

Compassion, Moral Imagination, and Action

The relationship between compassionate feelings and compassionate action is a complex one. Compassion that *never* resulted in action would hardly be compassion. Yet we can imagine situations in which the compassion is genuine, and yet due to unusual circumstances action is not possible. Compassion always involves the *desire* to do something about the situation, but it does not guarantee the opportunity to do so.

Even when the opportunity to act is present, compassionate feelings do not always tell us what the right course of action is. In order for compassionate feelings to be translated into actions, we need good judgment and often moral imagination as well. Recall the example of Le Chambon. For Jean-Pierre to bring a gift to Steckler on the bus, for the village to sing a song of affection and farewell to him—these were compassionate actions that showed an impressive amount of moral imagination as well.

It is precisely this element of moral imagination that traditional moral theories such as Kant's or Bentham's neglect. They seek to provide us with a set of *rules* for living the moral life, but moral imagination and creativity are precisely what take us beyond the rules. We might liken this observation to the difference between painting-by-the-numbers and painting one's own composition. When I was young, we used to get "paint-by-number" kits that contained a picture that was already outlined and in each space was the number of the color to be painted there. Some people hope that the moral life is this way: your moral principles will tell you exactly what to do. My own view is that the moral life is more like painting your own picture: ultimately you have to sketch out your own picture and, based on your best knowledge and training, choose your own colors.

Compassion and Pity

One final element in our definition of compassion is worth noting here: the difference between pity and compassion. The distinction centers around the issue of equality. When we pity someone, we look down on them, we see them as less than we are. Pity is essentially a response that promotes *inequality*, establishing the superiority of the pitier over the pitied. Part of the moral ambiguity of pity is that in the act of pitying someone, we both pull them up (by trying to help them) and put them down (by treating them as less than we are). It is little wonder that few people want to be pitied. When they are the object of pity, they pay a high price for the help they receive.

Compassion, on the other hand, presupposes a certain kind of *moral equality*. The villagers of Le Chambon did not look down on those they helped, but rather realized that "There, but for the grace of God, go I," which is why it is so much better to be the object of compassion rather than pity. If people feel compassion toward you, they see you as an equal who happens to be suffering. Their emotive response joins with you rather than separates itself from you. You feel affirmed and supported rather than put down.

The Moral Extremes

If you recall Aristotle's strategy for analyzing the virtues, you will remember that he suggests that they can be bracketed between the two extremes of excess and deficiency. Aristotle does not discuss compassion, probably because he did not see it as a virtue. (He does discuss well-wishing in Book IX of the *Nichomachean Ethics*, but that is the closest he comes to something like compassion.) Yet compassion offers an interesting challenge to the general claim that there can be both an excess and a deficiency in regard to any particular virtue. Let us look at this more closely.

Moral Callousness

There is relatively little difficulty with discussing what a deficiency of compassion would be like. It is a type of moral insensitivity or callousness, a state in which we fail to respond, either in feeling or action, to the suffering of other people.

In extreme cases, this lack of responsiveness may reach pathological dimensions. Sociopaths are individuals who seem to lack all feeling about the suffering of others, including the suffering that they may directly or indirectly inflict.

Other cases are less extreme, either in their intensity or their range. Some individuals may find that their level of compassion for anyone is low. Kant, in the passage cited in Chapter VI, talks of the man in whose heart "nature had implanted little sympathy." Such people have a generally low level of responsiveness to the suffering of anyone around them. At other times our lack of compassion is selective: certain individuals, groups, genders, or races fall outside the domain of those whom we are willing to perceive compassionately. In either type of case, we want to count it as a moral failing.

Moral Education

The degree of compassion we are capable of feeling is not fixed and immutable, although it cannot be changed instantaneously by a sheer act of the will. We have a natural disposition toward compassion, but whether that sense grows or atrophies depends on many factors, especially on childhood experience and education. Barriers to the growth of compassion may be mild or severe. A person's capacity for compassion is often dependent on childhood role models, usually parents. If our parents showed little or no compassion for the suffering of others, or if their compassion systematically eliminated certain individuals or groups as undeserving of compassion, we will probably have a tendency to be like them. In extreme cases such as when a child has been brutalized throughout childhood, whether physically, sexually, or emotionally, the capacity for compassion may be all but extinguished.

There are various ways in which our capacity for compassion may be educated. The word "education" goes back to the Latin word *educare*, which means "to lead out of." Usually, moral education is a matter of leading us out of our narrowness and provincialism. Literature and the arts are especially powerful in accomplishing this task, for they develop both our understanding and our emotions at the same time. They help us to see the world through other people's eyes and to understand the richness of their perceptions.

Sometimes the barriers to compassion are much stronger. Individuals who have been brutalized as children, for example, often have erected amazingly high and thick walls that prevent them from recognizing the suffering of others. In such cases, intensive psychotherapy is often the only way of dismantling those walls. Such therapy, when successful, liberates people from the walls that imprison them and cut them off from their own capacity for compassion. As such, it too is a form of moral education.

Can We Have Too Much Compassion?

The question of whether it is possible to have too much compassion may seem a strange one that only philosophers would ask. After all, an overabundance of compassion is hardly our major social problem. If anything, our society needs to find ways of increasing compassion; it does not have to worry about having too much of it. Yet there is a value in asking this question, for it rounds out our discussion of compassion by drawing our attention to two final points about compassion.

Indeed, we find that the charge of "too much compassion" is made in our society when we claim that someone is a "bleeding heart." Those who make such a charge rarely explain what they mean, but we can outline two interpretations of the "bleeding heart" criticism that will help us understand compassion better.

First, to call people "bleeding hearts" may imply that they do not know how to *act* properly on their compassion. At times, our compassion for others' suffering may lead us to act in ways that decrease those other people's responsibility for their own lives. If, for example, we see an older man with shaky hands trying to pour a glass of milk, we may take the pitcher and pour it for him as an act of compassion. In the process, however, we may rob him of a sense of his own autonomy and dignity, giving us, then, one interpretation of the "bleeding heart" charge: bleeding hearts may be individuals who feel a proper amount of compassion but act on it in inappropriate, albeit understandable, ways. From this example we learn that it is not enough to feel compassion; we must also have the good judgment to know how best to act on it.

There is a second interpretation of the "bleeding heart" charge that gives us another insight into the nature of compassion. The charge might imply that the virtue of compassion has been given disproportionately great weight in either of two ways. First, our compassion for another's suffering may outweigh our perception of other characteristics of the individual. Our compassion for the suffering of a prisoner facing execution may overshadow our perception of the atrocious character of the prisoner's crimes. Second, which is often a corollary of the first point, our compassion may outweigh other appropriate virtues, such as anger or justice. This suggests that we do not have to worry about having too much compassion as long as we are sure that it is balanced by other virtues.

The answer is not to decrease the amount of compassion we have, but rather to increase the strength of the virtues that balance compassion.

Gender and Compassion

In recent years extensive work has been done on the relationship between gender and ethics, and much of it has centered around the role of compassion in women's moral lives. We will be examining this issue in more depth in the next chapter, but several comments are in order here.

Compassion, Courage, and Gender

There is an interesting symmetry in the relationship between courage and masculinity and the relationship between compassion and femininity in our society. Just as an absence of courage counts against a man's masculinity, so an absence of compassion often counts against a woman's femininity.

There is another interesting barrier to the expression of compassion, a barrier that may be encountered more frequently by men than women. Often we encounter situations in which we want to show compassion, but we do not know what to *do*. We see someone crying in grief, we see a homeless, lost soul on the street, or we might even see someone dealing with the frustrations of aging. Because we do not know what to do, and because we are uncomfortable with our own impotence, we often push away these feelings of compassion. We do so because we cannot stand the feelings of impotence and frustration that we experience when we cannot act on our compassionate feelings. This powerlessness is more likely to be a problem for individuals who have been socialized into believing that they must always respond to situations through action. Insofar as men in our society are more likely to be socialized in this way, they are more likely to encounter this barrier than women are.

Self-Love

Until she met Shug, Celie—the central character in Alice Walker's *The Color Purple*—was terrified. She never thought that she deserved much, if anything at all, in life. So her treatment at her husband's hands hardly came as a surprise. But the terror remained, for she feared each moment could be worse than the preceding one. From her earliest days, she felt that what she wanted just did not count. Indeed, she hardly knew what she wanted. And then she met Shug.

Shug—short for "Sugar"—taught Celie what it meant to love herself. Sometimes she taught Celie by telling her—telling her how to act, telling her that it was OK to feel certain things. But her most powerful teaching came through her life: she taught Celie how to love herself by the way she lived her entire life. *The Color Purple* tells the story of Celie's journey toward self-love—and of her courage in persisting in this journey. And it is precisely this self-love or proper pride that Aristotle claims in the *Nicomachean Ethics* is the central virtue upon which all the other virtues rest.

The Definition of Self-Love

Self-love, like other virtues we have discussed, has both an emotive and a behavioral component. It involves having certain *feelings* as well as *acting* in certain ways. We can understand it initially by comparing it with love for other people.

Loving Others

My wife and I love each other, and certain kinds of feelings and actions are typical of that love. We feel a real tenderness for each other, a sense of deep joy that we are in the world and that we are in each other's lives. I cherish her and I want her to be happy; she feels the same about me. We both want what is best for the other person. *Love wants to see the other person flourish.* These feelings come out in the way we act as well. Besides many hugs and other displays of affection, we do many things to take care of each other. If we are overworking, one of us may plan a vacation for us to get away and just relax—or just go out for a nice long, relaxing dinner or an enjoyable movie.

Of course, none of this is perfect. We have our disagreements and arguments about things. We do not simply agree with one another: love contains plenty of room for disagreement, criticism, and even disapproval. When I want to order thick-sliced bacon for breakfast, my wife does not hesitate to remind me about cholesterol and calories. When she volunteers for one more committee, I do not hesitate to remind her about leaving some time to have a personal life. We find a real peace and harmony in our love for one another, but we still have plenty of room for disagreement, criticism, and growth.

Nor does our love for each other eliminate our love and concern for the rest of the world. For example, we both love our own families that we grew up in, and our love for each other certainly does not eliminate our love for them. We love each other first and foremost, but certainly not solely.

Loving Ourselves

We can understand the meaning of self-love by first looking at love of another person. First, it involves having certain kinds of *feelings* toward ourselves, feelings of positive regard, respect, and concern. Notice that this definition does not preclude self-criticism. *Self-love is not unconditionally positive self-approval.* It may include rigorous self-examination, but it does so within the context of a deep concern for the genuine welfare of the self. Similarly, self-love involves *acting* in certain ways toward ourselves. People who genuinely love themselves act in ways that promote their flourishing, even when that is difficult. Alcoholics who are clean and sober are acting in ways that show a genuine self-love, even though it might be extremely difficult for them to do so. *Self-love does not mean doing whatever you want to do.* Rather, it means doing whatever promotes your genuine flourishing.

The Vices of Deficiency

Recall again the story of *The Color Purple.* Celie provides us with a striking example of someone who has too little self-love.

A deficiency of self-love manifests itself in various ways. Some people are *self-deprecating*, putting themselves and their accomplishments down whenever possible. Others are *self-effacing*, hiding themselves and their achievements from notice by others. Some are *servile*, making their own needs and desires subservient to the needs and desires of others. When they behave subserviently by trying to please the people around them, they are *obsequious*. Some are simply *unaware of themselves*, for they have never come to know themselves well enough to be certain of their own likes and dislikes, their own hopes and fears, their own beliefs and doubts.

Usually the behavior associated with these attitudes toward the self is easy to recognize. Yet sometimes it manifests itself in opposite ways. Someone with very low self-esteem may behave in straightforwardly self-effacing or self-deprecating ways. However, they may compensate for their feelings of inadequacy by going to the other extreme, acting in arrogant or conceited ways.

What, if anything, is wrong with these traits? Within Aristotle's perspective, the answer is clear: they detract from flourishing. People who always put themselves down, who hide their own accomplishments, and who put their needs behind everyone else's are less likely to flourish. They suffer from a kind of *anorexia of the spirit* in which they starve themselves from the nourishment of relationships of equality with other people.

The Vices of Excess

Excesses of self-love take many forms: arrogance, conceit, egoism, vanity, and narcissism are but a few of the ways in which we can err in this direction. (The richness of our vocabulary here suggests that this type of vice is either more common than the vices of deficiency or else we focus more carefully on this type when it occurs.) In some cases there is an excess of attention to the self, an absorption in the self (*narcissism*); other cases involve valuing the self too highly (*conceit*); some involve patterns of behavior that show little regard for the welfare of others (*arrogance*); still others involve too great an attention to some aspect of one's appearance (*vanity*).

Self-Love and Friendship

One area in which the need for proper self-love emerges most clearly is friendship. Aristotle suggested that it is difficult, if not impossible, to have good friendships without proper self-love. There is good evidence to suggest that he is right in this regard. Reciprocity and mutual concern are at the heart of friendship, and either too much or too little self-love throws these factors out of balance.

The Obsequious Friend

We have all seen people who are so desperate to have friends that they will do anything for the other person. They give up themselves in order to be accepted by the other person as a friend. Such friendships usually are doomed. The obsequious friend is constantly vulnerable to abuse, since the friendship often is valued at all costs. Moreover, who would want that person for a friend once the person's true character is evident? We depend on our friends to help us see things in our lives we may be missing or misinterpreting. But the obsequious friend is unwilling to stand up to a friend, to articulate a different vision of reality. Obsequious friends simply mirror back what they think we want them to see and say.

The Narcissistic Friend

The situation is hardly any better when friends are narcissists, for this behavior also upsets the reciprocity and mutual concern that are so central to friendship. Narcissists are so self-absorbed that they cannot be genuinely concerned for the welfare of their friends. An essential part of being a good friend is being concerned about one's friends for their own sake. This does not mean that friends are purely altruistic, but it does mean that they are not concerned solely about themselves.

Both too little self-love and too much self-love destroy the balance between self-love and love for the other person which is the foundation of genuine friendships.

Self-Love and Moral Traditions

Egoism

As we saw in Chapter Five, ethical egoism had a very important moral insight: we ought to value ourselves. It fell short of the mark, however, on two counts. First, it failed to provide an adequate account of how we ought to act in order to value ourselves. Second, it mistook part of the story (valuing oneself) for the whole story. Aristotle, in stressing the centrality of the virtue of self-love, manages to capture the insights of ethical egoism without repeating its mistakes.

Self-Love, Self-Respect, and Kant

Kant's categorical imperative emphasized the importance of respect for oneself as well as for other people. That notion of self-respect, which contemporary Kantian philosophers such as Thomas Hill have explored in fascinating detail, has important similarities to Aristotle's notion of self-love. Yet there are important differences which center in part around the more general differences between love and respect. Love contains a broader and richer affective component than respect does. We can respect a stranger we do not even care about personally; we can hardly love such a stranger without knowing him better or without caring about him. There is an intimacy to love that is not necessarily present in respect. Also, love and respect result in different actions, for love is much more active and concerned about the other person than respect is.

The Place of Self-Love in the Utilitarian Calculus

One of Bernard Williams's principal criticisms of utilitarianism centered around the way in which it failed to give adequate weight to the individual agent's fundamental projects. An ethics of virtue which makes self-love the cornerstone of the moral life avoids this trap. Self-love involves giving a privileged place to one's own fundamental projects, to those hopes and dreams and values that are central to one's identity as a person, for these are usually crucial to flourishing.

Pride, Humility, and the Christian Tradition

Initially, one of the startling contrasts between the Aristotelian and Christian traditions centers around the question of what counts as proper self-love or pride. On the surface, the contrast is stark: Aristotle calls pride a central virtue, while Aquinas condemns it as a cardinal vice, the root of all other vices.

When we look below the surface, however, the disagreement is less clear-cut and more nuanced. In fact, Aristotle (and Greek society in general) had something akin to what Aquinas calls "pride." For the Greeks, *hubris* was the overstepping on the bounds established by the gods. It is their equivalent of the Christian sin of pride. On the other side of the fence, Aquinas stresses the importance of the virtue of proper self-love. Part of the disagreement between Aristotle and Aquinas thus proves to be verbal. The same words (actually, the Greek and Latin equivalents of those words) mean different things. What Aquinas condemns as pride may be closer to what Aristotle calls *hubris* than what he calls pride. Indeed, Lucifer's pride is quite close to Oedipus's *hubris*.

But this explanation is only part of the story. For Aquinas, *humility* is clearly a central virtue, but not so for Aristotle. This fact reflects a larger difference in worldviews. Humility essentially consists in knowing one's place and in not overvaluing one's self and one's achievements. One's "place" is more clearly and firmly articulated in a Christian worldview than it was for the Greeks, and there has been a more elaborate institutional structure in Christianity to remind people of exactly what their place was. To encourage humility as a virtue is to promote a stable and placid social and political order.

Wisdom, Moral Pluralism, and the Good Life

One of the principal criticisms levelled against Aristotle's approach to ethics is that it fails to tells us how to act. Despite all the illuminating things that Aristotle has to say about good character, we are still left without answers to pressing moral questions such as abortion, euthanasia, the death penalty, and the allocation of scarce medical resources.

There is much merit in this criticism, which is a good reason for saying that virtue ethics is seriously incomplete without the moral traditions we have considered earlier in this book. An ethics of character must be completed by an ethics of action, of this point there is no doubt. We can cultivate the virtue of compassion, for example, but when we act compassionately, we must still be aware of the moral concerns raised by other traditions. When we act compassionately toward other people, we must also be aware of their rights, take into account the consequences of our compassionate actions, and treat other persons as ends-in-themselves. Good character, in other words, does not obviate the need for other types of moral consideration.

However, an ethics of action is equally in need of an ethics of character for at least two reasons. First, one of the single greatest difficulties that act-oriented moral philosophies face is in applying a moral theory to a particular case. A morally sensitive character is more likely to insure that we apply a principle with insight and creativity. Without good character, we often only will be able to apply more principles in a mechanical manner, largely insensitive to the nuances of the situation. Second, as we have seen throughout this book, there are several different moral traditions which are relevant to our considerations of how to act. The virtue of practical wisdom consists, in part, of being able to balance such potentially competing concerns about rights, duty, and consequences. The wise person is the individual who is able to know when the concerns of one tradition take precedence over the concerns of the other traditions.

Bibliographical Essay

The classic source for discussions of the virtues is Aristotle's *Nicomachean Ethics* (abbreviated EN). It is available in a number of translations. Helpful **commentaries/introductions** to EN include Christopher Biffle's *A Guided*

Tour of Selections from Aristotle's "Nicomachean Ethics" (Mountain View, California; Mayfield Publishing Company, 1991) and Roger Sullivan's *Morality and the Good Life* (Memphis: Memphis State University, 1977). The account of the virtues in EN is supplemented, and occasionally contradicted, in Aristotle's other major work in ethics, the *Eudemian Ethics* (EE). For a translation and commentary on Books I, II, and VIII of EE, see Michael Woods, *Aristotle's "Eudemian Ethics"* (Oxford: Clarendon Press, 1982). In addition to EN and EE, Aristotle's *Politics* and his *Rhetoric* contain important sections relating to the virtues.

General works on Aristotle include Sir David Ross's *Aristotle* (New York: Barnes and Noble, 1966), W. K. C. Guthrie's work on Aristotle in Vol. 6 of his *A History of Greek Philosophy* (Cambridge: Cambridge University Press, 1981). **Works specifically on his ethics** include Nancy Sherman's *The Fabric of Character: Aristotle's Theory of Virtue* (Oxford: Clarendon Press, 1989); John Cooper's *Reason and Human Good in Aristotle* (Cambridge: Harvard University Press, 1975); W. F. R. Hardie's *Aristotle's Ethical Theory* (Oxford: Clarendon Press, 1980); Richard Kraut's *Aristotle on the Human Good* (Princeton: Princeton University Press, 1989); and Troels Engberg-Pedersen's *Aristotle's Theory of Moral Insight* (Oxford: Clarendon Press, 1983). Two excellent anthologies of articles on Aristotle's ethics are Amélie Rorty's *Essays on Aristotle's Ethics* (Berkeley: University of California Press, 1980), and Barnes, Schofield, and Sorabji's *Articles on Aristotle: 2; Ethics and Politics* (New York: St. Martin's, 1977); the latter contains an excellent bibliography. One of the most fascinating treatments of Aristotle's ethics is to be found in part three of Martha Nussbaum's *The Fragility of Goodness: Luck and Ethics in Greek Tragedy and Philosophy* (Cambridge: Harvard University Press, 1986). For a perceptive discussion and evaluation of Aristotle's ethics in light of current work in feminist ethics, see Marcia Homiak, "Feminism and Aristotle's Rational Ideal," in *A Mind of One's Own: Feminist Essays on Reason and Objectivity* (Boulder, Colo.: Westview Press, 1993), pp. 1–18.

The **contemporary resurgence of interest in the virtues** begins with Philippa Foot's "Virtues and Vices" in her *Virtues and Vices and Other Essays In Moral Philosophy* (Berkeley and Los Angeles: University of California Press, 1978), pp. 1–18, and Alsadair MacIntyre's *After Virtue*, 2d edition (Notre Dame: University of Notre Dame Press, 1984). Several **reviews of the recent literature** are noteworthy: Arthur Fleming's "Reviewing the Virtues," *Ethics*, Vol. 90, No. 3 (1980), pp. 587–95; Gregory Pence's "Recent Work on the Virtues," *American Philosophical Quarterly*, Vol. 21, No. 4 (October, 1984), pp. 281–97; Marcia Baron's "Varieties of Ethics of Virtue," *American Philosophical Quarterly*, Vol. 22, No. 1 (January, 1985), 47–53; Gregory Trianosky's "What Is Virtue Ethics All About?" *American Philosophical Quarterly*, Vol. 27, No. 4 (October, 1990), pp. 335–44; and Phillip Montague, "Virtue Ethics: A Qualified Success Story," *American Philosophical Quarterly*, Vol. 29, No. 1

(January, 1992), pp. 53–61. For an insightful analysis into **historical views of virtue,** see Richard White, "Historical Perspectives on the Morality of Virtue," *The Journal of Value Inquiry,* Vol. 25 (1991), pp. 217–31. Also see the excellent bibliography in *The Virtues,* edited by Robert B. Kruschwitz and Robert C. Roberts (Belmont, California: Wadsworth, 1987). Other collections of contemporary articles on virtues and vices include Sommers and Sommers, *Vice and Virtue in Everyday Life* (San Diego: Harcourt Brace Jovanovich, 1989); Vol. XIII of *Midwest Studies in Philosophy* (1988) on virtue theory; the special double issue on the virtues in *Philosophia,* Vol. 20 (1990); Flanagan and Rorty's *Identity, Character, and Morality* (Cambridge: MIT Press, 1990); Halberstam's *Virtues and Values* (Englewood Cliffs, New Jersey: Prentice-Hall, 1988); and John Deigh's *Ethics and Personality: Essays in Moral Psychology* (Chicago: University of Chicago Press, 1992). Joel Kupperman's *Character* (New York: Oxford University Press, 1991) presents a character-based ethical theory that places the discussion of particular virtues and vices within the context of the individual's character. For a utilitarian approach to virtue, see John Kilcullen, "Utilitarianism and Virtue," *Ethics,* Vol. 93, No. 3 (April, 1983), pp. 451–66.

Aristotle's discussion of *courage* appears primarily in his *Nichomachean Ethics,* Book III, chapters six through nine. David Pears's "Courage as a Mean" in Rorty's *Essays on Aristotle's Ethics* (Berkeley: University of California Press, 1980) is an insightful, detailed consideration of Aristotle's views on this virtue; for a critique of Pears's position, see Michael Stocker's "Courage, the Doctrine of the Mean, and the Possibility of Evaluative and Emotional Coherence" in his *Plural and Conflicting Values* (Oxford: Clarendon Press, 1990), pp. 129–64. Douglas Walton's *Courage* (Berkeley: University of California Press, 1986) provides a standard account of courage that focuses on courageous actions rather than character, while Lee Yearle's *Mencius and Aquinas: Theories of Virtue and Conceptions of Courage* (Albany: State University of New York Press, 1990) offers an interesting cross-cultural comparison between the thought of an early Confucian and a medieval Christian. For a provocative picture of courage that also recognizes its negative side, see Amélie Rorty's "Two Faces of Courage" in her *Mind in Action* (Boston: Beacon Press, 1988). Also see chapter two, "Courage," in John Casey's *Pagan Virtue* (Oxford: Clarendon Press, 1990). On ordinary courage in adolescent girls, see Lyn Mikel Brown and Carol Gilligan, *Meeting at the Crossroads: Women's Psychology and Girls' Development* (Cambridge: Harvard University Press, 1992) and Annie Rogers's paper, "The Development of Courage in Girls and Women," is available from the Harvard Project on the Psychology of Women and the Development of Girls, Harvard Graduate School of Education, and will be published in the *Harvard Educational Review.* For an account of Rhonda Cornum's experiences as a prisoner of war, *She Went to War* by Rhonda Cornum as told to Peter Copeland (Novato, California: Presidio Press, 1992).

The explicitly philosophical literature on **compassion** is relatively limited. The best pieces are Lawrence Blum's "Compassion," *Explaining Emotions,* edited by A. O. Rorty (Berkeley: University of California Press, 1980), pp. 507–18; Nancy Snow's "Compassion," *American Philosophical Quarterly,* Vol. 28, No. 3 (July, 1991), pp. 195–205; and Adrian M. S. Piper, "Impartiality, Compassion, and Modal Imagination," *Ethics,* Vol. 101, No. 4 (July, 1991), pp. 726–57; also see the section on compassion in Richard Taylor's *Good and Evil* (New York: Macmillan, 1970). For a perceptive and intriguing discussion of the place of compassion in contemporary American life, see Robert Wuthnow's *Acts of Compassion* (Princeton: Princeton University Press, 1991). The story of the village of the Le Chambon is recounted in Philip Hallie's *Lest Innocent Blood Be Shed* (New York: Harper Colophon, 1979) and his articles, "Skepticism, Narrative, and Holocaust Ethics," *Philosophical Forum,* Vol. XVI, No. 1–2 (Fall-Winter, 1984–85) pp. 33–49, and his "From Cruelty to Goodness," *Vice and Virtue in Everyday Life,* edited by Christina Sommers and Fred Sommers (San Diego: Harcourt Brace Jovanovich, 1989), pp. 9–24.

There is an extensive literature on the issue of **self-love** and **self-respect.** For an insightful discussion of Aristotle's position on this issue, see Marcia Homiak's "Virtue and Self-Love in Aristotle's Ethics," *The Canadian Journal of Philosophy,* Vol. 11, No. 4 (December, 1981), pp. 633–51. On the relationship between self-love and friendship in Aristotle, see especially Richard Kraut's *Aristotle on Human Good* (Princeton: Princeton University Press, 1989). One of the most influential contemporary philosophical articles on self-respect is Thomas Hill's "Servility and Self-Respect," reprinted in his *Autonomy and Self-Respect* (Cambridge: Cambridge University Press, 1991). Interesting responses to Hill's article include Larry Blum, Marcia Homiak, Judy Housman, and Naomi Scheman, "Altruism and Women's Oppression," *Philosophical Forum,* Vol. 5 (1975), pp. 222–47; George Sher, "Our Preferences, Ourselves" *Philosophy and Public Affairs,* Vol. 12, No. 1 (Winter, 1983), pp. 34–50, and Marilyn Friedman's "Moral Integrity and the Deferential Wife," *Philosophical Studies,* Vol. 47, No. 1 (1985), pp. 141–50. On the relationship between self-respect and race, see Michelle M. Moody-Adams, "Race, Class, and the Social Construction of Self-Respect," *Philosophical Forum,* Vol. XXIV, Nos. 1–3 (Fall-spring, 1992–93), pp. 251–66.

The story of Shug is found in Alice Walker, *The Color Purple* (New York: Harcourt Brace Jovanovich, 1982).

Citations. Philip Hallie's description of Le Chambon is drawn from "Scepticism, Narrative, and Holocaust Ethics" p. 40. The quotation from Aristotle's *Nichomachean Ethics* is from Book II, chapter six, 1106a16-24 in Irwin's translation with minor changes. Nussbaum's chart of the virtues is found in her "Non-relative Virtues," *Midwest Studies in Philosophy,* Vol. 13 (1988), p. 35. The woman's comments about Le Chambon are quoted in Hallie, *Midwest Studies in Philosophy,* Vol. 13 (1988), p. 44.

Discussion Questions

1. Recall your rating in the Ethical Inventory of statement 43: "Morality is mainly a matter of what kind of person you are."
   (a) After having studied several other approaches to ethics in addition to Aristotle's, what do you think the main arguments against this statement are?
   (b) Has your rating of this item changed after reading this chapter? If so, in what way? If your rating has not changed, are your reasons for your rating any different now than they were when you first responded to this statement?
2. Recall your response to statement 44: "Sometimes courage seems to go too far."
   (a) Is courage a simple virtue or does it have several components? If it is complex, what are its constituent parts?
   (b) If you agreed with this statement, give an example of when courage goes too far.
   (c) Has your rating of this item changed after reading this chapter? If so, in what way? If your rating has not changed, are your reasons for your rating any different now than they were when you first responded to this statement?
3. Recall your rating of statement 45: "Compassion for the suffering of others is an important character trait."
   (a) In your view, can a person ever have too much compassion? Explain.
   (b) Has your rating of this item changed after reading this chapter? If so, in what way? If your rating has not changed, are your reasons for your rating any different now than they were when you first responded to this statement?
4. Your rating of statement 46 ("It is important to care about yourself.") gives an indication of your views on the importance of self-love as a virtue.
   (a) Explain what it means to care about yourself. Give an example of doing so and an example of failing to do so. How important a virtue is this?
   (b) Has your rating of this item changed after reading this chapter? If so, in what way? If your rating has not changed, are your reasons for your rating any different now than they were when you first responded to this statement?
5. For Aristotle, virtues are those strengths of character that promote human flourishing. But exactly what is human flourishing? Address

yourself to both the substantive and the epistemological issues that this question raises. Can you give any examples of someone who clearly is not flourishing? Are there any difficulties in *knowing* whether someone is flourishing? Are there many different legitimate conceptions of human flourishing? If so, how do you deal with these difficulties?

6. I have suggested that there are typically some gender differences in our society in regard to virtues such as courage and compassion. Based on your own experience, do you think this statement is true? Are there any other virtues in our society that exhibit gender differences? Are there any vices that are valued differently in men and women? Are there reasons why virtues and vices *should* be different for women and for men?
7. One of the virtues not discussed in this chapter is forgiveness. Think about the place of forgiveness in a person's character. Is it ever possible to be too forgiving? not forgiving enough? Does *not* forgiving sometimes play a positive role in our lives? How does too little forgiveness detract from human flourishing? Why is it sometimes hard not to forgive another? If it is possible to be too forgiving, how could it detract from human flourishing? Why is it sometimes hard to forgive? How does forgiving—and not forgiving—yourself relate to human flourishing? How does self-forgiveness differ from forgiveness of other people? Explain.
8. Aristotle said "count no man happy until he is dead." What does this statement mean? Is it true? Why must virtue (and human flourishing) wait that long?
9. The movies *Glory* and *The Color Purple* present quite different views of courage. Compare these two movies in regard to the relationship between courage and gender. What does such a comparison suggest about this relationship?
10. Is Gandhi courageous? If so, what does that suggest about the relationship between courage and violence? How does this contrast with the picture of the relationship between courage and violence in *Glory*? Is the willingness to fight necessarily a sign of courage?

CHAPTER 11

The Ethics of Diversity: Gender, Ethnicity, and Individuality

Introduction

We are puzzled, both as citizens and as philosophers, about diversity. The very motto of our country, "*e pluribus unum*," speaks eloquently of a national hope: "out of many, one." Yet the pithiness of the Latin gives a misleading impression of clarity. What do we mean by "*unum*"? If we are seeking to be "one," does it mean that diversity should be eliminated? Surely uniformity is not our goal. Americans often have criticized societies such as that of contemporary China precisely because of their uniformity. Moreover, the American tradition of individualism would seem to value "the many" over "the one." Yet what should be the relationship between the one and the many, between unity and diversity? Often, our answers to this question are posed in terms of metaphors. For several decades, the metaphor of a melting pot captured our national ideal, if not our political realities. However, in the eyes of many, this metaphor threatened diversity and individuality, for in a melting pot everything gradually becomes the same. More recently, Jesse Jackson's metaphor of a patchwork quilt has challenged the melting pot metaphor, offering more hope of preserving uniqueness and difference within a context of unity. Yet we remain undecided, as a country and often as individuals, about exactly which metaphor most accurately captures the proper mix between the unity and diversity that we strive to achieve. Most of us reject the extremes of complete uniformity and complete diversity. We do not want everyone to be the same, but neither do we want such diversity

Where Politics and Philosophy Meet: The General Education Requirements

One of the interesting ways in which this debate about cultural diversity touches the lives of college students is in the general education requirements of their particular college or university. At one time, general education was grounded firmly in a shared understanding of the classics of the Western tradition: Homer, Plato, Aristotle, Aeschylus, Euripides, Cicero, Augustine, Aquinas, Erasmus, Dante, Shakespeare, Montaigne, Descartes, Hume, Goethe, Cervantes, Kant, and Hegel. Now there is much less agreement among academics about (a) what constitutes the 'canon' of essential writings and (b) about whether we ought to expect students to study that canon. One of the obvious advantages of having and studying a canon is that there is a common ground of shared traditions and experiences that provide a basis for a more finely textured understanding among people. Yet one of the clear disadvantages has been that the canon, at least as traditionally understood, left out certain groups in society (such as racial and ethnic minorities, non-Europeans, and women) and neglected material vital both to their understanding of themselves and to our understanding of one another. The traditional core general education program in American universities, for example, contained nothing from or about Native Americans, even though they obviously are crucial to our understanding of ourselves as a country.

that there is no meaningful sense in which we can call ourselves one people. Being part of a community means having things in common.

The issue of community and commonalities is not a purely political question. It is also an issue of lively disagreement among philosophers. For the last seventy years, philosophers have become increasingly discontented with, and mistrustful of, the philosophical 'canon' of essential writings and the Enlightenment belief in the universality of reason. Whereas initially this mistrust had a distinctively Marxist flavor, in the last thirty years post-structuralist thinkers such as Jacques Derrida, a contemporary French philosopher of the traditional structures of philosophy, have increasingly carried out a critique of the basic presuppositions of the modern age. Derrida, for example, has urged us to reread and rewrite the history of philosophy, paying attention precisely to those elements which usually are relegated to the margins of philosophy. The result has been a partial tearing down (or "deconstruction," to use a term introduced by Jacques Derrida), a radical reshuffling which brings to the fore previously neglected thinkers and ideas. With this reorientation, at least ideally, comes a greater receptivity to diversity.

The Neglect of Diversity

If we are to understand the proper role of diversity in the moral life, we must first have some understanding of why it seems to have little place in ethical theory. In recent years, there has been a growing emphasis on cultural diversity. This new emphasis raises intriguing issues for ethics. Some of these issues already have been dealt with in the chapter on ethical relativism, since the recognition of cultural diversity was a major motivating factor in the development of ethical relativism. There are other issues, however, which have not been as fully explored that relate directly to the way in which this issue is posed in contemporary discussions in America of cultural diversity.

The Impartiality of the Moral Agent

Traditional ethical theories have ignored issues of ethnicity and cultural diversity for at least two reasons. The first of these centers around the notion of the moral agent which is at the heart of traditional ethical theories. Both Kantian and utilitarian theories are committed deeply to a notion of the moral agent radically stripped of almost all vestiges of individuality, and hence quite different from a unique moral decision-maker.

The Kantian Moral Agent

For Kant, moral agents are rational self-legislators, autonomous beings who give the moral law to themselves. Cultural background and ethnicity are excluded from relevance, for the question is how *any* rational agent would act. The very idea of universalizability implies that one acts in the same way as any rational agent would act in the same type of situation. Any considerations of individuality, gender, or culture would be set aside in order to act as a purely rational being.

The Utilitarian Calculator

Utilitarians exhibit a similar impartiality. The utilitarian moral agent is essentially an *impartial calculator*, a person who disinterestedly computes the utility of competing courses of action and chooses the one that maximizes utility. In calculating utility, the utilitarian may include factors relating to gender and ethnicity in the overall equation, but the utilitarian moral agent as such exhibits no allegiance to a specific individual identity, gender, or ethnicity. Cultural diversity would seem to have no more place in utilitarianism than it does in calculus.

Thus we see one of the principal philosophical reasons for the neglect of diversity: the two major traditions in ethics both presuppose a notion of the moral agent that is so reified, so abstracted from the concrete situation, that no traces of individuality, gender or ethnicity remain.

Gender, Ethnicity, and the Philosophical Canon

There is a second reason why gender, ethnicity, and cultural background have played a relatively minor role in moral theory. Most of the work done in classical moral theory (and in many other areas as well) has been written by white males, about white males, and for white males. Historically, it has been difficult for women and members of minorities to acquire the university positions and research facilities that often are taken for granted in mainstream work. When they have done first-rate work, it often has been unrecognized, both during their lifetimes and afterward. Think of the major figures covered in standard histories of philosophy before the twentieth century: Plato, Aristotle, Aquinas, Montaigne, Descartes, Hume, Kant, Hegel, Marx, and Kierkegaard are but a few of the major figures. All of these figures in philosophy are men and all are part of our mainstream (largely Caucasian) European heritage.

This limitation had serious, although probably largely unintended, implications for the development of moral theory. Precisely because white males were the majority, there was virtually no need for them to be aware of their own ethnicity or gender, although it does not mean that they were unaffected by their own gender and ethnicity. On the contrary, their views often were profoundly affected by their gender and their cultural background on at least two levels. First, the problems they selected for study, the methods they employed, and the conclusions they reached were all often significantly influenced by their gender and cultural background. We shall call these *first-order influences*. There is also a *second-order influence*, one which helps to conceal the presence of the first-order influences. Because they were in the clear majority, these philosophers had no need to define themselves in opposition to some other group. Consequently, they did not have to acknowledge the presence of those first-order influences. Instead, they simply treated their own worldview as if it were the whole of reality itself.

This experience was not true for women and members of ethnic and cultural minorities, who by virtue of their situation in society had to define themselves in opposition to, or at least in contrast with, the dominant societal group. The awareness of difference is much closer to the heart of self-awareness for women and minorities than it is for white males. Consequently, women and minorities may be subject to just as many (although different) first-order influences as their white male counterparts, but they are much less likely to experience the second-order influences that encourage masking the first-order influences: they are much more likely to acknowledge their voices as women's voices, Native American voices, Chicano voices, African-American voices. White males, in contrast, are much less likely to acknowledge their own voices as white male voices; instead, white males are much more likely to think of their own voices simply as the voices of reason, of science, or of objectivity.

Questioning the Canon

Recently, the traditional canon (of the "classics") has come under increasing attack. The work of Carol Gilligan has profoundly influenced the way we understand the relevance of gender to morality. Much less work has been done by philosophers about the relevance of culture and ethnicity to ethics, so we shall have to mark out more of that conceptual terrain ourselves. Let us first consider the relationship between gender and ethics.

GENDER AND ETHICS

The Kohlbergian Background

Kohlberg's Question

Lawrence Kohlberg's work in the psychology of moral development set the stage for discussions of moral development in the second half of the twentieth century in America. As a young man, Kohlberg was affected profoundly by World War II and its aftermath, including the events leading to the founding of the state of Israel. When Israel was still struggling for statehood, it was under a strict embargo that was intended to prevent the importation of food, medicine, and armaments as well as the immigration of people. Some people defied this ban, thereby breaking the law, in order to participate in the founding of the state of Israel. Kohlberg, deeply moved by their actions, wondered why some people would break the written law for the sake of what they held to be a higher good, a higher law. Clearly, many of them were not doing so for their own gain; indeed, breaking the law often actually cost them money and sometimes even their freedom or their lives. How was it, Kohlberg wondered, that some people obeyed this higher law while others refused to deviate from the letter of the law?

The Six Stages

Kohlberg spent his life working out an answer to this question. What he found is that people pass through *stages* of moral development, some progressing farther than others, most never getting beyond the fourth of six stages. The first two stages, which Kohlberg labels **preconventional morality,** usually are seen early in childhood. Stage one is dominated by the desire to avoid punishment, while stage two embodies an attitude of "You scratch my back, I'll scratch yours." Stages three and four, which comprise **conventional morality,** usually are found in adolescence and adulthood. The third stage is what Kohlberg calls "the 'good boy/nice girl' orientation" in which the principal motivation is the desire to be a good person in one's own eyes as well as in the eyes of others. Stage four is characterized by following the rules of duly constituted authorities—a "law and order" mentality. The final two stages, comprising the level of **postconventional morality,** usually are never reached by most of the population. Kohlberg describes stage five as a social contract orientation, in which individual rights are given acceptance and revised in the light of well-reasoned critical discussions. The sixth and highest stage, which only a few persons such as Mother Teresa, Gandhi, and Martin Luther King, Jr., have reached, is characterized by an orientation toward universal ethical principles of justice, reciprocity, equality, and respect. These principles are arrived at through reason and are freely accepted.

Characteristics of the Stages

Kohlberg sees these stages as universal, sequential, and irreversible. His initial research covered a Malaysian aboriginal village, villages in Turkey and the Yucatan, and urban populations in Mexico and the United States. He found that the boys and young men in these cultures all went through the same sequence of stages, irrespective of such factors as ethnicity, religion, or class. He found, further, that one could not skip over a stage, moving, say, from stage three to stage five without going through stage four. Nor, Kohlberg claimed, could one go back a stage; movement could only be forward. Finally, we should note an ambiguity in Kohlberg's scale, one which has a significant impact on how we understand his work. On one hand, his stage theory is *descriptive* in character. That is, it simply claims to present the facts about how individuals change morally. On the other hand, his theory is also *normative* in character insofar as it claims that later stages are better than earlier ones. Indeed, this very notion of *development*—as opposed to mere *change*—suggests that later stages are preferable to earlier ones.

The Stages and Traditional Moral Theories

Obviously, Kohlberg's later stages bear striking resemblances to some traditional moral theories. Stage five clearly reflects social contract theories and rule utilitarianism, while stage six stresses Kantian themes of universalizability and rationality. (I suspect Kohlberg was influenced by John Rawls, whose *Theory of Justice* circulated in manuscript form for many years before its publication in 1971; in that work, Rawls notes some of his differences with Kohlberg.) Clearly, the more impartial and the more universal one's moral reasoning is, the better it is for Kohlberg.

Gilligan's Starting Point

When Carol Gilligan began her research into moral development, she had no particular interest in gender issues. She was, however, interested in Kohlberg's work, and in the early seventies she began to study the moral reasoning of draft resisters. What attracted her to this study was that it presented precisely the same problem Kohlberg originally had grappled with: how is it that some people come to obey a higher law than the written law of the land? Then something happened to Gilligan's study that social scientists have nightmares about. President Nixon cancelled the draft. Although this change was politically welcome, it obviously undermined Gilligan's research project since there was no longer any draft to resist! Fortunately, she was still at an early stage of her research, and she shifted to study another difficult moral choice in our society: abortion.

Now, the interesting thing about this story is that Gilligan did not set out to study women's moral voices; indeed, if the draft had not been cancelled, her subject pool—just like Kohlberg's—would have been composed entirely of men. (It is an interesting sign of the times that twenty-five years ago research could be confined solely to males and virtually no one would object—or even notice.) It was initially only a quirk of political fate that directed her attention toward an exclusively female group of subjects for her research. Yet it was Gilligan's sensitivity to what she then heard from her subjects that led to her tremendously influential work. When she began her research with women who faced the decision about abortion, she realized that what she was hearing did not fit into the framework that Kohlberg had established. We began to realize that women speak about their moral lives in a distinctive voice, one which Kohlberg's theory is unable to appreciate.

Women's Moral Voices

The Metaphor of Voice

In 1982 Carol Gilligan published a collection of her articles as a book entitled *In a Different Voice: Psychological Theory and Women's Development*. Its impact has been profound, not just in Gilligan's own field of developmental psychology, but in a wide variety of other areas as well. Philosophy, religious studies, clinical psychology, communication studies, history, political science, literature, and art criticism are but a few of the traditional disciplines influenced by her work. The metaphor of "voice" became a particularly powerful one, and women in a number of different fields concentrated on the challenge of "finding their own voice" in their specific disciplines.

The metaphor of voice struck a chord, as it were, with many women, and it is worth pausing for a moment to consider its power. By talking about women's

In her novels, poetry and essays, Alice Walker (1944–) gives voice to the experiences of African-American women.

voices instead of their theories or perspectives, Gilligan chose a focus that was more concrete and potentially more capable of integrating differences harmoniously than other, more common metaphors for moral diversity. Throughout this book, we have seen how the language of theories leads quickly to competitive and combative accounts of morality in which ultimately only one theory can be correct. Appealing to perspectives instead of theories offers more room for diversity, but there is virtually no trace of individuality in the perspectives themselves. To speak of voices, however, is immediately to conjure up something concrete, something with tone, texture, and cadence. Think, for example, of the distinctive voice of a singer such as Whitney Houston, of politicians such as Barbara Jordan and Margaret Thatcher, of a poet such as Maya Angelou, or of actresses such as Meryl Streep, Dolly Parton, and Whoopi Goldberg. Their voices are rich, nuanced, evocative, and utterly distinctive. The finely textured specificity found in the appeal to voices is not found in talk about theories or perspectives.

Three other characteristics of voices are particularly noteworthy. First, voices combine both emotion and content. *How* something is said is tied closely to *what* is being said. Voices are *embodied* in a way that theories are not. Second, voices are described and assessed in a wide range of terms, most of which have little to do with "true" and "false" or "right" and "wrong." Voices may be strong or weak, full-bodied or hollow, lilting or deep, strident or sweet, excited or dull, trembling and hesitant, or clear and confident. Third, voices may be different without excluding one another. Think of the ways in which people sing together. Their voices may blend in a choir. They may sing harmony, one voice in distinctive counterpoint to another. They may toss a melody back and forth from one person to another, taking turns singing. One may be the lead singer, others may sing background. There are, in other words, numerous different ways in which voices may interact with one another.

Think about this point in regard to yourself. If you were asked to describe your moral *theory*, it would probably be in impersonal language that gave little clue to who you are as an individual. On the other hand, if you were asked to describe your moral *voice*, it would be much more specific, much more indicative of who you are as a person, much more recognizable to your friends as *you*. It might be quiet or loud, questioning or obedient, strident or cajoling, authoritative or confused, stiff or supple, humorous or serious, fearful or reckless. Although we certainly can describe different types of voices, even the types have a concreteness and specificity about them that theories lack.

Let us now examine what Gilligan found about women's moral voices. We will begin by contrasting women's voices with men's voices, and then look more specifically at the voices which characterize the stages of women's moral development.

Men's Voices and Women's Voices

When Gilligan began doing her research with female subjects, she noticed that their responses did not seem to fit neatly into Kohlberg's framework. It is not that the responses could not be squeezed into that framework, but rather that something essential and distinctive was lost in the process and other things were misinterpreted or misvalued. Gilligan's study showed, first of all, that women tended much more often than the men of Kohlberg's studies to see the moral life in terms of *care* rather than *justice*, in terms of *responsibility* rather than *rights*. Whereas men see things as moral issues when they involve competing claims about *rights*, women see problems as moral when they involve the *suffering* of other people. Whereas men see the primary moral imperative as centering around *treating everyone fairly*, women see that moral imperative as centering around *caring* about others and about themselves. Men typically make moral decisions by *applying rules fairly and impartially*, whereas women are more likely to seek resolutions that *preserve emotional connectedness* for everyone. Similarly, men tend to look back and to judge whether a moral decision was correct or not by asking whether the rules were applied properly, whereas women tend to ask whether relationships were preserved and whether people were hurt. The quality of the relationships, rather than the impartiality of the decisions, is the standard for evaluating decisions for women. The meaning of responsibility also changes. For men, being responsible is primarily a matter of being *answerable* for actions, for having followed (or failed to follow) the relevant rules. For women, the focus of responsibility is in taking care of the other person, including (and sometimes especially emphasizing) their feelings. Moreover, it is directed toward what the other person actually feels and suffers, not what "anyone" (that is, an abstract moral agent) would experience. Responsibility is directed toward real individuals, not to abstract codes of conduct.

These differences tend to reflect deeper differences between men and women, differences in the ways in which they conceive of the self. Men are much more likely to see the self in terms of autonomy, freedom, independence, separateness, and hierarchy. Rules guide the interactions among people, and roles establish each individual's place in the hierarchy. In contrast, women tend to see the self in terms of relatedness, interdependence, emotional connectedness, and responsiveness to the needs of others. Instead of depending on rules as men do, women are much more likely to show an immediate response to the plight of the other person. They experience themselves, first and foremost, as *connected*; the self is its network of relationships.

These differences also affect what men and women will tend to experience as comfortable or threatening. Typically, men will think of the top of a social or professional hierarchy as appealing, as attractive to their sense of autonomy, as compatible with their sense of separateness. Women are more likely to experience it as isolated and detached, as threatening to their sense of connectedness. Conversely, men are more likely to feel at risk in situations which threaten their sense of autonomy and separateness—especially in situations of dependency and intimacy. Women are more likely to feel at risk in situations that threaten their sense of responsiveness and connectedness—and these are typically situations of independence and hierarchy.

The Stages of Women's Moral Development

Gilligan sees women as developing through stages of moral growth, just as men do, but the stages are different in important respects. She divides her schema into three levels, just as Kohlberg did. However, instead of having two stages under each level, Gilligan has three full stages and a transitional period between each stage. Thus there are three full stages and two transitional stages.

Moral development for females begins, according to Gilligan, with the concern for *individual survival* as paramount, which is the first level of moral development, corresponding to Kohlberg's preconventional level. It is followed by the *transition from selfishness to responsibility*, in which women start to become aware of morality as requiring that they be responsible for the well-being of others. Level two, which corresponds to Kohlberg's level of conventional morality, is one in which *goodness comes to be equated with self-sacrifice.* Many of us probably have had mothers or grandmothers who saw their lives in precisely these terms: to be a good person was to take care of other people (husband, children, family) at the expense of themselves. For them, it was not a struggle to motivate themselves to take care of other people—the struggle came when they tried to give themselves permission to take care of *themselves.* It is precisely this struggle to include the self that constitutes the second transitional phase. It is often a difficult struggle, for initially it feels more like moral regression than moral progress, since morality is equated with self-sacrifice. Gradually, however, this experience gives way to a third level, one in which moral goodness is seen as *caring for both self and others.* This highest level is one which takes inclusiveness and nonviolence as ideals and which condemns exploitation and hurt.

The Voice of Care

A clear theme emerges throughout these stages: women's moral voices are voices of care. Whether it be a narrowly defined care for one's own survival, an altruistic care for other people, or an inclusive care for both self and others, *morality is primarily about caring.* It is not about rules, universalizability, the impartial computation of consequences, or anything like that. It is about a direct relationship of emotional responsiveness to the suffering of persons, both self and other.

Gilligan's Traditionalism

One of the striking things about Gilligan's work, especially in light of its strong impact on feminist thinking, is the traditional, almost stereotypical picture of women that it seems to promote. Women emerge as more concerned about relationships, emotional connectedness, and caregiving than men, who seem more independent, rule-oriented, and emotionally detached. Gilligan herself states that her findings are only generalizations and that it is certainly possible that some individuals do not fit into the pattern she associates with their biological sex. It seems that the danger here is that this moral theory may perpetuate traditional sex-based stereotypes. Yet I think there is a way of retaining many of Gilligan's insights about *masculinity* and *femininity* without necessarily tying those as closely to *males* and *females* as she does. Let us look at the issues raised by this gender-based morality.

Integrating Diverse Voices

A deep ambiguity runs through Gilligan's work. Clearly, her work is *descriptive*. It articulates women's moral voices and the differences between their voices and men's without necessarily making any value judgments about which are better. However, at times her work also seems to have *normative* implications, suggesting that one voice may be as good as, perhaps even better than, another. Some of Gilligan's statements suggest that she thinks both men's voices and women's voices are of equal value in morality; other statements suggest that she sees women's voices as superior. In this context, we can set aside the question of what Gilligan herself says about this question and look at the various possible positions on this issue and consider them on their own merits.

The Separate but Equal Thesis

Assuming that, in general, men and women have different moral voices, one of the ways in which we could deal with the differences is to keep the two separate but equal. Men and women have different moral voices. Men's voices are right for men, women's voices for women. Neither is superior to the other; they are just different.

The problem with this thesis is fourfold. First, it is very difficult to retain the "but equal" part of such a position. Once the two voices have been separated, it is all too easy to dismiss the second voice as less important. Second, such a position tends to perpetuate gender-based stereotyping, since only males are given male voices and only females are given female voices. Third, it suggests that men and women have nothing to learn from one another, since each sex has its own moral voice. Fourth, males who have a "female voice" and females who have a "male voice" are looked down upon. The separate but equal approach is, as it were, a form of sex-based isolationism.

The Superiority Thesis

The second possible position is to maintain that one of these two voices is superior to the other. Historically, this belief has been the dominant position, most often with men maintaining (usually implicitly, occasionally explicitly) that men's voices are superior to women's voices in morality. In recent times, the roles have sometimes been reversed, with women claiming the superiority of women's voices.

There are two problems with this position. First, to say that one voice is completely true for everyone in all situations is interesting but obviously false. To say that one voice is partially true for some people in some situations is accurate, but it is so vague as to be unhelpful without further elaboration of the particular conditions under which one voice takes precedence over the other. Such additional elaboration then yields a position that is significantly different from the original thesis.

The second problem with this position is that it is exclusionary. It excludes whichever position is seen as not true—and that usually means that we cannot learn from that other excluded voice. If, on the other hand, we admit that we can learn from the other voice, then we find ourselves defending a version of one of the next two positions.

The Integrationist Thesis

The integrationist maintains that there is ultimately *only one moral voice*, a voice which may be the integration of many different voices. The integrationist need not claim to know precisely what this voice is, but must be committed to the claim that ultimately there is only one voice.

The principal difficulty with the integrationist thesis is that it is susceptible to losing the richness that comes from diversity. The integrationist position tends to be assimilationist, blurring the distinctive identities of the sources of its components. It celebrates a moral androgyny as a replacement for the sex-based voices.

The Diversity Thesis

The final thesis claims that we have diverse moral voices and that this diversity is a principal source of richness and growth in the moral life. We can learn from one another's differences as well as from similarities. The diversity thesis in the area of gender most closely embodies the pluralistic approach characteristic of this book.

The diversity thesis has two complementary sides. First, there is the *external diversity thesis* which suggests that different individuals have different (gender-based) moral voices, and that here is a fruitful difference from which we can learn. Men can learn from women, just as women can learn from men. What makes this claim an *external* diversity thesis is that it sees diversity as something that exists among separate individuals.

THE BEM SCALE

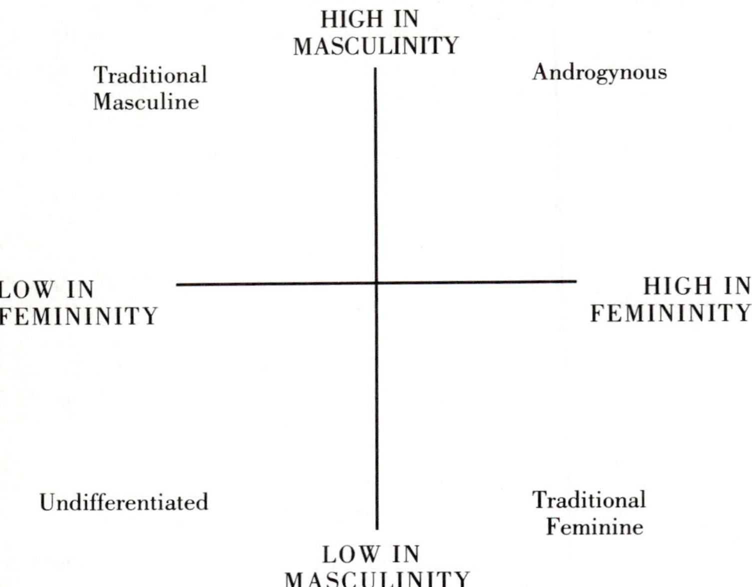

The *internal diversity thesis* sees diversity as also existing *within* each individual. Each of us, in other words, has both masculine and feminine moral voices within us, and this diversity of internal voices is considered a positive thing. One of the attractions of this position is that it minimizes gender stereotyping, for it denies that men have an exclusive claim to masculinity or that only women can have a feminine dimension. Men can have both masculine and feminine dimensions to their moral voices, just as women can have both.

Nor is it necessary to think an increase in one type of voice necessarily leads to a decrease in another. Sandra Bem has suggested that masculine and feminine traits in general may be mapped along two different axes, such that an individual may be high in both (androgynous), low in both (undifferentiated), high in femininity but low in masculinity (traditional feminine), or high in masculinity but low in femininity (traditional masculine). This approach leads to the schema given above.

The principal strength of this scale is that it does not make masculinity and femininity mutually exclusive traits, which is in sharp contrast to models that plot masculinity and femininity on a single axis with "strongly feminine" and "strongly masculine" at the opposing ends of the scale. On Bem's scale, one can be high in both, or low in both, as well as high in just one or the other. More often than not, males identify with a masculine gender and females with a feminine gender. We are probably most familiar with figures who are high on only one of these scales, but we have occasional examples of individuals who are high on both scales.

One World, Two Genders

We all live in the same world. The moral challenge facing us is to decide how to do so in a way that promotes respect, understanding, and community. Separatist approaches to diversity offer the hope of preserving differences, but they offer little encouragement for learning from one another or for forging a genuine community. Those who espouse the superiority of one voice (usually their own) over others not only refuse to learn from the other gender, but also often fail to develop the understanding of the other gender necessary to genuine respect. The final voice offers the best hope of preserving uniqueness and simultaneously celebrating differences within the larger context of community.

Caring and Act Utilitarianism

Interestingly, there are some similarities between an ethics of caring and act utilitarianism. They are both, generally speaking, consequentialist theories, that is, both see morality primarily as a matter of consequences. Both are concerned with weighing the consequences of projected actions, and both see those consequences—broadly speaking—in terms of the pleasure or pain that they might cause.

But the differences are equally instructive. The act utilitarian usually employs some kind of calculus, some method of computing the total amount of pleasure and pain that would result from various courses of action. Gilligan's ethics of caring is consequentialist, but differs from act utilitarianism both in (a) what kinds of consequences count and (b) how they are measured. The care ethic focuses primarily on two kinds of consequences: (1) the extent to which people might be *hurt* by a particular decision and (2) the degree to which a particular decision might diminish the *sense of connectedness* among the participants in the situation. Connectedness itself becomes a moral value. Moreover, the method by which these consequences are determined has a strongly intersubjective component. Whereas utilitarian calculators might well attempt to weigh consequences in the isolation of their offices, the caring person attempts to weigh consequences by talking with the participants and allowing them to participate actively in the process. For those assuming the standpoint of an ethic of care, there is an essentially intersubjective moment to the decision-making process. Both *what* is valued and *how* it is valued have a strong intersubjective dimension.

Emotions play a much more significant role in the ethics of caring than they do in the utilitarian calculus. First, in an ethics of caring, emotions (especially compassion and empathy) are necessary in order to know how much pleasure or pain a particular action causes. How can you know how much pain a particular action may inflict on friends if you do not listen to what they say about their feelings and try to understand those feelings? This process of listening and understanding is not only an intellectual one, but also involves an emotional, or affective, component.

Second, there is another emotive dimension to the ethics of caring that is absent from act utilitarianism. Caring has an irremediably emotive component to it. To care about someone is not just to act in particular ways; it is also, and necessarily, to *feel* in particular ways. There would be something odd if a parent tried to add up impersonally all the hedons and dolors for a particular choice that will affect the family. Part of caring is to feel something for the other person. (There is also a double kind of evaluation going on: understanding how much the other person values a particular action of ours and how much we value them.)

This approach suggests a way of understanding the relationship between act utilitarianism and the ethics of caring. In an impersonal context where we are dealing with large numbers of people who are strangers to us, act utilitarian considerations may well be relevant. In personal contexts where we are dealing with people we know and care about, the ethics of caring may better capture the moral insights that utilitarianism captures in the other, larger scale contexts.

Ethics, Ethnicity, and Cultural Diversity

As we already have indicated, ethicists in the past typically have conceived of the moral agent in such abstract terms that the moral agent seemed to possess little personal identity. Although recent feminist scholarship has begun to explore ways in which women and men have different moral voices, virtually no comparable work has been done by philosophers in regard to ethnicity. Certainly, no one has done for the moral voices of ethnic diversity what Carol Gilligan has done for the moral voices of gender diversity. The following remarks are offered in a tentative and exploratory vein as an attempt to begin to map out the conceptual territory within which a discussion of the relationship between ethics and ethnicity can take place.

Differences between Gender, Race, and Ethnicity

Both gender and ethnicity present issues of diversity, but the issues are not completely parallel. Consider some of the differences between gender and ethnicity.

- There are only two genders, whereas there are numerous ethnic identities.
- Gender commonly is regarded as an "either/or" matter (male or female); however, one can have more than one racial or ethnic identity.
- Although there is a biological imperative that demands men and women interact, there is no comparable imperative for people with different ethnic backgrounds. Nothing comparable to sexual attraction exists between different ethnic groups or cultures.

Despite these differences, it is clear that race and ethnicity have been used as a basis for discrimination at least as frequently as has gender. Indeed, precisely because different ethnic or racial groups can live without each other, the possibilities for discrimination—in its most extreme form, culminating in slavery and genocide—are even greater.

Race, Ethnicity, and Cultural Diversity

Race and ethnicity are distinct concepts, although they may overlap. **Race** is primarily a *biological* phenomenon that manifests itself in characteristics such as skin color, hair texture, body shape, and the like. Ethnologists generally distinguish among three main racial groups: Caucasoid, Negroid, and Mongoloid. Despite beliefs to the contrary, race is not a very precise concept, for there is a tremendous amount of variation within racial groups and a significant amount of overlap among them as well, as Steven Jay Gould has shown in *The Mismeasure of Man*. These variations are intensified by interracial reproduction. **Ethnicity**, on the other hand, is primarily a *cultural* phenomenon. It refers principally to an individual's identification with a particular cultural group. There are many more cultural groups than there are races, and often differences in cultures are overlooked by outsiders. There are, for example, many southeast Asian cultures, but non-Asians often lump them all together as "Indochinese," which would be roughly equivalent to lumping the English, the Irish, the Portuguese, the Finns, the Spanish, the Italians, the Lithuanians, the French, and the Germans together as "Europeans." Although it is true that they all come from countries in Europe, they often perceive themselves primarily in terms of national and ethnic identities. But, they are only Europeans to outsiders. **Cultural background** refers directly to individuals' ethnicity and only indirectly and accidentally to their race. For example, a Caucasian American infant raised in Thailand by Thai parents may well be Caucasoid by race but ethnically and culturally Thai.

One can be high on several different cultural scales simultaneously. Think of an Italian who has married into a Jewish family. That person may become steeped in traditional Jewish customs without giving up an Italian heritage. Being at home in one culture does not necessarily preclude being at home in

Dr. Martin Luther King, Jr. (1929–1968) was one of the strongest moral voices speaking for racial equality.

another, although there may be points of incompatibility between specific cultures. We can belong to two, or perhaps even more, cultures at the same time. This is not to say that there will not be some conflicts, but to be strongly identified with both traditions is to be committed to working out such conflicts in a way that respects both traditions as much as possible.

The Facts of Diversity

Do different cultures have distinctive moral voices? The obvious answer is "of course they do." In our consideration of descriptive moral relativism in Chapter Two, we saw that distinctive voices were clearly the case, at least in regard to (a) the particular actions which a given culture sanctions or condemns and (b) the peripheral values it accepts. Whether there is disagreement on central values is another question, and we have seen good evidence to suggest that there is widespread (but not total) agreement on certain values such as respect for innocent life.

To say that moral voices are distinctive is not to say that they are necessarily incompatible. We might find a much stronger emphasis on the concept of honor in Japanese society than we encounter in contemporary American society, but that does not necessarily make them incompatible, only different. Incompatibility, at least in the strict sense, occurs only when there are clearly opposing value judgments such as "honor is good" and "honor is bad." (For strict incompatibility, there must also be rough equivalence in the meaning of shared terms such as "honor." Cross-cultural comparisons of this type presuppose that understanding and judgment between cultures is possible; such comparisons also often demand a high degree of sensitivity to the nuances of another culture's worldview.) Differences alone do not constitute incompatibility. Often the relevant question is not whether different cultures have distinctive moral voices, but whether they can learn to sing together harmoniously when necessary.

Let us turn to a concrete example of the way in which a culture has distinctive voices so that we can understand more fully the nuances of the issues involved.

The Moral Voices of African-Americans

Consider the diversity of voices that are included in the African-American experience. Martin Luther King, Jr., Malcolm X, Alice Walker, and Maya Angelou are among the most powerful African-American moral voices of the second half of this century. These voices have many distinctive characteristics, but here I shall concentrate on just one element that is found in all four of these voices: *affirmation of self-respect in the face of oppression.* Self-respect is a value found in virtually all cultures, as is opposition to oppression. In this respect, African-American culture is not unique. However, the affirmation of self-respect in the face of daunting oppression is a moral value which ranks higher on the scale in African-American culture than it does in, say, white American culture where the same on-going experience of oppression is not present. The speeches and writings of Dr. King and Malcolm X resonate with a deep affirmation of the self-respect of African-Americans, an opposition to any attempts to deny the worth of African-Americans, and a commitment to bringing about the social, political, and legal changes necessary to sustain and enhance that sense of self-worth among African-Americans. Martin Luther King's "Letter from Birmingham Jail" eloquently details the ways in which segregation "distorts the soul and degrades human personality" for all involved, those who perpetuate segregation as well as those toward whom segregation is directed. Malcolm X's *Autobiography* is a superb example of moral autobiography, a description of his journey toward an increasingly well-founded sense of self-respect.

The novels, poetry, and journals of Alice Walker and Maya Angelou demonstrate a similar commitment. They have given voice to those African-Americans whose suffering had previously been endured in silence. In *The Color Purple*, for example, Alice Walker traces the journey toward self-respect of an African-American woman whose life began in oppression and moved gradually toward autonomy. In a similar way, we find an account of the journey from oppression to increasingly full self-respect and self-determination in Maya Angelou's autobiography *I Know Why the Caged Bird Sings.*

Against this rich background of diverse African-American moral voices, we now can understand better the conceptual issues involved in linking ethnicity to ethics. There are two ways of forging this link, one considerably strong than the other.

Externalist and Internalist Accounts of Ethnicity and Ethics

The first way of linking ethnicity and ethics, the *externalist approach*, is through a shared set of social experiences and problems that are seen as largely independent of the identity of the persons in question. In the case of African-Americans, the heritage of slavery and the ongoing presence of racism in American society figure prominently among the shared experiences of African-Americans. The argument here would be that African-Americans have to deal with a set of moral problems that are not usually encountered (at least in the same way) by the dominant white, male population of the United States. This way of understanding the link between ethnicity and ethics suggests that the connection is largely an external one. The analogy that suggests itself here is with professional groups that face particular moral problems not shared by the population as a whole. Physicians and psychologists, for example, must deal with questions of confidentiality and trust not shared in the same way by the population as a whole. African-Americans face a certain set of external problems not shared by the population as a whole; consequently, they develop distinctive moral voices to deal with those problems.

The drawback of this first approach is that it draws a comparatively sharp distinction between the group and the special moral problems it faces, and consequently, misses the ways in which specific moral problems partially constitute the identity of a particular group. The problems themselves are seen as largely external to the identity of the group itself. the distinctiveness of the voice derives primarily from the problems that it addresses, not from the members of the group themselves. The externalist account seems to miss the intimate connection between those problems and the very identity of the members of the group.

Ethics and ethnicity can be linked in a second, more intimate way through an *internalist account*. For example, the heritage of slavery and the experience of racism are powerful factors that are partially constitutive of the identity of African-Americans. Their voices are partially shaped by these forces, and it is misleading to think of their identity as something completely external to them. A particular sensitivity to the affirmation of self-respect in the face of oppression is one of the distinctive characteristics of African-American moral voices, and an internalist account of the link between ethics and ethnicity recognizes the extent to which this sensitivity is partially constitutive of the identity of African-Americans at this point in history.

"Thick" and "Thin" Conceptions of the Moral Self

These two approaches differ significantly in regard to the conception of the self that underlies each. The first approach is characterized by a "thin" conception of the self that sees the identity of the person as largely independent of empirical factors such as environment and ethnicity. As we saw in Chapter Seven, Immanuel Kant strongly exemplifies this attitude. For Kant, the self was constituted primarily by reason and will; empirical conditions were generally excluded from the core identity of the moral agent. In our critique of Kant, we suggested a "thicker" conception of the self, one that included more empirical factors, as central to an individual's identity. In such thicker conceptions of the self, ethnicity may become an important part of identity. One's identity as a person, in other words, may in part be constituted by certain experiences largely unique to one's ethnic or racial group.

Ethnic identity is constituted by shared experiences. In the case of African-Americans, one of the most significant of these shared experiences is that of being subjected to racial discrimination. In other words, an important part of their ethnic identity is precisely the experience of having their ethnic identity devalued and degraded. It is, as African-American philosophers such as Laurence Thomas have pointed out, an experience that has a profound impact on self-respect and self-esteem. The affirmation of self-worth against a background that denies or diminishes that self-worth is a particular value for any group that has been the object of systematic and long-standing oppression. Among African-Americans, the experience of racism is certainly an experience that is partially constitutive of their identity, and this common experience partially shapes their distinctive moral voices. Their ethnic identity is part of who they are, part of their personal identity as moral agents, and ought to be affirmed in part because it was the object of discrimination in the past.

Thus we see why there is a special moral justification for Black pride or Latino pride in a way that there is not for Caucasian pride. It is not because Caucasians should not be proud, but rather because there is no special moral need for them to be proud specifically *of their ethnicity* in the way in which there is for Blacks, Latinos, and others who have been discriminated against precisely because of their ethnicity. Consequently, self-respect for them involves an affirmation of their ethnicity (against a background that has devalued their ethnicity) in a way that is not true for their Caucasian counterparts.

Normative Options

We have now seen one of the ways in which different cultures may have (partially) different values. The central normative question we face is how we should act in light of this fact. The range of possible responses is similar to those options regarding issues of gender.

Separatists

Again, we can begin our discussion by noting two extreme positions. On one hand, we have the voice of the *separatists*, who maintain that cultures ought to retain their own voices through isolating themselves from the cultures around them. The drive toward separatism is particularly strong when the gap between cultures is wide and the difference in power is great. Separatists often fear being swallowed up by the larger culture and losing their identity in the process. Indeed, they feel that there is much to be gained from having a community of people with shared values, experiences, interests, and history. Such a community not only provides security, but also eliminates the need to start over in every conversation. Persons of color do not need to prove that racism still exists or show that it still has pernicious effects when talking with those who have shared their experiences. For example, recent Vietnamese immigrants share understandings of cultural alienation in their new homeland. They can take such common ground for granted and move on to a discussion of further issues within this shared context.

Yet *strict separatism* is rarely a long-term viable option, because it usually will increase the power differential between the larger and smaller culture. Eventually this option leads to an even greater marginalization of the smaller, less powerful culture, in some instances leading even to its extinction. There are groups in America who still pursue this path, of course. Amish communities in Pennsylvania and other states are a highly visible example of a largely separatist tradition that has managed to survive and in certain respects flourish. Some Native American communities, such as the members of the Acoma Pueblo, also have pursued a largely separatist course, preserving traditional values in comparative isolation from white society. African-American leaders such as W. E. B. Du Bois advocated the value of separatism in part as a way of preserving the uniqueness of the African-American tradition. The long-term prospects for such communities remain unclear, especially in an increasingly technological and computerized society.

If the prospects for strict separatism appear cloudy, the same cannot necessarily be said for *limited separatism.* Many groups in our society have long pursued a course of limited separatism, interacting with the larger culture yet simultaneously retaining a distinctive sense of group identity. Religious groups, fraternal organizations, and ethnic clubs are but a few types of such communities. They often flourish in part by maintaining a place within the larger community, but at the same time retaining a limited sense of their own separate identity.

Supremacists

On the other hand, *supremacists* argue that (a) there is one culture that is morally superior to all others, and that (b) that superior culture is their own. In American society, we have seen this attitude in both white supremacist movements like the Aryan Nation and Posse Comitatus and Ku Klux Klan, and in some ethnic supremacist movements as well. The supremacist attitude is suspect on several counts. Historically, it often has been associated with hatred, intolerance, and cruelty. Philosophically, in those instances in which it rests on an *a priori* judgment that everything in one culture is superior to everything in another one, it is simply wrong. Indeed, supremacists depend on discrimination precisely in order to obtain a sense of their own self-worth.

Interestingly, we would rarely consider separatism to be an acceptable option for the dominant group in society, presumably in part because we recognize that such a course of action would cut off the smaller cultural groups from valued goods and resources. We recognize that there may be a value in having traditionally African-American colleges in America, or organizations for Latino students on campus, but we would be hesitant to endorse the same options for Caucasians alone. There are at least two reasons for this. The first is one that we have already discussed. There is a special moral justification for the affirmation of ethnicity among groups that have been discriminated against precisely because of their ethnicity. For such groups, the affirmation of self-respect necessarily involves the affirmation of their ethnicity in a way that is not true for groups that have not been discriminated against on the basis of ethnicity or who even have been the perpetuators of discrimination.

The second reason for this difference is historical. Dominant ethnic groups often have functioned unjustly to disenfranchise and to disempower minority groups. Historical examples of this phenomenon are all too common. The Turkish attempt to exterminate the Armenians, the German attempt to wipe out the Jews and the Gypsies and enslave other ethnic groups such as the Poles, and recent Bosnian calls for "ethnic cleansing"—these are but a few of the most prominent examples of this tendency in our own century. Presumably separatist minority groups do not serve this same function. They do not attempt to disenfranchise or to disempower the majority group, since such minority groups do not control the distribution of power in the same way that the majority group does. If they were to function in this way, they too would be morally suspect, for they would turn into supremacist groups.

Integrationists and Assimilationists

The integrationist position in regard to ethnic and cultural diversity has a somewhat different shape than it does in regard to gender. Although we recognized that both males and females can have both masculine and feminine voices, there is still a strong and pervasive cultural pressure to identify people as either male or female. For example, English grammar forces us to classify individuals as male or female but not as Latino or French. The pressure in regard to ethnic and cultural identification is weaker. Moreover, individuals obviously could be from more than one ethnic tradition—for example, both Irish and Jewish. Such diversity in regard to being male or female is, at best, a much more subtle matter.

There are several possible models of integration, and these can be ranked according to the degree of sameness they seek to achieve. Some strive for assimilation and uniformity, while others emphasize cooperation within a context of at least minimally shared rules of interaction. At the far end of the spectrum, some models of integration shade into pluralism.

Pluralists

The middle ground between these extremes is essentially the same one described at the end of our chapter on relativism: a *cultural pluralism* that sees diversity as a source of strength, emphasizes the value of *dialogue*, and approaches such dialogues with a *fallibilistic* attitude. It is a pluralism that sees value in limited separatism, but also recognizes that we need to learn to live together while honoring our differences. We have much to learn from other cultures, just as they have much to learn from us. As pluralists, we can recognize that there are many ways of being right without giving up the possibility of taking a stand in those instances when we are convinced something is seriously wrong.

Consider the value of affirming self-respect in the face of oppression. As we have seen, given historical conditions, it is hardly surprising that this is an important value in African-American culture. Among groups who have not suffered such discrimination, the affirmation of self-respect may be a much less prominent value and may not involve an affirmation of ethnicity as part of self-respect. Thus, although white Americans also value self-respect, they may well not value it to the same extent or in the same way as their African-American counterparts. This is an excellent example of value pluralism, one in which different groups have partially different (but not necessarily incompatible) values. The advantage of a pluralistic approach to values is that it is able to understand and appreciate such differences in values without resorting to an attitude of "anything goes." However, not all differences in values are as easily understood and appreciated as this one is. We shall consider how we live with diversity, and especially how we deal with moral conflicts in a pluralistic society, later in this chapter. Before turning to that issue, let us consider one last source of diversity.

VALUING INDIVIDUALITY

Individuals are the *loci*, the meeting points, of diversity. We already have seen some of the principal influences on an individual's identity: gender, ethnicity, and culture. Each of these factors, often along with other influences such as our religious background and our socioeconomic class, help to shape who we are. What place does individuality play in the moral life?

Negative and Positive Morality

Morality sometimes is seen as having negative and positive elements. The negative elements are prohibitions that establish the *moral minimum* that is acceptable. To be concerned only with the moral minimum is like taking a course on a pass/fail basis: we are concerned primarily with what we need just to get by, to pass with a "C − ." While being concerned with the moral minimum is preferable to not being concerned at all, it is still a long way from moral excellence. The positive element of morality focuses on *moral excellence*. Individuality finds its true place in the realm of the search for moral excellence, for there are often many different individual ways in which we can excel.

Moral Excellence

As we saw in Chapter Nine in our discussion of moral saints, genuine saints need not be cardboard figures. Consider the great moral figures of the twentieth century. Each is characterized by the quest for excellence in a certain area. Gandhi shows us the power of nonviolence in the twentieth century. He was, if anything, tenaciously, insistently nonviolent. Think of Mother Teresa. Her compassion and her spontaneous and joyful love set her apart from the rest of us and constitute her moral individuality. Yet it would be inaccurate to think of either of them as extensions of a theory or applications of some single principle. Their lives show a richness and vibrancy that is a sign of robust moral health.

Moral excellence is not restricted to public figures. We all know, or perhaps are, people with a special moral excellence. Think of the friend who truly can be depended upon, even under the toughest of circumstances. That is moral excellence, and it is one that we might choose to strive to embody. Or think of the friend who is able, even in the most difficult of circumstances, to put defensiveness aside and to listen genuinely to the concerns of the other person, which, too, is moral excellence. Or the person who is always fair, even in the face of great opposing pressures. Or the person who always can be counted on to respond in a caring and compassionate manner to the suffering of others. Moral excellences come in many different shapes and sizes.

Forging Our Moral Identity

We are all born as human beings into particular moral communities and traditions. We are not impartial, purely rational moral agents lacking in particularity. We are individual women and men, born at a particular time and place, having a particular ethnic and cultural background, specific likes and dislikes, individual hopes and dreams. The task for each of us as moral individuals is to forge our own moral identity.

Moral pluralism suggests that there is room for choice and creativity in the shaping of our individual moral identity and our moral values. In other words, although our moral values set some minimal limits within which we must act, we have a considerable degree of latitude within those limits to shape our own moral identity. Moral pluralism establishes the negative limits on behavior and points out possibilities for us, but it is our own individual choice to create our own identity. It is here that virtue ethics is of particular relevance, for it provides the most guidance to us in answering the question "What kind of person do I want to be?" The guiding concern here is not that our moral identity be unique in the sense that it be different from anyone else's; rather, the crucial concern is that it be *ours*, that is, a freely chosen embodiment of the person we want to be.

The formation of our individuality involves more than just our moral values; it also involves striking a balance between our moral values and our non-moral values. Many of our choices in life about career, family, friends, and leisure involve non-moral values as well as moral ones. Finally, it is important for us to note that the development of individuality does not take place in a vacuum. We are always concrete individuals, situated in a particular time and place as members of various groups and communities. We can think of a community as a moral arena in which we have the opportunity to aspire to moral excellence.

Living with Moral Diversity

There is a richness in the diversity of theory as well as the diversity of experience which we (especially philosophers) have been too ready to ignore. One of the principal aims of this book has been to recognize and to value such diversity. Yet this goal is easier said than done, for moral conflicts—both real and imagined—present roadblocks on the path of the moral life. In order to complete our pluralistic account of moral values and to show the ways in which we can live with genuine diversity, we need an account of how to deal with moral conflicts. There are several ways in which we can respond to moral diversity and apparent moral conflict.

- We can live with diversity.
- We can seek imaginative ways of resolving conflicts.
- We can seek a compromise that all parties can live with.
- We can change our own behavior without demanding that others act differently.
- We can refuse to compromise and demand that others change.

Before turning to examine these options, a cautionary word is in order about the way in which internal conflicts come to be perceived as purely external ones.

Internal and External Diversity

In discussing cases of moral conflict, it is easy to focus on *external* moral conflicts between two or more people with differing and conflicting values commitments. While these conflicts are the more visible type, we should be aware that there are also *internal* conflicts in which a single individual experiences the pull of conflicting values.

There is a danger, especially in situations of sharp conflict, that internal conflicts come to be seen as purely external in character. In situations such as the abortion debate in which external conflicts are starkly polarized, participants easily can lose sight of the degree to which they also experience the conflict as an internal one. Pro-choice advocates might lose sight of their own moral qualms about abortion, just as pro-life advocates might neglect their own feelings of empathy for some women with unwanted pregnancies. The danger is that people on both sides will ignore their own reservations because the other side already is advocating them so strongly. Psychologically, what happens in polarized situations such as these is that people allow their opponents to carry the burden of their own dissenting convictions. Most of us have had the experience of strongly defending a position, having our opponent capitulate, and then having doubts about our own position. These feelings are not merely the product of some perverse desire to take the opposite side in every issue. They may also be the result of letting the opposition carry the minority side of our own feelings. When we are able to acknowledge the full and sometimes conflicting range of our own values and feelings, we may well find that there is more common ground between ourselves and those "on the other side" than we thought.

Living with Moral Diversity

In Peter Weir's 1985 film *Witness*, we are presented with an interesting example of moral diversity. The movie skillfully plays off two ways of life, both moral within their own traditions and yet apparently mutually exclusive. Harrison Ford plays police detective John Book, who must live in disguise in an Amish community during his pursuit of a killer. The movie portrays Book sympathetically as a detective genuinely committed to seeing justice done. If violence is necessary to accomplish this goal, Book does not shrink from it; but neither does he pursue violence for its own sake. The members of the Amish community, on the other hand, eschew violence; their commitment to pacifism lies at the core of their religious and moral identity. To betray that commitment would be to betray their deepest selves.

In one of the more striking scenes of the movie, a member of the Amish community named Daniel is confronted in town by several bullies who proceed to taunt him. Daniel does not fight back, but Book finally steps in and flattens the lead bully. Most non-pacifists would cheer, at least silently, when the bully gets what was coming to him. Yet I think that we can step back from a scene such as this one and draw several conclusions.

First, even if we are not pacifists, we might be glad that there are pacifists in our world. Even if we are happy to see Book punch the bully in the nose, we might still feel that our world is a better place because there are also people like Daniel in it. Daniel reminds us of another moral ideal, perhaps not our own, but one we can appreciate. Indeed, if there were more people like Daniel in the world, perhaps there would be both less violence and less need for violence. Daniel's presence in our own world may well prompt us to look harder for nonviolent alternatives before we resort to violence. We need not agree with Daniel in order to be happy that he is in our world.

Second, while there is an obvious moral conflict here about the moral value of violence, there is also a widespread area of agreement. If there is disagreement about whether justice can ever be brought about through violence, there is agreement that justice should be fostered. Indeed, there is also fairly widespread agreement about what counts as justice. Similarly, there is significant agreement about such issues as truthfulness, cooperation, and respect. Much moral diversity takes place within the larger context of moral agreement.

There is an added reason for valuing such diversity. It takes little reflection for us to realize that our values are not perfect. All we need to do is to look at virtually everyone else's values throughout history in order to see that none of them was without any moral blind spots at all. So, too, we can be assured that we are not immune to moral myopia, distortion, and blindness. We can be certain that some of our moral perceptions and judgments are off the mark—but the difficulty is that we cannot know *which* ones are. It is here that we depend on the values of others, for their blind spots may not be the same as ours. We count on others to help us see what we miss.

Thus we see the first way in which we can live with moral diversity: we can acknowledge it and encourage it, glad that there are others who see the world differently than we do. We might not agree with them, but *we may feel* our moral life as a whole could be more secure because they are part of our world.

Moral Imagination

The second way in which we can respond to moral diversity is imaginatively to seek new ways of acting that synthesize the diversity of apparently conflicting values. Some situations appear to be cases of moral conflict, but the conflict only exists because we lack the creative insight to devise a course of action that resolves the conflicting interests and values. Often a moral conflict has the following structure. One side says to do A because of value x; the other side says to do not-A because of value y. A morally imaginative solution would involve finding a course of action, B, that is compatible with both x and y.

Consider the following example, which *may* be a successful example of moral imagination. For the past several decades, our country has been experiencing a conflict that centers around the issue of poverty. On the one hand, some in our society—call them liberals for the convenience of the label—feel that the government must intervene to break the cycle of poverty. On the other hand, others in our society—we will stay with the standard labels and call them conservatives—feel that individuals are (or at least should be) responsible for their own lives and that government has no business intervening in the private sector and creating dependency on government by giving people food and other necessities of life. Recently, there have been attempts to develop a third possibility (in addition to welfare or no support at all) that *may* synthesize these apparently conflicting values. Workfare, as it is currently known, would be a government program that provides the standard support usually associated with welfare but (in cases where appropriate) only for a limited time and under conditions that include job training and eventual employment. Undoubtedly many liberals and conservatives would perceive workfare as a compromise, that is, as temporarily setting aside some of their values for the sake of reaching a wider consensus on a course of action. Others, however, might experience it as a morally imaginative solution that does not involve giving up any of their values, a third possibility where previously they had seen only two alternatives. If such a possibility could be worked out properly (which is not a small "if"), it might provide for some individuals on both sides of the issue just the kind of morally imaginative synthesis we have been discussing here. The interests and values of liberals would be satisfied insofar as the program helped to break the cycle of poverty and provided a compassionate response to the economically less fortunate in our society. The interests and values of conservatives also would be honored insofar as the program reduced dependency, encouraged personal responsibility, and was directed toward minimizing the government's intervention in the private sphere. Much, of course, would depend on how well-developed the program was and how sensitively it could be administered. The success of the program also would depend on how well it dealt with recalcitrant cases, that is, those who apparently could develop work skills but in fact did not do so, despite apparent opportunities. Finally, it would depend upon how well the program responded to the issue of the suffering of children, none of whom had a choice about the economic or social conditions of the family into which they were born.

One of the results of moral imagination is that it allows us to forge a new course of action that incorporates the previously apparently conflicting values. When this solution occurs, the participants in the situation are not compromising, for they are not denying any of their values. Instead, they are revising their values and wholeheartedly committing themselves to a course of action that they now perceive as consistent with their values.

Moral Compromise

Sometimes, in the face of moral conflict, we are unable to find a morally imaginative solution that synthesizes the conflicting values of the various parties. Compromise becomes necessary. Although "compromise" sometimes carries the connotation of "betrayal" or "selling out," not all compromises are betrayals. A compromise is an agreement that partially preserves the interests of all parties in a consensus that is acceptable to everyone. There are times when moral compromise is appropriate and morally praiseworthy.

In his book *Splitting the Difference*, Martin Benjamin has elaborated a number of the reasons why it is often appropriate to reach a compromise. First, compromise fosters the continuation of a communal life. Disagreements, including disagreements in values, are inevitable. Unless we are able to compromise in at least some of the cases, our common life would grind to a halt. Second, we may be more willing to compromise because we are not absolutely certain about what the right course of action is. This uncertainty may stem from either of two sources. There may be factual uncertainties. For example, how we act—especially if we are utilitarians—often depends on what we anticipate the results of our action to be. Yet these results are notoriously difficult to predict. We could find that a given situation is so morally complex that we are not completely sure about how we should act. Benjamin compares these situations to judging an Olympic figure skating competition. There may be as many as seven different judges, with each judge evaluating a performance to the best of his or her ability. Generally we recognize that there is room for legitimate disagreement, and the final score is a compromise among the various scores. These are judgment calls in which compromise is eminently reasonable. Third, we may compromise because *some* decision has to be taken immediately and there simply is not time to find an alternative that does not involve compromise. Finally, we may find ourselves in a situation of scarce resources that force compromises on us that in situations of more ample resources would not be necessary.

When Not to Compromise—and How

There are times when compromise is simply unacceptable. The moral price is too high, the suffering too great. There has been no shortage of such situations: the various genocidal programs of the twentieth century offer one set of examples, but they are not the only cases. Cases of child abuse offer another set of examples, ones that are often closer to home than is genocide. The moral theories we have examined help to articulate the moral minimum below which we should not allow ourselves or others to sink.

When discussing situations in which compromise is not acceptable, it is helpful to distinguish two types of cases. The first involves situations in which we will not compromise by acting, or agreeing to act, in ways which violate our moral values. Here the focus is on our own actions, on our refusal to cooperate with a possible compromise. In a second kind of situation we not only refuse to cooperate, but also actively try to stop other people from engaging in the objectionable activity. If we were to use abortion as an example, those in the first category would refuse to get abortions themselves if they were pregnant. Those in the second category would not only refuse to get abortions themselves if pregnant, but would also try to prevent others from getting abortions. Both are refusals to compromise, but the second involves an active intervention in a way that the first does not.

In both of these types of situations, it is important to reflect on *how* we refuse to compromise. Three points are noteworthy here. First, it is important to find ways of refusing to compromise that minimize polarization. We must look for ways of remaining connected with those with whom we disagree, which is often extremely difficult to do, but not always impossible. Often in such situations it is helpful to distinguish between people and their actions. We may refuse to cooperate with someone's actions, but we try to keep open other modes of communication and emotional connectedness with them.

Second, we can refuse to compromise, but do so *with respect*. Such respect was one of the striking characteristics of Gandhi's eventual refusal to cooperate with British rule of India. He refused to compromise on the large issue of Indian independence and he always agreed to compromise solutions on intermediate goals, but he never treated the British with disrespect. For a second example, recall the example of the villagers of Le Chambon given at the beginning of Chapter Ten. One of the startling aspects of their refusal to cooperate with the Nazis is that they were concerned with the welfare of the German soldiers as well as the Jews they sheltered. They wanted to be sure that *no one* was killed, including the German soldiers.

Third, we can refuse to compromise, but do so *imaginatively*, perhaps even *cleverly*. As the example of the villagers of Le Chambon shows, sometimes we can refuse to compromise without resorting to violence. When we resist, we hope to find ways of resisting that eventually will convert our adversaries to our viewpoint rather than beat them into submission.

LIVING MORALLY

Let me conclude with a different kind of metaphor in terms of which we can understand the issues of diversity—diversity in culture, in gender, and even in age. Think of ethics as architecture. Certainly there are occasionally matters of clear-cut right and wrong in architecture. From time to time, poorly constructed buildings do fall down, and people accidentally are killed or injured. Yet most of the time, other questions than those mathematical relations of size, weight, shape, and stress are much more interesting and relevant. Once we decide that a given group of buildings will not fall down, we can move on to more interesting questions about what life would be like in such a place. For example, what kind of balance is implied between communal living and individual privacy in the architecture? Buildings with few walls put a premium on communal life, perhaps at the expense of individual privacy. Buildings composed primarily of small, isolated rooms with no communal areas give relatively little value to a shared life, and emphasize the isolated individual as the primary unit. Our architecture reflects our values. For example, note the shift in American building away from large houses to small apartments and the implications for family life, both nuclear and extended.

We can learn about the moral life by studying different cultures in the same way that we learn about our everyday life from studying different architecture. Together, we might be able to build moral homes in which we can all live with dignity and mutual respect and in which each of us can flourish.

Bibliographical Essay

Lawrence **Kohlberg**'s major works on moral development are contained in the two volumes of his *Essays in Moral Development* (New York: Harper and Row, 1981 and 1984). Carol **Gilligan**'s *In a Different Voice* (Cambridge: Harvard University Press) appeared in 1982, and since then has continued to have a profound impact in a wide range of disciplines, including psychology, religious studies, philosophy, sociology, communications, and literature. It has become the best-selling paperback that Harvard University Press has ever published. Gilligan's more recent work is found in a collection of essays that she co-edited with Janie Victoria Ward and Jill McLean Taylor, *Mapping the Moral Domain* (Cambridge: Center for the Study of Gender, Education and Human Development, 1988) and in Lyn Mikel Brown and Carol Gilligan, *Meeting at the Crossroads: Women's Psychology and Girls' Development* (Cambridge: Harvard University Press, 1992). Nel Noddings's *Caring* (Berkeley: University of California Press, 1984) and, more recently, her book *Evil* (Berkeley: University of California Press, 1989) also have had a significant impact in articulating a specifically feminine voice in ethics. My presentation of Gilligan's position is indebted strongly to the (largely unpublished) work of Michelle Dumont. I owe my familiarity with the Bem scale to Linda A. M. Perry.

The work of Gilligan and others has stirred up a healthy debate among philosophers about the implications of her work, and of feminism in general, for ethics. Several journal exchanges are also of particular relevance here, most of which have appeared in *Ethics*: the Kohlberg-Flanagan exchange on "Virtue, Sex, and Gender" *Ethics*, Vol. 92, No. 3 (April, 1982), pp. 499–532; Lawrence Blum's "Gilligan and Kohlberg: Implications for Moral Theory" *Ethics*, Vol. 98, No. 3 (April, 1988), pp. 472–91; and the symposium on "Feminism and Political Theory," *Ethics*, Vol. 99, No. 2 (January, 1989). Owen Flanagan's *Varieties of Moral Personality* (Cambridge: Harvard University Press, 1991) contains several excellent chapters (especially chapters nine through eleven) on this issue.

It is worth noting that the voice of caring that Gilligan, Noddings, and others describe is not limited to feminist writers. The work of **Martin Buber** particularly is striking in this regard. His *I and Thou*, translated by Ronald Gregor Smith (New York: Scribner and Sons, 1960), is an insightful work that is certainly compatible with the type of framework that Gilligan and others are articulating.

Five **anthologies** contain a number of important papers **on feminism and ethics:** Eva Feder Kittay and Diana Meyer's *Women and Moral Theory* (Savage, Md.: Rowman & Littlefield, 1987); *Feminism and Political Theory*, edited by Cass R. Sunstein (Chicago: University of Chicago Press, 1990); Claudia Card's *Feminist Ethics* (Lawrence, Kansas: University of Kansas Press,

1991); *Explorations in Feminist Ethics*, edited by Eva Browning Cole and Susan Coultrap-McQuin (Bloomington: Indiana University Press, 1992); and *Ethics: A Feminist Reader*, edited by Elizabeth Frazer, Jennifer Hornsby, and Sabina Lovibond (Oxford: Blackwell, 1992). Claudia Card's anthology also has an excellent bibliography.

One of the main issues in regard to gender differences is whether we are espousing a moral ideal that either combines both masculine and feminine elements or is gender-neutral. See Joyce Trebilcot's "Two Forms of Androgynism," *Journal of Social Philosophy*, Vol. 8, No. 1 (January, 1977), pp. 4–8, for a key discussion of two different ways in which the ideal of **androgyny** can be understood.

Relatively little work has been done by philosophers around the issue of **ethnic and cultural diversity,** although much of traditional ethics—with its emphasis on universality and its "thin" notion of a moral agent—has minimized the value of such diversity. The *Philosophical Forum* has been in the lead in this area. See the double issue on "Philosophy and the Black Experience," *Philosophical Forum*, Vol. IX, Nos. 2–3 (Winter–Spring, 1977–78) and the triple issue on "African-American Perspectives and Philosophical Traditions," *Philosophical Forum*, Vol. XXIV, Nos. 1–3 (Fall–Spring, 1992–93). Also see the papers by Anthony Appiah, Maria C. Lugones, and Thomas Wartenberg presented at an APA symposium on Gender, Race, Ethnicity: Anthony Appiah, " 'But Would That Still Be Me?' Notes on Gender, 'Race,' Ethnicity, as Sources of 'Identity,' " *The Journal of Philosophy*, Vol. 87, No. 10 (October, 1990), pp. 493–99, and the commentaries by Lugones and Wartenberg. Also see the papers on multiculturalism and philosophy in *Teaching Philosophy*, Vol. 14, No. 2 (June, 1991), especially Larry Blum's "Philosophy and the Values of a Multicultural Community," pp. 127–34. For a recent discussion of some of these issues from a sociological standpoint, see Anthony J. Cortese, *Ethnic Ethics: The Restructuring of Moral Theory* (Albany: State University of New York, 1990).

A number of works recently have appeared on **moral conflict.** For two recent influential arguments in favor of the plurality of moral values and the consequent unavoidability of moral conflict, see Bernard Williams, "Conflicts of Values," *Moral Luck* (Cambridge: Cambridge University Press, 1981), pp. 71–82, and Thomas Nagel, "The Fragmentation of Value," *Mortal Questions* (Cambridge: Cambridge University Press, 1979), pp. 128–41. Also see Stuart Hampshire, "Morality and Conflict," *Morality and Conflict* (Cambridge: Harvard University Press, 1983), pp. 140–70. For a discussion of the problems that moral conflict poses for liberalism, see Steven Lukes, "Making Sense of Moral Conflict," *Liberalism and the Moral Life*, edited by Nancy L. Rosenblum (Cambridge: Harvard University Press, 1989), pp. 127–42. John Kekes's "Pluralism and Conflict in Morality," *The Journal of Value Inquiry*, Vol. 26 (1992), pp. 37–50, argues in favor of pluralism but againt the claim that our everyday mortal lives are characterized by fundamental moral conflicts. For a contextualist account of the resolution of moral conflicts, see James D. Wallace, *Moral Relevance and Moral Conflict* (Ithaca: Cornell University Press, 1988). Richard W. Miller's *Moral Differences: Truth, Justice and Conscience in a World of Conflict* (Princeton: Princeton University Press, 1992) is a nuanced defense of a limited version of moral realism.

There also has been an increase in work on **moral pluralism** lately. The Symposium on Pluralism and Ethical Theory in *Ethics*, Vol. 102, No. 4 (July, 1992) contains a number of important papers on pluralism. The (forthcoming) issue of *Social Philosophy & Policy*, Vol. 11, No. 1 (Winter, 1994) is devoted to "Cultural Pluralism and Moral Knowledge." On the benefits of moral diversity, see Amélie O. Rorty, "The Advantages of Moral Diversity," *Social Philosophy & Policy*, Vol. 9, No. 2 (Summer, 1992), pp. 38–62. Also see the works on pluralism discussed in the bibliographical essay at the end of Chapter Three.

The issue of pluralism raises important questions about **pluralism and the limits of the liberal state.** For a provocative position on this issue, see Charles Taylor, *Multiculturalism and "The Politics of Recognition,"* with a commentary by Amy Gutmann, Steven C. Rockefeller, Michael Walzer, and Susan Wolf (Princeton: Princeton University Press, 1992); John Kekes, "The Incompatibility of Liberalism and Pluralism," *American Philosophical Quarterly*, Vol. 29, No. 2 (April, 1992) and John Kekes, *The Morality of Pluralism* (Princeton: Princeton University Press, 1993).

On the notion of **moral compromise,** see Martin Benjamin, *Splitting the Difference: Compromise and Integrity in Ethics and Politics* (Lawrence, Kansas: University of Kansas Press, 1990) and David Wong's "Coping with Moral Conflict and Ambiguity," *Ethics*, Vol. 102, No. 4 (July, 1992), pp. 763–84, for a related discussion of moral accommodation.

Citations. Susan Wolf offers a perceptive discussion of the movie *Witness* and moral pluralism in her article, "Two Levels of Pluralism," *Ethics*, Vol. 102, No. 4 (July, 1992), pp. 792 ff. The quotation from Dr. King's "Letter from Birmingham Jail" is found in Martin Luther King, Jr., *Why We Can't Wait* (New York: Mentor Books, 1964), p. 82.

Discussion Questions

1. Recall your rating of statement 48: "Morality should reflect an individual's ethnic and cultural background."
   (a) Has your rating of this item changed after reading this chapter? If so, in what way? If your rating has not changed, are your

reasons for your rating any different now than they were when you first responded to this statement?

(b) Does your own ethnic or cultural background affect your moral views? If so, in what ways? Do you think that this is appropriate?

2. Recall your rating of statement 49: "Moral disagreements are a good thing in society."
   (a) Has your rating of this item changed after reading this chapter? If so, in what way? If your rating has not changed, are your reasons for your rating any different now than they were when you first responded to this statement?
   (b) Give an example of a moral disagreement that proved to be a good thing for society. Give an example of one that was harmful to society. What accounts for the difference between the two outcomes?
3. Each of us has a moral voice—or, more likely, several moral voices. Try to describe your own moral voice. In part, the theories presented in this book may help you to identify different voices: the voice of the egoist, the voice of the utilitarian, the voice of the religious believer, the voice of rights, and the voice of duty. Yet often what is most distinctive about our individual moral voices may not be captured by the theory they embody. Try to describe the timber, the tone, the texture of your voice. Try to isolate that which is distinctively *you*. It might help to imagine that you are trying to help another person get to know you morally.

   This exercise may be difficult, for it is often much harder to hear ourselves than it is to hear others clearly. Let me suggest something that might help. Remember the first time you heard a tape recording of your voice? Did you think it sounded like you? Did other people's voices sound more natural to you? We may encounter the same thing in regard to our moral voices. We may find that they sound different from the inside than they do from the outside. Ask your friends and family what they think your moral voices sound like. Do they hear you as strict, harsh, tentative, sympathetic, blaming, indecisive, bullying, and so on? Do they hear you as more rule-oriented or feeling-oriented? Do they hear your voice as primarily one of care or one of justice? Do they hear your individuality? Do they hear your culture, your ethnicity?
4. Here's an even more difficult assignment: Try to describe your *immoral* voices. This exercise is harder because these voices are usually silent—we act on them, but we rarely express them in a public way.
5. What is the difference (if any) between "guy talk" and "girl talk," or between the ways men speak to each other, the ways women speak

to each other, and the way(s) in which men and women speak to each other? Do these differences matter morally or only socially? Are they fixed or can we change them? How does this relate to your response to statement 47 in the Ethical Inventory?

6. Suppose a visitor from another planet came down to Earth, and did not understand why gender was even an issue for so many members of our species. What would you say to explain (or excuse) it? What might the "alien" say in return?
7. The actress Sigorney Weaver, for example, often plays film roles (for example, in the *Alien* series or *Gorillas in the Mist*) that are high in both femininity and masculinity. Who can you think of among males who ranks high on both scales?
8. We have discussed the issue of moral compromise at some length. Recall your response to statement 50 in the Ethical Inventory.
   (a) Has your rating of this item changed after reading this chapter? If so, in what way? If your rating has not changed, are your reasons for your rating any different now than they were when you first responded to this statement?
   (b) What values are so important to you that you would never compromise them by cooperating with others? What values are so important that you would go out of your way to actively prevent other people from engaging in behavior that violates those values?

A P P E N D I X

Writing Papers about Theories: Tips and Traps

Introduction

Writing about ethical theories often can be daunting. Here are some suggestions that may make it a little easier.

Choosing and Defining a Topic

If the topic for your paper is not assigned by your instructor, here are some suggestions about how to proceed.

- *Choose a topic you are interested in.* Papers are simply much easier to do if you are interested in the topic you are working on, and—all other things being equal—you will do a better paper as a result.
- *Choose a topic you will learn something from.* Your time is too valuable to do things that are not worth your while. If, for example, you are already clear about your position on a particular moral issue and have already thought through the arguments on both sides, you will probably learn more by doing a paper on some other moral issue about which you are still perplexed or uncertain.
- *Choose a topic that you can cover within the time you have available and space limits of the assignment.* Do not, in other words, bite off more than you can chew.
- *Sit down and figure out what* **you** *believe.* Sometimes it is difficult to know what your own views are, especially when you see many different arguments for and against a position. If this happens, you may find

it helpful simply to sit down and start to list (a) the things you think are true in regard to your topic and (b) the claims you think are false. It gives you a starting point for developing your own ideas.

- *Develop and continually refine your thesis.* In most cases in ethics papers, you will be developing and refining a *thesis*, that is, a claim which you are defending through reasoned arguments. In the course of working on your thesis, you will usually find yourself narrowing it down and making it more precise, more finely textured. You might begin, for example, with some general claim that euthanasia is wrong, and gradually refine it to a much more specific thesis about the role of physicians in voluntary euthanasia for persons with very painful non-fatal diseases.
- *Consider the objections to your thesis.* Your thesis is developed and refined through a dialogue with other thinkers about your topic. The process of considering objections to your own position and developing replies to those objections is an essential part of the intellectual life. Through this process, your own ideas become clearer and sharper.

Finding Sources

There are a number of helpful sources for gaining information about material on your topic.

- The *card catalogue* of college and university libraries usually contains both a subject index and an author index.
- The *Philosophers' Index* lists articles and books by specific topic; it also contains abstracts for many of the articles. It is available both in bound volumes and on-line for computerized searches through Dialog Information Service. Consult with your college librarian about how to choose keywords for searches.
- Several philosophy journals specialize in articles about ethics: *Ethics, Philosophy and Public Affairs, Journal of Value Inquiry, Social Philosophy & Policy,* the *Journal of Social Philosophy* and the *Hastings Center Report.* In addition, some journals have individual issues devoted to particular topics. *The Monist, Midwest Studies in Philosophy,* and *Philosophical Perspectives* for example, have had several issues devoted specifically to ethical issues.
- *Anthologies* are often an excellent source both of reprinted articles and bibliographies. Often they contain bibliographical essays or introductions that map out the current state of the discussion.
- Several excellent reference works are available in ethics, especially *The Encyclopedia of Ethics* (1992), edited by Lawrence and Charlotte

Becker; *A Companion to Ethics* (1991), edited by Peter Singer, and *The Encyclopedia of Philosophy* (1967), edited by Paul Edwards.
- Talk with your reference librarians. They often are delighted to help.

Format

Use the style sheet that your instructor suggests. The MLA (Modern Language Association) Handbook and the APA (American Psychological Association) are two of the most frequently used.

Quoting and Footnoting

There are a few easy and basic rules to keep in mind when using other sources in your writing.

- *Whenever you directly use the words of another person, these words must be enclosed in quotation marks and a reference to the source must be made.* To fail to do so is to plagiarize! **Tip:** When you are making notes on your readings, be sure to use quotation marks for any passages where you take the words directly from someone else. Otherwise, you may use your notes as part of your final draft and forget that they are composed in part of direct quotations.
- *Quote as little as possible.* In general, when instructors are reading your paper, they are trying (among other things) to reach as informed a judgment as possible about how well you have mastered the material under consideration. If you are able accurately to paraphrase difficult ideas instead of quoting them directly, it is much stronger evidence that you have mastered the position. If you give a long quotation, the evidence that you understand it (especially if you fail to discuss the interpretation of the quotation after you give it) is very weak. The longer the quotation, and the shorter your discussion of it, the less likely it is that you will convince anyone that you understand it.
- *Quote when it is important to draw the reader's attention to the exact language of the text.* Sometimes, especially when there is a controversy over exactly what a particular philosopher believes, it is necessary to quote the philosopher's exact words. Usually such quotations immediately will be followed by a discussion of specific points in the actual wording of the quotation.

  For example, Immanuel Kant tells us not to treat people only as a means to an end—but he does seem to allow that we may partially treat them as means to an end. He writes, "Always treat humanity, whether in yourself or in anyone else, as an end in itself and never merely as a means." The phrase ". . . and never merely as a means" suggests that it is permissible to treat other people (and oneself, for that matter) partially as a means. Quoting Kant directly in this context lends support to this claim, which is strengthened by the direct quotation. Clearly, quoting in this context is an indication that you have read the text closely and mastered it. In this context, quoting is not a substitute for understanding the text.

- *Whenever you are using someone else's ideas (but not their exact words), indicate so through a footnote or reference of some kind.* Again, to fail to do this documentation is plagiarism. **Tip:** It is easy to acknowledge your debts to other authors in passing with such simple phrases as "As Williams has pointed out . . . ," "Nozik has shown that . . . ," or "In light of Rorty's claim that . . . ,"

Some Common Pitfalls

There are a number of common pitfalls that you can easily avoid with a careful review of the draft of your paper before you submit it.

- *Avoid rhetorical questions.* Often we use rhetorical questions as a way of dismissing an idea. If the question is worth asking, it is worth answering. If you find yourself asking a question such as "Who's to say what is moral?," try to answer the question. This transforms it from a question into an assertion that can then be assessed on its merits.
- *Avoid clichés.* Sometimes we resort to stock phrases that we have heard time and again—but perhaps not really examined. How often have you heard someone reject an idea by claiming that "it's like saying that the end justifies the means." If you think about it for a minute, you will see that the end often justifies the means. Indeed, for pure consequentialists, it is the only thing that justifies any means. Similarly, "You can't legislate morality" is a cliché that must be avoided.
- *Be aware of exact meanings of words.* Do not use big words in order to sound impressive. Philosophers often use a specialized vocabulary that has a precise meaning within the philosophical community, just as any group of specialists does. Use this vocabulary when it is needed and when you have mastered it. (The glossary in this book is intended to help you gain a mastery of some of this vocabulary.) Do not use it if you do not know what it means or if it is not appropriate to the context and to your audience.
- *Be specific and concise.*
- *A spell-checker is not enough!* If you prepare your paper on a computer, use a spell-checker and, if available, a grammar-checker. However, after you have done that, check the text yourself. A spell-checker cannot differentiate between "there" and "their" or between "effect" and "affect." If you forget the "h" in "threat," it becomes a "treat."

- *Use gender-neutral language.* In recent years, we have become increasingly conscious of the ways in which our language gives the (sometimes unintended) impression that we are referring just to men when it is more appropriate to refer to both men and women. Many of us now try to avoid this problem. Some authors use constructions like "he/she" or "her or him"; others alternate, sometimes using feminine pronouns and at other times using masculine ones. My own inclination is to use plural forms whenever appropriate or to use constructions that avoid the need to employ gender-specific pronouns, since I find the other two ways stylistically awkward.
- *State what you are omitting.* It is usually impossible in a paper, or even a book, to cover all the relevant issues. There is nothing wrong with admitting this fact. Rather, it is often advisable to let your reader know that you are aware of important issues that you have chosen not to treat in that context. Often, this goal can be accomplished in a sentence or even a clause. Here are a couple of examples.

  > "I realize that Kant's philosophy is open to criticism on many fronts, but in this paper I will concentrate solely on issues about how maxims can be formulated and then subjected to the test of universality."

  > "Many thinkers have offered important insights into the nature of courage in a wide range of situations, but here I will be concerned only with instances of courage within a military context."

- *If you are undecided about an issue, say so.* It is OK to say that you are undecided about an issue. Sometimes you have reflected on an issue, seeing strong arguments on both sides of the question, not yet deciding where you stand. It is often appropriate to admit this ambiguity as long as you show a critical awareness of the arguments on both sides and give some indication of how you have progressed in your thinking on the issue.
- *When you make a mistake, learn from it.* Keep a list of the spelling and grammatical mistakes that you make in each of your papers, along with the appropriate corrections. Review it before you submit the final draft of your current paper and then proofread your current paper in light of the mistakes you typically make.

Styles of Argument

Different disciplines are characterized by different styles of writing. Most work in ethics is argumentative, sometimes even combative, in character. The usual structure of such writing is straightforward.

- *Show why the issue you are considering is interesting and important.*
- *State the thesis you are defending.*
- *Present the initial arguments in support of your thesis.*
- *Present the major possible objections to your thesis.*
- *Give your replies to those objections, refining your thesis in the process.*
- *Conclude with a more refined version of your thesis and an indication of its significance.*

Although a strong ethics paper usually will contain all of these elements, there is no need to follow this order rigidly.

The basic movement of this type of paper usually will be the back-and-forth movement of argument → objection → reply. The more precise and finely tuned that movement is, the better the paper will be. The process of presenting and replying to objections is crucial to this type of paper, for it is precisely in this dialogue with opposing viewpoints that your position is articulated.

By reading this book and other works in philosophy, you already have been exposed to a particular style of philosophical writing. Here are some of the characteristics of philosophical arguments that you may want to consider in your own writing.

Truth, Validity, and Soundness

As you construct your own arguments and evaluate the arguments of others, you will be focusing on two distinct questions:

- Are the premises of the argument true?
- Does the conclusion of the argument follow from its premises?

If both of these conditions are met, and the argument's conclusion is intended to follow *necessarily* from the premises, we have a **sound deductive argument.** (A deductive argument is simply an argument whose conclusion claims to follow necessarily from its premises.) An example of a sound deductive argument would be:

> All human beings are mortal;
> Socrates is a human being;
> Therefore, Socrates is mortal.

On the other hand, if both of these conditions are met and the argument's conclusion is intended to follow with *probability* from the premises, we have a **strong inductive argument.** (An inductive argument is an argument whose conclusion claims to follow with probability from its premises.) The following is a strong inductive argument.

> Every time I have given Jim advice in the past, he has gotten mad.
> I am going to give Jim advice this afternoon.
> Therefore, Jim will probably get mad this afternoon.

Notice that it is logically possible that the conclusion of a strong inductive argument could be false. It is impossible for the conclusion of a sound deductive argument to be false.

In evaluating arguments, we should always check to make sure that the premises are true. Consider the following argument.

Killing human beings is always wrong.
Abortion is the killing of a human being.
Therefore, abortion is always wrong.

This argument is **valid** because the conclusion follows necessarily from the premises. However, there is strong debate about whether the premises are true. Is it always wrong to kill human beings? What about war, self-defense, or capital punishment? Similarly, is abortion, especially in the earliest stages of pregnancy, the killing of a human being? We must answer questions such as these before we can decide whether the premises are true. If we conclude that one or more premises are false, then the argument is **valid but unsound.**

Sometimes arguments can have true premises, but the premises do not provide sufficient basis for asserting the conclusion. Here is an example:

All murder is wrong.
Errol Harris was executed in 1992.
Therefore, Errol Harris was murdered.

Both of these premises may well be true, but they do not support the conclusion that is drawn. In this instance, the first premise may be true, but it is not *relevant* to the conclusion. Whether murder is right or wrong is simply irrelevant to the question of whether Harris was murdered. For premises to support a conclusion, they must be relevant to that conclusion.

Sometimes arguments turn on a hidden **equivocation,** that is, an unacknowledged shift in the meaning of words. Consider the following argument in support of egoism.

Whatever anyone does is in his or her own self-interest.
All self-interested acts are selfish acts.
Everyone acts selfishly.

There is a sense in which the first premise might be true, but only if we take an extremely broad interpretation of "self-interest" which would include anything the self is interested in doing. On the other hand, the second premise demands a very narrow notion of self-interest if it is to be true. It is precisely this shift in meaning from one sense of self-interest to another that constitutes the fallacy in this argument.

When evaluating or constructing arguments, be sure that the premises are true and that the conclusion follows (whether necessarily or probably) from those premises. If both of these conditions are met, you have a good argument.

The Use of Counter-Examples

One of the most common ways of criticizing moral theories is through the use of counter-examples, which typically involves the following steps.

1. Show that a particular theory or principle necessarily leads to acting in a particular way in specific situations.
2. Show that that way of acting is clearly wrong or unacceptable.
3. Conclude that the theory or principle must be mistaken.

Let us consider an example of this type of argument.

Thomson's Violinist Example

In many discussions of abortion, many philosophers—both pro-life and pro-choice—have assumed that the central issue is whether the fetus is a person and thus entitled to the protection afforded by basic human rights. Both sides seem to assume that if the fetus is a person, then abortion is immoral because it is then the intentional killing of an innocent person, which is never acceptable. The principle being assumed by these discussions is the following:

It is morally wrong knowingly to kill an innocent person. Judith Jarvis Thomson, a philosopher at MIT, challenged that position by means of an ingenious counter-example.

> . . . now let me ask you to imagine this. You wake up in the morning and find yourself back to back in bed with an unconscious violinist. A famous unconscious violinist. He has been found to have a fatal kidney ailment, and the Society of Music Lovers has canvassed all the available medical records and found that you alone have the right blood type to help. They have therefore kidnapped you, and last night the violinist's circulatory system was plugged into yours, so that your kidneys can be used to extract poisons from his blood as well as your own. The director of the hospital now tells you, "Look, we're sorry the Society of Music Lovers did this to you—we would never have permitted it if we had known. But still, they did it, and the violinist now is plugged into you. To unplug you would be to kill him. But never mind, it's only for nine months. By then he will have recovered from his ailment, and can safely be unplugged from you."

The case of the violinist is, Thomson argues, similar enough to the abortion case that we should not get different answers in the two cases. We can grant that both the fetus and the violinist are human beings, that neither did anything to deserve being in the present predicament, and that neither the pregnant woman (at least in cases of rape or contraceptive failure) nor the person hooked up to the violinist did anything to deserve their fate. Yet most people would agree that you are not obligated to remain hooked up to the violinist, even if unplugging yourself would result in the violinist's death. Therefore the principle that it is morally wrong to do anything knowingly that will bring about the death of an innocent person is not valid without exception. Consequently, it does not in itself provide sufficient support for rejecting abortion as morally wrong.

There are at least two ways of trying to reply to such arguments. First, you can argue that the theory or principle really does not lead to that kind of judgment about the particular case. Usually this approach would be accomplished by showing that there are morally relevant dissimilarities between the two examples. Second, you can argue that our moral intuitions about that type of case are wrong, that in fact the theory's conclusions are correct. In this instance that would involve arguing that you are not permitted to disconnect yourself from the violinist. But Thomson has an ingenious rejoinder to such a claim. What, she asks, if we extended the length of time that you were connected to the violinist to, say, one year or five years or fifteen years? Surely at some point you would draw the line and say, "enough."

Showing the Unacceptable Implications of Your Opponent's Position

Another extremely common technique in philosophical argumentation is to take your opponent's position and show that it leads to unacceptable conclusions, perhaps even to logical contradictions. If you can show that it leads to a contradiction, then this type of refutation is called by its Latin name, *reductio ad absurdum*. There is no special name for the more common *reductio* that shows that your opponent's position entails a conclusion that is unacceptable. (The conclusion may be unacceptable for any number of different reasons, inluding that it is factually false or it is morally wrong.) Essentially, it simply says, "Look, if you really believe that, here's what it leads to. Obviously you don't accept that. Therefore you should toss out your theory."

When philosophers criticize utilitarianism, they sometimes argue in this way. First, they take a particular example—at times an extreme case—and describe the way in which a utilitarian would deal with it. Then they try to show that, if we deal with this situation in the approved utilitarian fashion, it will lead to acting in a way that runs counter to what we would normally expect morality to require of us. In other words, they seek to deduce what are called counter-intuitive consequences, that is, consequences which run counter to our standard ethical intuitions about the case in question. Once they have shown that utilitarianism yields such counter-intuitive results, they often directly conclude that utilitarianism must be wrong because it violates our everyday moral intuitions. In more sophisticated versions, critics both offer arguments in support of the correctness of our basic moral intuitions and also attempt to specify the precise factor in utilitarianism that leads us astray.

So a critic of utilitarianism may argue as follows. If a person attempts to assassinate the good and popular leader of a small impoverished country but his rifle shot misses the president and, instead, strikes a rock from which oil then begins to gush; if, furthermore, this accident leads to the discovery of a new natural resource for the country and thus eliminates starvation and poverty for a great number of people; then, from a utilitarian point of view, the attempted assassination would be a morally good act. If, however, a person—for purely humanitarian reasons and after taking all the necessary precautions—sets out to bring much needed medical care to a remote jungle area and inadvertently infects the jungle residents with a virus to which they have no immunity; if, as a result, a large segment of the population in that area dies; then, from a utilitarian standpoint, the individual's act of bringing medical care to that region would be a morally bad act. The critic of utilitarianism would then want to argue that in the first case, the act was obviously a bad one and that in the second case it was at least arguably a good act. Yet utilitarianism claims the former is good and the latter bad. Thus utilitarianism must be wrong.

There are several courses open to utilitarians in reply to these kinds of objections. First, they simply can say, "So much the worse for common sense morality; our moral intuitions must simply have been mistaken in those cases." Although this reply might suffice in some cases, it seems unlikely that there are not some cases in which the supporters of moral intuitions could not succeed in the argument. Second, they can argue that utilitarian principles do not necessarily lead to such consequences. Once again, however, it seems that the utilitarian reply will not suffice for all cases, although it may be relevant in a significant number of them. There are at least some cases in which utilitarian principles do seem to lead quite clearly to counter-intuitive conclusions about the moral worth of an action, even if these cases are fewer in number than critics of utilitarianism may suggest. Finally, and this one seems to be the weakest of the replies, the utilitarian could just admit that utilitarianism does not have an answer for this type of objection.

The Dilemma

When criticizing an opponent's position, philosophers often try to show that the opponent's position involves a dilemma. The word "dilemma" comes from the Greek; "*di*" means "two" and "*lemma*" means "proposition." In setting up a dilemma, you attempt to show that your opponent's position leads to either of two propositions and that neither of these propositions is acceptable.

We employed a version of the dilemma argument in criticizing deterministic ethical egoism. The first horn of the dilemma was to interpret deterministic ethical egoism as strongly deterministic, that is, as saying that all human beings are *determined* to act only in their own self-interest. Yet if that is true, then what is the point of telling them that they *should* act in this way? On the other hand, if deterministic ethical egoism is saying that we *ought* to behave in this fashion, then it is implying that we have a choice. But if we have a choice, then we are not determined and thus deterministic ethicial egoism cannot be true.

There are three ways of replying to this kind of attack. First, one can attempt to show that the position does not lead to the unacceptable conclusion. Second, one can try to show that the conclusion is not unacceptable. Third, one can try to go "between the horns of the dilemma," that is, to show that there is a third possibility that escapes the liabilities associated with the first two.

Metaphors and Similes

Often moral arguments depend on metaphors or similes in order support their point. (Both metaphors and similes understand one class of things in terms of some other class of things, but similes use the word "like" or its equivalent to describe the comparison. "Life is war" is a metaphor, while "life is like a war" is a simile.) Sometimes these metaphors are introduced merely by way of example, while at other times they lie at the core of the argument.

Consider the way in which evil is sometimes understood in terms of the disease metaphor. For example, some authors may think of an evil such as racism in terms of a disease such as cancer: "Racism is a cancer that infects the body politic." This metaphor can then be extended to justify particular social policies. If surgery is the preferred mode of treating cancer, then this metaphor might seem to justify social policies designed to "cut out" the cancer. Imagine the very different picture we obtain if we think of racism as "incorrect programming," using a computer metaphor. Instead of suggesting surgery we might well turn our attention toward reshaping educational policies.

Sometimes metaphors are woven into the very fabric of a theory. The weight or scale metaphor seems to function in this way in utilitarianism. Some consequences outweigh others, and so on. Similarly, spatial metaphors often seem to underlie talk of human rights. Rights establish a sphere of action that others cannot violate. Boundaries are set up, transgressions punished. There is nothing necessarily wrong with using such metaphors, but in evaluating moral theories it is important to be aware of our metaphors and to insure that they do not inadvertently lead us astray.

A Cautionary Conclusion about the Goals of Criticism

Philosophical criticism is often negative and combative in character. Many philosophical articles try to show that an opponent's position is flawed in some way—that it has some internal contradictions, that it leads to unacceptable consequences, and so on. Yet as we have seen in Chapter Nine, this adversial model is not the only legitimate paradigm of philosophical discourse. In writing philosophical papers, it is equally legitimate to advance and defend positive theses intead of attacking the positions of others. It is equally legitimate to build on the foundations of other philosophers, extending their insights and applying them to new areas.

Remember that writing papers is a process of discovery. The ultimate goal is to learn more than you knew before, to become clearer about an issue that was puzzling to you. Use your writing as an opportunity to do work that you will benefit from and to address issues that are important to you.

GLOSSARY

Absolutism. The belief that there is one and only one truth; those who espouse absolutism usually also believe that they *know* what this absolute truth is. In ethics, absolutism usually is contrasted with relativism.

Agnosticism. The conviction that one simply does not know whether God exists or not; it often is accompanied by a further conviction that one need not care whether God exists or not.

Altruism. A selfless concern for other people purely for their own sake. Altruism usually is contrasted wih selfishness or egoism in ethics.

Areté. The Greek word for "excellence" or "virtue." For the Greeks, it was not limited to human beings. A guitar, for example, has its *areté* in producing harmonious music, just as a hammer has its excellence or virtue in pounding nails into wood well. So, too, the virtue of an Olympic swimmer is in swimming well, and the virtue of a national leader lies in motivating people to work for the common good.

Atheism. The belief that God does not exist. In the last two centuries, some of the most influential atheistic philosophers have been Karl Marx, Friedrich Nietzsche, Bertrand Russell, and Jean-Paul Sartre.

Autonomy. The ability to freely determine one's own course in life. Etymologically, it goes back to the Greek words for "self" and "law." This term is most strongly associated with Immanuel Kant, for whom it meant the ability to give the moral law to oneself.

Calculus. A calculus is simply a means of computing something, and a **moral calculus** is just a means of calculating what the right moral decision is in a particular case.

Categorical Imperative. An unconditional command. For Immanuel Kant, all of morality depended on a single categorical imperative. One version of that imperative was "Always act in such a way that the maxim of your action can be willed as a universal law." See also **Hypothetical Imperative.**

Compatibilism. The belief that both determinism and freedom of the will are true.

Consequentialism. Any position in ethics that claims that the rightness or wrongness of actions depends on their consequences.

Counter-Example. An example that claims to undermine or refute the principle or theory against which it is advanced.

Cultural Relativism. See **Relativism.**

Deductive. A deductive argument is an argument whose conclusion follows necessarily from its premises. This type of reasoning contrasts to various kinds of inductive arguments, which offer only a degree of probability to support their conclusion.

Deontology. Any position in ethics that claims that the rightness or wrongness of actions depends on whether they correspond to our duty or not. The word derives from the Greek word for duty, *deon.*

Divine Command Theory. Any position in ethics that claims that the rightness or wrongness of actions depends on whether they correspond to God's commands or not.

Dolors. Utilitarian units of pain or displeasure. See also **Hedons.**

Emotivism. A philosophical theory that holds that moral judgments are simply expressions of positive or negative feelings.

Enlightenment. (1) An intellectual movement in modern Europe from the sixteenth until the eighteenth centuries marked by the belief in the power of human reason to understand the world and to guide human conduct. (2) For Buddhists, the state of Enlightenment or *nirvana* is the goal of human existence.

Ethical Egoism. A moral theory that in its most common version (*universal ethical egoism*) states that each person ought to act in his or her own self-interest. See also **Psychological Egoism.**

Ethics. The explicit, philosophical reflection on moral beliefs and practices. The difference between ethics and morality is similar to the difference between musicology and music. Ethics is a conscious stepping back and reflecting on morality, just as musicology is a conscious reflection on music. See also **Morality.**

Ethnicity. A person's ethnicity refers to that individual's affiliation with a particular cultural tradition that may be national (French) or regional (Sicilian) in character. Ethnicity differs from race in that ethnicity is a sociological concept whereas race is a biological phenomenon.

Eudaimonia. Aristotle uses this word for "happiness" or "flourishing." It comes from the Greek "*eu*," which means "happy" or "well" or "harmonious," and "*daimon*," which refers to the individual's spirit.

Flourishing. See **Eudaimonia.**

Gender. A person's gender refers to that individual's affiliation with either male or female social roles. Gender differs from sex in the same way that ethnicity differs from race: gender is a sociological concept, while sex is a biological one.

Hedons. This term is used by utilitarians to designate units of pleasure; the term "hedon" comes from the Greek word for pleasure. See also **Dolors.**

Hedonistic. Of, or pertaining to, pleasure.

Heteronomy. For Kant, heteronomy is the opposite of autonomy. Whereas an autonomous person is one whose will is self-determined, a heteronomous person is one whose will is determined by something outside of the person, such as overwhelming emotions. Etymologically, heteronomy goes back to the Greek words for "other" and "law."

Human Rights. See **Rights.**

Hypothetical Imperative. A conditional command, such as "If you want to lose weight, stop eating cookies." Some philosophers have claimed that morality is only a system of hypothetical imperatives, while others—such as Kant—have maintained that morality is a matter of categorical imperatives. Also see **Categorical Imperative.**

Impartiality. In ethics, an impartial standpoint is one that treats everyone as equal. For many philosophers, impartiality is an essential component of the moral point of view.

Imperative. A command. Philosophers often distinguish between **hypothetical imperatives** and **categorical imperatives;** see the entries under both of these topics.

Inclination. Used by Kant (actually, he used the German word *Neigung*), this word refers to our sensuous feelings, emotions, and desires. Kant contrasts inclination with reason. Whereas inclination was seen as physical, causally determined, and irrational, reason was portrayed as non-physical, free, and obviously rational.

Integrationist. Any position that attempts to reconcile apparently conflicting tendencies or values into a single framework. Integrationist positions are contrasted with separatist positions, which advocate keeping groups (usually defined by race, ethnicity, or gender) separate from one another.

Maxim. According to Kant, a maxim is the *subjective rule* that an individual uses in making a decision.

Mean. The arithmetical average of items in a group.

Means. Philosophers often contrast *means* and *ends*. The *ends* we seek are the goals we try to achieve, while the *means* are the actions or things that we use in order to accomplish those ends. A hammer provides the means for pounding a nail in a piece of wood. Some philosophers, most notably Immanuel Kant, have argued that we should never treat human beings merely as means to an end.

Moral Ballpark. The domain of actions, motives, traits, and so on, that are open to moral assessment, that is, that can be said to be morally good *or* morally bad.

Moral Isolationism. The view that we ought not to be morally concerned with, or involved with, people outside of our own immediate group. Moral isolationism is often a consequence of some versions of moral relativism.

Moral Luck. The phenomenon that the moral goodness or badness of some of our actions depends simply on chance. For example, the drunk driver may reach home safely without injuring anyone at all, or might accidentally kill several children who run out into the street while the drunken person is driving home. How bad the action of driving while drunk is in that case depends in part on luck.

Moral Rights. See **Rights.**

Morality. "Morality" refers to the first-order beliefs and practices about good and evil by means of which we guide our behavior. Contrast with **Ethics,** which is the second-order, reflective consideration of our moral beliefs and practices.

Narcissism. An excessive preoccupation with oneself. In mythology, Narcissus was a beautiful young man who fell in love with his own image reflected in a pool of water.

Natural Law. In ethics, believers in natural law hold that (a) there is a natural order to the human world, (b) this natural order is good, and (c) people therefore ought not to violate that order.

Natural Rights. See **Rights.**

Naturalism. In ethics, naturalism is the theory that moral values can be derived from facts about the world and human nature. The naturalist holds that "is" can imply "ought."

Naturalistic Fallacy. According to G. E. Moore, any argument which attempts to define the good in any terms whatsoever, including naturalistic terms. For Moore, Good is simple and indefinable. Some philosophers, most notably defenders of naturalism, have argued that Moore and others are wrong and that such arguments are not necessarily fallacious.

Negative Rights. See **Rights.**

Nihilism. The belief that there is no value or truth. Literally, a belief in nothing (*nihil*). Most philosophical discussions of nihilism arise out of a consideration of Fredrich Nietzsche's remarks on nihilism, especially in *The Will to Power.*

Noumenal. A Kantian term that refers to the unknowable world as it is in itself. According to Kant, we can know only the world as it apears to us, as a **phenomenon.** We can never know it as it is in itself, as a **noumenon.** The adjectival forms of these two words are "phenomenal" and "noumenal," respectively.

Particularity. In recent discussions, ethicists have contrasted particularity with universality and impartiality and asked how, if morality is necessarily universal and impartial, it can give adequate recognition to particularity. Particularity refers to specific attachments (friendships, loyalties, and so on) and desires (fundamental projects, personal hopes in life) that usually are seen as morally irrelevant to the rational moral self.

Phenomenal. See **Noumenal.**

Phronesis. According to Aristotle, *phronesis* is practical wisdom, the ability to make the right decision in difficult circumstances.

Pluralism. The belief that there are multiple perspectives on an issue, each of which contains part of the truth but none of which contains the whole truth. In ethics, moral pluralism is the belief that different moral theories each capture part of the truth of the moral life, but none of those theories has the entire answer.

Positive Rights. See **Rights.**

Prima Facie. In the original Latin, this phrase means "at first glance." In ethics, it usually occurs in discussions of duties. A *prima facie* duty is one that appears binding but which may, upon closer inspection, turn out to be overridden by other stronger duties.

Psychologism Egoism. The doctrine that all human motivation is ultimately selfish or egoistic.

Relativism. In ethics, there are two main types of relativism. *Descriptive ethical relativism* claims as a matter of fact that different people have different moral beliefs, but it takes no stand on whether those beliefs are valid or not. *Normative ethical relativism* claims that each culture's (or group's) beliefs are right within that culture, and that it is impossible validly to judge another culture's values from the outside.

Rights are entitlements to do something without interference from other people (*negative rights*) or entitlements that obligate others to do something positive to assist you (*positive rights*). Some rights (*natural rights, human rights*) belong to everyone by nature or simply by virtue of being human; some rights (*legal rights*) belong to people by virtue of their membership in a particular political state; other rights (*moral rights*) are based in acceptance of a particular moral theory.

Satisficing. A term utilitarians borrowed from economics to indicate how much utility we should try to create. Whereas maximizing utilitarians claim that we should strive to *maximize* utility, satisficing utilitarians claim that we need only try to produce *enough* utility to satisfy everyone. It is analogous to the difference between taking a course with the goal of getting an "A" and taking it pass-fail.

Skepticism. There are two senses of this term. In ancient Greece, the skeptics were inquirers who were dedicated to the investigation of concrete experience and wary of theories that might cloud or confuse that experience.

In modern times, skeptics have been wary of the trustworthiness of sense experience. Thus classical skepticism was skeptical primarily about theories, while skepticism is skeptical primarily about experience.

Subjectivism. An extreme version of relativism, subjectivism maintains that each person's beliefs are relative to that person alone and cannot be judged from the outside by any other person.

Supererogatory. Literally, "above the call of duty." A supererogatory act is one that is morally good and that goes beyond what is required by duty. Some ethical theories, such as certain versions of utilitarianism, that demand that we always do the act that yields the *most* good have no room for supererogatory acts.

Transcendental Argument. A type of argument, deriving from Kant, that seeks to establish the necessary conditions of the possibility of something's being the case. For example, we have to believe that we are free when we perform an action; thus belief in freedom is a necessary conditon of the possibility of action.

Universalizability. Immanuel Kant used this term when discussing the maxims, or subjective rules, that guide our actions. A maxim is universalizable if it can consistently be willed as a law that everyone ought to obey. The only maxims that are morally good are those that can be universalized. The test of universalizability ensures that everyone has the same moral obligations in morally similar situations.

Utilitarianism. A moral theory that says that what is morally right is whatever produces the greatest overall amount of pleasure (*hedonistic utilitarianism*) or happiness (*eudaimonistic utilitarianism*). Some utilitarians (*act utilitarians*) claim that we should weigh the consequences of each individual action, while others (*rule utilitarians*) maintain that we should look at the consequences of adopting particular rules of conduct.

Photo Credits

56	The Bettmann Archive
94	The Bettmann Archive
125	The Bettmann Archive
158	Culver Pictures, Inc.
193	The Bettmann Archive
220	The Bettmann Archive
270	The Bettmann Archive
291	J.L.G. Ferris, Pinx/Culver Pictures, Inc
328	Harcourt Brace & Company, Photo by Jean Weisinger
338	@1986 Flip Schulke, "King Remembered"

INDEX

D

E

F

G

H

O

P

Q

R

S

T

U

V

W

Y

Z